Mario Cuomo: The Myth and the Man

Other Books of Interest from St. Augustine's Press

Mario Cuomo:
The Myth and the Man
George J. Marlin

St. Augustine's Press

South Bend, Indiana

Manufactured in the United States of America.

1 2 3 4 5 6   26 25 24 23 22 21 20

Library of Congress Cataloging-in-Publication Data:
Names: Marlin, George J., 1952- author.
Title: Mario Cuomo : the myth and the man / George J. Marlin.
Identifiers: LCCN 2020032569
ISBN 9781587315077 (cloth)
ISBN 9781587315084 (ebook)
Subjects: LCSH: Cuomo, Mario M., 1932-2015.
Governors--New York
(State)--Biography.
New York (State)--Politics and government--1951-
Classification: LCC F125.3.C86 M27 2020
DDC 974.7/043092 [B]--dc23
LC record available at https://lccn.loc.gov/2020032569

∞ The paper used in this publication meets the minimum requirements of the American National Standard for Information Sciences – Permanence of Paper for Printed Materials, ANSI Z39.48-1984.

St. Augustine's Press
www.staugustine.net

My efforts are dedicated to

Michael M. Uhlmann, LL.B., Ph.D.
(1939–2019)

Special White House Assistant
to President Ronald Reagan

Friend and Mentor

Uhlmann's Razor:
"When stupidity is a sufficient explanation,
there is no need to have recourse to any other."

TABLE OF CONTENTS

PREFACE

I first met Mario Cuomo in 1970 at the law offices of New York Republican-Conservative Assemblyman John T. Gallagher, located on Roosevelt Avenue in downtown Flushing, Queens.

Cuomo and Gallagher were long-time friends and were both graduates of St. John's University School of Law class of 1956.

Gallagher was a noted trial attorney and Cuomo handled many of his appeals in New York's appellate courts.

At that time, I was a freshman at Iona College and a volunteer in Gallagher's campaign to win a fourth term representing northeastern Queens in the New York State Legislature.

My first encounter with Cuomo was exasperating to say the least.

After being introduced, he grilled me with a rapid-fire barrage of questions: Where was I going to school? What was I studying? Why I was majoring in Political Science and not American History? Why a second major in Philosophy and not English Literature? Why was I supporting a "bum" like Gallagher? Why was I a conservative? And on it went.

When, finally, I found breathing room to ask *him* a question—he questioned my question.

Little did I know that I was experiencing the sort of verbal assault that was to become Mario Cuomo's trademark in public life.

Although he intimidated me that day, I came away actually liking him.

When I was thirteen years old, I had cut my political teeth campaigning on street corners for William F. Buckley Jr. during his 1965 New York City mayoral race. Like many young conservatives, I was inspired to join my school debating team after watching Buckley sparring on television with his opponents. And I thought I was pretty good on my feet . . . until that day with Cuomo.

I admired Cuomo's debating style, and I liked his acerbic humor *and* that he was proud of being an Italian-American guy who grew up on the streets of a borough other than Manhattan.

After that meeting, Assemblyman Gallagher told me to keep an eye on Cuomo because he would be going places politically.

Two years later Cuomo made headlines when he brokered a resolution to the dispute in Forest Hills over low-income housing plans proposed by the administration of New York City mayor, John Lindsay. I later gobbled up his book, *Forest Hills Diary,* when it came out in 1974.

In 1973, Cuomo ran briefly for mayor himself and didn't like the experience. After the Queens Democratic leader, Matt Troy, threw Cuomo over the side for another Italian candidate, Congressman Mario Biaggi of the Bronx, he withdrew saying, "I am not running and may never run for mayor." He added, "politics stinks."

What is interesting about Cuomo's first foray into politics is that he came across as somewhat conservative, not as a flaming liberal. "People in Manhattan," his friend, Richard Sharkey said, "thought he was very conservative. He talked about anarchy sweeping the City. It was a very right-of-center speech."

Despite this early bad experience, Cuomo couldn't avoid (nor, really, had he any intention of avoiding) the political arena. He entered the Democratic primary for lieutenant governor in 1974 and came in second in a three-way race.

At that time, and in a subsequent unsuccessful race for mayor in 1977, Cuomo was the hero of many neighborhood Catholics as well as the hierarchy of the Roman Catholic Diocese of Brooklyn.

In 1974, he ran as a pro-life candidate saying he would have voted against the 1970 state legislation permitting abortions. He also opposed the so-called "Gay Rights" bill being pushed in the New York City Council.

Although I worked for Barry Farber, the Conservative Party candidate for mayor in 1977, I closely followed Cuomo's unsuccessful campaign against the winner, Edward I. Koch.

Cuomo lost the Democratic mayoral primary to Ed Koch but continued to run in the fall on the ballot lines of the Liberal Party and his own newly created Neighborhood Preservation Party.

During that race, I began to realize that Cuomo had a dual political personality. On the one hand, he was a proud "New Deal" Democrat, supportive of big-government welfare programs. Yet on the other hand, he couldn't resist being a Queens County "in-your-face" street fighter who

sought the support of conservative ethnic voters in the outerborough neighborhoods.

A Cuomo pollster summed up his candidate thusly, "He thought the
liberal ideals were more admirable—he aspired to them—but by instinct
and impulse he was not a liberal."

Journalist Jonathan Mahler agreed. In his book, *The Bronx is Burning*,
he wrote, "There was an intense competition for Cuomo's ear that reflected
the paradox at the candidate's core: His conservative, outer borough instincts were perpetually at war with his loftier liberal ideals."

After losing the mayor's race, Cuomo moved further left on social issues, particularly abortion, in order to succeed in New York Democratic
politics. The subject of abortion receives significant attention in this book.

In 1993, when I was the Conservative Party candidate for Mayor of
New York City, opposing Mayor David Dinkins and Republican-Liberal
Rudy Giuliani, I sat down with then-Governor Cuomo at his 2 World
Trade Center office on September 9, 1993 to discuss the issues.

At that meeting, after admiring his copy of the Holbein portrait of St.
Thomas More on his wall, and reminding him how we first met in 1970,
we got down to brass tacks.

The author with Governor Cuomo, September 9, 1993

The governor began by stating that during our conversation we would stay away from certain social issues because of our divergent opinions. As for fiscal issues, Cuomo—in his rapid-fire approach—argued that we were likeminded. He portrayed himself as a fiscal conservative who cut taxes numerous times and tried to impose discipline on the big spending Legislature. We also talked about crime in the streets and neighborhood policing.

At the end of the meeting, he asked if he could be helpful in any way. I suggested that he use whatever influence he had to make sure I was invited to participate in the televised debates with Dinkins and Giuliani. This he agreed to do.

Knowing that I would be meeting members of the press when I left, I told Cuomo that I would tell them that "we agreed to disagree about everything except Rudolph Giuliani."

I was surprised and flattered later that day when Governor Cuomo, in an appearance on a NY1 television show hosted by *New York Times* reporter, Sam Roberts, said the following:

> I met today with an intriguing guy, George Marlin, who is the Conservative candidate and a very bright guy.... He came in alone, it was just George and I, we're both from Queens, we have a lot of friends in common. I'll tell you this, I'm not surprised Rudy doesn't want to be on the same platform with him, not because Rudy isn't as bright as he is and you know, couldn't handle himself in a debate because Rudy surely can, but what this man does is remind you that Rudy's positions are very difficult to justify for a lot of conservatives and that's presumably why he didn't get the Conservative nomination. That's good if Rudy wants Democratic votes which obviously, he wants and he's getting but it's not so good if he wants Conservative votes and this guy means to make clear his case and he's very very good at it. Um... I talked to him today about crime, and the cop on the street and drugs, etc. and I thought he had some very enlightening points of view. I hope that the debates start soon and I hope that he's in the debates because I think he will

bring a very interesting dimension. I think New Yorkers should hear what George Marlin has to say.

Governor Cuomo kept his word to me about the debates.

The following year, I crossed swords with Cuomo on the death penalty in the editorial pages of *Newsday*, and I campaigned for George Pataki, who went on to unseat Cuomo after twelve years as New York's governor.

In the post-Cuomo gubernatorial years, we met on a few occasions and chatted from time to time on the phone. My last conversation with Cuomo was at his son Andrew's first gubernatorial inaugural on January 1, 2011.

Even though I worked against him, publicly criticized his record in Albany, and was disappointed by his positions on social issues that mattered to me, I still found him to be an intriguing figure.

This interest led me to write *Mario Cuomo: The Myth and the Man*.

This book is not an academic biography. It is an examination of the political background, public performance and paradoxes of Mario Cuomo from the perspective of a life-long New York conservative who had the privilege, at times, of having a front row seat in the political arena.

During the past thirty years, I have written scores of articles and op-ed pieces on New York politics and finances, and I have written four books in which Mario Cuomo appears: *Fighting the Good Fight: A History of the Conservative Party of New York*, *The American Catholic Voter: Two Hundred Years of Political Impact*, *Squandered Opportunities: New York's Pataki Years*, and, with my co-author Brad Miner, *Sons of St. Patrick: A History of the Archbishop's of New York*.

Some material in this volume has been drawn from those books and relevant columns I have written for various publications.

My thanks to the people who knew or worked for Mario and Andrew Cuomo, for discussing with me their opinions about them. I respect their requests to remain anonymous.

I am, as always, most grateful for the great assistance and patience of my beloved wife, Barbara, in preparing the manuscript. Without her, I could have never completed this work.

Heartfelt thanks as well to my friend and colleague, the aforementioned Brad Miner, for reviewing and commenting on the entire manuscript.

Dr. Michael Uhlmann, to whom this book is dedicated, was a great help before his untimely death on October 8, 2019. He critiqued the chapters devoted to Cuomo as public intellectual.

I am indebted to these friends, and I hope their kindness is vindicated by this present work. I, alone, am responsible for any errors, inaccuracies, or follies in what follows.

George J. Marlin
May, 2020

PART I

THE DECLINE OF NEW YORK AND

THE RISE OF MARIO CUOMO

CHAPTER 1

NEW YORK 1945-1975: FROM THE EMPIRE
STATE TO THE LEVIATHAN STATE

At the start of the post-World War II era, New York was truly the Empire State. Indeed, New York was the leading industrial state in the nation and the most powerful politically, with a population of 16.7 million, and—more important in terms of its influence on the nation's politics—possessing the largest block of electoral votes at 45. Twenty-five of America's top 50 companies were headquartered in New York, and nearly 2 million people were employed in manufacturing. The state's industrial base was diverse, both in terms of size and importance: apparel and textiles topped the list followed by printing, food production, machinery of various kinds, sundry chemicals, fabricated metals, and transportation equipment.

A few highlights of the state's post-war boom include:

- The ever-bustling Greater City of New York—the "Naked City" with its 8 million people in five boroughs—was the nation's leader in economic activity. Twenty-six percent of all employment was in manufacturing with printing, publishing, and apparel leading the way. And the city's arts and culture, especially in television production, made it the world's communications hub.

- In 1946, the rapidly growing suburban areas of Nassau, Rockland, Suffolk, and Westchester counties had a combined population of 1.25 million. By 1960, thanks in large measure to home mortgages provided by both the GI Bill and the FHA, these areas skyrocketed by nearly two-and-a-half times to a population of nearly 3 million. The boom came from the second- and third-generation descendants of nineteenth-century immigrants: Italian-Americans, Irish-Americans, and other hyphenated Americans, many of them World War II veterans, began raising families and commuting every day into New York City.

- Upstate New York was as economically diverse as any region in the United States. The fifty-three upstate counties had 6 million people and some of the most gorgeous real estate anywhere in America: the northern St. Lawrence region and the Mohawk Valley; the eastern shore of Lake Erie, the Finger Lakes region, the Catskills, and Niagara Falls. It was—and is—beautiful country, and it was complemented by manufacturing, high-tech R&D; by agriculture and dairy. There were glass factories, paper mills, electronics facilities, pottery kilns, mines producing iron ore, hydroelectric power plants, textile mills, furniture makers, and craftsmen making rugs and footwear.

But beginning in the late 1950s, New York began to experience an economic decline which continues to this day. It's a decline that invites medical metaphors. Commentators speak of the need for "life support" and warn that the state's condition is "grave" and "perilous."

As to those primarily responsible for New York's initial decline, one can point to three elected officials who dominated the political landscape between 1959 and 1973: Governor Nelson Rockefeller (1959–1973) and two New York City mayors, Robert F. Wagner (1953–1965) and John V. Lindsay (1966–1973). Their policies and fiscal excesses contributed to the erosion of the economy and brought the state to the edge of insolvency and the city to the edge of bankruptcy.

Nelson Rockefeller

In early 1958, Nelson Aldrich Rockefeller, the fifty-year-old multimillionaire grandson of John D. Rockefeller, the founder of the Standard Oil Company, was a frustrated man. Stints in the Roosevelt, Truman, and Eisenhower administrations did not satisfy him. Nor did his Washington assignments put him on the road to achieve his ultimate goal, a lease on the White House.

To be taken seriously as a candidate for president, Rockefeller decided he needed to prove to the nation his abilities by running his own operation in an executive position. The obvious post was governor of New York. Rockefeller grew up in New York, albeit on a grand estate, Pocantico Hills, in affluent Westchester County and on the exclusive Upper East Side of Manhattan, a/k/a, the Silk-Stocking District.

Electorally, New York was considered a swing state in the 1950s. The upstate regions were predominantly Republican, with some Democratic pockets in blue-collar working towns like Buffalo. New York City was heavily Democratic and very liberal, while the surrounding suburban areas were more conservative and were dominated by Republican machines.

Control of the state Legislature throughout the first half of the twentieth century would pass back and forth between the Democrats and Republicans. In the post-World War II era, the GOP had majorities in both houses for all but two years until 1974.

As for the office of governor, between 1900 and 1958, Republicans controlled the executive mansion for twenty-eight years and Democrats, thirty years. Republican governors, however, were not of the Ronald Reagan variety; they were sort of centrists who were more comfortable calling themselves Progressives in the Teddy Roosevelt mold.

Republican Governor Thomas E. Dewey served three terms between 1942 and 1954. Twice he was the Republican presidential nominee, losing to Franklin Roosevelt in 1944 and to Harry Truman in 1948.

For years, Dewey was the undisputed leader of what was known as the progressive Eastern Establishment. Conservative opposition within the Republican Party nationally was led by Senator Robert A. Taft of Ohio, known as "Mr. Republican."

When it came to governing, Dewey called himself a pragmatic liberal and ruled with an iron fist. *New York Times* political reporter, Warren Moscow, described Dewey thusly:

> [He] assumed complete control of his party. County leaders who opposed him were broken by cold, hard-bitten use of the patronage of the governor's office. Legislators suffered a similar fate. He brooked no interference ... for nearly a quarter of a century [Dewey] was the cold, efficient behind the scenes boss of the Republican Party and the state. He directed the election of legislative leaders, passed on nominees for the judiciary selected statewide tickets.... His domination of the party was more complete than Charles F. Murphy's had ever been in Tammany Hall.[1]

5

At the end of the war, Dewey took the state surplus and funneled the money into the Post-war Reconstruction Fund to finance infrastructure projects (i.e., N.Y.S. Thruway)—a move that enhanced his national profile. When more conservative Republican legislators objected, preferring a tax cut, he suggested they "stop bellyaching" and directed them to read the 1948 GOP platform, of which he insisted, "Unless it was designed to deceive, its various sections say and mean that we are a liberal and progressive party."[2]

And Dewey was able to impose his will, particularly when it came to spending, despite the cries of fiscal conservatives.

Total expenditures to accommodate a population that grew approximately 12% during his tenure (General Fund and Related Accounts), increased from $493.6 million in 1946 and hit $1.179 billion in his last year in office. The average annual increase was 11.5%.

As for debt, direct General Obligation (G.O.) debt grew modestly because its issuance required approval by the voters. In 1946, the G.O. debt was $388 million and $738 million in 1954. A different form of debt, for funding public authorities, began to grow.

For the first six years of the Dewey administration, there was no public authority debt. However, due to the creation of the New York Thruway Authority, the debt figure escalated by 1952 to $60 million, and by 1954, it had grown to $250 million.

Governor Dewey's handpicked successor in 1954 was U.S. Senator Irving Ives. A member of the U.S. Senate from 1947, Ives, Republican, had served previously as minority leader, majority leader, and speaker of the Assembly. Challenging him was the heir to the great Harriman railroad fortune, W. Averell Harriman. This former presidential advisor, ambassador, railroad executive and banker, wanted—as had Dewey before him and as would Rockefeller after him—to be governor in large measure as a stepping stone to the presidency.

That November, New Yorkers witnessed the closest gubernatorial election in the state's history. Harriman won with 49.6% to 49.4% for Ives. The difference was only 11,000 votes.

While Harriman considered himself a Franklin Roosevelt New Deal liberal, he was tightfisted when it came to money, and not only with his own money, but with the taxpayers' as well.

Biographer Rudy Abramson has written that Harriman "looked on the governor's office as a boardroom in which he was called upon to defend the returns he produced on stockholders' investment."[3]

"When all was said and done," Abramson concluded, "Harriman slipped through his term with his pledge against a general tax increase intact, saved by tight budgets, bond issues, and fingers gingerly put into the diminished construction-fund sugar bowl that had been so successfully raided by Dewey. The price for his stolid, conservative handling of the New York purse was an unremarkable record as leader."[4]

Total expenditures in Harriman's first year as governor (1955) were $1.262 billion and in his last (1958), $1.688 billion, for a total average increase of 8.4% annually. The state's general obligation debt increased slightly; from $69 million to $74 million. Public authority debt increased only $48 million to $499 million.

In 1958, the November elections were expected to go badly for Republicans. Although President Eisenhower remained popular after six years in office, he never had any genuine "coattails," and the "IN" party historically suffers significant losses on the federal and state levels in a two-term president's second midterm elections.

The political prognostication for 1958 seemed to be good news for Harriman, and he was hoping for a huge second term victory that might well make him the front-runner for the 1960 Democratic presidential nomination.

But self-inflicted wounds would prevent him from achieving his goal.

Never suspecting that his old pal and fellow millionaire from the Roosevelt and Truman administrations harbored his own political ambitions, Harriman had appointed Nelson Rockefeller to chair a state commission that would prepare for a potential constitutional convention.

The New York State Constitution requires the electorate, every 20 years, to answer this question: "Shall there be a convention to revise the Constitution and amend the same?" And Governor Harriman, expecting the electorate to vote yes (they didn't), wanted someone above the fray, like Rockefeller, to prepare for what he hoped would be a monumental event.

Rockefeller happily accepted the appointment because it allowed him to travel the state and lay the groundwork for his own run against Harriman.

Harriman's second debacle was his performance at the 1958 state Democratic convention. The state chairman, Carmine DeSapio, the last boss of Tammany Hall, wanted an ethnically balanced ticket to complement the WASP governor. DeSapio's choices were the Irish-Catholic District Attorney of Manhattan, Frank Hogan, for U.S. Senator and the prominent Jewish lawyer Arthur Levitt for state comptroller.

America's top liberal reformer, Eleanor Roosevelt, and the former New York governor and U.S. senator, Herbert Lehman, were appalled by the choices of the boss-controlled convention and walked out of the convention angry over Harriman's passive acceptance of DeSapio's selections. To Harriman's dismay, the party remained disunited throughout the election.

Rockefeller, on the other hand, was gliding towards the Republican nomination. His chairmanship of the convention commission had served him well, providing him with a first-rate education about the demographics of New York's sixty-two counties.

Along the way, he befriended Malcolm Wilson, the well-respected Catholic and conservative state assemblyman from Yonkers who would serve for 15 years as Rockefeller's lieutenant governor.

The two men drove around the state in Wilson's beat-up car, and Rockefeller was introduced to party faithful from Montauk Point to Buffalo.

"No baggage, no sycophants, no P.R. men—nothing but us," Wilson once said, and then he added, "And I paid for it personally."[5]

Rockefeller was easily nominated for governor on the first ballot and organized the best financed campaign organization in state history.

Nationally-syndicated columnist Stewart Alsop described the battle of the millionaires this way: "The voters of New York State are being asked to choose between a couple of extremely rich Siamese twins."[6] And journalist Garry Wills quipped: "First generation millionaires tend to give us libraries. The second and third generations think they should give us themselves."[7]

There was one big difference between these two rich liberals: Rocky—as he was now known—was a natural campaigner. He loved mixing with voters, kissing babies, eating hot dogs from stands and pastrami sandwiches from delis. Harriman, on the other hand, was a walking cadaver on the campaign trail.

On Election Day 1958, as Republicans suffered heavy losses across the nation (losing nine governorships, thirteen U.S. Senate seats and forty-seven house seats), Rocky beat Harriman by 500,000 votes.

"New York is a big, dynamic, high-powered state," Rocky's in-house intellectual Dr. William Ronan said, "and it wants a big, dynamic high-powered man for its governor."[8]

Unlike the laid-back Averell Harriman, the hyperkinetic Rockefeller hit the ground running on January 1, 1959, and his inaugural address, William Rodgers wrote in *Rockefeller's Follies*, "sounded like a presidential campaign speech."[9]

The new governor pressed forward with expansive plans to enhance the lives of New Yorkers. The expected success of his agenda, he believed, would impress the nation and make his ascension to the presidency inevitable.

But Rocky had to face political and financial realities immediately after unveiling his first budget, which called for expenses to increase by a whopping 13%, totaling $2 billion.

To achieve the balanced budget required by state law, Rockefeller was encumbered by two pledges he made during the campaign: no new taxes and pay-as-you-go financing for state projects.

So, he argued that his request for five new taxes that were expected to raise $277 million were necessary because Governor Harriman was guilty of overspending, which resulted in a fiscal mess.

Many members of the state Legislature were shocked by the governor's budget proposal. The Republicans who controlled both houses of the Legislature fairly choked over what they called "creeping socialism" and were aghast at the proposal to increase state income tax revenues by $150 million.[10] The more liberal Democratic minority, sensing political advantage, actually opposed any increase in taxes.

Downstate Democrats and upstate Republicans allied themselves to stop what they considered a Rockefeller tax juggernaut.

Rocky also had to contend with another powerful dissenter, State Comptroller Arthur Levitt. A nominal Democrat, Levitt viewed his office as non-partisan and was widely respected by the financial community and the voters during his 23 years in office as a fiscal watchdog.

Levitt was shocked by Rocky's cavalier attitude toward him. "He never got used to the idea of my being an independently elected official," Levitt said. "He expected acquiescence. He was accustomed to getting his way, and he wasn't about to let me stand in his way."[11]

Realizing his administration could be doomed from the get-go, Rockefeller rolled up his sleeves and went to work bargaining with individual legislators.

After three weeks of intense negotiation, Rocky gave a little to get a lot. He cut spending by about $40 million and agreed to a tax credit for low-income earners. Republicans, bought off, as some might say, with budgetary goodies for their home districts, reluctantly supported the tax increases. Democrats voted unanimously against the taxes but admitted that they were impressed by the determined governor. "He's a tough customer, this Rockefeller," one Democrat said. "He sure knows how to get what he wants."[12]

Rockefeller came away from the experience learning that a combination of personal charm and political hardball over patronage appointments paid off. And he believed he proved he was tough in promoting tax increases. Later, when questioned about his role in the legislative battle, he boasted, "Don't talk to me about guts, I had the guts to ask for $200 million in new taxes right after I took office. You try that sometime and then go down to New York City to give an address and stand up and be booed for five minutes."[13]

The New York Times applauded him for raising taxes and "succeed[ing] in this momentous test of leadership," adding that Rockefeller "thus set a standard for fiscal courage at a time when deficit financing and deferred reckoning have become so habitual as to be accepted as orthodox government."[14]

While Rockefeller came out of his first budget process with only minor bruises, he realized that his expensive and grandiose plans for transportation, education, housing, hospital, nursing homes, urban development, etc., would have tough sailing through the Legislature. Thus, the governor was determined to find ways to circumvent the Legislature and state constitutional spending and debt limitations.

To achieve what Comptroller Levitt called a subterfuge to undermine the state constitution, Rockefeller would spend the subsequent 14 years bullying weak Republicans and buying off liberal Democrats to create a shadow government that moved "a sizeable amount of the State's business outside the direct aegis of state government."[15] His success in creating this Leviathan—public benefit corporations that were not answerable to the people or the Legislature—contributed to skyrocketing debt, a declining economy, and helped push the state to the edge of insolvency and the City of New York to the brink of bankruptcy.

Rockefeller's Spending Spree 1959 - 1973

Nelson Rockefeller's 1958 campaign for governor and his 1959 budget battle taught him lessons that he would utilize during his remaining fourteen years as New York's chief executive.

The most important lesson was that money matters. As a trust-fund baby, Rockefeller had plenty of money and was not afraid to spread it around.

In his race against Governor Harriman, Rockefeller spent $1.8 million versus the incumbent's $1.1 million, making the 1958 gubernatorial campaign the most expensive in the state and the nation's history to that point.

But for Rocky, that was only a prelude to later campaign spending sprees.

In 1962, he spent $2.2 million versus Democrat Henry Morgenthau's $420 thousand. In a surprisingly close race in 1966, Rockefeller basically gave his political consultants a blank check. Although he was re-elected with only 44.6% of the vote, his campaign's expenditures totaled approximately $5.2 million, whereas his lackluster Democratic opponent, Frank O'Connor, raised a paltry $576,000.

Four years later, campaigning for an unprecedented four-year term, Rockefeller easily beat former U.S. Supreme Court Justice, Arthur Goldberg 52.4% to 40.3%. The price tag, $6.9 million versus Goldberg's $1.3 million.[16]

Despite cries of outrage from his Democratic opponents, Governor Rockefeller was not embarrassed by his bottomless campaign war chest. "Rockefeller's position was that the costs of campaigning were outrageous and that he would comply with any limiting legislation but that in the absence of such legislation, he would use all means at his disposal to win."[17]

Rockefeller also spent money to hire talent. His campaign staff had the most seasoned and competent members money could buy. He paid them to employ the latest and most sophisticated media and polling techniques.

For his most talented gubernatorial staff, whose state salaries were inadequate to retain them for long, Rocky provided low interest loans totaling $2.8 million that, for the most part, were forgiven over time.

Top beneficiaries of Rockefeller's largesse were his first chief of staff, William J. Ronan, who received $625,000 in loans; his second chief of staff, Alton G. Marshall, $306,000; and the Urban Development Corporation Chairman, Edward Logue was loaned $145,000.[18]

Rockefeller also sought to make sure loyalists took control of the state Republican Party, spending lavishly to build the party and to entertain local GOP leaders, helping to cement their friendship.

Over time, thanks to his checkbook and hard work, the joke in Albany was that Rocky owned the state Republican Party and that the Democratic Party was a subsidiary. Indeed, in exchange for their influence in persuading Democratic legislators to sign on to his programs, he gave the New York City Democrats running City Hall the fiscal powers that would eventually bring the city to the brink of financial collapse in 1975.

Rockefeller realized that a subset of Republican members of the state Legislature aligned with the fledging Conservative Party, founded in 1962, would oppose his tax and spend politics, so he sought to endear himself to both Republican and Democratic legislators who were more interested in power and perks than in principles.

Thus, he became the chief dispenser of ten thousand patronage jobs to legislators and political leaders of whom he asked nothing more than that they do exactly what he wanted them to do. These legislators then received benefits for their districts, usually hidden in the state budget. In later years, these emoluments became known as "member items."

Robert H. Connelly and Gerald Benjamin, in their book *Rockefeller of New York*, concluded that the governor "had come a long way from his posture 'above politics' of early 1959. He had learned that quid pro quo was a vital tool in seeking his policy ends. By the time of the 1970 campaign, Rockefeller could proclaim himself, in a speech before assembled party leaders, to be a firm believer in the patronage system."[19]

And despite occasional, short-lived outbursts of opposition throughout his tenure, Rockefeller got from the Legislature most of what he wanted in his annual budgets, as the following chart shows:

Fiscal year	Expenditure requested	Expenditure Authorized	Percentage Received
1960	2,041	1,994	98%
1961	2,035	2,092	103%
1962	2,395	2,324	97%
1963	2,591	2,595	100%
1964	2,889	2,781	96%
1965	2,920	2,894	99%
1966	3,488	3,460	99%
1967	3,987	4,022	101%
1968	4,686	4,629	99%
1969	5,494	5,519	100%
1970	6,417	6,207	97%
1971	7,257	6,748	93%
1972	8,450	7,422	88%
1973	7,900	7,785	99%

Source: New York State, *The Executive Budget*, 1945-78

Spending during the Rockefeller years (1959–1973) went up a remarkable 333%, with average annual increases of 22%. The bulk of the increased spending went to Rocky's favored projects, education and health.

Changes in annual spending in constant 1972 dollars, in millions of dollars:[20]

Category	1946–55 (Dewey)	1955–59 (Harriman)	1959–74 (Rockefeller)
Higher Education	28.5	15.0	927.8
Aid to Public Schools	221.3	292.5	1566.1
Other Education	41.2	30.4	559.4
Health	60.0	7.2	160.3
Mental Hygiene	104.4	70.9	489.0
Medicare/Medicaid – State	0.0	0.0	500.4
Medicare/Medicaid – Federal	0.0	0.0	1036.4

Not surprisingly, Rockefeller was not bashful about raising taxes to pay for this spending spree.

Between 1959 and 1973, the bank tax increased 5 times; the cigarette tax 4 times; the corporate and utilities tax 4 times; the corporate franchise tax 4 times; the pari-mutuel 4 times; the motor fuel tax 3 times; the personal income tax 3 times; the sales and use tax 3 times; estate taxes 2 times; insurance premium tax 2 times; and taxes went up just once on alcohol, highway use, motor vehicles, stock transfers, and unincorporated businesses.

Yet despite imposing on New Yorkers the highest tax burden in America, there still was not enough money to finance Rockefeller's dream programs for the Empire State. This was a serious problem in a state with a constitutionally required balanced budget.

So Rocky permitted his budget director to use every conceivable gimmick to give the appearance of a balanced budget. These abuses included "accounting procedures that utilized 'rollovers,' inaccurate revenue projections, and complicated tax deferrals and accelerated payment schedules...."[21]

Rockefeller was able to juggle the books because the state used cash-basis accounting, not accrual accounting. Under cash-basis accounting, budget directors delay paying bills and accelerate the receipt of revenues. This fiscal abuse conceals the true surplus or deficit but permits the governor to proclaim the budget is balanced.

One of Rocky's budget directors, Richard Dunham, had an epiphany moment when he accidently blurted, "any budget director who can't make a $100 million appear and disappear isn't worth his salt."[22]

Abusing the cash-basis system incurred a structural deficit that was rolled over every year, which by the 1980s was over $4 billion.

Throughout the Rockefeller years, the state's highly respected comptroller, Arthur Levitt, frequently condemned the cash-basis budgeting and on one occasion said, "In truth, the [Rockefeller] administration is not pay-as-you-go and never has been."[23] He abhorred the accounting that permitted the governor to achieve a balanced budget by "manipulating reserve funds, using one-time payments, accelerating expenditures, rolling over expenditures and employing other services at the end of the fiscal year."[24]

Rockefeller despised Levitt, cavalierly dismissing his criticisms by saying, "If you believe I am acting unconstitutionally, sue me."[25]

In fact, when the state Legislature passed a law in 1980 requiring the executive branch to implement Generally Accepted Accounting Principles (GAAP), then-Governor Hugh Cary vetoed the bill. *The New York Times* reported that the law was rejected because it "would have required the executive branch to give the Legislature large amounts of new information in the generally secretive budgeting process."[26]

Tax increases and "sleight of hand" accounting did not provide enough money for Rocky's grandiose plans, hence he turned to the bond market to raise money by issuing long-term debt.

There was, however, the familiar roadblock: that constitutional requirement that all proposed general-obligation debt be approved by voters.

During the Depression of the 1840s, New York almost became insolvent due to debt-payment guarantees on the construction of the Erie Canal and other privately- and publicly-funded building projects. To prevent future abuses, the New York Constitutional Convention drafted provisions mandating voter referendums forcing long-term debt—the only exceptions (found in Article VII, Sections 2 and 3) are for "debt in anticipation of the receipt of taxes and revenues," and "the State may contract debts to repel invasion, suppress insurrection, or defend the State in war."

These limitations, Rockefeller believed, tied his hands to fund his plans for the Empire State. So, to circumvent public approval and to evade public scrutiny, he began creating scores of state agencies and authorities which could borrow and spend billions of dollars outside the state budget.

This dubious technique became commonly known as "backdoor borrowing." In other words, a given agency issues debt to finance a gubernatorial-approved capital project for which the state is bound, often by a lease-back, to appropriate funds annually in its budget to cover principal and interest payments on the agency bonded debt.

In a December 2014 report, New York Comptroller Thomas DiNapoli pointed out that this kind of backdoor borrowing, "eliminates the opportunities to have input on major borrowing decisions that affect them financially; transferring control to public authority boards [appointed by the governor] and thus further limiting accountability and transparency."

During his time in office, Rocky created more statewide perpetual authorities than any governor who proceeded or succeeded him:

Authority, commission, or corporation	Year created
East Hudson Parkway Authority	1960
New York State Housing Finance Agency	1960
Adirondack Mountain Authority	1960
New York State Job Development Authority	1961
New York State Atomic Research and Space Development Authority[a] (Energy Research Development Authority)	1962
Manhattan and Bronx Surface Transit Operating Authority	1962
State University Construction Fund	1962
Mental Hygiene Facilities Inpatient Fund	1963
Metropolitan Commuter Transportation Authority (Metropolitan Transportation Authority)	1965
Long Island Rail Road	1966
Niagara Frontier Transportation Authority	1967
Battery Park City Authority	1968
United Nations Development Corporation	1968
Urban Development Corporation	1968
Rochester-Genesee Regional Transportation Authority	1969
Environmental Facilities Corporation	1970
State of New York Mortgage Agency	1970
Capital District Transportation Authority	1970
Central New York Transportation Authority	1970
New York Municipal Bond Bank Agency	1972
Medical Care Facilities Finance Agency	1973

[a]   Note: Rockefeller, expecting to occupy the White House one day, prepared himself for leading the nation in the Space Age by creating the New York State Atomic Research and Space Development Authority in 1962. The Authority's goals were to establish "a pulse reactor facility as the first component of a 'Space Technology and Radiation Center'" and to develop Western N.Y. Nuclear Service Center. The authority failed to achieve its space goals and its title was later changed to the Energy Research Development Authority.

When Nelson Rockefeller took office in 1959, direct debt, authorities, and state debt guarantees totaled $1.4 billion. When he left office, it stood at $11.8 billion—the highest of the states in the nation. New York's share of the total outstanding debt of the 50 states was 20%.[27]

Here's the breakdown:

Total debt and debtlike commitments of New York State[28]
1958-1974 ($ millions)

Years	State Full faith and credit debt	Authorities Full faith and credit debt	Lease-purchase agreements	"Moral obligation" debt	Total
1974	3,448	566	2,954	4,246	11,214
1973	3,451	582	2,702	3,079	9,814
1972	3,362	581	2,284	2,149	8,376
1971	3,130	558	1,836	1,596	7,120
1970	2,523	571	1,537	1,101	5,732
1969	2,258	547	1,270	842	4,917
1968	1,769	523	1,073	663	4,028
1967	1,323	505	777	462	3,067
1966	1,236	499	537	418	2,690
1965	1,089	503	433	410	2,435
1964	1,082	505	191	333	2,111
1963	1,072	504	46	254	1,876
1962	1,050	493	28	60	1,631
1961	1,035	495	19	60	1,609
1960	988	498	15	—	1,501
1959	897	499	14	—	1,410
1958	744	500	14	—	1,258

These shadow governments were designed to evade the will of the people. Comptroller Arthur Levitt sounded alarms about this sprawling leviathan. "The inherent evil in the excess we use of the authority structure is obvious," he declared. "There is a loss of public control and of legislative understanding. Control must be restored if our democratic process is to remain meaningful."[29]

Shortly after being sworn in as governor in 1975, Hugh Carey said this about Rockefeller's financial machinations: "He's constructed a perpetuity. The way he's set up the authorities, boards, and commissions with term appointments it's almost beyond the reach of a governor to effectuate policy because he had these overlapping directorships in so many ways that their policy—which used to be his policy—becomes state policy without the intervention of the public. To call it a dynasty is one thing, but it is feudal."[30]

The most egregious financing scheme was "Moral Obligation" bonds. The brain child of the legendary municipal bond attorney, John Mitchell—later of Watergate fame—who argued that bonds could be issued through any one of the state's agencies and sold to the rating firms and to investors with the assurance that the State of New York would consider itself to have a "moral obligation" to repay the debt incurred should the bonds default.

Mind you, this was a moral and not a legal obligation. Years later, Mitchell was asked if moral obligation bonds weren't "a form of political elitism" that simply bypasses voters. "That's exactly the purpose of them," he said.

Here's an excerpt concerning moral obligation bonds, from Mitchell's 1984 interview with *The Bond Buyer*:

Q. How did the idea for the moral obligation bond come about?

A. [When] Nelson Rockefeller was elected the governor of New York in 1958, the voters turned down all the propositions that had to be voted under the state constitution—for housing, mental health, etc. His director of housing was telling me about the state's problems.

In order to keep the interest cost down and have a security that would be marketable, I transferred over to the Housing Finance Agency a concept [of moral obligation bonds] that had been used temporarily in connection with school districts.

I just took that and adapted it to the Housing Finance Agency and structured the mechanics of it. It went very, very well and the bonds were marketable, the interest rates were more than reasonable, and, of course, we took it from there.

The technique worked. The bond rating agencies accepted it, and the Office of the Comptroller of the Currency ruled that banks could buy and underwrite the bonds when it declared the debt was much the same as general obligation.[31]

Over the years, Rockefeller expanded the state's moral obligation to finance the State University Construction Fund, nursing, nonprofit housing, and health facility and hospital programs. The Battery Park City Authority and the City University Dormitory Authority also managed to obtain the state's moral obligation.

In 1968, after the assassination of Martin Luther King, Rockefeller convinced the state legislature to approve the creation of the Urban Development Corporation. Backed with the state's moral obligation, the UDC's mandate was to build housing in "substandard, blighted areas."

Then in 1973, perhaps sensing that he was on a sinking fiscal ship, Rockefeller jumped overboard and on December 18 he resigned as New York's 49th governor, ostensibly to become Chairman of the Commission on Critical Choices for America, a study group initiated by President Richard M. Nixon. But Rocky told one aide the real reason for leaving before his fourth term was up: "There's no more money," he admitted.[32]

Nelson Rockefeller not only left the state's coffers severely depleted, his 15-year run of taxing and spending and his social and regulatory policies impaired New York's private economy.

At the end of the Rockefeller era, every industry in the state was in decline, over 2 million jobs were lost between 1960 and 1974. Manufacturing took the biggest hit, losing more than 500,000 jobs between 1970 and 1976.

In the early seventies, manufacturing plants were closing or moving out of the state at the rate of one per day. And every week, two thousand citizens were packing their bags and leaving New York in search of greater and more stable economic opportunities.

Throughout the 1960s and the early 1970s, New York was lagging the nation in population growth, employment growth and in per capita income. Compared to the economic growth in the fifty states, New York came in at the bottom. The state's per capita income dropped from 120% of the national average to 106% in the 1970s.

A survey taken shortly after Rockefeller left office by the Fantus Company, placed the Empire State "for attractiveness of business climate" dead last.[33]

Unemployment, which in the early Rockefeller years was lower than the national average, exceeded it by the end of his tenure.

Unemployment[34]
U.S.A. vs. New York

Year	U.S.A.	New York State	N.Y. City
1958	6.8	6.3	6.1
1959	5.5	5.4	5.3
1960	5.5	5.0	5.0
1961	6.7	6.0	5.6
1962	5.5	5.2	5.0
1963	5.7	5.4	5.3
1964	5.2	5.1	4.9
1965	4.5	4.6	4.6
1966	3.8	4.2	4.2
1967	3.8	3.9	3.7
1968	3.6	3.5	3.2
1969	3.5	3.5	3.1
1970	4.9	4.5	4.8
1971	5.9	6.6	6.7
1972	5.6	6.7	7.0
1973	4.9	5.4	6.0
1974	5.6	6.4	7.2

Employment trends were depressing between 1960 and 1970. While employment grew nationally by 30.80% and in neighboring New Jersey by 29.35%, in New York it grew by only 15.74%.

In Rockefeller's last term in office, 1969-1973, for every 19 new companies that opened, 35 closed.

Between 1961 and 1973, of the 1,054 companies employing 144,551 people that moved out of the state, 49% relocated in New Jersey, 9% in Pennsylvania, and 10% landed in Connecticut.[35]

The primary reason companies were leaving New York was the state's taxes. By 1973, the state had the highest state and local per-capita tax rate in the country—a distinction it holds to this day.

Rockefeller pushed the top state income tax rate to 15%. A 1974 report generated by the U.S. Advisory Commission on Intergovernmental Relations, concluded that New York had little remaining taxing capacity.

Another study indicated that a comparison of individual tax rates of adjacent state "cast a pall upon the merits of remaining in the Empire State." The study concluded, "for top corporate executives contemplating a move out of New York City, this translates into a prospective saving in total personal income taxes of better than 60%."[36]

Other reasons companies were running to the exit doors: high cost of living, high wages, expensive space, high utility costs, as well as the decline in public services and ever-increasing crime.

Reviewing the business climate in 1975, Governor Hugh Carey's Commerce Commissioner, John Dyson, said: "For over ten years now, New York State has built up a bad taste in a lot of mouths. And I realize better than anyone else we have no one to blame but ourselves. Too long we took business for granted." Dyson also admitted, "there are more laws and duties impeding business here than in any other state."[37]

Businesses were beginning to look southward because the fledging sunbelt states were business-friendly, had cheap labor, cheap space and low taxes.

Nelson Rockefeller, less a Republican and more a committed New Deal, Fair Deal, Great Society social engineer, had proclaimed in 1959 that New York would "help to lead America toward new horizons of wellbeing and equal opportunity for all citizens." He left office failing to meet those goals. In fact, he exacerbated New York's fiscal, economic and cultural woes.

"This was a man," political economists Peter McClelland and Alan Magdovitz observed, "with a propensity for overdoing, for triumphs on a grand scale, and for failures on a grand scale. Impatient when constrained and impetuous when not, a spender more than a planner, a doer more than a thinker, he prodded, cajoled, and bullied the state into a spending spree that, in retrospect, was often as intemperate as the man."[38]

And the intemperate Rockefeller also stood by as New York City was sinking into the fiscal abyss.

CHAPTER 2
THE UNMAKING OF GOTHAM

Throughout the twentieth century, New York's governing class viewed their city as the bastion of urban liberalism. There were no social problems, they boasted, that could not be solved. It would merely take money, social engineering formulas, and political will.

During the Depression Era, Mayor Fiorello H. LaGuardia, a nominal Republican, became the poster boy for big government. He ruled City Hall from 1934 through 1945, and subscribed to a philosophy of growth that had no limits. He spent lavishly to build and support schools, parks, airports, public housing, municipal hospitals, a tuition-free City University, and a burgeoning welfare system.

To finance his ambitious plans LaGuardia began to employ fiscal gimmicks to mask his overspending.

"The city faces a crisis in its fiscal affairs," the Citizens Budget Commission announced shortly after the 1941 election, detailing the price that the city was paying for its modern, caring government. In 15 years, annual city expenditures, exclusive of emergency unemployment relief, had grown three times more rapidly than the city population, while the debt multiplied five and a half times the population growth.

Rather than accept this as the price of good intentions and large government, LaGuardia used every possible financial artifice to hide the full cost of his leftist urban policies. During the war, LaGuardia was able to camouflage growing municipal costs by taking advantage of the forced savings produced by the war economy (supply shortages prevented some expenditures that had already been approved and budgeted from being implemented, and the draft pulled a large number of civil servants off the salary rolls). Yet still he overspent. At the end of a given fiscal year, when the city was behind in its receipts, Comptroller Joseph D. McGoldrick would roll over unpaid bills to the next year's budget. *Brooklyn Eagle* columnist William Heffernan referred to the camouflaged budget as "the final stage of a municipal rake's progress ... the gimme philosophy raised to the nth degree, the legacy of a 'government that has spent without discretion and taxed without care.'"[1]

The investment banking firm of Lazard Freres and Co. declared in a credit report that the city lacked "proper retrenchment in expenditures for both current and capital purposes." The city insisted on expanding government services; yet as the Citizens Budget Commission pointed out, the programs rested on an "insubstantial fiscal foundation."[2]

Historian Thomas Kessner concluded: "By the time he [LaGuardia] left office, the city had been transformed into the colossal metropolis; it was saddled with debt, an infrastructure too expensive to maintain comfortably, dangerously expanding citizen expectations, and snowballing bureaucracy."[3]

The post-war boom helped lift the city from its fiscal malaise. However, during this period, the ideological seeds were planted that eventually wrecked its financial and economic base.

In the second half of the twentieth century, the two mayors primarily responsible for the unmaking of Gotham were Robert F. Wagner, Jr. (1954–1965) and John V. Lindsay (1966–1973).

As for their personal and political lineage, the two men came from different sides of the tracks.

Robert Wagner, Jr. was the son of the Democratic liberal icon, U.S. Senator Robert Wagner, Sr. Senator Wagner was revered by both Tammany Hall bosses and elitist reformers as the man responsible for the passage of the 1935 Act that bore his name and granted workers the right to organize unions and to engage in collective bargaining.

Robert Wagner, Sr. was born in Nastätten, Germany in 1877. His family moved to New York when he was eight years old. He went on to graduate from City College and earned his law degree from the New York School of Law in 1900.

As a young lawyer, Wagner became a member in good standing of Tammany Hall when it was led by Boss Charles Murphy. Unlike most bosses, Murphy appreciated talent and was unafraid to sponsor and promote men of quality and principles like Wagner and future governor and presidential candidate Alfred E. Smith. Murphy's Tammany Hall, Wagner said in 1937, "was the cradle of modern liberalism."[4]

The "Charles Murphy Institute," as it was called, permitted men like Wagner, Smith, Edward Flynn, and James Farley to become significant players in the political process. Murphy explained it this way:

> Formerly, it was difficult for young men of talent and ambition to get into public life. They were discouraged at every step by those already in who wished to keep the influence within as narrow bounds as possible. I encouraged the selection of young men for public office, particularly for legislative positions, encouraged them to develop their talent, to keep free from demoralizing influences, to speak their minds, do what was right and develop character and a reputation which would do credit to themselves and reflect favorably upon the organization and my leadership. These young men went out into public life and made good.... They gave you a different viewpoint of what Tammany Hall is and its aims and aspirations.[5]

Wagner began his climb up the political ladder when he was elected to the New York State Assembly in 1905. Three years later, he moved up to the state Senate where he was to serve for ten years, eight of them as the Senate's Democratic leader. After the impeachment trial of Governor William Sulzer, who was removed from office, Wagner became acting lieutenant governor.

In 1918, Wagner was elected to New York's Supreme Court and was later elevated to the Appellate Division. Elected to the U.S. Senate after accepting the Democratic Party's nomination in 1926, he was a fighting liberal. Wagner successfully pushed for social and labor legislation and was President Franklin D. Roosevelt's top Senate ally during the New Deal era. He served in the Senate until he resigned due to ill health on June 28, 1949. He died on May 4, 1953 at the age of 75.

Wagner, a baptized Lutheran, was married in 1908 to Margaret Marie McTague, a Roman Catholic. He converted to Catholicism in 1946. The couple had one son, Robert F. Wagner, Jr.

Born on April 20, 1910, Robert Ferdinand Wagner, Jr. was weaned on politics. After graduating from Manhattan's Loyola Catholic grammar school and the Taft School, he went on to receive his bachelor's degree and law degree from Yale University.

He followed his father's footsteps into politics when he was elected to the New York state Assembly from Manhattan in November 1937. On January 13, 1942, he resigned from the Legislature and joined the Army Air Corp, attaining the rank of Captain.

After being discharged from the service, Wagner went to work for New York City government serving as Tax Commissioner and Chairman of the City Planning Commission. In 1950, he jumped back into the political arena and was elected Manhattan borough president.

Three years later, Wagner made it known in various political circles that he was available for the Democratic mayoral nomination if the county bosses wanted him.

In 1950, Mayor William O'Dwyer, politically wounded by revelations of a police corruption scandal and fearing indictment, convinced President Harry Truman to appoint him Ambassador to Mexico. He resigned on August 31, 1950 and was succeeded by Vincent R. Impellitteri, the president of the New York City Council.

Viewed by the political establishment as a bungler, the Democratic Party refused to support Impellitteri in the November 1950 special election. Impellitteri thumbed his nose at the party bosses, ran as an independent on the newly created Experience Party, and won.

Impellitteri was a hapless mayor. Governor Thomas E. Dewey, state legislators, and Mike Quill of the Transit Workers Union walked all over him. "A survey taken of five hundred prominent civic leaders, failed to yield a single endorsement for the incumbent, and the City Club, a good government group, reported a great influx of new young members because 'the Impellitteri administration's faults have aroused young businessmen and lawyers as nothing else has in recent years.'"[6]

As a result, the low-key Borough President Bob Wagner, viewed as honest and practical, became the consensus choice of most Democratic leaders to rid themselves of Impellitteri.

But the incumbent mayor refused to step aside and entered the primary.

As historian Chris McNickle has pointed out, Wagner "outclassed" Impellitteri in every respect: He was "more well spoken to a listener's ear, more competent in spite of the mayor's incumbency, better respected for his integrity than the [mayor] who lunched regularly with [mobster] Tommy Luchese, and whose staff gave city jobs to dolts with impunity...."[7]

Wagner easily defeated Impellitteri in the primary by garnering 66% of the votes. He carried all the counties by large margins except heavily Italian Staten Island. That November, in a four-way race, Wagner won his first of three mayoral terms.

Born in Manhattan in 1921, John Vliet Lindsay grew up the quintessential WASP. He attended the Buckley School and prepped at St. Paul's School in New Hampshire.

Like Wagner, he received his undergraduate and law degrees from Yale. He also joined the armed services during World War II. As a naval officer, he served in both the Atlantic and Pacific theaters.

That's where the comparison ends. After the war, Lindsay joined a white-shoe law firm and became a member in good standing in the elitist "Republican Eastern Establishment."

When fellow GOP Manhattanite Herbert Brownell went to Washington in 1953 to take command of President Eisenhower's Justice Department, he hired Lindsay as the special assistant to the Attorney General. Realizing that Lindsay was a well-bred progressive Republican, Attorney General Brownell—a longtime crony of Governor Thomas E. Dewey—took the young assistant under his wing and began educating him in the ways of New York politics.

In 1958, Lindsay returned to New York to seek the Republican nomination in Manhattan's Seventeenth Congressional District. Lindsay was running in an area that was described by Bill Buckley "as probably the most fabled in the United States. It shelters not only just about all the residential financial, social, and artistic elite of New York but also probably the densest national concentration of vegetarians, pacifists, hermaphrodites, junkies, Communists, Randites, clam juice and betel nut eaters...."[8]

Thanks in part to the efforts of Brownell, the WASP establishment rallied around Lindsay. The incumbent, Republican Congressman Frederic Coudert, was literally scared out of the primary, and Lindsay, "one of the bright hopes of the Republican Party" (as *The New York Times* described him), went on to beat his Democrat-Liberal opponent.

Lindsay became one of the most liberal members of the House of Representatives. By 1964, he was voting with the Democrats half the time, and the left-wing Americans for Democratic Action gave him a rating of 87%. Lindsay went out of his way to infuriate conservative Republicans: he sponsored bills to abolish the House Un-American Activities Committee; refused to sign the annual statement opposing admission of Red China to the UN; opposed an amendment to permit prayer in public schools; voted against the reaffirmation of the Monroe Doctrine; and supported all of Lyndon Johnson's domestic initiatives.

Lindsay refused to endorse Barry Goldwater in 1964 and repudiated the GOP platform. He would remind his constituents that: "I am not running as a Republican, I am running as Lindsay." His campaign slogan was "John V. Lindsay—The District's Pride, the Nation's Hope." While Republicans all over the state went down in flames, better than 70% of the "Silk Stocking District" voted to return Lindsay to Congress. *The New York Times* saw Lindsay's "Stature Enhanced by Vote"; The *New York Post* called him "The Big Winner."

Analyzing the 1964 results, Lindsay described his party as "a pile of rubble." He lectured that liberals "are among the Republicans who will have to rebuild the party out of the ashes. We hope we can work with other moderate groups throughout the country to return the party to the tradition of Lincoln."[9]

With Nelson Rockefeller announcing in early 1965 that he would seek a third term as governor in 1966, and with Republican Jacob Javits and Democrat Robert Kennedy sitting tight on their Senate seats, Lindsay's options for political advancement were limited. After much vacillation, and after Rockefeller promised a substantial financial contribution, Lindsay announced his candidacy for the office of mayor of New York City. In a city where Republicans represented less than a quarter of the voting population, Lindsay declared that to build a winning coalition, he would run as a "fusion" candidate.

Lindsay told the New York Liberal Party screening committee that, "I have been a liberal Republican in Congress. Everybody knows that I have been independent in my decisions.... I want a non-partisan city administration and not a Republican administration. I want a fusion ticket with a qualified Democrat and a qualified Liberal along-side myself.... I will get as far away from the Republican Party as possible." And to guarantee that he would receive the Liberal nomination, the "Good-Government," "Reform," "Fusion" candidate agreed that "liberals would receive one-third of all city jobs and judgeships, a chunk of money to use during the campaign, and the right to name one of Lindsay's running mates."[10]

On May 28, 1965, Mayor Wagner announced that he would not seek a fourth term. He said that he had promised his wife, who died of lung cancer in 1964, that he would leave public life to attend to the upbringing of his young sons.

With Wagner out, the Democratic Primary became a free-for-all. City Comptroller Abraham Beame went on to beat City Council President Paul Screvane, Manhattan Congressman William Ryan, and Manhattan Councilman-at-large Paul O'Dwyer, brother of the disgraced former mayor, William O'Dwyer. Beame, an accountant from Brooklyn, won with a 45% plurality and was the first Jew to be nominated by Democrats for mayor of New York City.

Adding to the mayoral race's volatility was the announcement of William F. Buckley Jr., the editor of the conservative journal *National Review*, that he would seek the nomination of the four-year-old Conservative Party of New York State.

In his first press conference as a candidate at the Overseas Press Club on June 21, Buckley made it clear that he was running primarily against Lindsay whose brand of Republicanism he abhorred.

I propose to run for Mayor of New York.

I am a Republican. And I intend, for so long as I find it possible to do so—which is into the visible future—to remain a Republican. I seek the honorable designation of the Conservative Party, because the Republican designation is not, in New York, available nowadays to anyone in the mainstream of Republican opinion. As witness the behavior of the Republican Party's candidate, Mr. John Lindsay, who, having got hold of the Republican Party, now disdains the association; and spends his days, instead, stressing his acceptability to the leftward most party in New York, the Liberal Party. A year ago, Mr. Lindsay declined to support the choice of the national Republican Party—and of 27 million Republican voters—for President. Mr. Lindsay's Republican Party is a rump affair, captive in his and others' hands, no more representative of the body of Republican thought than the Democratic Party in Mississippi is representative of the Democratic Party nationally.[11]

And concerning his Democratic opponent, Buckley quipped: "The differences between Mr. Beame and Mr. Lindsay are biological, not political."[12]

Thanks to Buckley's presence in the 1965 race, it was the most memorable in New York's modern political history. Journalists and historians still talk about it, over fifty years later.

The race is also remembered because of a three-week newspaper strike that commenced just as the fall campaign was beginning. This meant that television debates, where Buckley could excel, became the prime media forum in the mayoral campaign.

It's fair to say that Buckley trounced his opponents in the numerous debates. Lindsay, with his chiseled good looks and sonorous voice, may have sounded great when he was fully scripted, but in the debate format, which emphasized spontaneous wit and a ready command of facts, he sometimes came across as dull-witted. The four-foot-eleven accountant, Abe Beame, looked and sounded like an IRS agent discussing an income-tax audit.

The mayoral slugfest ended on November 2, 1965 with John Lindsey narrowly winning with a plurality. He received 43% to Beame's 39% and Buckley's 14%.

Four years later, John Lindsay, after losing the Republican primary to State Senator John Marchi of Staten Island, would go on to win a second term as the Liberal Party candidate, receiving 43% of votes cast.

Robert Wagner and John Lindsay had very different political personalities. Wagner, a Roman Catholic of Irish and German descent, could mix comfortably with the Tammany Hall crowd and he instinctively understood the needs of the neighborhood blue-collar ethics.

Lindsay, an Episcopalian, with an attitude of "noblesse oblige" was more comfortable in the company of Upper East Side progressives and the good government crowd (goo-goos, as they were known), sipping cocktails at the Knickerbocker Club. And unlike Wagner, Lindsay knew nothing about the city's outer boroughs—Queens, Brooklyn, the Bronx, and Staten Island. He couldn't find his way on a subway to the city's working-class neighborhoods.

Lindsay's budget director, Peter Goldmark, admitted, "We all failed to come to grips with what a neighborhood is." Another Lindsay staffer, Nancy Seifer, said "There was a whole world out there that nobody at city hall knew anything about.... The guys around Lindsay didn't know what a neighborhood was. If you didn't live on Central Park West, you were some kind of a lesser being."[13]

However, what made Lindsay and Wagner similar was they both laid claim to the proud banner of liberalism. Both were committed to the left's insatiable appetite for expansive government and the imposition of their ideological formulas regardless of the cost.

Mayor Wagner set the tone for the liberal approach to governing when he said, "I do not propose to permit our fiscal problems to set the limits of our commitments to meet the essential needs of the people of the city."[14]

That guiding philosophy led to social policies that affected the city socially, economically, and fiscally and caused its financial collapse in 1975. What follows is an overview of what historian Charles Morris called New York City's "liberal experiment."

The Changing City

Throughout the first half of the twentieth century, a large majority of people living in New York City neighborhoods were white ethnics: Irish, Italians, and Eastern Europeans. In the 1940s, about 40% of the city's population were Catholic and 25% Jewish. And these ethnics held approximately 66% of the city's blue-collar jobs.[15]

At the end of World War II there were plenty of working-class jobs in the city. Employment was at an all-time high, surpassing job records set during the 1920s boom. Manufacturing in 1950, for instance, accounted for 30% of city jobs and employed 916,000 people.

But the post-war boom was short-lived. The city's population and job base began to rapidly change as millions of working-class folks moved to the suburbs.

Leftist social scientists often attribute the massive exit of white ethnics to racism because the city's African-American and Hispanic populations were growing at a brisk pace, but this claim is fallacious. The movement to the suburbs began long before the racial strife of the 1960s. "During the 1940s," labor historian Joshua Freeman has written, "nearly half a million New Yorkers left the city; during the 1950s, 1.2 million; and during the 1960s, another half million."[16]

In 1940, Nassau County's population was 406,000 and by 1960 it stood at 1,300,000—an astonishing increase of 320%. Similarly, Suffolk's 1940 population of 197,000 grew 338% to 666,000.

The flight to the suburbs of people and jobs can be attributed to several government policies: the Servicemen's Readjustment Act (better known as the G.I. Bill), FHA/VA Housing loans, the Federal Highway Trust Fund, and urban renewal.

The G.I. Bill, signed into law by Franklin Roosevelt in June 1944, contained various provisions including tuition vouchers for college and vocational training, guaranteed small business loans, the creation of veteran hospitals and vocational rehabilitation centers, and the most popular of all, FHA/VA home loans with no down payments.

When drafting these new policies and programs, New Deal social engineers made sure their fingerprints were all over the final documents. In the name of "urban planning," the Federal Housing Administration "encouraged banks to lend on millions of new low risk suburban homes while refusing to stake money on older city properties."[17] To ensure there were few exceptions in this anti-neighborhood lending program, the FHA designed requirements on lot size, house width, and distance from adjacent homes that effectively eliminated categories of inner-city dwellings such as the sixteen-foot row house. Historian Kenneth T. Jackson, in his award-winning work, *Crabgrass Frontier: The Suburbanization of the United States*, concluded that "Unfortunately ... [these] programs hastened the decay of inner-city neighborhoods by stripping them of much of their middle-class constituency."[18]

One FHA manual actually informed lending institutions that "crowded neighborhoods lessen desirability [and] older properties in a neighborhood have a tendency to accelerate the transition to lower class occupancy." And to further ensure policy compliance, federal tax-code changes gave developers incentives to build new structures in suburbia instead of improving old ones in city neighborhoods. Since many inner-city single-family homes were disqualified from receiving loans, the mass exodus to "Levittown" settlements commenced.

Between 1946 and 1979, 65% of all FHA/VA home loans in N.Y.C.'s metropolitan area went to finance suburban homes. Nassau County received 162,669 home loans; Suffolk County, 76,543 loans; and 29,660 went to Westchester. During the same period, New York City, which never developed a program to combat the exodus of working-class citizens to suburbia, received only 146,691 FHA/VA loans.

As for the people who left the city, urbanologist Edward C. Banfield observed, "Allowing for exceptions, however, the 'flight' of the middle class to the suburbs was not properly speaking a flight at all. Most of those who left did so neither from fear of violence or of blight, but simply because they wanted and could afford newer and more spacious houses and neighborhoods."[19]

Sociologist Herbert J. Gans, author of *Levittown*, agrees. In his study he found "that only 9% of those interviewed volunteered the inadequacy of their old neighborhood or community as their important reason for leaving it. The desire to own a spacious, free-standing house was the most frequent and important motivation."[20]

FHA/VA-guaranteed loans, which were risk-free for bankers and developers, in effect subsidized the movement of white working-class folks, "while at the same time penalizing investment in the rehabilitation of the rundown neighborhoods of older cities."[21]

The next issue that drove the exodus was transportation.

The emphasis of Robert Moses, New York State's "master builder," and other planners, was on road and bridge construction to the suburbs while mass transportation was generally ignored. On June 29, 1956, the Federal Highway Trust Fund was created and $2.2 billion of its funds were allotted to New York State for the construction of 1,246 miles of roads. In 1977, a Commerce Department study concluded: "In earlier stages of our national development, firms and individuals were willing to pay the higher costs of living and doing business in the Northeast's centers of high population and economic concentration.... The benefits of close proximity outweighed the costs, but modern transportation, together with electronic communications, have eroded the once-premium advantage of concentration. Instead, they are underwriting a decentralization of our national economy and population."

And then there was the ultimate scheme of meddling social engineers' intent on destroying the old ethnic neighborhoods, urban renewal.

To further their agenda, these big-government architects stripped away the planning powers of urban municipalities and directed the flow of federal dollars to big-time developers like the Levitts, who owned large pieces of undeveloped land in the suburbs, and to master builders like Moses.

Moses' Pulitzer Prize-winning biographer, Robert Caro, points out that 350,000 New Yorkers were driven from their one- and two-family homes thanks to his policies. With the clear intention of destroying certain New York City neighborhoods, Moses built several elevated roadways (e.g., Brooklyn's Gowanus Parkway, the Cross-Bronx Expressway, and the Grand Central Parkway in Queens) right through the ethnic enclaves. "The ethnic neighborhood embodied everything Moses considered retrograde and to use his term, he took a 'meat-ax' to the neighborhood and chopped it to death."[22]

Even America's leading prelate, New York's Francis Cardinal Spellman, succumbed to the temptation. To implement plans to build Lincoln Center on Manhattan's West Side, Robert Moses knew he would have to eliminate several Catholic parishes and their environs through the power of eminent domain, and he knew the residents would protest. So, he solicited and won the support of Cardinal Spellman and the Jesuits of Fordham University. In exchange for the land needed to build Lincoln Center, Moses offered Fordham the chance to build a Manhattan campus. Cost of the property to Fordham? One dollar. The real price for the property? The dislocation of 7,000 mostly Catholic families along with the destruction of St. Matthew's Parish on West 68th Street.

"Don't let's spend too much time with an individual pastor who thinks his jurisdiction and membership may be somewhat reduced," Moses lectured his planners. "There must be adjustments in the churches," he told them, "to keep pace with adjustments of the general population."[23] New York's churchmen actually went along with this cynical view. Cardinal Spellman blessed the deal, and St. Matthew's was bulldozed to make way for Fordham's Graduate School, which included a School of Theology.

"Urban renewal and public works," Joshua Freeman concludes in his prescient book, *Working Class New York: Life and Labor Since World War II*, "demolished the homes of hundreds of thousands of New Yorkers, leaving them no choice but to relocate even if they had no desire to do so."[24]

Sociologist Scott Greer lamented in 1965 that "the Urban Renewal Agency (URA) [after spending $3 billion dollars] has succeeded in materially reducing the supply of low-cost housing in American cities."[25]

New York City's Deindustrialization: The Decline of Working-Class Jobs

Historically, New York City was the manufacturing capital of the United States. At the turn of the twentieth century, manufacturers turned out clothing, books and periodicals, leather goods, textiles, cigarettes, and cigars.[26] "The expansion of low-wage factory work led to a rise in immigration, and in 1900 factory workers in the city accounted for 11% of the national total."[27]

During the 1920s economic boom, manufacturing jobs hit an all-time high of 1 million. When the Great Depression hit New York, the numbers dropped to 750,000. But, thanks to the war economy, the manufacturing sector grew by leaps and bounds reaching 916,000 by 1950 and hit a high in 1959 of 963,000, 7% of the national total.[28]

However, during the sixties, New York experienced a great decline in its manufacturing sector that has continued into the twenty-first century.

Manufacturing Job Loss[29]
New York City

Year	Total Manufacturing Jobs
1960	946.8
1961	914.0
1962	911.7
1963	878.7
1964	865.5
1965	865.1
1966	863.7
1967	846.7
1968	840.0
1969	825.8
1970	766.0
1971	702.2
1972	675.8
1973	652.8
1974	602.1
1975	536.9

In 1946, about 40% of the city's labor force were craftsmen, operators, and blue-collar workers. By 1970, that number was down to 29%.[30]

An important component of the city's manufacturing sector was the apparel industry whose workers were represented by the powerful International Ladies Garment Workers Union (ILGWU). Despite the ILGWU's political clout in the Democratic Party, it wasn't enough to stop the outflow of jobs in the clothing industry to suburbia, the South, and eventually to overseas markets that employed cheap labor. In 1950, there were 340,000 workers in the garment industry; in 1960, 247,000 workers; by 1965, it declined to 241,000; and in 1975, the total employed dropped to 142,000.[31] (The number of garment workers in New York City in 2018 was about 5,000.)

Why this decline? A host of reasons. Numerous industries followed the movement of the labor force out of the city to suburbia to be closer to the workforce and to build new plants on cheap land. One study indicated that manufacturers that left the city between 1961 and 1973 doubled their workable space for the same price they were paying in the city.[32]

Other reasons for leaving: "Many government policies made economic retardation worse. The repeated escalation of taxes, the tightening of environmental restrictions, the underfunding of mass transit in New York City, the souring of New York's business climate by intransigent bureaucrats and unsympathetic politicians. . . ."[33]

In 1953, New York City had 56% of the manufacturing jobs in the metropolitan region. Thirteen years later, 1966, the suburbs had a majority of the jobs.[34]

Just how the movement of industry hurt the city was succinctly described by historian Joshua Freeman:

> First, it diminished the tax base. Second, workers entering the city job market, especially with limited skills, found fewer employment possibilities. The 1954 decline in manufacturing employment hit Puerto Rican workers particularly hard, given their clustering in low-skilled jobs and lack of seniority. Third, job relocation deepened the lines of racial segregation. Since housing markets in areas to which industry moved generally

discriminated against nonwhites (in 1960, Levittown, near Nassau County's burgeoning defense industry, did not have a single African-American among its eighty-two thousand residents), blacks and Puerto Ricans could not easily follow manufacturing outward. Nonwhite urban newcomers found themselves locked out of the industrial jobs that had provided ladders of social mobility for previous generations. Fourth, the industrial exodus excluded the city, already largely outside the Fordist economy, from important sectors of economic growth. The relocation of electronic and aircraft equipment manufacturers to Long Island, for example, meant that New York benefited little from the Cold War boom in armaments spending. In 1963, only 3.5% of New York's manufacturing employees engaged in defense-oriented production, in contrast to over half in Nassau County.[35]

During the Wagner/Lindsay days, the city did experience job growth in other sectors. Between 1955 and 1970, service industry employment grew by 46%, finance services and insurance by 36%, and government employment by 44%.[36]

For the most part, however, the jobs generated in these sectors, which came to dominate the city's employment base, were what are described as "White Collar" positions. This phenomenon did not help the rapidly growing minority population that was mostly unskilled.

Throughout the 1950s, 1960s, and 1970s the city's population remained relatively flat but racially the demographic was changing.

In the 1950s, on average, 41,000 Puerto Ricans were moving into New York City annually. In 1960, their total number was 613,000 or 8% of the population. By 1970, it hit 812,000. The African-American population was also growing at a fast clip. In 1950, African-American population totaled 728,000, in 1960 it stood at 1,060,000, and 1,526,000 in 1970.

With the outflow of working-class jobs from the city, this created a serious problem for the many minority migrants because they had, relative to the white population, "fewer skills, less education and a greater incidence of poverty."[38]

New York City Population[37]
1930-1980

Year	Puerto Rican	Black	White
1930	—	328,000	6,540,000
1940	61,000	450,000	6,925,000
1950	187,000	728,000	6,891,000
1960	430,000	1,060,000	6,052,000
1970	847,000	1,526,000	4,973,000
1980	853,000	1,695,000	3,703,000

"The population shuffle, then—minorities in and whites out—" analysts Peter McClelland and Alan Magdovitz noted, "has brought a downward pressure on the income-generating potential of the region." This helps explain why New York City's per capita income declined from 143% to 116% of the national average between 1950 and 1974.[39]

The risk of minorities moving to the city and not finding a working-class job was mitigated by New York City's very generous welfare benefits. The welfare population in the city increased from 338,000 in 1960 to 530,000 in 1965. By 1971, recipients totaled an incredible 1,165,000.[40]

Welfare City

In America's first century, local governments and charities took care of the downtrodden in their communities. For most citizens and their elected representatives, there were two types of poor people. The first were those who were incapable of providing for themselves due to no fault of their own. The second group were those who were lazy, immoral, or alcoholics; in other words, the unworthy poor.

Eligibility for any financial aid was generally only for those perceived as the worthy poor—the disabled, the old or children of widowed mothers.

Assistance was often limited to long-time residents of a given locality, not drifters or newly arrived immigrants.

The guiding social philosophy was, "it is not bread the poor need, it is soul; it is not soup; it is spirit." In other words, temperance and a solid moral foundation "were believed to be the keys to rehabilitation and self-reliance."[41]

Most of those considered worthy poor in the late nineteenth and early twentieth centuries were widowed or single mothers with children. Believing that the basic unit of society—the family—was sacrosanct, social reformers attempted to maintain the home life of recipients of aid. Taking away a child from a mother and placing the child in an orphanage was, as a matter of social policy, expected to be rare.

A White House conference held by President Theodore Roosevelt in 1909 concluded that "home life is the highest and finest product of civilization. It is the great molding force of mind and character." Hence, state welfare assistance was expected to be designed to prevent the breakup of families. No child, the conference white paper concluded, "should be deprived of his family by reason of poverty alone."[42]

Many state legislatures responded by passing laws that required welfare workers to determine if the home life of recipients was good for the child. "Suitable home laws often contained specific behavioral prohibition or requirements on adult caretakers."[43]

The Great Depression dramatically changed the overall welfare philosophy that had previously been employed. Federal policy makers came to believe that state and local governments were incapable of handling the huge growth in the number of poverty-stricken families, and that citizens were not at fault and that their plight was the "byproduct of larger social and economic forces."[44] Accordingly, the New Deal created federal entitlements based on the "general welfare" clause found in Article 1, Section 8 of the U.S. Constitution.

While President Franklin D. Roosevelt expanded the federal government's role in providing relief to millions of suffering Americans, he warned the nation that "continued dependence upon relief induces a spiritual and moral disintegration fundamentally destructive to the national fiber. . . . [I]t is precisely the permanent guarantee of benefits that induces dependency."[45]

Thanks to this perspective, FDR created programs like the Civilian Conservation Corps (CCC) and the Work Projects Administration (WPA) that gave people a salary to work on various government-funded projects.

President Roosevelt argued that "as our Constitution tells us, our federal government was established among other things 'to promote the general welfare,' it is our plain duty to provide for that security upon which welfare depends."[46] On August 14, 1935, FDR signed into law the Social Security Act, which established new welfare programs: Aid to Dependent Children (ADC), Old Age Assistance, and Aid to the Blind, as well as the Unemployment Insurance Program.

Roosevelt was particularly pleased that participants who would receive retirement benefits earned the privilege. That is because the benefit was to be funded by a payroll tax placed on each person's annual earnings, not from the federal government's general fund revenues. The retirement benefit "should be self-sustaining in the sense that funds for the payment of insurance benefits should not come from the proceeds of general taxation."[47]

Roosevelt's vision that the Social Security fund would, over time, have a large reserve and be self-funding was short-lived.

In the post-World War II-era, Congress, not surprisingly, couldn't keep its hands off the reserve funds, and the Social Security retirement-fund surplus was spent on new benefits for other programs, the largest of which was Aid to Dependent Children. Welfare payments made to support children of divorced and widowed mothers was expanded to include the children of women who were never married.

Federal bureaucracies coerced the states to lower their eligibility rules. As a result, state moral (i.e., suitable home) codes were eliminated and the parent's behavior no longer mattered. A 1950s New Jersey grand jury investigation reviewing the state's expanded ADC program, concluded "There is no ... logic, justice or morality ... in granting state welfare funds to a mother who has had two, three, four or even five illegitimate children fathered by two or three different [men]. Immorality, promiscuity, and unwed motherhood seemed to be rewarded and encouraged by the easy allowance made upon a simple application of need."[48]

The other major cause of expanding welfare rolls was government regulatory and judicial decisions that ruled people had a legal right to receive welfare benefits.

Three landmark Supreme Court decisions were pivotal in creating an individual entitlement right to public assistance benefits, and all three cases involved the AFDC program. *King v. Smith*, decided in 1968, struck down the man-in-the-house rule and, along with it, a host of other state eligibility regulations as violations of the Social Security Act. *Thompson v. Shapiro*, decided the following year, struck down state welfare residency requirements as a violation of the Constitution's implied right to travel. *Goldberg v. Kelly*, decided in 1970, ruled that welfare was akin to property and therefore was protected by the Constitution's due process provisions.[49]

Writing in *Goldberg v. Kelly*, the noted liberal, Justice William Brennan, forcefully rejected F.D.R.'s belief that welfare was destructive, and described a new view of welfare: "We have come to recognize that forces not within the control of the poor contributed to their poverty…. Welfare, by meeting the basic demands of subsistence, can help bring within the reach of the poor, the same opportunities that are available to others to participate meaningfully in the community."[50]

Residency requirements, living arrangements, seeking employment, and proof of citizenship were eliminated because such regulations were considered intrusive.

These various regulatory and judicial decisions that relaxed standards, and 1960s Great Society programs, caused the welfare rolls to explode. And this was most evident in New York City.

In 1945, approximately 300,000 people receiving welfare benefits cost New York City $70 million. Five years later, the cost was $168 million—up 140%. By 1955, welfare costs had jumped 300% since the end of World War II to $280 million. During that same period, city spending on education had increased only 80%.

That ten-year period was only the beginning of the welfare explosion in New York City. The number of recipients continued to grow in both good and bad economic times because the system's policies had the effect of rewarding women for giving birth to children, regardless of the mother's marital status.

Over time, welfare became a way of life because leftists controlling the city government believed it was a right without the corresponding obligation to even seek a job—even that a work requirement was demeaning.

In 1965, Assistant Secretary of Labor, Daniel Patrick Moynihan, was one social scientist who recognized that these trends during the heyday of President Johnson's Great Society—when the federal government was writing blank checks to finance many hastily conceived and dubious social welfare programs—were unsustainable.

In his groundbreaking report, *The Negro Family: The Case for National Action*, the "Moynihan Report," as it famously became known, painted a bleak picture of the nation's inner-city African-American poor.

Moynihan found that many poor black people were caught up in a "tangle of pathology" thanks to U.S. welfare systems that simply "pensioned the Negros off." The expansion of Aid to Families with Dependent Children (AFDC)—which was originally created in 1935 to provide help to needy orphans and widows—actually encouraged black men to abandon their children because AFDC could not be paid to families where fathers were in the home. This also contributed to a sharp rise in out-of-wedlock black births.

Moynihan added that the absence of male figures damaged family stability and contributed to an "entire sub-culture of dependency, alienation, and despair." It also pushed black families into "a matriarchal structure, which, because it is so out of touch with the rest of American Society, seriously retards the progress of the group as a whole and imposes a crushing burden on the Negro male and, in consequence, on a great many Negro women as well."[51]

Moynihan was brought up Catholic and lived in a fatherless home, so he understood the importance of family, religious, and neighborhood ties, and "the enduring power of ethnic and racial cultures." And he approached the problem of the disintegrating black family from a different perspective than was typical at the time.

In *Freedom Is Not Enough*, a book on the Moynihan Report, historian James T. Patterson points out that Moynihan, influenced by "Catholic social welfare philosophy (which placed family well-being at the core of the good society) ... favored enactment of family allowances that would be given to *all* families with children." He also argued for programs that would give "men proper jobs and a respectable place in the community and family."

Great controversy arose after President Lyndon Johnson said in a June 1965 commencement speech at Howard University, based on Moynihan's findings, that if the black family unit did not become more cohesive, all the civil-rights gains would become meaningless.

Moynihan was assaulted by members of the Civil Rights movement, the poverty industry, and the fledging feminist movement for his "unflattering description of matriarchy" and for leaving the "impression that lower-class black women having babies out of wedlock were irresponsible." Patricia Harris, an African-American lawyer and activist, complained that the family issue was not *the* explanation for the problems of black people, but rather the "white discrimination against them, the white assumption of black inferiority." Dr. Benjamin F. Payton, a black sociologist, denounced Moynihan as a "crypto-racist."[52]

Lyndon Johnson quickly distanced himself from the speech and his administration repudiated the Moynihan Report. As a result, those destructive anti-poverty programs continued to be funded.

Total New York City welfare recipients during the Wagner Administration grew most years at a rapid pace.

Welfare Recipients

Year	Total recipients	
	Number in Thousands	Percent change over year
1958	331.4	--
1959	327.5	-1.2
1960	324.2	-1.0
1961	345.2	6.5
1962	360.5	4.4
1963	393.3	9.1
1964	446.6	13.6
1965	503.8	12.8

Source: N.Y.C. Department of Social Services

If the 12.8% increase in 1965 became the norm, the number of people receiving benefits would double in six years.

When John Lindsay took office on January 1, 1966, he had to contend with the budding welfare-rights movement promoted by federally-funded community organizers.

The original intent of the "War on Poverty" was to encourage "maximum feasible participation" of inner-city residents in their quest for community. However, social diagnosticians and policy makers changed the language in the Economic Opportunity Act of 1964 to read that there be "maximum feasible participation of public agencies and non-profits" in poor neighborhoods, the effect of which was the creation of a permanent poverty industry.

That simple clause was responsible for the rise of community organizers whom Daniel Patrick Moynihan described as "guerillas living off the administrative countryside" exercising power without the corresponding responsibility. Unlike elected politicians who were accountable to the people, these activists had no fear of punishment for ineffective or unpopular actions. Many of them subscribed to the radical rule of Saul Alinsky that one must organize to "rub raw the sores of discontent" because conflict is the basis of community organization.

In this spirit, a 1969 draft of the Office of Economic Opportunity's "Trainer's Manual for Community Action Agency Heads" actually encouraged "threat power" as an appropriate tool for community organizers:

> *Threat power*—the ultimate threat power is the riot. This is clearly against the public law, the national standards of conduct and the rules of OEO, and it is most destructive to the citizens most in need. But it is important that Board members recognize the *threat power* of rioting as a very real power and possibility.[53]

Hundreds of millions of dollars that poured into community action programs were dedicated to supporting professional organizers and sometimes rabble-rousers, not the downtrodden. Mayor Wagner complained to the White House in 1965 that community organizers were "becoming full-time paid agitators and organizers for extremist groups." One activist and later Green Party campaigner, Stanley Aronowitz, who was chairman of Manhattan's West Side Committee for Independent Political Action, conceded that the only benefit of the Great Society's largesse was that "it has given employment to the organizers."[54]

After studying the community organizing programs of the sixties, Moynihan concluded that they consisted of soaring rhetoric, minimum performance, feigned constancy, and private betrayal. There was not "maximum feasible participation" but "maximum feasible misunderstanding."

In the early Lindsay years, community organizers began a campaign to enroll eligible people to become welfare recipients. As Charles Morris, in his 1980 book, *The Cost of Good Intentions*, reports, "It became something of a badge of honor for case workers to manipulate the regulations to build the largest possible grant for a client, and the union included welfare liberalization as part of its bargaining demands."[55]

It became so easy to apply for welfare benefits that the *Daily News* called Lindsay's welfare commissioner, Mitchell Ginsburg, "Come and Get it Ginsburg."

Welfare rolls exploded during the Lindsay years and by the early 1970s, 30% of the city's population were on welfare.

Lindsay Years
Welfare Recipients

Year	Total recipients	
	Number in Thousands	Percent change over year
1966	566.6	12.5
1967	707.6	24.9
1968	889.3	25.7
1969	1,016.5	14.3
1970	1,094.7	7.7
1971	1,206.5	10.2
1972	1,265.3	4.8
1973	1,198.9	-5.2

Source: N.Y.C. Department of Social Services

The cost of welfare also skyrocketed. Welfare spending in 1965 was $400 million and by the end of Lindsay's first term in 1969, it stood at $1 billion.[56]

Another major cost to the city was Medicaid.

The Federal Social Security Act of 1965 established a Medicaid program that the states could join in order to provide medical services to welfare recipients. If a state agreed to participate in the program, the Feds paid half the cost.

Unable to turn down any opportunity to get a massive infusion of "free money" from Washington, then-Governor Rockefeller persuaded the Albany Legislature to pass a Medicaid bill.

But not only welfare recipients were eligible; the legislation included nearly all the "poor."

By late April 1966, Rockefeller had made enough deals with Democrats to secure passage of the Medicaid package. "With the eligibility benchmark set at $6,000 a year for a family of four, and the state promising to cover services from eyeglasses to surgery, New York was effectively offering free medical care to one in three of its residents."[57]

However, unlike the other states that joined the Medicaid program, New York State did not agree to absorb the entire 50% matching contribution with the Feds. Albany's legislation mandated that New York City and county governments pay half of the state's contribution, i.e., for every dollar expended, the Feds would pony up 50 cents, the state 25 cents, and local governments would be on the hook for 25 cents. Thus, did Medicaid become a staggering unfunded mandate for New York City taxpayers.

By 1970, there were in New York City, 546,157 Medicaid recipients—70% of the state total—for a total cost of $666 million. When Mayor Lindsay left office on December 31, 1963, it was costing $1.4 billion to service 663,034 recipients.

In his book *The Future Once Happened Here*, renowned social scientist Fred Siegel wrote of New York City's welfare revolution that:

> The irony was that in the name of redressing old injustices that treated African-Americans as less than full citizens, it recreated their second-class standing through liberal paternalism. In the name of antipoverty, it trapped people in dependency; in the name of eliminating invidious distinctions, it effaced the importance of character; in the name of the old Leninist dogma of "the worse, the better," it left the city far worse.[58]

Daniel Patrick Moynihan agreed. In fact, he forecasted in 1966 the impact of flawed poverty programs.

> [There] is one unmistakable lesson in American history: a community that allows large numbers of young men to grow up in broken

families, dominated by women, never acquiring any stable relationship to male authority, never acquiring any set of rational expectations about the future—that community asks for and gets chaos. Crime, violence, unrest, disorder ... are not only to be expected, they are very near to inevitable. *And they are richly deserved.*[59]

CRIME CITY

When William F. Buckley Jr. was running for mayor in 1965, he published a position paper describing New York City's rampant crime, its causes, and its remedies. The title was "In New York, It Pays," and in it he argued:

The first mark of the civilized community is the ability to control its criminal element. By this standard New York City has lapsed into barbarism. . . .

The basic cause of increased crime is, of course, the increasing moral and social disorder that mark contemporary society, and is thus less a problem for civil magistrates than for our churchmen and educators. . . .

Current welfare and housing policies have resulted in an undue concentration in New York City of idle and demoralized persons in an environment which breeds crime and criminals. No program to restore law and order to the city can be effective without coming to grips with New York's grave social problems.[60]

The liberal Daniel Patrick Moynihan agreed. The welfare system, in his judgment, was not only encouraging the breakdown of families, it was causing widespread problems including an increase in crime.

Moynihan voiced his concerns when serving as Assistant Secretary of Labor in a March 1965 memorandum to President Lyndon Johnson:

The breakdown of the Negro family is the principal cause of all the problems of delinquency, crime, school dropout, unemployment, and poverty which are bankrupting our cities, and could very easily lead to a kind of political anarchy unlike anything we have known.

- Last summer there were Negro riots in New York, Rochester, Jersey City, Elizabeth, Paterson, Dixmoor, and Philadelphia. Mostly made up of young Negro youth who know how bad off they are. There will be more.

- Last year the number of persons on welfare in New York City went up by one-eighth.

- In most of our cities, about three-quarters of the crimes of murder, forcible rape, and aggravated assault are committed by Negroes. Given the childhood experience of most of these youth, psychologists state that their later behavior is entirely predictable.

The point is this: Most of the welfare assistance, the special education efforts, the community action programs which we are now doubling and redoubling are essentially the provision of surrogate family services. Society is trying to do for these young persons what in normal circumstances parents do for their children. Only these children have no parents.

We can go on providing this kind of welfare assistance forever. The evidence of a quarter-century is that it does not change anything.

- In 1940 there were a quarter-million AFDC children whose fathers were absent—i.e., had deserted them. In 1963, there were nearly 2 million. Two-thirds of the increase were Negroes.[61]

In 1945, the total of New York City crimes reported—which included murder, rape, robbery, assault, burglary, and petty theft was 32,843. There were 292 murders that year.

Ten years later, during Mayor Wagner's first term in office, total crimes were 137,254; 306 of them murder.

During Wagner's last year in office, 1965, the number of criminal offenses reported were 187,795, and murders had jumped to 681.

This was only the beginning of the crime wave, as the following chart reveals:[62]

Year	Total Crimes	Murder
1966	323,107	734
1967	396,421	809
1968	482,990	976
1969	478,990	1,116
1970	517,716	1,201
1971	529,447	1,513
1972	434,303	1,757
1973	475,855	1,740

Under Mayor John Lindsay's watch, New York's murder rate jumped 137%. "New York's rate of increase and rank among [U.S.] cities in car thefts was 84%, rank fifth; robberies 209%, rank seventh; and rapes 112%, rank eleventh."[63]

As crime soared, John Lindsay and the self-righteous liberal allies who dominated his administration appeared to accept it as a norm. Historian Vincent Cannato has suggested that John Lindsay was so frightened of the impact of more aggressive policing against crime in minority neighborhoods that the mayor "seemed to be saying [more crime] was the price to be paid to avoid riots."[64]

But under Lindsay policing did change. The role of the beat cop, who often knew the neighborhood like the back of his hand, was degraded. The police no longer had a strong presence on the streets of the city's precincts. Cops were no longer pro-active. Instead they drove around, cocooned in patrol cars and merely reacting to incidents.

An NAACP report demanding the city tackle "the reign of criminal terror in Harlem" by putting more policemen on the streets, by more vigorously enforcing anti-vagrancy laws, and by seeking harsher punishment for convicted murderers and drug dealers, fell on deaf ears.[65]

Because Mayor Lindsay shared the liberal belief that "Society," not individuals, bears responsible for urban ills—that, in fact, minority crime arose from social injustice and criminals themselves are actually victims— he denounced calls for "law and order" as racist.

In his 1968 commencement speech at Vassar College's graduation ceremony in Poughkeepsie, New York, John Lindsay sought to answer his critics: "Peace cannot be imposed on our cities by force or arms," he said, "nor can people be converted at the point of a gun. . . . A shotgun aimed at the black teenager will no sooner achieve stability than a gasoline-filled bottle in the hand of that teenager will erase poverty."[66]

But in the late 1960s, New Yorkers were witnessing a city in decline. Staggering welfare rolls, decaying infrastructure, skyrocketing taxes and spending, rampant crime, graffiti-laden subways, and filthy streets were taking a toll on the psyche and pocketbooks of the city's residents. And it was into this political and social milieu that a young and ambitious Queens County lawyer, named Mario Cuomo, waded into when he took on the cause of Italian homeowners in Corona Queens in the late 1960s.

CHAPTER 3
THE RISE OF MARIO CUOMO

Mario Matthew Cuomo was born on June 15, 1932 to Andrea Cuomo and Immaculata Giordano Cuomo in a small apartment above the family grocery store in South Jamaica, Queens.

Mario's family lineage is an interesting one. His grandfather, Donato, born in the Province of Salerno in 1870, Italy, left for America in 1896 when he was 26 years old. After his son Andrea was born in 1901, and Donato had earned enough money to buy a home in his Italian village, he took his wife Maria and their four-year old son and moved back to Salerno.

In the 1920s, young Andrea moved to the village of Tramonti where he met Immaculata. Shortly thereafter they were married in 1925. Andrea, an American citizen by birth, then left for America in 1926 to find work and to set up a household before his pregnant wife—who was to give birth to their first child, Frank—would follow Andrea to Jersey City in 1927.

After working long hours as a day laborer for his uncle in Jersey City, Andrea took his savings in 1931 and bought a grocery store in Queens, New York.

Prior to moving to New York City, Immaculata gave birth to Marie in 1928. Her third child named Mario, born in 1930, died before his second birthday. Two years later, Mario Matthew was born.

The South Jamaica neighborhood of Mario's youth was predominantly Roman Catholic: Italians, Irish, and Poles. It was the golden age of the Catholic Church in New York when ethnic groups identified themselves by their parish.

When the Cuomo children were not in school, they spent most of their free time working in the store and making deliveries. Papa Andrea was a tough taskmaster and the undisputed head of the family. Because he appreciated the value of an education, he expected his children to devote their energies not only to their chores, but also to studying hard.

Although Mario served as an altar boy at St. Monica's Church, he did not go to the parish parochial school. Instead he entered P.S. 50 and attended C.C.D. classes after school to learn the tenets of his Church and to qualify for Confirmation. Mario initially had a tough time in P.S. 50 because he spoke very little English. Italian was the primary language in the Cuomo household.

In his teen years, Mario worked summers as a stock boy at the Gertz Department Store in Jamaica. He also developed a love for baseball and coached neighborhood youth teams. Playing ball, he developed his lifelong reputation as a ruthless competitor who hated to lose. And at one point, he even hoped to follow in the footsteps of his hero, Joe DiMaggio, and become a professional ball player.

Mario was not the typical street-corner kid. He never joined a gang and did not participate in typical teenage hijinks. Outside of baseball, his other passion was reading.

Another factor that kept Mario on the path of righteousness was his father's decision to move out of South Jamaica to a more residential neighborhood, Holliswood, Queens.

He was fortunate in receiving his parent's permission to attend St. John's Preparatory High School run by the Vincentian Priests and located in the Bedford Stuyvesant section of Brooklyn. He was especially fortunate that he did not have to attend the school most of the neighborhood wise guys attended—Jamaica High.

Paying fifteen dollars a month tuition was a heavy lift for the Cuomo family, until Mario was granted a full scholarship in his sophomore year.

At St. John's Prep, Mario came into contact with a student body that was mostly Irish, kids whose parents had been in the United States for generations.

Although Mario had top grades, was inducted to the More Honor Society and was a varsity baseball player, he felt like a fish out of water. The Irish at St. John's considered themselves elite, and Mario did not fit in.

Later in life, he admitted (and regretted) that he had been ashamed to have his parents attend school functions because they were working-class folks and spoke poor English. "They wouldn't have understood the language. I would have embarrassed them and embarrassed myself. . . . I didn't like those kids but I didn't want them to know that my parents didn't speak English well."[1]

Turning down an athletic scholarship to Hofstra, Mario accepted an academic scholarship to the Vincentians' St. John's University, then located in Brooklyn (now located in Queens).

At the university, Cuomo came into his own. He excelled academically. He made it into the America's Universities Who's Who and was tapped for the top scholastic society, the Skull and Circle Honor Fraternity. He also played varsity baseball.

During his years at St. John's, Cuomo developed his reputation as a self-assured, cocky, argumentative person. He loved to stir the waters and thought nothing of provoking arguments with students, professors, and priests. His close friend and classmate, Fabian Palomino, put it this way, Mario "could be withering, harsh and petulant."[2]

Mario also perfected a style he would employ his whole life: answering a question with a question. In a *New Yorker* profile, Ken Auletta described how Cuomo used the technique when he was caught smoking by a dean in one of the university buildings and was ordered to the cleric's office:

"What for?" Cuomo asked.

"You're not supposed to smoke," the dean said.

"Did you see me smoking, Father?" Cuomo asked. "Is there a rule against carrying a lighted cigarette?"

"Are you going to tell me you weren't smoking?" the dean asked.

"No, Father. But I'm not going to tell you that I was. I have shoes on, and yet I'm not walking."[3]

In 1951, Cuomo was offered a contract and a $2,000 signing bonus to join the Pittsburgh Pirates organization. Mario convinced his parents and his future wife, Matilda Raffa, that it was a great opportunity, and he signed the contract in the Cuomo grocery store in August of 1951.

Cuomo took a leave from St. John's and went to play for the Pirates minor-league team, the Brunswick Pirates in the Class-D Georgia–Florida League. "Matt" Cuomo, as he became known, garnered a reputation as an aggressive player with a short fuse. One Pirate employee said Cuomo was willing to "run over you if you get in his way."[4]

But after being knocked unconscious by a fastball that resulted in a concussion and caused a blood clot in his head, Mario decided there was more to life than baseball and went back to school and graduated from St. John's in 1953—*summa cum laude.*

Before he entered St. John's Law School with a scholarship in the fall of 1954, Cuomo married Matilda, a graduate of St. John's Teaching College.

To support the family—a daughter, Margaret, was born in 1955—Matilda taught at the Dutch Broadway School in Queens; Mario worked summers at his father-in-law's company and wrote briefs for a local law firm.

Cuomo excelled in law school. The dean's list student was accepted by the U.S. Attorney's Southern District office as a student assistant. And he was a founding editor of the school publication, *The Catholic Lawyer.*

Accepted by the Delta Theta Phi Law Fraternity, Cuomo tied for first in his law-school class with Patrick Rohan.

There were several future political stars in the St. John's Law School class of 1956, as well as two future deans of the law school, Patrick Rohan and John Murphy. Two classmates who would be his good friends for decades to come were Fabian Palomino and John T. Gallagher.

Thanks to the efforts of the dean of St. John's Law School, Cuomo met and was hired by Judge Adrian Paul Burke, a jurist on New York's highest court, the Court of Appeals. However, the post required Cuomo, who was living in an apartment with his family in the Cunningham Heights part of Queens, to spend many weeks in Albany.

Because Matilda preferred to raise their two children, Margaret and Andrew, (born in 1958) close to her family, she declined to move to Albany. To save money, Cuomo shared a room in Albany's cheapest hotel with fellow clerk and friend, Fabian Palomino. The two friends traveled to Albany together, worked long hours, and for leisure fiercely debated legal and political issues into the wee hours.

Clerkship terms are for only two years, so in 1958, Cuomo started looking for a full-time job with a law firm. Having worked for a respected judge and having graduated at the top of his class, Cuomo sought employment with some of Manhattan's most prestigious law firms.

What Cuomo quickly learned is that, in the 1950s, the old-line Anglo-Saxon Protestant firms frowned upon hiring Catholics, in general, and Italians, in particular. They even frowned upon people from the outer boroughs (i.e., Queens, Brooklyn, Staten Island, and the Bronx) because they deemed them socially inferior as, in their opinion, they were from "parochial" law schools like St. John's.

Being denied interviews by all the top-tier law firms hit Cuomo hard. One law school friend, John T. Gallagher—a future Cuomo appointee to the New York Court of Claims—told the author that Cuomo had a big chip on his shoulder because of those rejections and took great pleasure in verbally torturing WASP lawyers he came across during his legal career.

So, Cuomo accepted an offer from the Brooklyn firm of Corner, Weisbrod, Froeb & Charles. He also convinced his friend, Fabian Palomino, to join the firm.

Cuomo's new employer, like many others in the borough, was located near Court Street in downtown Brooklyn. It was a general practice firm that handled a variety of legal issues. But Cuomo, who would become a partner in 1963, preferred litigation and pushed the firm in that direction. It was during this period that he developed a love and a knack for appellate work. Although he was good in court litigation, over time he specialized in researching, writing, and arguing appeals. He also took on pro bono defense work for people facing criminal indictments. His experiences in the criminal courthouse influenced his thinking on the death penalty, which was to become a key issue in his political career.

Cuomo worked hard, often seven days a week. He never took vacations and expected his legal associates to follow his example. In whatever down time that was left, Cuomo became an adjunct professor at St. John's School of Law where for the next decade he taught several nights a week.

During the 1960s, Cuomo became active in civic affairs. He joined the boards of the Committee on Catholic-Jewish Relations, the Catholic Interracial Council, the Legal Aid Society, the St. John's Alumni Federation Board, and went on to serve as president of the Brooklyn Catholic Lawyers Guild and later the Queens County Catholic Lawyers Guild.

Cuomo took on community legal battles that most observers considered lost causes. He even took on the legendary "Master Builder" himself, Robert Moses, when he was president of the 1964–1965 World's Fair Corporation.

It happened this way: For decades, scrap metal dealers worked out of an industrial-zoned area in Willets Point, Queens, but Moses now considered the eviction of these dealers (by the expedient of eminent domain) an essential part of his blueprint for the World's Fair.

Cuomo took on the case of the scrap yard owners, despite pressure on him and his law partners to reject the case.

In a face to face meeting with Moses, Cuomo always claimed to have stared him down. Cuomo biographer, Robert S. McElvaine, described the confrontational thusly:

"Well," Moses said, shifting arguments, "we have to get the junkyards out of the way, because the whole *world* is coming to see the World's Fair, and this is a blight."

Cuomo told him to put tall trees around the junkyards "and pass a regulation that says you can't pile cars or scrap above a certain height. Then nobody will see it, except from the air."

"No, that's not good enough," Moses insisted. "We'll pay them generously."

"They don't want to be paid generously," Cuomo said, "because there's no place else that they can do this business. This whole city is zoned against heavy industrial use. If you had another location, it would be something else. But you're putting them out of business. These are people who are war heroes, people who won all kinds of awards for cooperating with the government—even those who weren't in the service. These are people who are very hardworking. They're not highly skilled; they're not commercially mobile; they have limited abilities—they're very good at what they do. You're trying to take away their livelihood."

"No. You've got to surrender," Moses demanded.[5]

In the ensuing court battle, Cuomo went up against Leo Larkin, Mayor Wagner's corporation counsel. The case went all the way to New York's highest court, the Court of Appeals, that ruled in favor of Cuomo's clients.

Beating the legendary Moses enhanced Cuomo's standing in the legal profession and his visibility in local communities, particularly in his home borough of Queens. He was called on to be guest speaker at numerous civic association meetings and took on some of their battles against City Hall. Despite his reputation as an argumentative bomb-thrower, he became known in community circles as a power broker himself, capable of negotiating fair compromises between conflicting forces.

One case Cuomo took on that made major headlines was the Corona, Queens scatter-site housing project.

Cuomo vs. City Hall

Mayor John Lindsay's administration was devoted to slum clearance in poor minority neighborhoods, a part of which was the decision to build "scatter-site" housing in old ethnic neighborhoods and to move those displaced by slum clearance into the new developments. "The City," historian Vincent Cannato has written, "would force middle-income communities to accept low-income housing in the name of integration and social justice."[6] Lindsay's advisors, many of whom probably didn't know what subway to take into Queens, certainly had no idea of the cohesiveness of these neighborhoods and were thrown off-guard when they met defiance from outerborough residents.

When it was announced that one such project was to be built in the Italian working-class neighborhood of Corona, Queens, residents rallied against it. The thought that sixty-nine of their one-family homes would be condemned for no other reason than to satisfy the ideological agenda of a remote mayor was beyond the pale.

To take on the city, the neighborhood folks turned to Mario Cuomo to lead the charge.

At first Cuomo was reluctant to accept the case. He had just finished with the scrap metal case, which took up plenty of time for little compensation. And the thought of another David versus Goliath case seemed too much to take on.

Yet, after meeting with what he described in his subsequent book, *Forest Hills Diary,* as "nice gentle family people, simple, hardworking, law abiding. . . . A vanishing breed"—he could not bring himself to say no.

Armed with legal briefs and demographic data, Cuomo and community leaders went to the Site Selection Board meeting at City Hall to plead their case. Cuomo was appalled that the Lindsay-controlled board dismissed them without a fair hearing and unanimously approved the Corona project.

Cuomo's next move was to tie up the matter in the courts. Although he eventually lost in the Court of Appeals in April 1969, he did manage to delay any city action for two years.

But the cause of the Corona Sixty-Nine did not die. Columnist Jimmy Breslin made their plight the subject of numerous columns. A local rabble-rouser, Vito Battista—founder of the United Taxpayers Party and a future assemblyman from Queens—led protests at civic association meetings and at City Hall.

To get the issue off the dime, Cuomo sat down with Lindsay's top deputy mayor and proposed a compromise that would permit most of the houses to remain standing. Others, he suggested, could be moved to a vacant lot.

The plan that Cuomo negotiated with the city was announced in December 1970. Twenty-eight homes were to survive and thirty-three would be moved. When State legislation was finally signed into law by Governor Rockefeller in 1962, only four homes were to be relocated.

The Cuomo compromise did not please everyone, particularly the professional agitators. But it was the first time the city had actually reversed a condemnation decision—and that was a significant victory for Cuomo.

In a letter to the Corona Taxpayers Association, dated June 9, 1972, Cuomo—who was paid only $12 thousand for his years of work—wrote the following:

> What does it all mean? Most of us have been so busy with the actual fray that we've not paused long enough to think through what it was really all about. Sure, it involved the homes and your right to stay in them and to make your lives there. But it involved a great deal more. It involved the integrity of the whole governmental system. A mistake was made. Everyone knew it. The question was: Would the System be big enough to confess and correct its own blunder? And the System did. And it did so not because it was forced to by vast political strength—we had none of that—it did so not because of the financial power of our group—because we were all practically beggars. In the end all we had on our side was the rightness of what we were saying. And in the end, it was rightness that prevailed.[7]

Cuomo took on this cause because he understood the importance of the neighborhood. He knew that for millions of immigrants who had come to America in the early twentieth century, their neighborhoods served as a social harbor where one was accepted, which was often not the case in the big city itself.

In New York's "Little Italy," for instance, relations were so tight that a given block would be inhabited by immigrants from the same town or village. These people struggled to secure a piece of land they could call their own. As social philosopher Michael Novak pointed out, to achieve moderate success in America, these immigrants took the route of "loyalty, hard work, discipline, and gradual self-development."[8]

It was certainly so for the Italian residents of Corona.

Cuomo had grown up in a similar neighborhood and knew from experience what Catholic sociologist Father Andrew Greeley described in his 1977 work *Neighborhood*: "The neighborhood asserts the importance of the primordial, the local, the geographic, the familial against the demands of the bureaucratized, rationalized, scientific, corporate society. . . . The neighborhood is rejected by our intellectual and cultural elites because the neighborhood is not modern and what is not modern is conservative, reactionary, unprogressive, unenlightened, superstitious, and just plain wrong."[9]

Cuomo opposed what he called "the city's elusive—and sometimes baffling—site selection process" because he believed it was wrong to destroy a cohesive community.[10] Cuomo told Robert McElvaine that the controversy was not about race but of class, a "clash between working and non-working people."[11]

Thanks to the publicity he received for his role in the Corona crisis, Cuomo found himself shortly thereafter embroiled in another controversy only a few blocks south of Corona in Forest Hills.

The Crisis of Low-Income Housing

In 1971, the Lindsay administration imposed upon the Jewish neighborhood of Forest Hills a plan to construct three twenty-four-story low income apartment buildings on an empty lot on 108th Street, slightly south of the Long Island Expressway.

Irate residents in this solid middle-class neighborhood, many of whom voted for Mayor Lindsay in 1965 and 1969, formed the Forest Hills Resident Association to oppose the housing project. Taking to the streets, they picketed the site carrying signs that read:

"Lindsay Is Trying to Destroy Queens.
Now Queens Will Destroy Lindsay"

and

"Down With Adolf Lindsay And His Project"

and

"Save Forest Hills, Save Middle-Class America"

and

"Forest Hills Doesn't Want Welfare
Towers on 108ᵗʰ St."

While Lindsay's apparatchiks dismissed the protesters as bigots, as in Corona they failed to understand the mindset of Forest Hills' mostly Jewish residents. Samuel Rabinove of the American Jewish Committee, in a 1972 letter to Jewish community leader Albert Vorspan, summarized the concerns and fears:

> Forest Hills residents survey the wreckage of the other NYC neighborhoods where Jews used to live in relative peace— Brownsville, Crown Heights, Williamsburg, East New York, Hunts Point, and now Far Rockaway. They see 80-year-old women thrown to the sidewalk by youths who steal their pocketbooks, armed robbery and burglary virtually epidemic, children beaten up and subjected to extortion in schools, which are no longer scholastic achievement-oriented, all kinds of property vandalized and destroyed. . . . They are not willing to sacrifice their own children on the altar of black revenge. Can anyone blame them?[12]

It is hard not to account Mayor Lindsay's denseness to a kind of elitist snobbery to which he was all but completely blind. His response to protests about his housing policies not only caused the mayor grief on the local level, it was also negatively impacting his hopes to oppose President Richard Nixon as the Democratic Party's 1972 presidential nominee. Forest Hills residents were contacting their retired relatives in Florida to vote against Lindsay in that state's Democratic primary. (Planes were hired to carry a banner that read "Lindsay Spells *Tsuris*"—Yiddish for "trouble.") Lindsay's poor showing in the primary ended his quest for the presidency.

Coming to the aid of the beleaguered Forest Hills residents, Cuomo's long-time friend and law school classmate, Jack Gallagher, now a Republican-Conservative assemblyman representing northeastern Queens, and Republican State Senator Martin Knorr from Ridgewood, introduced legislation crafted to kill the housing project. But when the bill arrived on the desk of Governor Rockefeller, he vetoed it claiming it was poorly written and probably unconstitutional.

The Lindsay Administration, now in damage-control mode, was in search of a way out of the dilemma. The solution: bring in their nemesis from the Corona debacle, Mario Cuomo, to negotiate a compromise solution.

Cuomo readily accepted the assignment. After all, wasn't he the great conciliator and defender of the outer boroughs? So, on May 17, 1972, he agreed "to make an independent exploration of possible revisions of the Forest Hills project and the overall planning for low-income housing in Queens, and to make recommendations to the Mayor, the City Council and the Board of Estimate for any changes." He also had the "freedom to make any recommendations [I] think appropriate."[13]

After extensive discussions with all parties on both sides, Cuomo presented a 10,000-word report to Mayor Lindsay on July 25, 1972.

To prevent accusations of racial bias, and to appear evenhanded, Cuomo's approach was analytical in nature.

As for the relocation of welfare recipients to Forest Hills, Cuomo wrote:

> By placing the emphasis upon the reality of the hostility in the Forest Hills community without respect to its justification or lack thereof, I do not mean to suggest that I regard that concern as utterly baseless. Certainly, the perfidious generalization that all low income, or for that matter welfare people are vandals and criminals would be universally rejected by reasonable men. On the other hand, to deny the poverty and social problems are related would be to deny the testimony of history and our own experience in this City. . . . One need only to travel through

this City to confirm the deterioration that has been occasioned by the spread of poverty areas. This hard experience is fresh in the minds of many of the Forest Hills residents who fled from that kind of erosion in Brooklyn, the Bronx and Manhattan into Forest Hills where, by dint of their own efforts and the benediction of the fates, they have been able to create a community and a life style relatively free from the kinds of problems that oppress the ghetto dweller.[14]

As for the city's proposed housing plan, Cuomo concluded that the project was too large to implement, and he recommended the city compromise with the local community and decrease its scope by 50%, and with 60% of the apartments going to low-income families and 40% to seniors.

Meeting with various parties to review the draft of his report, Cuomo wrote in his diary on July 22, four days before the actual release of his findings, ". . . they're all unhappy, I think, but none of them attempted to push me."[15]

He was right; neither community leaders nor city bureaucrats were happy with the report. Nevertheless, both sides swallowed hard and accepted Cuomo's conclusion:

> The position I recommend will call for political courage on the part of those who assume it, since criticism and pressure from both sides is inevitable. Hopefully, however, the criticism will be outweighed by a predominant reasonableness which recognizes and appreciates what was stated by a great man long ago:
>
> > "All government—indeed, every human benefit and enjoyment, every virtue and every prudent act—is founded on compromise. . . ." – Edmund Burke (*Speech on conciliation with America, March 22, 1775.*)[16]

Cuomo's reference to the intellectual founder of the modern conservative movement sealed his case.

Mayor Lindsay, who claimed he would never abandon his ideological-driven position, surrendered, reluctantly accepting the Cuomo compromise.

Most Queens politicians applauded Cuomo's report, including the Queens Democratic leader, Matty Troy. One elected official from Manhattan, who joined the protesters in Forest Hills and endorsed Cuomo's report, was a little-known Manhattan Congressman named Edward I. Koch. Ed Koch claimed his membership on the House Banking Committee, which oversees housing, compelled him to take a stand. Few suspected at the time, including Cuomo, that Koch was contemplating a race for mayor down the road.

But then and there, Cuomo was on a roll. Newspaper editorials and members of the Board of Estimate—the entity that gave final approval to the Cuomo plan—praised his efforts. He parlayed the diaries he wrote and the report into a book that was published by Random House, one of America's most prestigious publishers. To add pizzazz to the work, the noted political columnist, Jimmy Breslin, wrote the preface, and Dr. Richard Sennett, professor of Urban Studies at Princeton, contributed the afterword.

First Political Stirrings

With all this notoriety, the 40-year-old Cuomo began thinking about entering the political arena.

The notoriety Mario Cuomo received from his "split the difference" settlements in the Corona and Forest Hills public-housing cases gave him the political bug. But he cloaked his ambition by claiming government service was a calling, a "religious need to participate in this world and try to improve it."[17] Believing "integrity" was rare in politics, he portrayed himself as a twentieth-century Thomas More, giving up the quiet life to serve others. He would be an ombudsman who supplied, as he wrote in his Forest Hills diary, "an intelligent balanced alternative that this town will understand and respect if it is properly and honestly articulated."[18]

Of course, there were other driving forces, not least his ambition and his certainty he was smarter than most others in public life. He admitted to his biographer that he had an obligation to run for office ". . . because I for so long stayed out of the system and took shots at it . . . and excoriated John Lindsay, Nelson Rockefeller, Bob Moses and everybody else. . . . I reached the point where I felt like a hypocrite taking shots at the establishment. Nothing is easier than that."[19]

That quote sounds like the Mario the author first met in 1970 in the Flushing law office of his classmate, Assemblyman John T. Gallagher. My first impression was of a very smart man, possessed of a very sharp tongue who couldn't resist a wise crack.

Journalists Jimmy Breslin and Jack Newfield, as well as former Bobby Kennedy aide Adam Walinsky, were pressuring him to enter public life. They saw him as a new kind of liberal, an "urban populist."

Breslin claimed that Congressman Hugh Carey considered Cuomo a genius. When Carey was thinking about running for mayor in 1969, he allegedly "begged" Mario to join his ticket as City Council president.[20]

Cuomo turned down that spot as well as positions in the Lindsay administration—which would have been political dead ends considering how unpopular Lindsay was at the end of his second term in 1973.

When Cuomo's name was bandied about for mayor in 1973 by his friends in the press, Mario received plenty of resistance from his wife, Matilda. Yet, that did not stop him from sitting down with the Queens County Democratic boss, City Councilman Matthew Troy, Jr. Because Troy had supported Cuomo's Forest Hills compromise, Mario was initially convinced that Troy was a man of his word. (Cuomo would later learn the hard way that Troy—who eventually did a term in prison—was, in Cuomo's words, "one of the great liars in political history."[21])

Putting his toe into the mayoral waters, Cuomo did not present himself as a flaming liberal; nor did he paint himself as an outerborough right-winger. Nevertheless, as his friend J. Richard Sharkey observed, "People in Manhattan thought he was very conservative. He talked about the anarchy sweeping the city. It was a very right-of-center speech."[22]

At Matt Troy's Queens Democratic club, Cuomo came up against Ed Koch for the first time. Koch was also considering a mayoral run and developing the "shtick" that would serve him well four years later—as a kind of recovering Manhattan super liberal sympathetic to the fears of neighborhood white folks.

Cuomo took a different approach. For lack of a better description, call it "shock therapy"—the truth from the Queens guy who knows the mind of working-class white residents.

At Councilman Troy's meeting, Cuomo bluntly told his listeners:

> You've got all these blacks and Puerto Ricans down in South Jamaica where I was born and raised. You think they're *all* bad because they're the ones who are coming up here mugging and raping you and breaking into your houses. And you're saying "We don't want them in our neighborhoods. We don't want them anywhere near us? Leave them where they are. They should all die."

> Well, the net result of that attitude is their poverty will get worse and they'll produce more muggers and rapists. The truth is *we can't get far enough away from them to be safe.*

> Okay, the liberals come and tell you that it's our moral obligation to help those people because we oppressed them—the blacks anyway—for 400 years. That's what John Lindsay told you, right? However, here in Queens, how can I tell my father that? My father who for so many years had a grocery store in South Jamaica. In that store he never punished a black or hurt a black or enslaved a black. If you tell me about his "moral obligation," he won't know what you're talking about. Here's what you have to say to my father. "Whether you love them or not, whether you have an obligation to them or not, is between you and God. When you go to confession on a Saturday, talk to the priest about it. But unless you do something about where they are now, how they live now, they will continue to come into your neighborhoods and mug and rape."

> Where are you going to next? Wyandanch? Then where? Montauk? You know what's going to happen? In time, they'll be three miles away from Montauk and your daughter is going to get caught because next is the water and it's all over. You can't run forever. You have to find ways to break up segregated neighborhoods.

And most of all, you have to find ways to get them jobs. Real Jobs. And that, in part, means electing people who will really do that. Remember, we have to do this because we love ourselves, not because we love them. In the end, the only thing that works is self-interest.[23]

As Cuomo was organizing a campaign team, figuring out ways to raise money and preparing his official announcement, Matt Troy was getting cold feet.

After eight years of elitist government led by John Lindsay, the social scientists, editorial writers, pundits, union leaders, neighborhood pols, and the people were exasperated and angry over the fiscal, economic, and social decline of their city.

The left-wing journalist, Murray Kempton, who created the 1965 slogan, "Lindsay—he is fresh, everyone else is tired," conceded that "The substantive achievement does not exist: under Lindsay, the air is fouler, the streets dirtier, the bicycle thieves more vigilant, the labor contracts more abandoned in their disregard for the public good, the Board of Education more dedicated to the manufacture of illiteracy than any of these elements ever were under Wagner."[24]

At *The New York Times*, John Corry wrote: "The problem was that Lindsay had been a myth to begin with, and when a myth dies, it leaves a huge void. Lindsay critics were like disappointed lovers. They had offered him their hearts, but now they pursed their lips and shook their heads."[25]

Jack Newfield of the *Village Voice*, with co-author Paul DeBrul, concluded in their book *The Abuse of Power* that:

Lindsay turned out to be a disappointment, almost a tragedy, as mayor, given his potential and hopes invested in him. . . . Lindsay dramatized the role of mayor, but he couldn't *do* it. He was the mayor of America, but not of Queens. From St. Paul's School and Yale, he lived in the bubble of Manhattan culture. He was a WASP running the greatest ethnic city on earth, and he did not understand the ordinary lives of ordinary people in the four other boroughs. Lindsay was an activist with poor judgment. Lindsay was an actor with no self-knowledge.[26]

Dr. Fred Siegel summed up Lindsay's eight years in office thusly: "Lindsay wasn't incompetent or foolish or corrupt, but he was actively destructive."[27]

And Norman Franks of the Patrolmen's Benevolent Association said this about the Lindsay record: "In every area that is central to our survival, the city is literally coming apart at the seams. And as crisis piles upon crisis, as tragedy follows on the heels of disaster . . . the official response at the highest levels has consisted of indecisiveness, procrastination, empty gestures, futile attempts at administration reform and repeated adventures in brinkmanship."[28]

Lindsay's low standing with the public led Matt Troy and other Democratic leaders to believe the time was ripe for them to take back control of City Hall and the patronage that went with it. And Troy, anxious to be in the winner's circle with the next mayor, concluded that Cuomo was not the right Mario to rally the angry ethnic voters in Queens, Brooklyn, and Staten Island.

So, in March of 1973, Troy pulled the rug out from under Cuomo and endorsed another Mario: Bronx congressman Mario Biaggi. In Troy's mind, the congressman was a much better fit. Biaggi, a 23-year veteran of the New York City Police Department, was wounded eleven times in the line of duty. He was the recipient of the Department's highest award, the Medal of Honor—and twenty-seven other decorations as well.

As a "Law and Order" candidate, Biaggi also received the nomination of the Conservative Party, which had impressive ballot box clout in the outer boroughs.

Cuomo, angry that he was passed over by Troy, told his supporters he was thinking about running without any organizational support. But as he worried about what to do next, Cuomo revealed a side of his character that reappeared throughout his political career: he privately "agonized and procrastinated" over whether to stay in the race or get out.[29] After days of indecision, Cuomo finally concluded it just couldn't work. Even if he managed to file enough petitions to get on the ballot, he didn't have the money to finance a credible campaign; and anyway, the two Italians, Biaggi and Cuomo, would split the votes of their working-class constituents and cancel each other out.

At a late-March mayoral candidates' night at a civics association in Jackson Heights, Queens, Cuomo announced, "I am not running and may never run for mayor." Clearly disgusted, he added, "politics stinks."[30]

From this unhappy experience, Cuomo made several decisions he would adhere to for the rest of his political career; decisions that some would argue, despite the successes to come, later cost him his election to a fourth term as governor and closed the doors to a presidential run. He decided he would never again trust anyone in politics. He would rely only on family and a very, very close circle of friends. And he would play the game of politics by his own rules, not the conventional ones.

As it turned out, the Biaggi campaign was a disaster. In May, reports surfaced at both the New York *Daily News* and *The New York Times* that Biaggi had invoked the Fifth Amendment when questioned by a federal grand jury in 1971. Although Biaggi denied the accusation, leaked grand jury minutes proved he had.

Biaggi plummeted in the polls and came in third in the Democratic primary with just 14.7% of the vote.

The two top vote-getters, Comptroller Abraham Beame and Congressman Herman Badillo, having received under 40% of total votes cast, had to face each other in a runoff. Beame easily beat Badillo, garnering 60.7% of the vote. He went on in November to be elected the first Jewish mayor of New York City.

Cuomo's hatred of politics did not last very long. Councilman Troy's top political crony in Queens, Borough President Donald Manes, offered Cuomo a consolation prize in late 1973: ombudsman for complaints filed with the New York State Public Service Commission.

The Public Service Commission (PSC), created in 1907, regulates the gas, electric, water and telecommunication industries throughout the state. According to the 1973 edition of the *New York State Red Book*, the PSC "has jurisdiction over the rates, services, and long-range planning of all electric, gas, steam, telephone and telegraph corporations, and of water works corporations having a value of $30,000 or more, and of the rates of smaller water works corporations. The Commission also has licensing jurisdiction over the siting of electric and gas transmission lines."

When Don Manes was sworn in as Queens County's 16th Borough President on September 22, 1971, he pledged to use the somewhat ceremonial office "as an ombudsman—a conduit for complaints and a watchdog over services supplied by various city agencies."[31]

So, he appointed Cuomo to a made-up, unsalaried position to advocate for citizens filing complaints with the State agency. While the position was legally powerless, it gave Cuomo a public platform to generate news as the guardian angel of the powerless. It was a perfect position for Cuomo. He could be a critic without any responsibilities.

Knowing that Cuomo still had the political bug, his friends, led by Adam Walinsky, now tried to convince him to run for governor in 1974. After 16 years of Republican rule, it was the conventional wisdom that the State House was ripe pickings for the Democrats.

Cuomo declined, claiming he was not qualified. But he also had to suspect that he didn't have the clout, money, or organization to get the top prize. Compared to the front-runners, millionaire Howard Samuels and Congressmen Hugh Carey, Cuomo was still a never-been-elected-to-anything neophyte.

But Walinksy was unwilling to give up and urged Mario to go for the second spot on the ticket, lieutenant governor.

At first, Cuomo displayed his Hamlet, "to be or not to be" side. He told Walinsky that, logically, if he were not qualified to be governor, he couldn't be qualified to be the lieutenant, since he'd become governor were lightning to strike.

His friends persisted and convinced Cuomo otherwise, and he entered the political fray for the second time despite the fact that Matt Troy made it clear the Queens organization would not support him.

While Cuomo—to the surprise of the political class—became the lieutenant governor nominee at the Democratic Party convention—the events surrounding his victory are murky at best.

Although Cuomo didn't have Troy's support, he believed he had the support of Brooklyn Boss Meade Esposito and a host of other leaders.

At the convention, however, the dynamics were constantly changing. The state party chairman, Joe Crangle of Buffalo, tried to impose Assemblyman John LaFalce of Western New York on the convention as lieutenant governor. In an attempt to dissuade Cuomo from seeking the lieutenant governor spot, Troy was authorized to offer him the nomination for U.S. Senator. Knowing it was merely a sop, Cuomo made it clear he would not be a sacrificial lamb against the incumbent Senator Jacob Javits, and told Troy to forget about it.

Cuomo claimed he was initially for Carey at the convention, had convinced political guru, David Garth, to run Carey's campaign, and hoped to join up with Carey on his ticket.

Later on, Cuomo insisted Carey "screwed" him. "He stayed away from me at the convention. I tried to find him, but he made a deal with the leaders which I didn't know. They would give him 25% of the delegate vote that he needed to get on the ballot without petition, but in return he would have to stay away from me or any lieutenant governor candidate."[32]

Cuomo then endorsed Howard Samuels and said Carey called him up and said, "You're screwing me—you're going with Samuels"! Cuomo replied, "Boy, you've got some nerve!"[33]

Hugh Carey had a different version. After Cuomo endorsed Samuels, Carey says he spoke to Cuomo and said "Why did you do that? Don't you know that Samuels is running against me and that he has already said that he wants [State Assemblyman Antonio G.] Olivieri for lieutenant governor?" Carey claimed that Cuomo replied, "I know that, but Samuels said he is really for me and that he will give me money for my campaign after the convention."[34]

The Democratic Convention in Buffalo nominated Howard Samuels for governor. Samuels was from the Rochester area and had an impressive resume. A graduate of the Massachusetts Institute of Technology, he had served as President Johnson's Undersecretary of Commerce and President Carter's Director of the Small Business Administration. Later, he headed up New York City's Off-Track Betting operation and became well-known as "Howie the Horse."

Samuels, a self-made millionaire, served as Frank O'Connor's lieutenant governor candidate in his unsuccessful run against Nelson Rockefeller in 1966. Four years later, Samuels lost the Democratic gubernatorial primary to former U.S. Supreme Court Justice Arthur Goldberg.

Hugh Carey, who was not endorsed by any of the state's county leaders, managed to rack up 31% of the convention's votes. By breaking 25%, he did not have to go the laborious and expensive petition route to get on the primary ballot.

When it came to the lieutenant governor spot, Samuels remained neutral and party leaders began feuding.

At one point, Crangle pulled his support for LaFalce and put up state Senator MaryAnne Krupsak from Buffalo thinking a woman candidate would shut out Cuomo and Olivieri. Although Troy supported her, he lost control of his angry Queens delegation which voted for Cuomo.

On the first ballot, no one received the majority. On the second ballot, Cuomo began to pick up steam thanks to the efforts of Nassau's Democratic Chairman Jack English and District 37 union boss, Victor Gotbaum. On the third ballot, Cuomo easily went over the top receiving 65% of the vote.

During the balloting, his opponents both received 25% of the vote and MaryAnne Krupsak and Antonio Olivieri announced they would contest the nomination in the primary.

Although Cuomo was the official nominee, his running mate, Howard Samuels, appears not to have been an enthusiastic supporter. After the convention, it took party leaders two weeks of cajoling to get Samuels to publicly endorse his running mate. That fact belies an earlier claim that Samuels had promised to donate campaign money to Cuomo.

By all accounts, Cuomo was an awful candidate, as he himself later admitted. But there was more to it. Cuomo ran as an obnoxious bull in a china shop. He portrayed himself as an in-your-face "urban" populist.

He described his lieutenant governor designation as an "accident" and despised the public impression he was the choice of party bosses.

At speaking engagements, Cuomo would tell attendees, "I don't like schlepping on the beach and I don't like balloons."[35]

When he couldn't get meetings with publishers of newspapers and leading members of Manhattan's political elites, he told Nat Hentoff of the *Village Voice*, "I suppose they thought it would be a total waste of time to talk to some crude Italian Catholic. After all, they were liberals."[36]

When Cuomo's opponents declared they would not maintain private law practices if elected, he quipped, "The only difference is that they don't have law practices to give up and I do."

Lacking funds to finance his campaign and gaining little traction with voters, Cuomo told a member of his staff, "Sometimes I wonder why I am doing this. I ask myself where I get the nerve to think people should listen to me."[37]

Cuomo was the anti-candidate always giving the public impression that he was a reluctant participant in the public arena. He wanted to give back but was fearful he wasn't qualified or too much of an introvert to be a glad-hander.

During the 1974 campaign, the urban populist also ran as a loyal son of the Roman Catholic Church. He was a favorite of the bishop of the Brooklyn Diocese, Francis J. Mugavero. The bishop was a left-wing social worker whose diocese was known as the "Reno of the Church" because it granted more annulments annually than the rest of the American Church combined.

Cuomo revealed his Catholic stripes during the one and only debate with Olivieri. (Due to a flat tire, Krupsak failed to appear.)

Cuomo, the *Times* reported, "said that if had he been a member of the [State] Legislature, he would have voted against the 1970 law that relaxed abortion curbs in the State. The Queens lawyer also said he would have supported laws providing State aid to non-public schools."[38] (On another occasion, he declared that he was against selling contraceptives and opposed so-called "gay rights" bills proposed by N.Y.C. councilmen.)

Olivieri, a baptized Catholic, was "defending his vote for the more permissive abortion law, saying he personally opposed abortion but supported freedom of choice for others. He said he had voted against state aid to non-public schools as unconstitutional, a position the courts have upheld."[39] Ironically, Olivieri's "personally opposed" language would later be embraced by Cuomo—and famously so.

While the bishop of Brooklyn could not publicly embrace Cuomo, he attempted to help in small ways. Word got around to the local Knights of Columbus chapters and the various parish fraternal organizations that Cuomo was one of them.

The Brooklyn diocesan newspaper, *The Tablet*, published letters to the editor with suggestive headlines in their August 29th and September 5th editions:

Cuomo Means Quality

It hardly seems fair that the one name which has not so far been mentioned in this column is Mario Cuomo, candidate for lieutenant governor. He deserves the loud and enthusiastic endorsement of Right to Life—but they've been too busy attacking Carey. Mario, in my personal opinion, is quality—tried and true, through and through.

NOTA BENE: *The Tablet* and its columnists discuss political issues but we do not endorsee (sic) candidates. However, we do endorse voting in the Primary on Tuesday, Sept. 10.

Olivieri Pro-Abortion

Dear Sir: *The New York Times* of Aug. 24 reported the taping of a TV debate between Mario M. Cuomo and Antonio G. Olivieri, two candidates for the Democratic nomination for Lieutenant Governor. In that debate Mr. Cuomo stated that he supports laws providing state aid to non-public schools and that he is strongly opposed to abortion.

Mr. Olivieri repeated his support for the permissive abortion law which he warmly supported as a member of the Assembly and defended his repeated votes against state aid for non-public schools. It should be noted that not only did Mr. Olivieri vote for the abortion-on-demand bills, but he also voted against the "conscience clause" bill which was overwhelmingly passed by the Legislature in 1961 to protect the rights and consciences of doctors and nurses opposed to their own participation in abortion procedures.

On Primary Day, Tuesday, September 10, the political establishment was shocked to learn that Democrats embraced Hugh Carey over Howard Samuels, 55% to 45%, a near rout. Carey carried New York City, the suburban counties and most of upstate.

Carey's easy victory did not, however, help Cuomo. He came in second to State Senator MaryAnn Krupsak receiving 32% to her 42%. Olivieri came in a distant third place, garnering 26% of votes cast.

The fact that Krupsak was a woman probably helped her cause. The other major reason for her victory was that Cuomo and Olivieri split the Italian vote. In 1974, New York still had large white ethnic voting blocks in its city's working-class neighborhoods. Being Catholic and Italian or Irish mattered, hence the concept of balanced Democratic tickets that generally included Irish, Italian, and Jewish candidates.

While Cuomo was licking his wounds, Hugh Carey went on to win a smashing victory in November. Incumbent Republican governor, Malcolm Wilson, who had taken over the governorship in 1973 after Nelson Rockefeller resigned to become Gerald Ford's vice president, couldn't survive the post-Watergate Democratic tide. He went down receiving only 40% to Carey's 60%. Carey managed to carry 61 of New York's 62 counties.

Mario Cuomo, despite his political failures in 1973 and 1974, and despite his claim that he hated politics, couldn't stay away. He made it clear that he was available for an appointed position—specifically, as New York's Secretary of State.

Curiously, the first appointment Carey announced was that of Cuomo to just that office. But why? After all, Carey owed Cuomo nothing. They had fought at the state Democratic convention. And Cuomo's claim that he talked political guru Dave Garth into taking on Carey's campaign was ludicrous. Garth told Carey's biographers, Seymour Lachman and Robert Polner, that it was Carey's ailing wife, Helen, whom Garth had met on a D.C. shuttle plane, who had convinced him to run Carey's media campaign.[40]

One long-time Carey aide claims that Bishop Mugavero appealed to Carey to give Cuomo the post. During the campaign, Carey equivocated on the abortion issue. He said he opposed abortion but also opposed a constitutional amendment prohibiting abortion and supported state funding of abortion. So, it is possible Carey agreed to a appoint Cuomo as Secretary of State as a way to placate the bishop and to get back into his good graces. Or maybe Carey may have wanted the ambitious Cuomo, in the phrase frequently used by President Lyndon Johnson, "inside his political tent pissing out instead of being outside the tent pissing in."

CHAPTER 4

HUGH CAREY TAKES THE HELM OF THE SINKING STATE AND CITY

Before Hugh Carey was sworn in as New York's 51st governor on January 1, 1975, his predecessor, Nelson Rockefeller quipped, "Poor Hugh. I spent all the money. And it's no fun being Governor of New York if you haven't got the money." He also gleefully told the new governor, "I had the champagne, you have the hangover."[1]

Carey understood the fiscal problems facing the state and he realized that, in addition to excessive spending, the national recessions of 1970 and 1974 had seriously hurt the state's economy, a point he made clear in his inaugural address:

> The first step on this journey is the recognition that it is time to change course in what this government does and how it does it. All around us, in this Capitol, are symbols of splendor, monuments of glass and marble. They stand as living embodiments of an idea of government as an ever-expanding institution, to be paid for from the ever-expanding riches of tomorrow.
>
> To the citizens of New York, I say: tomorrow is here. We have learned that every resource of this Earth is finite; so is the resource by which government sustains itself: the earnings of the people.
>
> This government will begin today the painful, difficult, imperative process of learning to live within its means. To further tax the poor, and those struggling for bare necessities, would be intolerable. We will not take that path.

This decision imposes responsibilities at every level of government.

To the people of New York, I pledge a state government that will not use the public payroll to provide private ease. Every job, every commission, every agency, every person paid by the public, must answer to a single overriding test: are you worth the people's trust, are you worth their compensation?

To mayors of our cities and towns, to the leaders of our counties and villages, I resolve to work with you to relieve unfair local burdens—to shape a state government that will, over the years, assume those responsibilities that are indeed statewide.

And from you, I ask a pledge to examine every one of your expenditures by the test of worth. We cannot continue to pass our responsibilities to the next generation of taxpayers. Now is the time, when economic hardship dramatizes needless spending, to bring government back into line with reality. A program that cannot be justified in hard times should never have been created in good times, and this is the time to rid ourselves of these drains on the pockets of the people.

One week later, in his first State of the State address to the Legislature, Carey painted an even drearier picture:

In the very simplest of terms, this government and we as a people have been living far beyond our means. There has been scarcely an activity, a category of public spending, in which we did not lead the nation. What we did was limited only by our imagination and our desire: our buildings were the tallest and most sumptuous, our civil service the most highly trained and paid, our public assistance programs the most expensive. Indeed, so lavish was the style of our government that we came to depend on it for life itself, forgetting that government was only the result of our industry and not its source. As the state's private economy stagnated, government became the principal growth industry in New York. Fewer New Yorkers are gainfully employed today than in 1958. But those who work now bear an enormously increased burden for the support of their fellows, and for the expenses of government. To pay for all of this, our taxes also became the highest in the nation . . . and every interest and group and advocate came to think of the state budget, and of state subsidy of local budgets, as a cornucopia, a never-ending horn of plenty that could pay for more and more each year.

Now the times of plenty, the days of wine and roses, are over. We were in the lead car of the roller coaster going up, and we are in the lead car coming down. So we must first recognize the immediate burdens we inherit. We do this not in a spirit of recrimination, nor in criticism of any man or party. There is responsibility enough to go around for all. But if we would master our fate, we must first acknowledge our condition.

Seven weeks later (February 25, 1975), the roller coaster hit its first obstacle—the Urban Development Corporation, created by Governor Rockefeller in 1968 to remove urban blight, defaulted on $104.5 million in short-term notes when the state Legislature refused to appropriate money. Ignoring the state's "moral obligation" to pay principal and interest due to U.D.C debt holders was devastating.

Of the financial mess Governor Carey said:

Sort of a preface to the crisis was the largest single moral obligation agency to default, the Urban Development Corporation, which was former Gov. Nelson Rockefeller's way to do quick mobilization to build things. They started building, but they didn't build economically and they didn't manage the house. . . . Rockefeller went to Washington to become Gerald Ford's vice president, I took over, and there was no way to meet the obligations for the UDC's debt.[2]

Suddenly the state, its agencies as well as its local municipalities, had trouble borrowing. New York City officials told the public that the "recent default by the state U.D.C. has created an unwarranted climate of suspicion in the marketplace."[3]

Carey realized that the state's financial situation was a house of financial cards built on sand and could collapse if even one agency failed to make its debt payments. On one occasion, he blurted out, "In New York State, we haven't found only back-door borrowing. We got side-door financing and New York's borrowing over the years—through the State government, its authorities and agencies and U.D.C. and M.T.A.—we got money going out the doors, the windows, and the portholes."[4]

Four weeks into the crisis, Carey persuaded the Legislature to come up with the money they "morally" owed. This payment added some sense of stability to the debt market.

Governor Carey skillfully managed the U.D.C crisis: he budged the Legislature to act and calmed jittery financial markets. But there was no time to bask in glory, for in a matter of months he had to face an even greater challenge, indeed the greatest crisis of his career: the financial collapse of New York City.

Gotham's Fiscal Meltdown

The city's spending spree, aided and abetted by increasingly large and powerful public employee unions, had continued unabated through the Wagner and Lindsay administrations.

In 1961, the city's operating budget was $2.7 billion; in 1965, it was $3.8 billion; $6.3 billion in 1969; and in Lindsay's last year in office, 1973, it hit $9.5 billion. Two years later when the city went bust, the operating budget stood at $12.2 billion.[5]

Between 1961 and 1969, the average increase of the city's operating budget was 11.1%. The average increase in spending in fiscal years 1969–1975 was 11.8%. In contrast, the average inflation rate between 1960 and 1969 was approximately 2.3%, and between 1969 and 1975 approximately 6.0%. What drove the spiraling costs? Welfare and public employee wages and benefits.

As noted earlier, the number of welfare recipients increased from 324,000 in 1961 to 1.2 million in 1973. The share of the city's budget to meet the costs of welfare during that period rose from 12% to 22% of operating expenditures.

As for labor costs, between 1965 and 1975 city operating expenditures increased by $8.3 billion and "43% was attributable to an increase in labor costs. . . ."[6]

Mayor Wagner had signed an executive order in March of 1958 allowing 100,000 city employees to join unions and bargain collectively.

Wagner ignored the advice that President Franklin D. Roosevelt had expressed in a 1937 letter to the National Federation of Federal Employees:

All Government employees should realize that the process of collective bargaining, as usually understood, cannot be transplanted into the public service. . . . The employer is the whole people, who speak by means of laws enacted by their representatives in Congress. . . . Particularly, I want to emphasize my conviction that militant tactics have no place in the functions of any organization of Government employees. Upon employees in the Federal service rests the obligation to serve the whole people, whose interests and welfare require orderliness and continuity in the conduct of Government activities. This obligation is paramount. Since their own services have to do with the functioning of the Government, a strike of public employees manifests nothing less than an intent on their part to prevent or obstruct the operations of Government until their demands are satisfied. Such action, looking toward the paralysis of Government by those who have sworn to support it, is unthinkable and intolerable.[7]

Mayor Lindsay doubled down on Wagner's decision. Despite being ill-treated by unions early in his first term, he signed Executive Order 52 (on September 29, 1967) that expanded public union bargaining rights. The order obligated the city to bargain in good faith "with the certified employee organizations of mayoral agency employees on wages (including but not limited to wage rates, pension, health and welfare benefits, uniform allowances and shift premiums), hours (including but not limited to overtime and time and leave benefits) and working conditions. . . ."[8]

In other words, Mayor Lindsay conceded routine management authority to collective bargaining negotiations. "What finally resulted over time," Raymond Horton concluded in *Municipal Labor Relations in New York City: Lessons of the Lindsay-Wagner Years*, "was that the scope of bargaining became a function of union influence and not law. Strong unions could bargain over more managerial issues than could weaker unions. By 1970 the major unions for all practical purposes bargained with the city government on whatever managerial issues they wanted and refused to bargain on those issues they wanted left alone. Civil service unions—not the city government—were refusing to bargain over managerial issues, a complete reversal of the position that existed less than a decade earlier with respect to managerial prerogatives."[9]

With the number of full-time employees in the city government increasing from 256,000 in 1960 to 333,000 in 1968, Victor Gotbaum, head of the powerful District Council 37 (part of the American Federation of State, County and Municipal Employees union), quipped, "We have the ability in a sense to elect our own boss."[10]

And by the end of his first mayoral term, Mayor Lindsay appeared to agree.

Fearing that the 300,000 city union employees and their families would punish him at the polls, and having tired of strikes by transit, sanitation, teachers and hospital workers, the Lindsay administration settled with the major unions in early 1969.

After analyzing the tremendous costs of the settlements, a *New York Times* editorial concluded that "a liberal outlay of public money has taken long steps . . . to establish peace on the turbulent municipal labor front."[11]

However, the abdication of managerial responsibility and adopting the short-run syndrome "buy labor peace now, worry about the costs later" was a major contribution to the city's financial crisis.

The costs associated with running New York City were now astronomical. The mayor's Temporary Commission on City Finances noted that from 1971 to 1975, "per employee compensation, despite the increasing severity of the city's financial problems, rose 51% in four years, higher than in either previous four-year period. . . ."[12]

The Bureau of the Budget revealed that between 1960 and 1975 wages jumped 316%. This was greater than the inflation rate and on comparable salary gains in the private sector. Twenty-year retirement at half-pay granted to the police in 1857 became the demand of every union. The Committee for Economic Development observed that between 1960 and 1970, the state enacted 54 city pension bills. According to the Temporary Commission of City Finances, retirement costs rose 469%, between 1961 and 1976, from $206 million to $1.48 billion. Unfunded pension liabilities hit $8 billion by 1977.

To fund an operating budget that paid for the ever-spiraling welfare and public employee costs, as well as 19 municipal hospitals, parks and pools, the City University system, daycare centers, radio and T.V. stations, public housing, as well as primary and secondary schools, police, fire and sanitation departments, Wagner and Lindsay raised taxes and employed fiscal abuses and financial and accounting gimmicks to give the appearance of balanced budgets.

In addition to property taxes, the city imposed on its citizens 19 other forms of taxation, all of which had to be approved by the state Legislature and the governor in a home-rule message. These taxes include: N.Y.C. Real Property Transfer Tax, N.Y.C. Mortgage Recording Tax, Commercial Rent Tax, Personal Income Tax, Sales and Use Tax, Cigarette Tax, Hotel Occupancy Tax, General Corporation Tax, Unincorporated Income Tax, N.Y.C. Bank Tax, Utility Tax, Commercial Motor Vehicle Tax, Auto Use Tax, Horse Race Admission Tax, Off-Track Betting Surcharge, and Fire Insurance Premium Tax.

Because the heavy tax load imposed on New Yorkers did not generate enough revenue to balance the city budget, the mayors employed fiscal gimmicks—most noticeably the issuance of short-term debt to fund the revenue deficit—to give the appearance of a balanced budget.

The addiction to temporary debt, which started at $250 million in 1965 and ballooned to $4.5 billion in 1975, actually began when voters approved N.Y.C. Charter revisions in 1961.

Those changes gave the mayor sole power to estimate revenues for a given fiscal year. "The significance of the charter change," the Citizens Budget Commission reported, "was that when you had a mayor operating with a Budget Bureau which was creative, the sky was the limit. There were no checks. You had creative budget officials playing the fifth violin, the piccolo and the kettle drum all by themselves." In order to create the illusion of a balanced budget, the mayor could overstate revenues and no one could challenge his projections.

To further enhance a mayor's budget juggling act, Governor Rockefeller rammed through the Legislature a change in the local finance law allowing the amount of Revenue Anticipation Notes (RANS) to be based on a mayor's estimates of the next fiscal year's revenues. Under the previous language of the law, RANS issued could not exceed the previous fiscal year's actual receipts. The new language permitted a mayor to overstate revenues expectation to increase the issuance of short-term debt.

To cover revenue estimate shortfalls later in a given fiscal year, a mayor would raid the city's rainy-day funds.

Albany continued to feed the city's growing hunger for budgetary gimmicks.

In 1964, Albany allowed the city to use capital project budget dollars—funded by long-term debt to improve the city's infrastructure—to pay current operating expenses. This abuse was expanded by a 1967 amendment to the local finance law that permitted the New York City to capitalize consulting, legal, and advertising costs. The lame rationale for this raid on infrastructure funds was that they had a 3-year period of probable usefulness.

In 1965, $28 million, 3.6% of the total $720 million capital budget funds, was allocated for current expenses. The amount raided from the capital project budget funds increased every year—from 9.7% of city capital project budget funds in 1966, to 18.9% in 1970, to 20% in 1973. And in 1975, 52.6% of the funds, $724 million out of $1.376 billion were transferred to cover current expenditures—a 2,500% increase in ten years.

The result: future generations were stuck paying for New York City's fiscal mismanagement and the city's infrastructure was rapidly deteriorating. And it's not as though Mayor Lindsay wasn't warned. In 1966, his own Temporary Commission on City Finances cautioned:

> That borrowing for current expenses is an unsound practice is generally recognized. Its unfavorable influence in the case of New York City may be summarized as follows:
>
> It encroaches on borrowing power needed for other purposes.
>
> It is detrimental to the City's credit standing.
>
> It results in unjustified interest cost.

It conceals and postpones the impact of current expenses on taxes.

It increases annual borrowing significantly and expands outstanding debt.

In 1971, Albany changed two more provisions of the Local Finance Law to permit a new form of short-term borrowing, known as Budget Notes, to cover distorted revenue estimates. The first change expanded the city's authority to issue Budget Notes up to 4% of the city budget. The second provision permitted the city to roll over the debt for three years.

When the $308 million in Budget Notes finally came due in 1974, and the city was unable to pay it off, Albany stepped in, as it had so often done, and created the N.Y.C. Stabilization Reserve Corporation (SRC). This so-called public benefit corporation's sole purpose was to issue debt up to $520 million to pay down the city's maturing Budget Notes. There was no guaranteed revenue stream to pay off SRC debt. There was only the moral obligation of the city.

The SRC, however, never got off the ground. By the time the courts ruled on a legal challenge questioning the constitutionality of the SRC, the city was in no position to issue more debt.

By 1975, city expenditures totaled $12.8 billion while revenues totaled only $10.9 billion.

A report issued by N.Y.C. Comptroller Jay Goldin, "City Debt: The Price of Deception," concluded "that more than 20% of all short-term debt ($1.5 billion) was attributed to 'gimmicks,' as was about 10% ($700 million) of all long-term debts."[13]

Senator Daniel Patrick Moynihan noted, "from Wagner's third term to Beame's second year [1975], the city was, in effect, printing money."[14]

With 1976 short-term debt needs projected at $7 billion, the financial markets closed their doors to New York City.

New York was brought to its knees because of its huge permanent short-term debt. As journalist Ken Auletta succinctly summarized: "The rollovers, false revenue estimates and plain lies have robbed the taxpayers of literally billions through excessive borrowings to cover up excessive fraud."

As for the question of who was to blame, Peter McClelland and Alan Magdovitz summed it up best in their book *Crisis in the Making*:

> Every city official who supported, actively or passively, proposals and policies for which the bottom line was more debt to finance current expenditures is, to use the legal phrasing, an accessory before the fact. So is every Albany legislator who was a party to the passage of laws that sanctioned this process. If the cast is large, the offense at least is well defined. The propensity of city and state officials to blame the unions, the banks, the federal government, is as predictable as it is misplaced. From a multitude of wellsprings came pressures for expenditures to outrun receipts. But theirs was the decision to give way, and in the giving way, to embark upon financial practices long recognized as the height of fiscal idiocy. They were the ones (again in legal phrasing) who had "the last clear chance" to stem a rising tide of red ink that would ultimately engulf nothing less than the financial capital of America. Their failure is both personal and professional. Their actions contravened the spirit of the Constitution if not the letter of the law, and well they knew that fact. "Things" were not in the saddle riding the city's fiscal might into the ground; people were—people elected or appointed to serve the public interest. Not their own interests, but the public's interest. The financial chaos they wrought is but one measure of how miserably they served that goal.

After years of mismanagement, budgetary gimmicks, phantom revenue, huge permanent short-term debt, and the capitalizing of operating expenses, the city was on the edge of the fiscal abyss.

In his book *The Bankers*, Martin Mayer wrote:

> On the simplest level, the story of New York's financial collapse is the tale of a Ponzi game in municipal paper—the regular and inevitably increasing issuance of notes to be paid off not by future taxes or revenue certified to be available for that purpose, but by the sale of future notes. Like all chain letter swindles,

Ponzi games self-destruct when the seller runs out of suckers, as New York did in spring 1975.

After taking a very close look at the city's financials, the "suckers"— the banks and broker-dealers—announced in April 1975 that the investment community would no longer underwrite the city's debt.

Knowing that default on debt payments or, worse yet, a municipal bankruptcy would wreak financial havoc on the state and the nation, Governor Carey had seen enough and began using his steely Brooklyn street smarts and his Irish charm to devise and implement a plan that could save New York City.

The governor's first move was to advance the city $800 million in state aid. This was only a stop-gap measure to give the governor time to construct a master plan for a bail-out.

To force the city to begin internal reforms, Carey convinced the Legislature to create the Municipal Assistance Corporation (M.A.C., usually pronounced "mac") in June 1975. M.A.C. was empowered to restructure the city's debt and to monitor its fiscal condition. It was also authorized to issue up to $3 billion in bonded debt secured by a first call on the city sales tax revenues.

To further placate the investment community, Carey and the Legislature created the Emergency Financial Control Board (E.F.C.B.) whose members included Carey, Mayor Beame, State Comptroller Levitt, City Comptroller Goldin and three so-called "wise men" from the financial community.

The E.F.C.B. possessed the authority to accept or reject the city's budget and any of its proposed contracts, and it had oversight of the three-year financial plan the city now had to present to the board.

The E.F.C.B. was granted significant oversight powers. The E.F.C.B. could accept or reject proposed city budgets and contracts. It could order the city to go back to the fiscal drawing boards, and if the city failed to comply, the E.F.C.B. could impose its own budget or order operating cuts. In effect, Mayor Beame and his executive staff became vassals of the E.F.C.B.

Employing the powers of M.A.C. and E.F.C.B., the governor announced in September 1975 that "far reaching steps were taken or agreed to by the city" that included:

• The formation of a Management Advisory Committee to assist in streamlining the city's management;

- A ceiling on the size of the city's budget;
- A moratorium on additional taxes;
- The dismissal of thousands of municipal workers, the elimination of thousands of positions from the city's budget, and a freeze on new hiring;
- A suspension of wage increases of city employees;
- An increase in public transit fare;
- A further reduction in the budget of the City University and an increase in student fees;
- A significant reduction of the capital budget;
- Appointment of a special mayoral deputy for finance.

These drastic measures were still not enough to convince the bankers and broker-dealers to open their doors to the city. Hence, in November 1975, the city defaulted by a decree of the state Legislature.

Moratorium payment legislation was enacted on $2.6 billion of notes. Those who held the defaulted paper were offered M.A.C. bonds in lieu of principal payments. Although the governor and his advisers conceded this scheme might be declared unconstitutional under the Contracts Clause, they were willing to take that chance to buy more time.

And time was exactly what they needed.

Aid from the federal government was needed to stem the tide, so Carey went to Washington to convince his former congressional colleagues and his old friend President Gerald Ford to propose and pass legislation permitting short-term loans up to $2.3 billion a year.

Ford initially and publicly pledged that he would veto a federal bailout. However, after much adverse publicity, including a *Daily News* front page headline **FORD TO CITY: DROP DEAD**, and after much cajoling by Governor Carey, the president reversed himself saying "he would approve legislation permitting federal guarantees for New York's debt—even if the state Legislature could not come up with a package that he deemed acceptable."[15]

The legislation eventually passed and was signed into law requiring the city to pay a steep price for guarantees. The city had to implement numerous tax increases and give the feds a first lien on all the city's revenue to ensure repayment.

Before final passage and approval by the feds, the N.Y. State Legislature passed tax increases in November 1975 "that raised the city income tax by 25%, increased sales tax on a host of items such as cigarettes and haircuts, and imposed a 50% surcharge on the estate tax in the city."[16] As promised, President Ford signed the legislation into law on December 9, 1975.

Just as remarkable was the successful negotiation with the city's public employee unions led by Carey ally, Richard Ravitch. Andrew Cuomo summed it up best in a *Daily News* editorial he authored years later:

> The state recovered through shared sacrifice and a balanced approach that did justice to the interests of both business and labor. . . . Famously tough labor leaders, like District Council 37 head Victor Gotbaum and Albert Shanker, president of the U.F.T. came to the rescue. The former agreed to shelve pay raises for municipal workers; the latter helped stave off bankruptcy by buying city bonds with pension funds.

Carey's leadership, the federal loan guarantees, Municipal Employee Union agreements, tax increases, and the tough monitoring of M.A.C. and E.F.C.B., permitted the city to avoid insolvency and from filing Chapter 11.

But the crisis was far from over. City operating deficits were projected for years to come. In fact, the city deficits, in accordance with Generally Accepted Accounting Principles (GAAP), were to hit $1.4 billion in 1975; $1.16 billion in 1976; and $1.0 billion in 1977.

Looking to the future and reflecting on what he had just witnessed, Governor Carey had become convinced that the one man incapable of grappling with the crisis was the incumbent mayor, Abraham D. Beame.

The Brooklyn-bred accountant and former city Comptroller, whose 1973 campaign slogan was, "He knows the Buck," had proved to be a weak chief executive who simply did not grasp the reality of the financial catastrophe he helped create.

Not only was Carey convinced that Beame had to go, as the 1977 mayoral elections approached, he had just the man in mind for the job: Mario Cuomo.

CHAPTER 5
SECRETARY OF STATE CUOMO

While Governor Carey was saving New York City, Mario Cuomo, who had no significant role in the crisis, was settling in as Secretary of State. Cuomo had accepted the post on the condition that the Office of Local Government and the Office of Planning Services be transferred to report to the Secretary of State's office. The governor obliged and Cuomo renamed it the Division of Community Affairs.

Cuomo also took over the Division of Economic Opportunity which according to *The New York State Redbook*, provided "technical assistance to community action agencies in formulating and implementing local economic opportunity programs reviews and coordinates reviews of other State agencies of local community action program applications for federal aid prior to submission to the Governor for approval. . . . "

For most of its history, the Department of State kept official records and controlled licensing services. The 1,200-page 1974 edition of *The New York Red Book*, which contains "information concerning New York State, its Departments and Political Subdivisions, and the officials who administer its Affairs," described the duties of the Secretary of State thusly:

> The Secretary of State is the general recording officer of the State; custodian of the Great Seal, and of documents issued under it, and many of the ancient documents of the State. He is the depositary of the original land records of the State including patents and certain maps, survey and title papers. The Secretary of State has custody of the State Laws, supervises publication and distribution of Session Laws, Legislative Manual, the Official Compilation of Codes, Rules and Regulations of the State of New York and the supplements thereto; and the preparation of election material for the county boards of elections; causes to be published

the abstracts and form of submission of proposed constitutional amendments and concurrent resolutions proposing amendments; monthly publication and distribution of the State Bulletin, the official State paper.

The 1975 Red Book description of the Secretary of State reads very differently:

The Secretary of State assists the Governor in coordinating the activities and services of state agencies and simplifying state procedures to the end of providing more effective services to local governments throughout the State. He keeps the Governor informed as to problems of local governments and advises and assists the Governor in developing policy and utilizing the resources of the State for the benefit of local governments. The Department serves as a clearinghouse of information and assistance and of state and federal services available to local governments. In working with communities throughout the State, the Secretary assists local governments to engage in cooperative efforts to develop solutions of their common problems, particularly in metropolitan and rapidly growing areas. In cooperation with local governments and the organizations which represent them, he encourages expansion and improvement of in-service training facilities and programs available to local officials.

The Secretary encourages cooperation among agencies and levels of government and with the private sector for the protection and development of human, natural and man-made resources. The Department advises and assists municipalities in their planning and development activities and compiles, formulates, and disseminates information, projections and techniques relating to development of resources.

The Secretary of State coordinates the campaigns, programs and activities of state agencies and political subdivisions in providing fire safety information, publicity, and instruction and assists in the development and execution of such programs. He maintains liaison with public and private fire service agencies and organizations and recommends to the Legislature and the Governor legislative proposals to promote fire safety and fire mobilization and control.

The Secretary of State is responsible for preparing and filing a State fire mobilization and mutual aid plan. He may appoint and remove a regional fire administrator for each zone established pursuant to the plan. He makes regulations and issues orders necessary to implement the plan, which shall be activated whenever a county, city, town, village or fire district requests or when the Governor determines that the public interest so requires.

Obviously, Cuomo had a very different perception of the Secretary's duties.

Cuomo sought the job because he realized the duties of the office extended throughout the state, and with offices in numerous counties, Cuomo would find reasons to visit them, and this gave him a chance to meet community leaders and learn their concerns. He quickly realized that a state official appearing in upstate communities was newsworthy. Editorial boards and reporters were always eager to meet him and most gave him positive coverage.

Veteran Albany reporters have said that in those days Mario was very open to the press. He would often personally handle routine calls from them.

In addition to learning what made people tick in the predominantly Republican counties upstate, Cuomo was able to establish relationships with staff in the county offices. These friendships would serve him well when he ran for governor in 1984.

It is fair to say the Department of State post gave Cuomo opportunities to lay the foundation for a future statewide race.

David Shaffer, an Albany reporter for the AP and a close watcher of the future governor, described Cuomo in the mid-Seventies as "a quietly ambitious man with a greater awareness of what the job can do for his political career and a greater willingness to work hard at it."[1]

One reason his plan worked is that Governor Carey and his senior staff were not micromanagers. They weren't particularly concerned with what Cuomo was up to—as long as his activities did not embarrass the governor.

Governor Carey was not afraid to have talented people around him. M.T.A. Chief Richard Ravitch told the author that Carey had a simple rule that he applied to subordinates: "Do a good job and I don't mind you getting the bulk of the public credit because some of the credit will fall on me. But if you screw up you take the fall."

This was a very different approach than both Mario and Andrew Cuomo would take as governors. They were, as the saying goes, "control freaks." They micro-managed every aspect of government. Nothing could happen without their approval. Department and agency heads feared the executive office and were afraid to make decisions, let alone make news.

Mario took advantage of the freedom to wander about the state and began to make news. He drafted legislation to stop legislators from accepting gifts from lobbyists. It failed to get anywhere, but it gave Cuomo an opportunity to lecture on the evil influence of Albany's lobbying class.

Cuomo also sought to make headlines in minority neighborhoods, and so directed his Division of Licensing Services to revoke the licenses of real estate companies that refused to rent apartments to African-Americans. Harlem's *Amsterdam News* applauded Cuomo in an editorial titled "Bravo Mario": "It has never been done before because no Secretary of State holding office prior to Cuomo has had the guts to do it. And therein lies the hope and beauty of Mr. Cuomo's action."[2]

While Governor Carey was grappling with the state fiscal mess, Cuomo, intent on proving he was a team player, identified cost-cutting measures in his department to the tune of $3.5 million. Over time, by utilizing "zero-based budgeting," he cut expenditures by 40%. One way he achieved savings was by pushing out Republican appointees and replacing them with Democrats at lower salaries. (Both Mario and Andrew frowned upon appointees making a decent salary, hence their inability to attract or to hold on to talented people during their gubernatorial years.)

Carey also used Cuomo to handle special situations that would arise from time to time. One such case in 1976 involved a rent strike at the state's largest housing project: Co-Op City in the Bronx.

Built between 1968 and 1973, Co-Op City, financed by a Federal Housing Finance Agency loan, housed close to 16,000 people.

Outraged by the poor construction and the incompetence of the management company, residents demanded action after a default on the federal loan. So the state fired the management company, took over management, and after due diligence was prepared to hit co-op owners with a 25% increase in maintenance fees. The residents, understandably unhappy with the proposed increases, commenced a rent strike.

The strike dragged out for six months until Governor Carey, wishing to avoid a political catastrophe, sent the Secretary of State to the rescue. Cuomo was the right fit due to his prior involvement with the Forest Hills housing controversy.

Just as he did with Corona and Forest Hills, Cuomo came up with a "split the difference" compromise memo of understanding (M.O.U.) between management and tenants, which he presented to the governor in February over the protest of Lee Goodwin, the State Housing Commissioner.

When the strike dragged on for several more months, Cuomo threatened to quit the negotiations unless the state signed on to his memo of understanding. This it did on June 29, 1976. Jack Newfield and Paul De Brul wrote in their book *The Abuse of Power* that the Cuomo M.O.U. provided "that the tenants would assume management of Co-Op City for six months in return for delivering all monies collected during the rent strike and promising to meet all mortgage interest payments. . . . They would, for the first time, democratically elect their own board of directors. No rent increases would be imposed during this time. Most importantly, they had embarked on the largest experiment with tenant management ever undertaken in the United States."[3]

The Co-Op City success encouraged Carey to assign Cuomo to put out other political fires. One was to settle a land dispute between the Mohawk Indians and State Park officials in 1977. Cuomo managed to work out a compromise to move the Indians out of the Adirondack State Park to 5,000 acres in Clinton County.

Cuomo also managed to convince the governor to create an Office of Indian Affairs that would report directly to him.

Cuomo, ever seeking ways to increase his visibility throughout New

York, instituted a state ombudsman's office that, of course, reported to the Secretary of State. Aggrieved citizens could now call an 800 number to file complaints. He also started writing a regular column that was distributed for free to newspapers throughout the state and many local media outlets—particularly weeklies always hungry for filler—printed his column.

Hugh Carey and Mario Cuomo had an odd relationship. They could never be social friends and they really didn't trust one another. Nevertheless, they shared a grudging respect. Carey thought Cuomo was one of the smartest guys he knew and admired his command of the English language. Meanwhile, Cuomo thought Carey was one of the smartest politicians he knew, and admired his command of numbers, particularly when it came to state and city financial matters.

But theirs was always a political marriage of convenience, and it was severely strained in 1977.

Cuomo for Mayor?

New York City Mayor Abraham Beame had to go; but he wouldn't leave quietly because he believed he would be vindicated if elected to a second term in November 1977.

To get onto the November ballot, however, Beame first had to win the Democratic primary. And other candidates, sensing the incumbent's weakness, were coming out of the woodwork.

Four from Manhattan announced their candidacies. The best known was the brashly exuberant left-wing congresswoman Bella Abzug, known nationally for her big mouth and her big hats. Next was Percy Sutton, the first African-American to be elected Manhattan borough president. He was a member in good standing of the Harlem Clubhouse—that included Charlie Rangel, David Dinkins, and Basil Paterson. Then there was Edward Koch, the little-known congressman who had taken over John Lindsay's Upper East Side seat when Lindsay became mayor in 1966. Finally, there was Joel Harnett, a wealthy entrepreneur who lived on Sutton Place and was a former head of the good government group, Citizens Union.

From the Bronx, there was Herman Badillo, the first Puerto Rican to be elected to Congress, who four years earlier had lost the mayoral run-off to Abe Beame.

Governor Carey was not thrilled with any of these contenders. He did meet with Ed Koch, but concluded he couldn't win.

So, Carey wanted Cuomo to be the Democratic standard bearer and he wasn't alone. Mario was the first choice of Queens boss Matt Troy—the man with whom Mario had locked horns at the 1974 Democratic state convention. And Mario had friends in the media—Jimmy Breslin and Nat Hentoff—who were also urging him to throw his hat in the ring.

But Cuomo said publicly, time and again, that he had no interest in running. Besides his wife, Matilda, was against it.

Yet, although Cuomo insisted he was not in, he never actually ruled himself completely out. As in 1974, he appeared to be indecisive—the Hamlet of Queens County.

He could have easily ended the speculation by endorsing one of the contenders. This he declined to do, probably because he found all of them wanting.

Then a determined Governor Carey came up with a plan to get Cuomo off the dime.

Carey leaned on the owners and editors of the *Daily News* and the *New York Post* to write editorials urging Cuomo to enter the race.

On March 2, 1977, the governor vetoed a bill establishing June 7 as Primary Day. Carey preferred to keep it on September 13 to give Cuomo more time to become more well known throughout the city.

Carey then convinced the N.Y. Liberal Party not to endorse State Senator Roy Goodman, a Manhattan liberal Republican and the GOP nominee, and to hold out instead for Cuomo. The Liberal Party, which was then more a patronage mill than a party of principles, obliged. Carey had already appointed several of their members to government positions, and it is likely the party expected more appointments down the road.

Then on Holy Thursday, April 7, 1977, Carey and top aide David Burke met with Cuomo and applied pressure on him.

"This is a fateful day, Mario," Carey said he told him. "Mario, after Holy Thursday, Good Friday came next, and the Savior had a vision of his crucifixion and he said, Oh my Father, please let this cup pass from me. In other words, He begged his Father to relieve him of the pain of crucifixion, but then He thought about it, and He went through with it. Now Mario, you can let this cup pass from you, or you can try to become mayor, and you do know that the city can use your leadership. I'm not going to push you, but by Easter morning I want you to let Dave here know if you'll let this cup pass from you."

On that note, Carey and Burke left Cuomo to contemplate his future.

Outside the meeting room, Burke said to Carey, "You son of a bitch. You trapped him. Now he's going to go around thinking he's Jesus Christ."[4]

On Good Friday, Cuomo was leaning towards running. Matilda was also coming around thanks to Carey, who had urged various people to talk to her about the importance of his candidacy.

In the end, Cuomo told journalist Peter Hamill that Matilda "began to understand that in some odd way, the family was likely to get stronger, not weaker."[5]

On Wednesday evening of Easter Week, Cuomo was told that the next day's edition of the *Daily News* would have a huge headline indicating Cuomo was running for mayor.

And so, Mario finally jumped off the fence. But before announcing, he secured from Carey two promises: that he would receive ample contributions to finance a credible campaign, and that Carey would support him to the bitter end—even if he lost the Democratic primary and ran solely on the Liberal Party line as Lindsay had—successfully—in 1969.

But before Mario finally announced, Carey had met with two other people.

The first meeting was with political media adviser David Garth. At lunch at the Plaza Hotel, Carey urged Garth to abandon Koch and to go to work for Cuomo. According to *New York* magazine, Garth basically said: "Hugh, you know I tried to get Cuomo to run for mayor last year. He said absolutely not. I went to Koch and I can't leave him. Sorry."[6]

So, later that same day, Carey reached out to Koch who told the *Times*.

"I remember being in my office, it was 3 p.m. and I had a call from Carey. 'Ed,' he said, and this is an exact quote, 'would you indulge me by meeting me at 4 p.m. at [former Mayor] Bob Wagner's house?' So, I said I would and then I called David Garth. I said 'Do you know what this is about?' and he said, 'Sure, because I just had lunch with the Governor, and he asked me if I'd work for Cuomo.' I went over to Bob Wagner's and [his wife] Phyllis Cerf Wagner leads me upstairs. Bob Wagner never says a word, though I think he's the major manipulator in this area, and [then the governor says] 'Ed, I want to tell you something before you read it in the press.' And I say, 'Governor, no matter what you say I still support you.' So he sort of says 'I want to stop Badillo and Beame because they'd be terrible for the City. You can't win, and Mario is going to announce tomorrow.'

"So, this goes on for 20 minutes. I never say a word. I'm a good listener. I'm not a bad talker, either. 'Governor, are you finished?' I finally said, 'I won nine times in 14 years. Mario did not support you in '74, and when he ran in '74 he was beaten by an unknown person upstate, Mary Anne Krupsak. Governor, can't we get together on this? Cuomo can run with me for City Council President.' And then Carey said, 'Well, I was thinking of it the other way around.'

"So, I told the Governor then that I represented the most prestigious district in Congress, and that for me, City Council President would be a step down, but that for Secretary of State Cuomo, it would be a step up. So I said good-bye then, and Carey said good-bye, and that was the last I heard from him until the night he endorsed me."[7]

When did Mario Cuomo finally make up his mind to enter the mayoral sweepstakes? Most likely in the second week of April. Nat Hentoff, in a very extensive article for the *Village Voice* published on April 18, 1977, and titled "Cuomo Rising: Will New York's Great Smart Hope Run for Mayor?," described a Good Friday conversation with Cuomo:

"Any change [on your candidacy]?" I asked him.
"No fixed change," said the secretary of state, "but there are all kinds of turbulences at work now."
"The *Daily News* editorial?"
"Flattering," Cuomo said, "but it's not what I mean."

"Then it must be Matilda."

"Yes, I think it's going to be different with Matilda. She now is almost convinced by people she's been talking to that the good I may be able to do for the city could justify depriving the family."

"So, it's all up to you now," I said.

Cuomo nodded, "It depends on whether I really would have a chance to do some good. Then it would be worth making the effort." Pause. "I think a sufficient chance exists."

"So, I can say you're going to run?"

A long pause.

"Let me put it this way," I suggested to the secretary of state. "If I write that you are going to be a candidate for mayor, will I come out looking like a schmuck?"

"No," the man of "almost zealous candor" said. "You will not."

CHAPTER 6
MARIO CUOMO FOR MAYOR, 1977

As the 1977 campaign for mayor began in earnest, four events had a significant impact on every candidate.

Son of Sam

On July 29, 1976, a lone person fired shots from a 44-caliber gun at two women chatting in a parked automobile in the Bronx. One woman died and the other was seriously wounded.

The serial killer, who signed his name "Son of Sam" in notes left at the crime scenes and also in letters sent to journalist Jimmy Breslin, ended up murdering five people and maiming six more in his first year on the loose. Most of his crimes were committed in quiet outer borough neighborhoods—Flushing, Forest Hills, Bellerose, Bayside, Floral Park in Queens, and Pelham Bay in the Bronx.

As the first anniversary of the murder spree approached, people in neighborhoods throughout the city were in a state of panic. They were afraid to go out at night, to walk their dogs, or visit their favorite restaurants and taverns. Women cut their hair short and wore high-collared coats to hide their faces.

The author of this book was stopped by police one Saturday night during the "Summer of Sam." I lived in Flushing, Queens and had missed the Q12 bus going east to Bayside and decided to walk the 25 plus blocks to Bell Boulevard to meet some friends at a favored watering hole, One Station Plaza.

When I reached Northern Boulevard and about 202nd St., not far from the "Eléphas" discotheque that Sam had struck in June, several cop cars surrounded me, and I was thrown up against the wall and searched.

After the police were satisfied I was not the culprit they were searching for, they informed me in no uncertain terms that I was a jerk for walking alone. They were right, and were kind enough to drop me off at Bell Boulevard.

Son of Sam struck for the last time on July 31, 1977 in the Bath Beach part of Brooklyn. He shot four bullets at a young couple sitting in a car. Stacy Moscowitz died in the hospital. Her boyfriend Robert Violante lived, but lost most of his vision due to the head wounds he received.

Then the police got a break. A woman out walking her dog had seen a man on a street near a car parked by a fire hydrant that had just been ticketed by the police. The man had looked at her in a way that frightened her, and she ran home. Then she heard shots fired. Although she waited four days before calling the police, her tip led to a quick search of ticketed cars in the area and the discovery of a Ford Galaxie registered to David Berkowitz of 35 Pine Street in Yonkers.

On August 10, 1977, the police nabbed Berkowitz outside his apartment.

"You got me," Berkowitz told the detective who approached him. The .44 caliber Bulldog revolver that was used in the shooting was found in a paper bag in the Ford Galaxie.

Claiming that demons and a neighbor's dog (that he later shot) ordered him to kill young women, he pleaded guilty.

Berkowitz was sentenced to 25-years-to-life in prison on June 12, 1978.

The Blackout

On Wednesday, July 13, 1977, beginning at approximately 8:30 p.m., a series of lightning strikes at electrical substations, coupled with human error at New York City's principal power provider, caused the entire electrical system to completely fail at approximately 9:30 p.m. and the city went dark.

Calling the blackout "Christmas in July," thousands of people in the five boroughs turned out to the streets and began rioting, looting, and destroying property.

More than 1,600 stores were looted, 1,000 fires were reported, nearly 4,000 people were arrested, and about 500 cops were injured in just a 12-hour period. "Of those arrested for participating in property damage and theft, 65% were Black, 30% Latino and 4% White."[1]

Sadly, most of the destruction occurred in poor minority neighborhoods. In the Bedford Stuyvesant part of Brooklyn, for instance, 35 blocks were wrecked, more than 130 stores were looted, and a third of them were set on fire.

The city's chief executive, the hapless Mayor Beame, was flabbergasted. While he condemned the event as "night of terror in many communities that have been wantonly looted and burned," the mayor appeared helpless.[2]

F.A.L.N. Bombing

To add to the pandemonium, on August 3, 1977, the Puerto Rican terrorist group, Fuerzas Armadas de Liberación Nacional Puertorriqueña (FALN) planted bombs that exploded in two East Side Manhattan office buildings, killing two people and injuring seven others. Scores of buildings, including the World Trade Center towers, evacuated over 100,000 workers. Visiting the sites of the bombing—342 Madison Ave. and the Mobil Oil Building, 150 E. 42nd St.—the mayor said, "This is an outrageous act of terrorism."[3]

SEC Report

After the financial collapse of the city in 1975, the Securities and Exchange Commission commenced an investigation to determine how and why it happened. Mayoral candidate Joel Harnett had filed a suit in a federal court early in 1977 calling on the SEC to make the report public. The SEC finally obliged exactly two weeks before Primary Day. The scathing 982-page report may be summarized thusly: Beame and City Comptroller Jay Goldin had "misled" investors by engaging in "deceptive practices masking the city's true and disastrous financial condition."[4]

Being exposed as the emperor with no clothes, Beame attacked the SEC report as a "hatchet job," a "shameless, vicious political document."[5]

These four events had a significant impact on all the candidates, particularly the perceived frontrunners Abe Beame and Bella Abzug.

Mayor Beame looked more and more like a befuddled accountant who had lost control of the city's finances, the unions, and crime in the streets. Out of sheer desperation, he abandoned his opposition to the death penalty and promoted a new slogan: "Mayor Beame: He's fighting your fight against crime."

Beame did make inroads with the municipal unions. Despite battles with him during the city's financial crisis, many union leaders preferred the devil they knew. Hence, some of the largest unions came out for Beame, including the United Federation of Teachers, the Central Labor Council, and the International Ladies Garment Workers Union.

The union support may have looked good on paper, but because many of the rank and file members lived outside the city, they were unlikely to provide the votes necessary to get Beame into a run-off.

Congresswoman Bella Abzug was considered the strongest challenger early in the campaign because she had come within 10,000 votes of being the Democratic candidate for U.S. Senator a year earlier. She had received 327,700 votes to Daniel Patrick Moynihan's 333,697.

But her reactions to the summer crises did not help her cause. After the blackout, she had turned her venom on Con Edison, not the rioters. She also insisted that police and firemen had a right to strike. That position may have sat well with the city's uniformed workers who lived on Long Island, but not with New York City's non-uniformed residents, who felt plagued by crime and were demanding law and order.

In *Ladies and Gentlemen: The Bronx is Burning*, author Jonathan Mahler related a classic confrontation between Abzug and residents of the Bushwick section of Brooklyn:

> "But what would you have done if the police had been on strike during the blackout?" one distressed community resident asked.
>
> "Mobilize the community organizations and get them into the streets," Abzug replied.
>
> "The community *was* mobilized," another resident volunteered. "They were all out looting."[6]

Abzug was also hurt by her support for school busing. She could not get past her liberal Manhattan attitudes and see that people in the outer boroughs wanted to preserve their communities, their neighborhood schools, and to be safe in their homes.

At community events she would lose her temper and shout at voters. After one elderly woman told Abzug she "didn't care about people like her," Abzug erupted and shouted, "Then go vote for that schmuck we have now."[7]

Pundits began to ridicule Abzug saying she had created a voter ailment, "Bellaphobia." Cuomo described her campaign style as "agree with me or I'll make you deaf."[8]

The political backlash after the blackout riots and looting also damaged the candidacies of Percy Sutton and Herman Badillo. "I think they were hurt very badly [after the lights went out]", said Bronx City Councilman Steven Kaufman.[9]

Knowing that he had to get votes outside of the black community to have a fighting chance of victory, Sutton, like Beame, began tilting to the right on the "law and order" issue. Several days after the riots, Sutton gave a 13-page sermon at Harlem's famous Abyssinian Baptist Church and condemned "the marauders" and "criminals" who were out to "drag an entire people backward and downward into the primeval ooze and slime of riot and disorder."[10] He went on to say, "You can't, on Tuesday, buy a television set that was stolen from the store around the corner and then on Sunday go to church and call yourself a Christian."[11] Sutton also demanded that "those who took advantage of the darkness to rip and plunder, to pillage, loot, and burn" must be severely punished.[12]

Later in the campaign, Sutton was seen marching around his neighborhood donning an auxiliary-police uniform.[13]

In the 1973 Democratic mayoral primary Herman Badillo had come in second behind Abe Beame, receiving 30% to Beame's 34.5%. But in the run-off, Democratic establishment voters and Mario Biaggi's "law and order" voters went for Beame, and Badillo had lost badly, receiving only 39.2% to Beame's 60.7%.

Badillo nursed a grudge, believing it was race prejudice and not candidate competence that had decided the primary. Now, four years later, he thought he had the best claim to be the first minority elected mayor. But the blackout and, especially, the FALN bombings did not help his chances.

The evening the city went dark, Badillo had camped out at his Bronx district attorney's office, and had told the media that, "People were breaking down gates, jumping into stores and taking as much as they could. It was disgraceful. People saw a chance to get food-stuff and jewelry for nothing and they took it. The police had no plan to protect merchants."[14]

The comment started well but ended badly, because attacking the police was a political blunder.

Badillo did come out for the death penalty but for the most part his campaign appealed only to his base. Writing in the September 5, 1977 issue of *New York* magazine, Doug Ireland observed:

> . . . Badillo is the only one in this campaign who pleads the cause of the poor. Because he came from poverty, he understands that we must bring the poor into the mainstream of the city's economy or face chronic summer rioting.

The two candidates best positioned to take advantage of the 1977 summer woes were Ed Koch and Mario Cuomo.

And the very best thing going for Ed Koch in 1977 was David Garth, who was running his media campaign. Without Garth, Koch would have lost. The irony of that, of course, is that the person who had steered Garth to the Koch camp was Mario Cuomo. Had Cuomo not procrastinated for months, Garth would likely have signed on with him and the course of the city's history might have been very different.

Upon taking command, Garth gave Koch the same marching orders he had given to Hugh Carey in 1974: lose weight, buy some decent suits and get a decent haircut.

Garth's strategy was based on securing second place for Koch in the primary. Garth figured that if either of the two favorites, the politically battered Abe Beame, or the Manhattan radical Bella Abzug, came in first and Koch second, he would be well positioned to win the run-off.

It was a risky strategy that Garth thought probably would not work, but one had to have a strategy.

Koch also knew that he had to make inroads outside of Manhattan, particularly in middle-class Jewish and working-class Catholic neighborhoods in the outer boroughs. That explains why years earlier, he had shown up during the Forest Hills housing controversy to voice his support for Jewish homeowners.

Koch's 1977 theme was a simple one: "After eight years of charisma [John Lindsay] and four years of the clubhouse [Abe Beame], why not try competence."

His campaign focused on the city's fiscal and economic problems, the continued threat of bankruptcy, and on one issue a mayor had nothing to do with: the death penalty. Even though it is a federal and state issue, Koch constantly stressed that he was a long-time proponent of imposing the death penalty.

Ed Koch's whole life was politics. Hence, as a candidate he worked at it day and night to overcome the "Ed Who?" image. He walked neighborhood streets introducing himself to voters and speaking to small crowds via a bullhorn. He traveled in a Winnebago "Kochmobile" covered with posters.

Garth commercials showed Ed Koch doing what he did best, talking to voters about serious issues. Koch was also a funny guy, so Garth produced one TV ad showing that side of the candidate. In that ad, Koch talks directly to the camera saying, "Most political campaigns lack humor, but it's obvious this one is going to be different. Four years ago, Abe Beame told us he knew the buck. When he was Mayor, we didn't have any bucks. . . . Now Mayor Beame is asking for four more years to finish the job. Finish the job! Hasn't he done enough?"[15]

Koch followed Garth's orders to stay "on message" concerning the city crisis. As historian Jonathan Soffer points out in his work, *Ed Koch and the Rebuilding of New York City*, "of all the candidates, Koch used the harshest rhetoric blaming the crisis on wrong leftists and 'poverty pimps,' but he also made more specific management proposals, including changes in work rules to increase productivity of city workers, bringing the Board of Education under mayor control, and the introduction of zero-based budgeting."[16]

Ed Koch had been campaigning vigorously for months when Mario Cuomo finally decided to enter the race. Cuomo's ultimate reason for running was not inspiring, "The governor had given me the opportunity to come into public service. I felt I owed him something."[17]

Surrounded by family and friends in his Rego Park, Queens headquarters,

Cuomo finally announced on May 10th his candidacy and set the tone of his campaign: "The record of the administration," he declared, "is on the faces of all those among us who have lost the sense of hope—of every old woman who lives behind triple-locked doors, waiting for day to return, afraid to venture onto the night streets or once look up at the night sky."[18]

The one significant advantage Mario Cuomo had over Ed Koch was that he was an ethnic Catholic who actually grew up and lived in an outer-borough working-class neighborhood. He truly understood what made his neighbors tick, and he had the oratorical skills to express empathy.

Cuomo also had the advantage of plenty of campaign money thanks to Governor Carey. This permitted him to hire the nationally known Democratic campaign strategists and pollsters, Gerald Rafshoon and Pat Caddell. Those two men had helped elect an obscure ex-governor of Georgia, Jimmy Carter, the 39th president of the United States the year before.

Despite these political advantages, candidate Cuomo and his campaign team never really clicked.

Most of the fault for the lackluster campaign and its antics rests on the shoulders of Cuomo, who could not make up his mind what kind of version of himself he wanted the public to see. In a sense he was a walking contradiction, trying to be a kindly philosopher and an angry "bull in the china shop" at one and the same time.

The angry man loved to poke you in the eye: his opponents, members of the press, and even many of the folks he met while campaigning. His biting humor and sarcasm were meant to hurt or diminish those with whom he crossed swords. He feared no man when it came to giving tongue-lashings.

Journalist Nat Hentoff describes one such encounter at a Cuomo meeting with the *The New York Times* editorial board:

> When Cuomo visited the *Times*, one of the more pietistic members of that paper's hierarchy asked Cuomo why he is so negative about Percy Sutton's chances.
>
> "Because there are more bigots than blacks in the city," says the secretary of state.

The questioner flushes, and says with some passion that "the people in this town are *better* than that." Cuomo, suddenly aware that he is close to being called a bigot himself for having told the truth, confronts the man from the *Times*. "I know this city. I've lived here all my life. Where do you live?"

"Scarsdale." The subject dropped.[19]

Reflecting on his angry-man behavior at the *Times*, Cuomo said, "I suppose it was out of place for me to react to him that way. He probably thought, 'Just like an Italian, this Cuomo speaks too loud and too much.' But one thing I try to do is not deceive myself."[20]

Cuomo's initial campaign slogan was "Put your anger to work." He said time and again at campaign stops, "I'm as angry as you are about a variety of issues."[21]

The candidate insisted that "law and order" was the number one issue in the campaign and he was going to be "tough." In a primary flyer distributed by the Cuomo for Mayor committee, he is quoted saying: "I am as angry as you about crime in our city. Criminals, not the people, should be afraid to walk the streets. . . . We need more cops, more judges, more people going to jail."

But instead of just running with this angry-man message which was music to the ears of his core constituency, the conciliatory side of him insisted on reminding voters that unlike Ed Koch, he was against the death penalty.

When speaking at civic association meetings and other public forums, particularly in the outer boroughs, Ed Koch would ask people who supported the death penalty to raise their hands. Playing to those who said "aye," he would let them know he was with them.

This Koch technique drove Cuomo crazy. Since the mayor had nothing to do with the imposition of the death penalty, he believed Koch was being a crass political opportunist. As a result, Mario could not keep his mouth shut about his own opposition to the death penalty.

In *The Bronx is Burning*, Jonathan Mahler describes how Cuomo handled the matter:

Cuomo typically prefaced his response to this question by pointing out that it was an issue over which the mayor had no jurisdiction. He would then proceed to explain that the electric chair would not make his seventy-seven-year-old parents any safer; that the only time anyone would actually burn, it would be some poor miserable person who couldn't afford an attorney to go up the ladder to the Supreme Court; that the electric chair wouldn't produce jobs or alleviate racial tension; that we as a society are better than capital punishment.[22]

Cuomo's position was a valid one. But instead of downplaying the issue or just simply saying "I'm morally opposed," he kept on obsessing about the death penalty, coming across as a self-righteous professor.

After the mayoral election, Cuomo actually conceded that his harping on the issue was a mistake. He told his biographer, Robert McElvaine, "It is one thing to have the death penalty position which I did but I kept bringing it up. I didn't like the idea, but I can't examine my motivation. But I know I brought it up more than I needed."[23]

Cuomo's campaign was also plagued by events beyond its control. One major problem was Governor Hugh Carey. It was Carey who convinced Cuomo to run, and it was Carey's contacts that permitted Cuomo's campaign to be the best funded in the primary.

But the man who saved New York City from bankruptcy was not all that popular himself. Carey had forced the mayor to make major cuts to the city budget that included huge layoffs, with the result that thousands of bureaucrats, teachers, cops, firemen, sanitation workers who were let go were not very happy with the governor.

Carey's unpopularity hurt Cuomo because he was perceived as the governor's puppet, his water carrier.

A former top Lindsay Administration appointee, Richard Aurelio, says Carey's public activities were "inartistic in the ways he helped Cuomo and the help haunted the Cuomo campaign throughout the entire summer."[24]

One Cuomo aide was much more blunt about the governor's role: "The Carey endorsement was a political albatross. It was killing us. The governor was either stupid or he was doing it simply to satisfy his ego."[25]

Even a good thing, *The New York Times* July 31st endorsement of

Cuomo, ultimately worked against him. Not only was it too early in the primary season, the endorsement caused the *New York Post* and possibly the *Daily News* to endorse Koch.

Cuomo felt betrayed because the two tabloids had urged him to enter the race.

It appears that Rupert Murdoch, the owner of the *Post*, was annoyed by the *Times'* endorsement. To him, Cuomo was now the *Times'* candidate and Murdoch wanted his own candidate. So, Koch received the *Post's* endorsement on August 19, 1977. And for reasons not really known, the *Daily News* also endorsed Koch days later. These two endorsements by papers that were read by Cuomo's natural constituency gave Koch the shot in the arm he needed as the candidates were reaching the finish line.

While there are developments during any political race that are beyond the control of a candidate and his supporters, there is no excuse for a candidate not making sure his campaign apparatus runs smoothly.

In this most important area, Cuomo was a near total failure. Early in his career and then later as governor, Cuomo was an indecisive micro-manager. Except for his son, Andrew, and a few very close aides, he didn't really trust anyone and constantly second-guessed his hired media gurus.

Gerald Rafshoon did not need to work for Mario Cuomo but he decided to join the campaign because he viewed Cuomo as an "urban, ethnic version of Jimmy Carter."[26]

Rafshoon quickly learned, however, that none of his creative work was good enough for Cuomo. The candidate claimed that the initial TV commercial that ended with the slogan, "Put your anger to work. Make New York what it can be again," was mortifying—even though it significantly improved his polling numbers.

Annoyed that his candidate looked down upon politics and his work, Rafshoon quit at one point. Although Cuomo talked him into returning, campaign management did not improve and was a constant nightmare for Rafshoon. There were too many kibitzers and too many changes in top management. Also, Cuomo insisted on making most decisions himself—a trait that is disastrous in a political campaign.

Ken Auletta was one of Cuomo's biggest fans but became disillusioned as he watched Mario in action. In a September 18, 1977 *Daily News* column titled "Falling out of Love with Mario," Auletta wrote:

At the beginning of this campaign I thought the people of New York would also fall in love with Mario. But a campaign tests a public man. We learn whether the candidate knows how to delegate authority, whether he surrounds himself with substantive people and listens to them, whether he is disciplined, decisive, calm under pressure, whether he understands management and has done his homework. Each are qualities demanded of a good mayor. By this test, Mario has failed. He has not proved a good delegator of authority.

Auletta went on to say that "Just as a mayor cannot run a city alone, so a candidate for major office cannot be his own campaign manager. Mario never understood this." It is practically the first rule in politics.

The Democratic turnout on Primary Day, Thursday, September 8, 1977, broke all records and the voters shocked the pundits. Ed Koch came in first place with 19.81% of the vote. Mario Cuomo came in second with 18.74%. The favorites, Abe Beame and Bella Abzug, trailed with 17.88% and 16.56% respectively. Results for the rest were: Percy Sutton (14.42%), Herman Badillo (10.97%) and Joel Harnett (1.53%).

What was most interesting: Koch came in first place without carrying one of the five boroughs by a plurality.

1977 Democratic Primary						
	Manhattan	The Bronx	Brooklyn	Queens	Staten Island	Total
Edward I. Koch	50,806	23,453	49,470	52,002	5,812	181,544
Mario M. Cuomo	25,331	23,028	54,845	56,698	10,430	170,332
Abraham D. Beame	23,758	25,747	63,304	44,607	7,337	164,753
Bella Abzug	56,045	20,435	37,236	33,883	4,314	151,913
Percy Sutton	35,012	24,801	42,903	28,525	1,399	132,640
Herman Badillo	27,193	35,007	28,909	9,051	876	101,036

Cuomo carried Queens and Staten Island; Beame carried Brooklyn, Abzug carried Manhattan; and Badillo carried the Bronx. Coming in second place in Manhattan, Queens, and Staten Island, plus a decent third-place showing in Brooklyn, was enough to give Koch the first-place finish.

Since no candidate received over 40% of the vote, Koch and Cuomo had to battle it out in a run-off primary scheduled ten days later, Monday, September 19, 1977.

With Koch and Cuomo receiving a combined primary vote of only 38.55%, a mad rush began immediately after the victory speeches to expand their bases by picking up a majority of the 61.45% of votes cast for the also-rans.

The first step in doing that was to secure the endorsements of the losers and the county bosses. In this arena, Koch excelled and Cuomo faltered—badly.

While Cuomo spent most of Wednesday, September 10, brooding, Koch began visiting his former opponents and cutting deals to win their support.

Both Koch and Cuomo met with Herman Badillo on September 11. Koch made a number of promises to Badillo, including a senior position in his administration and the chairmanship of his campaign.

Badillo complained to Koch that his meeting with Cuomo did not go well. "Cuomo didn't even ask me to have a cup of coffee," Badillo said.[27]

According to Badillo, he "couldn't get a straight answer from [Cuomo]. . . . He kept giving me the typical Cuomo philosophical discourse." When it came to discussing political spoils for the Hispanic community, Cuomo said, "Look, I'm not going to dish out jobs."[28]

So, on September 12, Badillo endorsed Koch. This endorsement was important because it gave Koch momentum by encouraging other minority leaders to take a second look at him.

Percy Sutton was not happy with what he perceived as racist overtones in Koch's primary campaign. Besides, he was, on the one hand, leaning toward Cuomo and, on the other, thinking about establishing an independent black political party.

This meant Koch had to look elsewhere for black support, so a meeting was held at the offices of Dave Garth on September 13 with other prominent political African-Americans led by Congressman Charles Rangel.

Koch claims in his memoir that he was "very eloquent" in that meeting. He told them how he had "gone to Mississippi in 1964 to help with black voter registration, how [he] had marched into Montgomery, Alabama, with the Reverend Martin Luther King."[29]

But there was more to the meeting, namely promises. Two people present at the two-hour session, Carl McCall and Basil Paterson, told historian Jonathan Soffer that Koch "promised not to abolish the anti-poverty agencies that were the financial mainstay of a portion of the black political elite and vowed to provide jobs to the black community. . . . [H]e also pledged that Sydenham Hospital in Harlem would remain open."[30]

Koch agreed to stop using terms such as "poverty pimps" and promised to "appoint more blacks than the Lindsay and Beame administrations combined."[31]

At the end of the meeting, Congressman Rangel told Koch, "We were going to wait till the morning to endorse but I can tell by the faces here, we'll go with you."[32]

The next day, the most important black leaders in the city, less Percy Sutton, publicly endorsed Koch over Cuomo. Sutton, realizing he had missed the boat, announced that he would remain neutral in the run-off primary.

For Mario Cuomo, losing Badillo and the African-American leadership was a major blow to his campaign. He mistakenly believed that, as a self-proclaimed "conciliator," it was logical to assume the black community would support him, which is why he refused to cut deals for endorsements. So Mario must have been shocked when the *Amsterdam News*, Harlem's leading newspaper, assailed him in an editorial as "self-righteous, arrogant, sarcastic, and unyielding."[33]

Another key endorsement would be Abe Beame's, because the old Democratic clubhouse supporters still looked to the mayor for guidance.

So, Koch effected a truce with the long-time Democratic Brooklyn boss, Meade Esposito. On Sunday, May 11, Ed Koch, Ed LoCicero, and David Garth paid a visit to Esposito at his mother's home in Brooklyn. Although they arrived an hour late, a very calm Esposito is reported to have said "I don't want anything. You're my man. Have some of [mother's] meatballs."[34]

Esposito's instant support for Koch was probably influenced by the treatment he had received from Cuomo. Mario did not want to be perceived as a flunky of the bosses, so he refused to meet with Brooklyn's Stanley Steingut, the powerful speaker of the New York Assembly. A brief meeting with Esposito got nowhere and Cuomo sent a message back to him, via a local district leader, that read: "Drop Dead. You're Finished. You've Exceeded Your Limit of Lying."[35]

Esposito even agreed to keep his support of Ed Koch a secret, so Koch would not be portrayed as a puppet.

The secret endorsement paid off. On Friday, September 16, Mayor Beame endorsed Koch before a crowd of ten thousand in Coney Island.

Koch had managed to secure the endorsement of Hispanic, Black and party regulars. That left just the Jews and Catholics in the outer boroughs. He received help with working-class Jews when he was endorsed by Deputy Mayor Stanley Friedman, an important political player in the Jewish neighborhoods in the Bronx.

It was becoming clear that several of Mario Cuomo's allies were leaning towards Koch. Even Queens Borough President Donald Manes was distancing himself from Cuomo. Although he publicly supported Cuomo, Manes got the word out to the Democratic leaders in Jewish neighborhoods that it was okay to tell their constituents to vote for Koch.

That left the white ethnic Catholics, and they were certainly in Cuomo's corner. But that did not stop the Koch campaign from putting Cuomo on the defensive by stressing his opposition to the death penalty and Koch's support of it.

At this point in the campaign, many Irish, Italian, and Polish Catholics felt unwanted in a Democratic Party led by Manhattan elites who frowned upon them, and these formerly solid Democrats had re-registered as members of the Republican and Conservative parties and, therefore, could not vote in the Democratic Party.

Cuomo's campaign was foundering. And David Garth's greatest fear was that the Cuomo camp would begin an overt whispering campaign about Koch's sexual orientation.

Was Ed Koch a homosexual? No one really knows to this day. The author had the pleasure of spending many hours with Koch discussing and debating various issues. I even penned a glowing review of his 1990 book *All the Best* for William F. Buckley Jr.'s *National Review*. And I agree with many political observers that Koch may have been asexual. He was obsessed with public life and his own public image. Little else mattered to him.

Nevertheless, this did not stop rumors about the 52-year-old bachelor who lived in Greenwich Village, despite a statement he made on WNEW in 1977: "I don't happen to be homosexual, but if I were, I would hope that I wouldn't be ashamed of it."[36]

In the 1970s, the homosexual movement's political influence at City Hall was growing. Starting in 1971 and every year until it was passed in

1986, a so-called homosexual rights bill was introduced to the City Council, the purpose of which was to amend the city's administrative code to outlaw discrimination based on "sexual orientation or affectional preference."

Attempts at passage in the 1970s failed due to a coalition of Democratic, Republican, and Conservative City Council legislators from the outer boroughs led by Democratic majority leader, Thomas Cuite.

To help defeat the legislation, the Roman Catholic Church, led by Terence Cardinal Cooke, would put out a statement opposing the bill. One typical statement read:

If the bill has an underlying purpose, to advocate and gain approval of homosexual behavior and lifestyle, then there is no way in which the Catholic Church in the City of New York may find it acceptable. And there is no way in which we can remain silent on the issue.

The Catholic Church's moral teaching differentiates between "orientation" and "behavior" for both homosexuals and heterosexuals. While a person's orientation is not subject to moral evaluation, there is no doubt that a person's behavior is subject to evaluation. Homosexual behavior and an attendant homosexual lifestyle are not in accord with Catholic moral teaching and are, in fact, harmful to all persons who become involved; heterosexuality is the norm for human behavior.[37]

Congressman Ed Koch had supported the passage of the legislation and testified annually at City Hall on its behalf.

A campaign flyer paid for by Gay Independent Democrats distributed during the run-off, endorsed Koch and declared "Gays Have a Choice For Change," "Isn't it time we had real friends at City Hall."

The piece went on to say that Koch had an outstanding record of proven support for civil rights for lesbians and gay men and added that Ed Koch:

- is the prime sponsor of the gay civil rights bill in Congress.
- has helped gays with immigration, child custody, prison abuses, the

military, and has succeeded in having anti-gay policies in governmental agencies reversed.

• successfully negotiated with the City Administration to win more police protection for gays in the wake of anti-gay gang violence, and has worked for an end to harassment of gays by police.

• supports the rights of gay teachers. His opponent, Mr. Cuomo, does not.

Before David Garth signed on to the Koch campaign, he asked Koch directly if the rumors about his sexual orientation were true. Koch said no, but Garth had him thoroughly investigated anyway.

As another precaution, Garth convinced Bess Myerson, the first Jewish woman to become Miss America, to join the campaign as Koch's constant companion. Garth promoted the message that Ed and Bess might even get married after the election. When asked about wedding bells in one interview, Koch said, "It's always a possibility, but I don't want to talk about it. She is an incredible person, a warm human being that I truly adore."[38]

Meanwhile, an increasingly desperate Cuomo campaign could not resist keeping the gay rumors alive. There were two reasons: Cuomo's base was Catholic and mostly opposed "gay rights," and he needed the votes of Hasidic and Orthodox Jews who also opposed the gay rights legislation.

Cuomo's primary campaign manager, Michael G. Dowd—a politically well-connected Queens County lawyer—had retained a private investigator to examine Koch's sexual life. (For immunity against prosecution, Dowd later confessed to paying bribes to Geoffrey Lindenauer, an aide to Queens Borough President Donald Manes. Dowd was disbarred in 1990 for five years.) The detective Dowd hired "reported directly to Cuomo's Brooklyn campaign coordinator Thomas Chardavoyne," historian Jonathan Soffer has written. "Dowd lamely claimed that he was looking into the charges 'on my own with a few friends' because he feared that Koch might be blackmailed if he were elected."[39]

When *The Village Voice* asked Cuomo about the investigation, Cuomo said: "Oh Christ. Holy Mother of God. I'm so . . . I'm so . . . disappointed. . . . Asking questions like that about someone can injure his reputation. What if you hurt this fellow and he wins? What you've done is you've scarred the reputation of the Mayor of the greatest city in the world."[40]

Koch justifiably complained that there was not "even an admonishment of Dowd or Chardavoyne, whereas the ethical thing would have been to fire these people on the spot."

On top of the Cuomo campaign investigation of Koch, flyers were distributed and taped to light poles throughout Catholic neighborhoods—particularly in Queens—that read "Vote for Cuomo Not the Homo." As a Republican-Conservative activist working in that campaign in my home county of Queens, the author can attest that the flyers existed. They appeared on Saturday nights around churches and church parking lots.

As for the origins of the flyer, historian Jonathan Soffer wrote, "One suspect was Cuomo's son Andrew. [Koch] supporters raged for years against the young Cuomo, then twenty years old, for allegedly plastering Queens with 'Vote for Cuomo, Not the Homo.'"[42]

While Andrew, to this day, denies any involvement in the matter, Koch's campaign field coordinator tells a different story. He sent a Koch volunteer to patrol streets in Queens who took down the license plate of a person putting up the flyer on poles. "Garth found out it belonged to someone who worked under Andrew Cuomo in the campaign, though there was no direct link."[43]

The New York Times journalist Howard Blum told Andrew's biographer, Michael Shnayerson, that "Koch had no doubt that Cuomo was behind the posters."

> That view was echoed in a videotaped interview made public after Koch's death. "That matter has affected our relationship from '77 through this year," Koch relayed about Mario and himself from the grave. "We get along, and we got along as mayor and governor, but I always held it against his son Andy Cuomo. Even though social relationships when we meet in public are good, underneath, he knows I know what I'm really thinking." The next words were bleeped, but they seemed to be, "You prick!"[44]

There were other more understated tactics employed to keep the "gay" issue alive, some of them quite subtle.

Cuomo campaign literature distributed during the run-off stressed that Mario was a family man. One piece had this bold headline, "Our City

Can Be A Better Place To Raise A Family." Below the headline was a photograph of the Cuomo family assembled in a living room. The caption below the photo read, "Mario and Matilda at home with their children and their parents." Cuomo would also describe Koch as a "Greenwich Village bachelor."

In 1974, as a candidate for lieutenant governor, Cuomo had stated his opposition to the proposed New York City gay rights bill. By 1977, he had flip-flopped and voiced his support for the legislation. But there was a caveat. At public forums and in debates with Koch, Cuomo said he would sign a gay rights bill into law but was opposed to "proselytization." Cuomo went so far as to charge "that Koch favored allowing teachers to 'proselytize in the classroom.'"[45]

The *Daily News* also reported on November 1 "that Cuomo would veto a gay rights bill that would give homosexual teachers the right to proselytize—or advocate—their lifestyle, adding 'Cuomo also urged Koch to debate the gay rights issue publicly, the way he did on capital punishment.'"[46]

"Proselytize" was an interesting choice of words. It can mean that one embraces, advocates, espouses a particular cause or belief, or it can mean brainwashing or evangelizing. Cuomo carefully chose the word "proselytize" to imply that a Koch administration would permit teachers to, essentially, brainwash children about the gay lifestyle—a policy that was anathema to Cuomo's base.

For his part, Koch was appalled by the accusation. In his memoirs, he wrote that "the bill did not advocate any such thing and no one in the race and certainly not I, supported such an idea."[47]

As for the Cuomo Campaign "gay" antics, the candidate was in denial.

As for the investigation into Koch's sexual orientation by the detective hired by Mario's campaign manager, Cuomo told *The Village Voice*, "I hope, I hope Mike [Dowd] made it absolutely clear to you that during the primary I said I didn't want it explored. And I don't want it explored, especially at the last minute."[48]

Saying it shouldn't be explored doesn't mean Cuomo did not know it was, in fact, being explored, and whether or not it came at the last minute is irrelevant.

Even Cuomo's sympathetic biographer, Robert S. McElvaine, concedes that this "was not Mario Cuomo's finest hour." Although he states that "there is no reason to disbelieve Cuomo's declarations that he personally had nothing to do with the attempts to investigate Koch's private life or spread rumors about him," he admits that Cuomo "did have something to do with it," because Cuomo "did help to create the whole atmosphere in which his supporters thought that such activities had a place in the campaign. Cuomo's responsibility begins with his lack of control over the campaign." Indeed, he adds, "Cuomo's 1977 campaign was largely beyond his control."[49]

Lack of control seems a flimsy excuse at best. As we have seen, key players in and observers of the Cuomo campaign have repeatedly stated that Mario Cuomo was a control freak, a micromanager—traits he exhibited throughout his entire political career.

Having watched that campaign and knowing how Cuomo operated, the present author finds it hard to believe that Cuomo wasn't very much aware of the detective's probe into Koch's private life and the "Vote for Cuomo Not the Homo" flyers.

It is possible that Cuomo, after hearing about potential dirty tricks, walked away from such discussions without approving or disapproving in order to have deniability if the antics backfired. But to suggest he was in the dark the entire campaign is just not plausible.

As for Cuomo's more subtle tactic of referring to Koch as a "bachelor who lives in Greenwich Village and champions secular solutions for most problems"[50] Cuomo, a first-rate wordsmith and a first-rate trial and appellate lawyer, knew exactly what he was doing: casting doubts about Koch's character and lifestyle.

In the final days of the run-off, the Cuomo campaign went on a negative offensive. With poll data indicating that former Mayor John Lindsay remained unpopular with the general public, a commercial was released that showed a picture of Koch morphing into Lindsay. Considering the fact that Lindsay gave Cuomo his first opportunity to serve the public, it was widely viewed as a low blow.

David Garth responded with a simple last-minute ad that had Bess Myerson looking into a camera saying, "Whatever happened to character, Mr. Cuomo? We thought your campaign would do better than that."

On Run-off Day, Monday, September 19, 1977 Ed Koch easily defeated Mario Cuomo.

1977 Democratic Primary Run-off					
	Manhattan	The Bronx	Brooklyn	Queens	Staten Island	Total
Edward I. Koch	115,251	69,612	131,271	107,033	9,835	433,002
Mario M. Cuomo	61,570	55,355	112,587	105,522	19,799	354,833

He received only 45% of total votes cast and even lost his home borough of Queens, where he received 49.52% versus Koch's 50.47%. He did manage to handily carry heavily Italian-Catholic Staten Island, but the total votes cast in that county amounted to only 7.5% of total votes cast.

Koch won by putting together a broad coalition. According to a News-Center 4 exit poll, he received 75% of the Jewish vote and an impressive 33% of the Catholic vote. His pro-death penalty strategy apparently succeeded in chipping away at Cuomo's Catholic base.

In his concession speech, Cuomo congratulated Koch but reminded him that he, Mario, was still the candidate of the Liberal Party. "I'll see you in November," he said.[51] The head of the party, Donald Harrington, told the *Daily News* that after it became apparent Cuomo had lost, he and colleague Ray Harding "had a long talk and he's in it to the end." He added, "It's not in the nature of the man to withdraw. We're sure we can win it with his hardcore Democratic votes and our Liberal Party votes."[52]

In defeat, Cuomo had roared that he would "go everywhere Ed Koch goes. I'll debate with him, I'll make use of every forum I can." And then he gave himself an escape hatch. "I'm in unless something drastic happens."[53]

When *The New York Times* asked if "something drastic could be outright rejection by Governor Carey?", Cuomo snapped back, "That's not dramatic enough."[54]

As Ed Koch was basking in victory and Mario Cuomo was licking his wounds, the man on the hot seat was Governor Hugh Carey.

On run-off primary night at the Terrace-on-the-Park in Queens for the victory party that was not to be, Cuomo said he had spoken to Carey, who congratulated him for the campaign he had run, but that the governor had made no promises about support in the upcoming general election.

Carey had also sent to Koch what the *Daily News* called a "cryptic" telegram saying he is "ready to play an appropriate role in the process of conciliation." This appeared to build on the comment he had made a few days earlier, "I will not ignore the mandate of the people."

Yes, Carey abandoned his pledge to the Liberal Party that he was in "all the way" if they nominated Cuomo.

The Democratic governor, who would be up for re-election himself the next year, didn't need to be embarrassed that his own Secretary of State was running against the duly chosen nominee of the Democratic Party.

Cuomo realized that if he abandoned the race, he would be helping Carey—because the governor then would not have to abandon his pledge to Cuomo and could happily endorse Koch.

In defeat, Cuomo's self-righteous persona was in full flower. He let the governor know that the promise he had made to the Liberal Party was that he would run, no matter what, and he made it clear to Carey that he would not let the governor off the hook: Mario still expected Carey's full support in the campaign ahead.

Before Carey publicly abandoned him, Cuomo insisted on a face-to-face meeting. Cuomo, *Time* reported, "felt betrayed and said so angrily. Stung, Carey started to rise out of his chair. 'Sit down, Hughie,' warned Cuomo, 'or I'll knock you right on your ass.' Carey leaned back into his chair."[55]

The following week Carey gave his "full and enthusiastic" endorsement to Edward I. Koch.

For the next seven weeks, Mario Cuomo ran as the candidate of the Liberal Party and the Neighborhood Preservation Party (NPP). The NPP was a creation of Andrew Cuomo. Petitions were circulated to get the NPP on the November ballot. This minor party was intended to be the ballot line hardcore Catholics and conservatives, who would never vote on the Liberal Party line, could cast a vote for Cuomo with a clear conscience.

In the general election campaign, Cuomo was a liberated candidate. He was no longer the favored candidate of the establishment and no longer could be accused of being Carey's stooge. Instead, he could be the candidate he preferred to be: a long-shot underdog.

Hitting New York City's streets in search of votes, Cuomo went on the attack. On Koch, he told the media, "The guy's a conservative," and he condemned the boss-controlled Democratic Party establishment that was supporting Koch. Koch responded sarcastically that "as Mr. Cuomo sees it, if a politician endorses Cuomo, 'It's because God told him to,' while if the same politician endorses me, 'it's a deal.'"[56]

Cuomo was a better candidate in the general election, but he simply could not overcome the built-in advantages Koch had as the nominee of the majority party in New York City.

Although Ed Koch won the election, it was with only 49.99% of the vote. Cuomo shocked the pundits with his strong second-place finish, 40.97% of the vote. The Republican candidate, State Senator Roy Goodman, garnered just 4%, as had the Conservative Party nominee, radio talk show host Barry Farber.

General Election							
		Manhattan	The Bronx	Brooklyn	Queens	Staten Island	Total
Democratic	Edward I. Koch	184,842	116,436	204,934	191,894	19,270	717,376
Liberal and Neighborhood	Mario M. Cuomo	77,531	87,421	173,321	208,748	40,932	587,913
Republican	Roy M. Goodman	19,321	6,102	11,491	18,460	3,229	58,606
Conservative	Barry M. Farber	9,070	7,624	16,576	20,453	3,714	57,437
Others		4,281	1,731	3,752	3,256	761	13,781

What was interesting about the results was that the vast majority of the votes for the Liberal Party candidate came from right-of-center white working-class folks—the so-called Nixon Democrats.

In 1965, Conservative Party mayoral candidate, William F. Buckley Jr., had received 341,226 votes—mostly from the outer boroughs. In the 1969 mayor's race, Republican-Conservative John Marchi garnered 542,411 votes. Four years later, Marchi, running solely on the GOP ticket, received 276,575 votes; and Conservative Mario Biaggi racked up 189,986 votes.

Contrast those totals with the 1977 results. Goodman received only 56,606 votes and Farber's total was 56,437. Cuomo actually outpolled them on the Neighborhood Preservation Party line, where he received 64,971 votes.

Goodman and Farber experienced a huge drop in support because their natural constituencies flocked to Cuomo. The *Times/*CBS exit poll revealed that 66% of Cuomo's support came from Catholics and 20% from Jews. Minorities broke overwhelmingly for Koch.

Cuomo carried Queens and Staten Island, and in many white working-class neighborhoods in the five counties, he won by landslide proportions. In the seven Assembly districts that sent Republican-Conservative legislators to Albany, Cuomo received, on average, 68% of the vote.

Here are a few examples of Cuomo's performance in conservative bastions:

Bay Ridge, Brooklyn	Cuomo – 74% of votes cast
Middle Village, Queens	Cuomo – 65%
Ridgewood, Queens	Cuomo – 65%
Throgs Neck, Bronx	Cuomo – 69%
Staten Island	Cuomo – 61%

President Richard Nixon had carried these neighborhoods overwhelmingly in 1972, and Ronald Reagan would carry them by even larger margins in 1980.

Before going down to address supporters gathered at the Starlight Room at the International Hotel at JFK Airport, Cuomo told his close supporters that, even in defeat, "We did it our way."

Referring to the narrow electoral margins, Cuomo lamented, "Under 10 points. I hate to lose by under 10 points. Under 10 points means I could have won. Under 10 means spending the rest of my life trying to figure out what I could have done different. Over 10, that's different. I hope it goes up."

On the elevator going down to the Starlight Room, Cuomo told his bodyguard, "It's like losing a baseball game 2-1 in the 16th inning. You go home and break your toe on a pail. I'd rather lose 10-1."

Speaking to the assembled crowd, Cuomo said, "Ed Koch is going to be the next Mayor of the City of New York. I congratulate him on his achievement and I know that the hundreds of thousands of people who voted for me today join me in wishing him well."

Cuomo told his supporters that the outcome was "shockingly close" and that he was "sorry we didn't have another week." He thanked them for "an honorable, indeed a beautiful campaign."

As Cuomo was leaving, many shouted "Mario for Governor." Cupping his ears, he shouted back, "I didn't hear that."

Departing the ballroom, Cuomo told reporters following him to the elevator that he would be back on the job as Secretary of State the next morning at 9:00 a.m. When asked how he felt going back to a governor who had deserted him, Cuomo told them that he had not heard from Carey, and then quipped: "I don't work under the governor, I work for the people of the State of New York."

Asked about a future run, Cuomo replied, "I have no idea. There is nothing about what happened in this campaign to discourage me."[57]

Not everyone agreed with that, and not everyone agreed that his campaign had been either "honorable" or "indeed beautiful."

A bold headline in the Wednesday, November 9, 1977 edition of the *New York Post* read "THE BIG SMEAR: Dirtiest campaign in memory."

The opening paragraphs in the article by Joyce Purnick, later of *New York Times* fame, read:

> The just-completed race for mayor was—to many observers— marred more heavily by smear tactics and rumor-mongering than any in recent memory.

> Little of what went on appeared in the press, but throughout this campaign—particularly in its last two weeks—the innuendos were rampant, centering on whispers that Edward Koch is a homosexual.

Purnick lists some of the "incidents" that had occurred in the campaign:

- Newspaper and wire service reporters were repeatedly told—sometimes by Cuomo aides—that there had been "incidents" in Koch's past involving homosexuality. No evidence to support the allegations was presented, and efforts by dozens of reporters to verify the rumors turned up no information whatsoever.

- Patrolmen's Benevolent Assn. president Samuel DeMilia told the Associated Press he had "information" damaging to Koch. Refusing to elaborate, he said: "If someone makes me mad, I'll do what I have to do." Craig Ammerman, AP City Bureau chief, wrote a story reporting on DeMilia's charges and threat, but decided not to release it until after the election.

- Seeking reaction to the story, AP reporters gave copies to Koch and Cuomo. Both agreed, Ammerman said, not to distribute or discuss it. But within hours, he said, the *Times* and *Daily News* had copies of the unreleased story, and a *Post* reporter was told about its contents by a top Cuomo aide.

- AP reported its New York office was "deluged" by calls from people who "falsely claimed to be reporters" urging that the story on DeMilia's charges against Koch be released.

- Although the issue of a gay rights bill pending before the City Council had been dormant through most of the campaign, a week before the election Cuomo aides called reporters to suggest they were missing a big story—that the homosexual community was angry with Cuomo over his position on the bill.

- Gay activists charged that Cuomo himself brought up his differences with Koch on the bill several times during the last 10 days of the campaign. Cuomo angrily denied the charge, saying he was responding only to attacks by gay activists on his position on the bill.

- Koch aides said Cuomo supporters had taken sound trucks through the Bronx chanting, "Vote for Cuomo, not the homo."

- Cuomo, meanwhile, charged that Koch supporters had driven sound trucks through the outer boroughs saying Cuomo has links to the Mafia and is anti-Semitic.

Mario Cuomo had been a flawed candidate in 1977. He tried to be St. Thomas More and Niccolò Machiavelli at one and the same time. While he wanted the general public to perceive him as a passionate liberal and a conciliator, he also revealed a dark side of his personality: the obnoxious lawyer who could not pass up an opportunity to make a hurtful wisecrack.

Of the first run-off primary debate on New York's Channel 13, Cuomo's biographer has observed that, "Cuomo appeared to be arrogant, practically a bully."[58] Richard Starkey, a Cuomo campaign aide, wrote that, "The debate is a major disappointment because Mario is reduced to a sniping role. He's testy instead of smooth and unruffled. He harps too much on the death penalty issue. . . . I had hoped for a decisive drubbing of Koch. This is at best a standoff, at worst a defeat for my man Mario."[59]

The noted columnist, Murray Kempton, agreed. Cuomo and Koch, in his judgment, had switched roles, "Cuomo was the hectoring bully; Koch the mild-mannered pacifier."[60]

When it came to the issues, Cuomo said when he joined the race on May 10, "The people of this city have a right to know, in the most precise detail, what their candidates intend to do."

One-time Cuomo admirer Ken Auletta complained, in his September 18, 1977 *Daily News* column, that Cuomo had not lived up to his pledge and that details had "been absent from Mario's campaign" and "his positions tend to be vague."

> Ask Mario about excessive fringe benefits—the $4,640 fringes' cost per city employee, the twenty "sick days" granted City University professors, the up to twenty-eight "chart days" off given police sergeants, the five weeks' paid vacation starting sanitation men get, the two days off given cops and the one day given firemen who donate blood—and he vaguely says this is a subject for "negotiation." Ask about rent control, decentralization, or Westway, and he promises studies. Ask Ed Koch about future layoffs, and he says they are unavoidable. Ask Mario, and he says they are "undesirable."[61]

A disenchanted Auletta concluded that Mario did not take the time to learn the issues.

Another liberal journalist, Doug Ireland, went ballistic on Mario in the pages of *New York* magazine:

He is probably the best orator on the hustings this fall, yet it is difficult at this late date to pin down his sense of the city. He wraps himself in the ethereal principle, but his attempt to deal cohesively with real issues in this campaign has too often been tortured, embarrassing to watch. He may be a philosopher king, but even Plato learned to walk erect among the poor. Cuomo recently took to television to say, "I hate to admit we're at a point now in society where you have to be as primitive as talking about how we lock up the animals who threaten us, but that's the fact of it now." When a former law prof postures like a street tough, mingling academese with up-from-the-streets rhetoric, watch out. And don't think for a minute that blacks and Puerto Ricans in New York are fooled by Mario's coded speech. One of the city's most sophisticated black leaders who knows the man well told me "it doesn't matter that Mario isn't a bigot and is a liberal at heart. If he is elected, it will be a signal to the blacks and Puerto Ricans to stay back, lie down, and keep quiet."[62]

In *The Bronx is Burning*, Jonathan Mahler made this apt observation about Cuomo and his campaign: "There was an intense competition for Cuomo's ear that reflected the paradox at the candidate's core: His conservative, outer borough instincts were perpetually at war with his loftier liberal ideals."

Cuomo's pollster, Robert Sullivan agreed. "He thought the liberal ideals were more admirable—he aspired to them—but by instinct and impulse he was not a liberal."[63]

Candidate Cuomo couldn't resist being the South Jamaica tough guy, the "in your face" street fighter. And that sometimes thuggish attitude was adopted by some of the campaign's young volunteers, particularly Cuomo's 20-year-old son, Andrew.

Two anecdotes from the 1977 campaign, one involving Mike Long, the long-time state chairman of the New York Conservative Party, and one involving the author, illustrate this.

At a mayoral forum at Fort Hamilton High School in Brooklyn, Cuomo boasted that his Neighborhood Preservation Party was the only political party in New York to have a platform. Hearing this, Mike Long—

then the Brooklyn chairman of the Conservative Party—interjected that Cuomo was wrong, and reminded him that the Conservative Party has a platform. When Cuomo told him he was wrong, Long yelled to him, "You're a liar!" What followed was a pushing match of the sort one would ordinarily expect to see in a schoolyard brawl. Long recalls: "Mario and I sneered at one another and began pushing back and forth. He pushed me through a swinging door and I pulled him along with me. The cops didn't know me but they certainly knew the mayoral candidate, so they broke things up and searched me while Cuomo left in his car."

"Moments later," Long continued, "Cuomo came back in the car and called me over under some trees to chat. He apologized, and when I told him we did have a platform, Cuomo asked for copies. Next day, I had State Headquarters send him a copy of every platform since the party's inception. Later I received a note from Cuomo conceding that the Conservative Party did indeed have a platform."[64]

The letter on "Mario Cuomo for Mayor" stationery, dated November 4, 1977 read:

Dear Mike:
You *do* have a platform. I will say it publicly the first chance I get.
Sincerely,
Mario

As for tough guy Andrew: In 1977, bishop of the Roman Catholic Diocese of Brooklyn, Francis Mugavero, brought in a Saul Alinsky-inspired group to organize members of the parishes in Brooklyn and Queens for community action.

Days before the September 9 primary, a rally of over 1,000 people representing dozens of parishes gathered at St. Sebastian's Parish auditorium in Woodside, Queens to meet and hear from all the candidates. Let the author now tell the story as I experienced it:

I attended the candidates' night forum with an old friend, Jack Swan—a community relations consultant to Terence Cardinal Cooke. We were there in part to escort in the Conservative Party candidate Barry Farber.

Mario—a favorite son of the Diocese despite his flip-flopping on abortion and gay rights—received a huge ovation when he was introduced.

There was, however, one "BOO!" from me. At six-foot-six inches tall, I could hardly be missed, particularly by young Andrew Cuomo, who with a couple of his buddies was standing in the back of the auditorium a few feet away from me.

When I stepped outside to see if I could find Farber—who was running late as usual—Swan overheard Cuomo say to his companions, "Let's beat the s**t out of that guy!" He followed them outside and when they got close to me, Swan waved his cane and yelled at them. Having second thoughts, they dispersed and went sheepishly back inside.

Looking back, Mario was probably fortunate he lost the mayoral race. Being mayor in a city like New York is not a contemplative job. One must make scores of instant decisions every day without hesitation. And Cuomo was not that kind of person. He preferred to debate every issue—often with himself—before deciding anything. He was actually better suited for a position in Albany, where there was plenty of time to ponder public policy.

CHAPTER 7
LIEUTENANT GOVERNOR CUOMO

In 1978, as Governor Hugh Carey geared up to run for a second term, he could look back with pride on his administration's accomplishments. He had saved New York City and the state itself from falling into the fiscal abyss. His administration was scandal-free. And unlike the way it had been during the big-spending Rockefeller years, Carey had kept annual increases in state expenditures below the rate of inflation.

Although he had reluctantly raised taxes in 1975 to the tune of $600 million in order to balance the budget, he knew very well that taxes were too high. In fact, New York's tax burden was stymying economic growth and driving the wealthy to low-tax states. So Governor Carey made it his mission in 1977 to convince the Legislature to reduce personal income taxes by $225 million.

In 1978, he told the Legislature, "If we are to provide jobs for our people and economic opportunity for our children, we must tear down the wall of high taxes that separates us from the rest of the nation."[1] He would successfully pursue his tax-cutting crusade in subsequent years.

During Carey's tenure, the top tax rate on earned income declined from 15% to 10%. There were also "increases in some personal deductions and exemptions, along with the phased elimination of the separate personal income tax profits from unincorporated businesses."[2]

Yet despite his successful attempts to tame the state and city leviathan, the governor was not especially popular with the political class or the voters in early 1978.

The major reasons for his unpopularity were his personality, his governing style, and his opposition to the death penalty.

While the governor enjoyed swapping political stories with cronies in neighborhood bars like P.J. Clarke's in midtown Manhattan, he was a very private person, a loner.

David Garth had a good way of describing Carey: "To me the guy is like a diamond, whichever way the light shines through, you see another reflection. He's a man nobody knows. . . . The guy has more faces than Lon Chaney."[3]

One state official said of him, "Like an octopus, he puts up a smoke (sic) screen, usually with a barrage of words. Most people we know, the one thing that makes them human is that they exchange feelings. You don't exchange feelings with Hugh Carey. His feelings about people come out in little bon-mots."[4]

Albany insiders viewed Carey as aloof and easily bored with mundane issues. He was not a micro-manager; with the exception of the state budget where he amazed the press and public with his mastery of the minutiae, he winged it on many other matters.

Carey was at his best when addressing a crisis and could be very demanding. James Tully, his tax commissioner, observed, "He's a tough man to work for. He can be demanding and sharp. He's the brightest man I know. His heart's in the right place, but you have to get to it."[5]

Many legislators didn't like Carey because he didn't hang out with them or stroke their egos, and this caused problems for his administration.

For example, for the first time in 153 years the Legislature refused to confirm a governor's nominee. They also overrode one of Carey's vetoes—something that had not happened for 104 years.

However, Carey's biggest problem in Albany was his lieutenant governor—Mary Anne Krupsak.

The state Constitution gives the lieutenant governor two roles: to preside over the Senate and to serve as acting-governor when the governor travels beyond the state's borders. Outside of those duties, the lieutenant governor is dependent on the largesse of the governor, who may delegate duties as he sees fit.

Having been a state senator, assemblywoman, lawyer, and public affairs consultant in the private sector, Krupsak had expected to be consulted by Carey and his staff on policy issues. She was not. Carey and his senior staff had no interest in what Krupsak thought, and basically ignored her.

From time to time, Carey did throw her a few bones. He doubled her office's budget, permitted her to open two regional offices and to serve as a state "ombudsman."

And in December 1977, Carey asked Krupsak to stay on the ticket in 1978, and she accepted.

Yet something happened only days before the Democratic Party's state convention that caused her to change her mind.

The storyline goes like this: After allegedly agreeing to appear on June 8 in the governor's stead at a Nassau County Democratic dinner, Krupsak took offense when State Commerce Commissioner John Dyson also appeared and spoke to the gathering about pertinent state issues.

Krupsak was furious and called the governor's chief of staff, Robert Morgado, at 1:00 in the morning and threatened to quit the ticket.

After appeals to her from Garth and Democratic chairman John Burns were of no avail, Carey called her on Sunday, June 11. "One more time I'm asking you," the governor said, "Will you be my lieutenant governor?" She answered, "No, thank you, sir." And Carey replied, "So be it."[6]

With the convention slated to commence in just three days, the mad rush to come up with a replacement began.

Historian Daniel Kramer claims that "Assistant Appointments Officer, John Marino, urged his chief, Judith Hope, to beg Carey to select Secretary of State Mario Cuomo."[7]

While this is probably true, the person who put the heaviest squeeze on Carey to pick Cuomo was David Garth.

Garth convinced Carey to put aside his pride. To win a second term, Carey needed to make inroads in New York City's white, ethnic, working-class neighborhoods that were then trending Republican, and Cuomo was the one man most likely to be helpful in those areas, because he had carried them in the mayoral race a year earlier. Also, as secretary of state, Cuomo had been working effectively upstate and could be a campaign asset in the Buffalo, Syracuse, and Rochester ethnic neighborhoods.

While the Carey campaign was momentarily stalled, Cuomo was not sitting still. Despite the fact that he was branded a three-time loser, there was still a significant subset of Democrats urging him to run for something statewide. The most attractive post was state Attorney General, especially because the famed "people's lawyer," Republican Louis Lefkowitz, was retiring after 20 years in office.

Convinced that as a "lawyer's lawyer" he was best qualified to be A.G., Cuomo faced one major problem: in 1977 he had promised Bronx Borough

President Robert Abrams that he would support him for that job in exchange for Abrams' endorsement of him for mayor.

A promise, Cuomo liked to say, was sacred to him. He had defied Carey and the Democratic establishment when he had refused to drop out of the race after losing the primary to Ed Koch, for the reason that he had given his word to the Liberal Party to run through November. His word was his bond.

But by late May 1978, Cuomo's ambition was more important than his word: he was ready to go to the Democratic convention to seek the A.G. nomination, Abrams or no Abrams.

Cuomo promoted himself as more suited for the job because, unlike Abrams, he had courtroom experience and was a legal scholar. "We need an attorney, not a general," he told potential supporters.[8]

Meanwhile, a reluctant Hugh Carey had decided Cuomo must be his guy. So, he sent Garth and Robert Morgado to offer the lieutenant governor slot to Mario.

Many of his supporters advised him to reject the offer, but Cuomo now convinced himself that he had a moral obligation to run. "Despite his serious difference with Carey," Robert McElvaine has written, "Cuomo believed he would be better for the state than the Republicans would. If he was needed to save the state from Republican rule, Cuomo thought, he must accept."[9] And there is little doubt that in the back of Cuomo's mind there was also the thought he could be Carey's successor in 1982, and that was better than being attorney general.

Cuomo did make one condition: Carey had to ask him face to face to take the post. The governor begrudgingly complied.

Before facing off against his general-election opponent, the Republican-Conservative Assemblyman Perry Duryea of Montauk, Carey had to hold off primary challengers Mary Anne Krupsak and Brooklyn State Senator Jeremiah Bloom.

As the incumbent governor, Carey had all the advantages in such a face-off, although there were concerns that Krupsak could do well upstate and Bloom could cut into the Jewish vote in New York City. However, there was a positive side: a well-fought primary would keep Carey's name in front of the public and would sharpen his campaign and debating skills for the fall election.

On Primary Day, September 12, 1978, a large number of registered Democrats (20%) turned out to vote. Carey won, but it was not a landslide victory. He received only 52% to Krupsak's 34% and Bloom's 14%.

This was a lukewarm endorsement by Democrats and did not bode well for the governor. As the general campaign commenced, public opinion polls had the Carey-Cuomo ticket thirty points behind the Duryea-Caputo ticket. (Bruce F. Caputo was a U.S. congressman from Yonkers.)

The Carey-Cuomo shotgun marriage did not start off well. The governor was furious over statements Cuomo made about him: "What makes Carey tick?" Cuomo told Ken Auletta. "Who cares, He's a good governor. Why not settle for that? Why do all this psychological probing?"[10] And when asked how he could run with Carey after he had deserted him in 1977, Cuomo replied that Carey had put himself between a rock and a hard place, "first by endorsing me and then making a commitment he couldn't keep. I don't think the Governor is much of a politician but I think he's a great governor."[11]

Carey angrily told Garth, "See, he is going to screw me. He's saying I'm not a good politician." Garth calmed down the governor by convincing him Cuomo's comment could actually be helpful. "You dummy," he said, "shut your mouth! This is the line we win with: 'He's a lousy politician, but a great governor.'"[12]

Carey was fortunate that his opponent, Perry Duryea, was a weak candidate. Conservatives were not thrilled with him because as speaker of the Assembly, he had cast the tie-breaking vote to approve the 1970 abortion law. Besides, Republicans had grown used to Nelson Rockefeller paying all the party's campaign bills and were reluctant to open their checkbooks for Duryea.

Although there was plenty to criticize in the Carey record, the governor easily bested Duryea in their thirteen debates. And Duryea's refusal to release his personal income tax returns really hurt him.

Accused of using tax shelters and other gimmicks to pay less tax than he actually owed, Duryea denied any wrongdoing but refused to release any returns except the most recent. Even Duryea's campaign consultant, John Deardourff, admitted that "a fundamental mistake was failing to deal with the personal finance issue early on. . . . It's our sermon to all candidates in the post-Watergate era to face up to the personal finances issue early on. I was never listened to on this one." Conservative Party Chairman Mike Long agrees: "Duryea lost credibility carrying around a briefcase that contained his taxes. He told everyone they were in the case, but he didn't show them to anyone. It was an important reason why he lost to Carey."[13]

Cuomo campaigned effectively around the state, particularly in the N.Y.C. neighborhoods he carried in 1977. He was an excellent counter-puncher to Duryea's Italian-American running mate, Bruce Caputo.

On November 7, 1978, Hugh Carey bucked a national trend. Whereas five Democratic governors around the country lost, he became the first Democratic governor of New York to be re-elected in forty years.

Carey beat Duryea 54% to 46%. It was not a landslide and his margin of victory, 400,000 votes, was down 50% from his 1974 election. Nevertheless, the Carey-Cuomo ticket won because the ticket made serious inroads in the more conservative neighborhoods in the city, carrying areas that had been dominated by Nixon Democrat voters who had elected Republican legislators to represent them in Albany: places such as Bay Ridge, Fort Hamilton, and Canarsie in Brooklyn; Douglaston, Bayside, Middle Village, Richmond Hill, Ridgewood, Glendale, and Maspeth in Queens. They also carried the bastion of conservatism, the heavily Italian-American Staten Island. And despite the fact that both Carey and Cuomo were pro-abortion, they managed to capture 52% of the Catholic vote.

There is no doubt that Cuomo helped flip some of the votes in the white ethnic neighborhoods, particularly the Italian ones.

However, the claim by Cuomo's biographer that "Cuomo's role in the 1978 Carey campaign amounted to almost that of a campaign manager ... "[14] doesn't hold up. In a post-election piece in the *New York Post* titled "The two brilliant men who engineered Gov. Carey's come-from-behind victory," author Arthur Greenspan wrote:

> Gov. Carey's spectacular comeback to win a second term when nobody thought he could was the result of a brilliant collaboration by a team which included media wizard David Garth, Carey himself, and a man little known to the general public, Robert J. Morgado, the Governor's secretary. . . .

Garth, whose reputation as a political king-maker is legend, is not one to hide behind false modesty but in the current campaign, he insists on sharing the credit.

"We're going to get a lot of credit, David Garth, the media this, the media that," he said in analyzing the victory for The Post. "But I'm telling you that it would have been nothing without Bob Morgado."

And he added: "If I were to give credit to anyone other than the candidate himself, I would credit Morgado with the victory."

Garth said there were three ingredients in the campaign, "confidence, cash and the incumbency."

"Cash is the money raised in the campaign. We had that," he said. "The confidence we had from the Governor, and the strategy. And then it was the use of the incumbency. We had a perfect blueprint, written by a man named Rockefeller. And Bob ran the incumbency."[15]

Another *Post* piece that contrasted the strategies of Duryea's media consultants and the Democrats' operation, reported that "In Carey's camp, his media advisor, David Garth, ran the show. In fact, it was said, Garth had such control of the operations that some factions, such as union supporters, objected."[16] There is no record of Cuomo having had any major input into the campaign strategy or that he served as a kind of de facto "campaign manager."

When Mario Cuomo was sworn in as New York's lieutenant governor on January 1, 1979, he finally achieved what he had been seeking throughout that decade—elective office.

But the office had little power. His staff was much, much smaller than the one he had as secretary of state. His biography and job description—which he approved—in the 1979–1980 edition of *The New York Red Book*, was significantly shorter than his secretary of state entry in previous editions.

One sentence that sticks out in the lieutenant governor biography: " . . . Mr. Cuomo earned a reputation as the most active Secretary of State in the State's history." Self-aggrandizement?

Cuomo also quickly learned that neither the governor nor his senior staff had any interest in him or his opinions. He would write bitterly in his diary about how little face-time he had with Carey.

On the plus side, Carey and his people really didn't care what Mario Cuomo did on a day to day basis; they did not micromanage his activities. Cuomo was free to accept speaking engagements and other appearances all over the state. And so he travelled widely, making contacts and friends he would later call on when he would make his move to succeed Carey in office.

Cuomo took his duty as presiding officer of the Senate seriously, particularly in his first year as lieutenant governor. He not only wanted to master the parliamentary procedures, he also wanted to get to know members. One longtime Albany lobbyist told the author that Cuomo paid particular attention to upstate Republican legislators. He wanted to learn what made them tick and, even more important, to learn what was on the minds of their constituents and the issues that mattered to them. Such knowledge would only help in his drive to become the state's chief executive.

The relations between Carey and Cuomo continued to be strained, and the governor would sometimes take public shots at Cuomo. On one occasion, when asked about Cuomo's role in the administration, Carey replied, "He doesn't do anything." Carey staff members ridiculed Cuomo memorandums to the governor, complaining that they read "like term papers."[17]

Then Cuomo struck back.

The jibes, he told a reporter, were made by "people with no vision, who believe in the grubby deal, who made the arrogant assumption that there is secret technique for running government."[18]

Despite claims by Cuomo's friends that the 1977 mayoral defeat had humbled him, that his attitude and approach was kinder and softer, that he was no longer the furious and indignant urban populist, there remained under the thin skin of the "New Cuomo" a simmering anger that could burst out in a heartbeat.

In 1980, the under-utilized Cuomo was approached by Jimmy Carter re-election campaign officials Pat Caddell and Gerald Rafshoon to oversee Carter's New York campaign. Cuomo wanted the job even though Carter was facing a strong challenge from Senator Ted Kennedy. Before accepting, however, he consulted with top elected officials in New York and cleared it with Governor Carey, who said, "Yes, go do it."[19]

Governor Carey did not like President Carter. In fact, Carey admitted in later years that he had voted for his long-time friend President Gerald Ford in 1976. As a result, several political wags believe Carey okayed Cuomo's role in the Carter campaign figuring he would fail.

Throughout 1979, Carey equivocated whenever there was talk about Carter's second-term prospects.

On one occasion when asked point blank if he supported Carter's re-election, Carey said, "I think we ought to have a political moratorium."

Another time he said, "I expect to support Carter."

On still another occasion, Carey said, "I have never announced for an unannounced candidate yet."

David Garth said Carey's position was one of "cemented neutrality." When Cuomo was asked about Carey's position on Carter, he said "How the hell do I know? It's all gas."[20]

Carey privately rooted for Ted Kennedy, who went on to decisively beat Carter in the New York's presidential primary: 59 to 41.

Even when it became obvious in the summer of 1980 that Kennedy could not overcome Carter's delegate lead, Carey further angered Cuomo and the Carter campaign by calling for an "open convention."[21]

Carter was re-nominated and Cuomo went on to serve as co-Chairman of the New York Carter-Mondale campaign. To assist him, Mario brought on board his son, Andrew, a student at Albany Law School.

While there is no doubt the Cuomos learned plenty about organizing a statewide campaign, their efforts were futile. On November 4, 1980, Republican-Conservative Ronald Reagan (also on the ballot in the Conservative Party's row C) carried liberal New York with 47% of the vote to Carter's 44%. Third party candidate, John Anderson, garnered 8%.

To add insult to injury, Town of Hempstead Supervisor Alphonse D'Amato, running as a Republican-Conservative, won the U.S. Senate seat held for 24 years by the very liberal Jacob Javits.

Throughout his two terms in office, Hugh Carey proved to be a fiscal conservative who managed to do more with less.

During the super-inflationary Carter years, the Empire Center has reported that "New York's per capita spending increased much more slowly than the average. In fact, the New York State budgets under Carey didn't grow at all after adjusting for inflation. . . ."[22]

Carey managed to do this and to cut taxes, by reducing Medicaid costs during his tenure by $2.3 billion, by cutting the state workforce by 20,000, and by imposing a wage freeze on government employees.

When the Republican-controlled Senate and Democratic Assembly revolted in his second term against his frugal budgets by passing legislation that increased spending, Carey fearlessly used his line item veto power.

After Carey vetoed $900 million in spending added to his budget in 1982, the Legislature did override some of the vetoes totaling $375 million.

"Thanks largely to Carey's budgets and tax policies," the Empire Center concluded, "the Empire State emerged from the oil price shocks and stagflation of the 1970s and early 80s well-positioned to gain from the national economic expansion that began in 1983."[23]

Yet, despite his fiscal and economic achievements, Carey remained an unpopular figure throughout the state.

He was certainly not loved by the members of the Legislature, who despised him for vetoing political pork for their districts.

The general public soured on him because of his soap opera-like personal life. On election night 1978, standing next to gal-pal Anne Ford Uzielli, he told the crowd assembled to celebrate his victory:

I know you've been waiting for me to make a personal announcement for some time, I'm prepared to make that announcement tonight. This is my announcement:

We've just come through a campaign. It was a long, hard campaign.

I announce that in order that I will not be aloof, alone, remote, inaccessible and grouchy, or any of those, tonight I shall embark on a new campaign.

I hope it will not be as long and as hard and as difficult as the last campaign.

He was referring to his campaign to convince Anne Uzielli to marry him. That was not to be, and shortly thereafter the governor began squiring around town Evangeline "Angie" Gouletas. Carey met the multi-millionaire real estate magnate at Ronald Reagan's presidential inaugural in January 1981 and quickly fell in love—after his earlier inamorata had rejected his marriage proposal for a second time.

The Carey-Gouletas courtship became "Page Six" gossip material. And it became a bad soap opera when it was revealed, after they announced their engagement, that Gouletas had lied about her previous husbands. Her "dead" first husband turned out to be alive, and she had not disclosed that she had had a third husband. A publicly humiliated Carey said shortly before the wedding, "I am certain in my own mind that I now possess all relevant facts about the life and marriages of Evangeline Gouletas prior to our marriage."[24]

Carey's public courtship, his night-life, the jokes about his fiancée that made all the gossip magazines and the national news stations, the fact—because Evangeline's marriages were never annulled—he was unable to marry in the Catholic Church, plus his long honeymoon abroad, did not sit well with the general public, particularly his core supporters, blue-collar Catholics. As a result, Carey's popularity plummeted.

To add fuel to the fire, Jimmy Breslin—a Cuomo friend—depicted Carey in his newspaper column as "Society Carey."

Breslin wrote:

> Society Carey hardly does anything except fly. He is the governor of New York and the discoverer of the 10-hour workweek. When he is on the ground, most of his time is spent driving to or from the airport. . . . He likes to fly around in the air with his girlfriend. . . .
>
> When you look at Society Carey with his new auburn hair and his girlfriend and his 10-hour workweek, with state pilots flying

him and the girlfriend around in the sky in state planes, with limousines waiting on the ground . . . you can see the reason why there is no other name in the world for Society Carey except . . . Society Carey.[25]

Watching "Society" Carey's poll numbers drop like a rock, several Democratic pols were thinking about challenging Carey in a primary or running for the nomination if the governor chose not to seek another term. And the name at the head of the list of wannabees was Mario Cuomo.

CHAPTER 8
CUOMO FOR GOVERNOR, 1982

The political death watch for Hugh Carey began in 1980. Cuomo and the other potential gubernatorial candidates—City Council President Carol Bellamy, Attorney General Bob Abrams, and Assembly Speaker Stanley Fink—studied Carey's every move hoping to get an indication of his plans for 1982.

During this period, Cuomo continued to play head games with himself. He told his biographer, "Remember I started the thing [politics] on one leg—never taking it seriously, or as seriously as I do now. I always had the feeling that I'd go back into private practice."[1]

That's hard to believe. Mario Cuomo was not only ambitious, he believed he could do a better job than other elected officials because he was smarter and sharper on his feet.

As early as 1971, there was talk among various St. John's Law School alums about who from the class of 1956 would someday be governor: John Gallagher or Mario Cuomo.

Gallagher, a long-time friend of the author (and the man who introduced the author to Cuomo in 1970), was elected to the Assembly from northeast Queens in 1965 as a Republican-Conservative. He served on the board of the law school and was considered an up and coming star. While Gallagher and Cuomo were good friends, Gallagher told the author they both had big political ambitions.

Gallagher went on to run for U.S. Congress in the newly reapportioned 6th Congressional District that covered northern Queens and Nassau in 1972. After he lost that closely contested race against incumbent Democrat Lester Wolff, his political star dimmed. Years later, Governor Cuomo appointed Gallagher to the N.Y.S. Court of Claims.

Continuing to downplay personal ambition, Cuomo attempted to portray himself as a modern version of St. Thomas More. He claimed he had an "obligation as a Christian of mercy to try to get himself into a position where he could do the most good."[2] The office of the State's chief executive fit that bill.

To understand Cuomo's behavior and thinking during his quest to become governor, his published diary is essential reading even though, as Assembly Speaker Stanley Fink suggested to *The New York Times*, "Mr. Cuomo keeps the diaries in loose-leaf notebooks so he can do plenty of judicious editing and rewriting." The entries from November 1980 until Carey announced he would not run for a third term on Friday, January 15, 1982, reveal a man who frequently was unsure about his political future; was often upset that he was ignored by Governor Carey and his staff; and enjoyed sticking it to the governor and his aides when he could.

Time and again, he complains about how he's ignored by Carey and misled by the governor's chief of staff, Bob Morgado.

When the governor did not include Cuomo on his committee dedicated to finding ways to aid the victims of the earthquake that hit the Village of Conza in South Italy in November 1980, in defiance of the governor he set up his own committee, the Italian Disaster Emergency Assistance, on December 2.

When Cuomo learned shortly before the governor was slated to deliver his 1981 State of the State address to the Legislature that Carey would name him "coordinator" of his criminal justice proposals, Cuomo declined the honor, citing disagreement with some of the recommendations.

The following month, a nervous Cuomo wrote in his diary of growing speculation that Carey wanted to dump Cuomo. The diary cites rumors and leaks that Carey is talking to others about being his running mate in 1982 and that the governor only talks to him when he wants something.

Carey did contact Cuomo late in the day on February 12, 1981 and Cuomo said his end of the conversation was "crisp." According to Cuomo, Carey insisted that Cuomo was responsible for the rumors about their poor relationship. An angry Cuomo refuted the charges and informed Carey that he, not the governor, would decide if he runs again for lieutenant governor.

A few days later, Mario discussed his future with his son Andrew, by then a 22-year-old student at Albany Law School. The young Cuomo believed Carey would have a tough time winning in 1982 because the public has become disgusted with Carey. After the discussion, Cuomo concludes, he will be uncommitted as to his future electoral plans.

Just how "uncommitted" Cuomo was is debatable. On March 14, Cuomo met with his most trusted political advisors, including son Andrew, and laid out a strategy for going forward. Parts of his plan included finding a core group of contributors; organizing a fundraiser for August; renting a "pre-campaign" office; commissioning a public opinion poll and spending as much time as possible pressing the flesh in New York City and the surrounding suburban counties.

The one significant disagreement among the attendees was whether or not Cuomo should challenge Carey in a primary. Mario and Andrew agreed that it would be difficult to run against Carey because they did not have a rational reason for breaking with him.

That position turned out to be a valid one. In the race against Republican Lew Lehrman, in 1982, Cuomo, running as a Carey ally, was able to run on his record of saving New York, cutting taxes, and reigning in spending, while labeling Rockefeller Republicans as tax-and-spend addicts.

To further advance his cause, Cuomo—the self-proclaimed urban populist who disliked rich Manhattanites—began meeting with captains of Wall Street. He sought the support and the financial backing of investment bankers including Dale Horowitz of Solomon Brothers and John Heiman, chairman of the executive committee of Warburg Paribas Becker.

On March 25, 1981, Cuomo wrote sarcastically in his diary, "The Governor appears to have dyed his hair again and that is being perceived as a sure sign he's running again. I'm sure he is . . . but I don't know if it's for Governor, for President, for Evangeline Gouletas or for all three."[3]

The Carey-Cuomo relationship deteriorated further when the *SoHo News*, in April 1981, ran a headline quoting Cuomo: "The people around the Governor are cowards and phonies and you can tell them I said so." Claiming the quote was taken out of context, Cuomo conceded that it widened the rift with the Governor.[4]

The rift widened further when Cuomo learned in early June that Carey told Richard Meislin at the *Times* that his lieutenant governor has not been around Albany very much. "He's been invited to all these functions [with legislative leaders], but he hasn't been around." When asked why, the governor, laughing, said "He's otherwise occupied. 'How'? I don't know."

A "stunned" Cuomo replied, "His ignorance of my activities may result from the fact I haven't heard from him since February. Incidentally, I don't need the communications from him to function well, but the communications could solve his problems of lack of information."[5]

Cuomo went on to tell the *Times* that he had "reactivated his independent campaign committee in preparation for next year's state-wide elections."

"I have a committee, I am raising money, I've scheduled a fund raiser," he said.

When asked what elected position he would seek in 1982, he gave this "Cuomoesque" answer: "I feel you don't make a decision until you have to. That's not ambivalence, that's prudence."

"I know that whatever I do next year, I'll have to run. If you wanted to be Lieutenant Governor, if you wanted to be Governor, if you wanted to be anything, you'd have to run. I'm ready for that."[6]

The Cuomo bandwagon was stalled in mid-October 1981 when the lieutenant governor learned that his top aide, Bill Cabin, had been committing fraud. Cabin had been forging Cuomo's signature, placing people on the state payroll, and then confiscating their paychecks and depositing them in his own account. Before getting caught, he had pocketed about $128,000.

Cuomo immediately turned the information over to the Albany County District Attorney, and on October 28, 1981, Cabin confessed his guilt to the State Police.

While not culpable, Cuomo admitted it was "a staggering blow" because he did bear responsibility for hiring Cabin in the first place. Cuomo feared his opponents would point fingers at him and ask how he could manage the state if he could not handle his chief of staff.[7]

Cuomo hoped the political damage was mitigated by his effective disclosure and the likely return of the stolen funds.[8]

Meanwhile the Cuomo-Carey relationship hit rock bottom on Monday, November 2, 1981 during an hour and a half meeting they had together. Cuomo claimed a bitter Carey was childish, rude, overly sensitive, defensive, and angry that his lieutenant governor might challenge him in 1982.[9]

Carey had a slightly different take on the relationship. He told the

Times, "It's very hard to share your confidence with a man who might run against you. Maybe I look for too much allegiance."[10]

Later that day, Cuomo had the unpleasant duty of announcing the Cabin scandal to the public. The press reports were not fatal, and 14 days after Cuomo blew the whistle, Cabin pleaded guilty and was sentenced to jail.

Cuomo, however, was still fearful that the Cabin matter would leave him open to criticism that he was not a good manager and top-notch administrator.[11]

While Cuomo and his campaign team continued to lay the foundation for a gubernatorial race in the last days of 1981, on January 2, Cuomo's diary reveals that he is still not sure what to do in 1982.

> How shall I try? Shall I leave public office voluntarily and commit myself to practicing law and teaching and perhaps finding a position from which I might continue to articulate?
>
> But this is an option I will be left with even if I am forced out of public service by a defeat in a campaign, so I don't have to sacrifice any other opportunities to achieve it.
>
> Well, then, how about staying in public service? In what position?
>
> Being Lieutenant Governor again makes no sense. . . .
>
> I'm left with the possibility of running for Governor or stepping aside. That's the case as of this moment, and things are sure to change, maybe even dramatically, but I mustn't do nothing while I'm waiting for all the facts. What I will do now is go forward even faster and harder with all preparations for the race. Things may change—let them. If I run, I will be a long shot, but so were Momma and Poppa.[12]

It was this kind of interior monologue, full of misgivings that, when manifest in later actions, would cause some political insiders to call Cuomo the "Hamlet of the Hudson." To others, of course, he would become an intellectual hero, a modern St. Thomas More, torn between the quiet life—teaching and practicing law—and duty to answer the call to serve the people.

Perhaps it was some sort of dramatic self-delusion: an ambitious man who wanted power but couldn't bring himself to admit it publicly, for fear that he would be seen to be—an ambitious man who wanted power.

During the second week of January 1982, several of Carey's people were whispering to Cuomo that Carey might not run. Cuomo was encouraged to be kind to Carey so he doesn't run again out of sheer spite.

Speculation came to an end on Friday, January 15, 1982 when Hugh Carey announced he would not seek a third term.

Even before Carey completed his statement, those seeking to replace him, including Cuomo, were already on the phones lining up support. Cuomo's first call was to David Garth, who said he would do Cuomo's campaign but warned him to "play it cool."[13]

Playing it "cool" was at that moment very important because of the sleeping giant in the political arena, Mayor Edward Koch, who could wake up at any moment and reach for the prize waiting in Albany.

By all accounts, Koch's first term as mayor (1978–1981) was a success. To get the Financial Control Board off his back, he bit the bullet and imposed significant budget cuts across the board, which included the elimination of 20,000 city jobs.

Koch strove to have a budget balanced according to Generally Accepted Accounting Principles (GAAP), by the end of his first term. The size of the deficit was declining according to GAAP every year. In Abe Beame's last year in office (1977), the deficit stood at $1.039 billion, and by 1978 it had declined to $712 million, then to $422 in 1979, and was down to $356 million in 1980. And thanks to unexpected economic growth, Koch was able to project a balanced budget for fiscal 1981, one year ahead of schedule.

Writing in *The New York Times*, in May 1981, Clyde Haberman conceded, "even those who think [Koch] is too quick at times to praise himself say that he took many key measures to restore fiscal order."[14]

New School professor, Marilyn Rubin, agreed, suggesting that "Koch deserved credit for maintaining tight spending controls, improving cash management, and increasing city revenues through imposition of user fees on such commodities as water. His fiscal prudence enabled the city to reduce income taxes from 10.8% of personal income when he took office to 9.3% of personal income at the end of his first term."[15]

Realizing that the base of his support came from Catholic and Jewish neighborhoods, Koch was moving to the center-right of the political spectrum, particularly on fiscal issues.

Koch called himself a "liberal with sanity." He publicly confessed that when he was in Congress, he was a "leading liberal." But, he explained, "when you're in Congress, you don't have to pay the cost of it, and we gave away the country. Now I go back to Congress, when I testified before committees, and say *Mea Culpa* and you, too."[16]

As for knee-jerk liberals, he said "I don't believe in half their crap. That government has to become bigger. . . . I have contempt for government. I should know. I'm in it."[17]

He also set his sight on elitist do-gooders: "The good government groups and social workers destroyed the city for twenty years and they resent bitterly anyone who wants to come in and reassert the balance."[18]

To prove New Yorkers were impressed with his *chutzpah*, Koch set his eyes on scoring a huge margin of victory in 1981 and so sought the nomination of both the Democratic and Republican parties.

On the Democratic side, four people came forward to challenge Koch in the primary: Brooklyn Assemblyman Frank Barbaro, a former longshoreman; Melvin Klenetsky, a supporter of the U.S. Labor Party; perennial presidential candidate Lyndon LaRouche; and medical doctor Jeronimo Dominguez.

On the Republican side, a majority of county leaders voted to permit Koch to enter the primary against Queens Assemblyman John Esposito.

David Garth's campaign theme that "Koch had saved the city from fiscal ruin and deserved four more years to get services on track again,"[19] struck a chord with voters.

Koch won the Democratic primary with 60% of the votes, and in the Republican primary, he won with 66%.

In November, Koch won big, receiving 74.6%.

Although Koch had made public a promise at Jerusalem's Western Wall never to run for higher office, his smashing victory prompted his political allies to urge him to throw his name in the mix for the 1982 gubernatorial race.

After the mayoral election, potential Republican and Democrat gubernatorial candidates, including Mario Cuomo, began calling on Koch—who now perceived himself a power broker.

Cuomo's post-election meeting with Koch was the second one in 1981. At the first meeting, on June 17, he had breakfast with the mayor, and according to Koch, Cuomo briefed him on his potential plans for 1982.

Here's Koch's version of the June meeting:

> He said he was considering running for Attorney General, but if Carey were to drop out, he said he would consider running for Governor. It was clear at that time that he was upset by the shabby way Carey had been treating him. . . .
>
> He said, "Well, if I run . . . well, what are your plans regarding endorsing someone for Governor?"
>
> I said, "The Governor fouled up the State takeover of Medicaid. Now the likelihood is that will cost the City of New York almost a billion dollars a year. I am not committed to the Governor. I will be keeping my options open."
>
> He said, "You know, your credibility Upstate is amazing. Normally a Jewish Mayor from New York would be just what they hate. But they like you."
>
> I said, "Oh? Isn't that nice."[20]

At their second meeting on December 21, 1981, Cuomo told Koch that he was pretty sure Carey would not run but if he did, he would not be running as Carey's running mate. In Koch's view, this meant it was implicit "that he would be running against [Carey] in the primary." Although he would later temper his view, Koch's immediate reaction was that a Governor Cuomo "couldn't be good, ultimately, for either me or the City of New

York—because I knew Mario and I suspected he would seek to torture me and therefore the city for beating him in 1977."[21]

Cuomo's impression of the meeting was similar. Cuomo made it clear he would not run for state comptroller because that might push incumbent Republican Ned Regan to run for governor, a race he could win.[22]

Shortly after Ed Koch was sworn in as mayor for a second time, he left New York with Dave Garth and other friends for an 8-day vacation in Spain.

During his absence, a draft "Koch for Governor" movement began, led by *New York Post* owner Rupert Murdoch who was "repelled by Cuomo's liberalism."[23]

When Koch returned from Spain, he was swamped by reporters asking if he was running. He said he would certainly think about it and the following day, he said he would make a decision in the next thirty days.

During this period, Cuomo did more handwringing about running for governor and rationalizing his reasons for doing so.

On Saturday, January 16, 1982, in a diary entry, Cuomo described a Carey press conference held the previous day. Carey was critical of Cuomo questioning his qualifications and said he didn't contribute many policy ideas. Cuomo feared such attacks could harm his future political plans.

He went on to describe how much a campaign requires and how difficult it will be to woo support "without losing your soul."[24]

This tortured man who fears "losing his soul" is the same one who discarded his opposition to abortion, gay rights, and birth control to satisfy his ambition to attain high office.

After all the philosophical handwringing in that same diary entry, Cuomo quickly changed gears and wrote of a morning meeting with his campaign team and the need to raise campaign money.

To raise money he went to the "power brokers" and "political bosses." His biographer's claim that Cuomo's eventual victory "was inclusive of everyone except the 'power brokers and political bosses'" is nonsense. Cuomo actively sought the support of the rich and powerful. He lists in the diary many of the key players, political bosses, union leaders, financiers, real estate moguls, and political hacks he reached out to including: Ray Harding, Vince Albanese, Harold Fisher, Mario Biaggi, Donald Manes,

Meade Esposito, Stanley Friedman, Steve Berger, Al Vann, Barry Feinstein, Felix Rohatyn, Robert Wagner, Charlie Rangel, Ed Costikyan, and Phil Caruso. (Three people on the list—Harding, Esposito and Friedman—were later convicted of crimes and did time in prison. A fourth, Manes, committed suicide before he was indicted on corruption charges.)

Cuomo also boasted about meeting with horseracing industry bigshots in Saratoga and receiving pledges of $30,000 in contributions from those elites.[25]

On Monday, February 8, 1982, Cuomo decides he will definitely run. His strategy if Koch should enter the race would be to debate him frequently.

Two days later, Cuomo informed Koch that he was entering the race and would formally announce on March 16. He wrote in his diary that he also asked for Koch's support. He pledged, if elected, to be helpful to the city he has lived in all his life.[26]

Interestingly, on February 16, 1982, the Most Reverend Joseph Sullivan, auxiliary bishop of the Roman Catholic Brooklyn Diocese, paid Koch a visit.

Sullivan, who was head of Catholic Charities in Brooklyn and Queens and was a Koch appointee to the board of New York City's Health and Hospitals Corporation, was a far-left radical both theologically and politically. (When asked to give an invocation at the annual dinner of the Catholic organization, The Cathedral Club of Brooklyn, Sullivan referred to the cassock he was wearing as a costume and appealed in his prayer to a "he-she God.")

Cuomo and Sullivan were close friends: He attended Sullivan's consecration as a bishop in November 1980, and he and Matilda attended receptions honoring "Bishop Joe" as Cuomo referred to him.

(Sullivan—not the ordinary of the Albany Diocese, Bishop Howard Hubbard—would give the homily at Albany's Immaculate Conception Cathedral during a special Mass on Cuomo's gubernatorial inauguration day, January 1, 1983.)

Bishop Sullivan, who was quoted in Cuomo's 1984 Notre Dame speech, once boasted to the author and Conservative Party Chairman Mike Long that he collaborated closely with Cuomo on that speech.

In his autobiography, Koch described what Bishop Sullivan said in their February meeting:

"I would like to tell you why I think you shouldn't run for Governor. You have done a marvelous job here in the City, and you have been able to speak out for New Yorkers. I don't know if you could do the same in Albany, where you would have to work with the State Legislature. It is not the same as working with the City Council. They are much more difficult. One thing that you have given the City that is well known is an intangible thing, and that is the spirit and excitement and the sense that we can overcome and the pride that New Yorkers now feel. As I have said on many occasions, 'If someday Ed Koch got up in the morning and said he no longer wanted to do the job, it would be all over for New York City. The spirit would end, and we could not recover from that.'"

I said, "You have been very kind to me."

He said, "I don't know if I am imposing or out of line."

I said, "Not at all. Your advice is very important to me. Now let me tell you why I might run. The power has shifted to Albany, as a result of the New Federalism and the block grants, which go directly to Albany from Washington. And when I look at the other candidates, I don't think they are terribly good."

Then he said, "You know, Mr. Mayor, two of our bishops went Upstate recently and both are complaining and want to come home. They are New Yorkers from the City, and they don't like it up there. I worry that you will not like it either. What will you do with yourself up there?"

I said, "Well, I think about the personal separation from my friends here in the City for long periods of time and missing the modest lifestyle that I have in New York City."

He said, "Yes. But I want you to know that whatever you decide to do, I wish you well."[27]

Did Cuomo put up Sullivan to make the appeal to Koch? It certainly is in the realm of possibility. In any case, the appeals fell on deaf ears. Koch announced he would seek the Democratic nomination for governor on Monday, February 22.

Cuomo vs. Koch Redux

Throughout January and February, Cuomo was in regular contact with Dave Garth. The campaign guru wanted to run Cuomo's campaign—and had earlier committed to it—but he told Cuomo he had to stick with Koch if he jumped into the race even though Garth had urged him not to run. Garth agreed with Cuomo that Ed Koch did not have a plausible rationale for seeking the office.

Shortly before the Koch announcement, Garth sat with Koch on the porch at Gracie Mansion and asked: "'Why the hell do you want to be governor?' There was a big pause. I said I knew all the mental reasons, but what do you want it for? He couldn't answer."[28]

Koch's best case for running: with states getting more money, block grants, etc. from President Reagan's "New Federalism," Albany will be the place to be to help people.

Few bought that line. Koch's real reason was ambition, or as he later wrote in his memoir, hubris.

Another compelling reason for not running: Koch was a dyed-in-the-wool city guy. He knew nothing about upstaters and couldn't have cared less about them.

This attitude became very evident when the *Playboy* interview Koch had sat for months earlier appeared in the magazine's April 1982 issue.

Answering a question about the suburbs, he answered: "Have you ever lived in the suburbs? It's sterile. It's nothing. It's wasting your life."

As for life in the country: "The country? Rural America? That's a joke!"

And when questioned if long subway rides were a waste of people's time, he replied: "As opposed to wasting time in a car? Or, out in the country wasting time in a pickup truck? When you have to drive 20 miles to buy a gingham dress or a Sears Roebuck suit?"

These wisecracks hit the airwaves all over New York and the nation and had a devastating impact on how the public perceived Koch. A poll taken shortly after the interview's release had Koch's negatives up 28 points and his positive rating down 25.

At first blush, Cuomo believed the interview would not have long-term damage.[29]

He was right in terms of the political establishment. Many downstate pols and power brokers feared Koch, so they either embraced him or stood on the sidelines. Others told Cuomo they were secretly rooting for him.

People who abandoned Cuomo fearing retaliation from Koch win or lose didn't realize that the Cuomos (Mario and Andrew) were also keeping lists of friends and foes—but more on that later in the book.

At the June 1982 Democratic State Convention held in Syracuse, Koch managed to get an impressive 61%. Cuomo, however, did much better than expected, garnering 39%. Having received more than 25% guaranteed Cuomo a spot on the primary ballot without having to circulate petitions— a costly and laborious process.

In this third Koch-Cuomo match, the mayor proved to be an awful candidate. Forced to spend most of his time campaigning upstate, it became evident to his handlers that he had no idea about upstate demographics. Most of the time he had no idea where he was and had no interest or knowledge in the issues and problems confronting local voters.

"Asked by a reporter in Cooperstown what county he was in, he replied, 'Oneonta.' He was, in fact, in Oswego County, as New York has no county named Oneonta, which is a city."[30]

In contrast, Cuomo having spent the previous eight years travelling the state speaking at conventions, civic associations, dedication ceremonies, charity dinners, club installations, etc. not only knew the state, but knew the regional issues.

As a result, while Cuomo played the underdog—a role he relished— he had to know in his heart that he had huge advantages over Koch. E.J. McMahon, presently president of the Albany think tank, the Empire Center for Public Policy, and who in 1982 was an Albany reporter, told the author that he was convinced from the beginning that Cuomo was going to win the primary and that Koch was really the weakest candidate to oppose him. McMahon said, "When I would see Cuomo in the Albany area, he appeared to have this Cheshire cat grin on his face when he talked about his uphill battle. That's because Cuomo had an upstate network, the endorsements of the State public employees' union, and Albany's long-time Mayor and power broker, Erastus Corning."

"That," McMahon concluded, "plus the fact that mayors of New York are historically unpopular upstate gave Mario an edge, and if he romped Koch upstate, it might be enough to overcome Koch's advantage in the city."

Because Cuomo could not come close to matching Koch dollar for dollar on the airwaves, the debates mattered. From July 7 to Primary Day, Thursday, September 23, 1981, there were nine television or radio confrontations. Koch did not attend the tenth debate scheduled for primary eve at 11:30 p.m. on New York City's Channel 5.

At the first face to face, sponsored by the *New York Post*, all agreed that Cuomo wiped up the floor with Koch. The "old Cuomo style," the lawyerly, aggressive, take no prisoners, was on display:

Koch: "I have a record of achievements as Mayor that can be duplicated as Governor."

Cuomo: "In a nutshell, Mr. Mayor, you take much too much credit and not nearly enough responsibility."

When Koch boasted that he appointed "excellent criminal judges," Cuomo demurred: "I remember the fellow who flipped a coin and took a defendant home."

Striking at Koch's Achilles' heel, Cuomo thundered, "We must have a Governor who knows the whole state, as I do, who can bring the state together."[31]

Koch had refused to prepare for the debate believing he could wing it. He failed.

At the second date on July 12, sponsored by the New York State Broadcasting Association at Grossinger's Hotel, Koch was better prepared and went on the offensive.

Koch jumped on the Cabin scandal: "It raises serious questions about your management abilities."

Cuomo came back sternly: "I caught Bill Cabin; I got the money back."

After the debate, Cuomo, pointed to Koch's drop in the polls, "If the Mayor were not in trouble," Mario said, "he would not have gone with Bill Cabin."[32]

The New York Times headline after the third debate on July 28, 1982, read "Cuomo-Koch Debate Bristles With Charges." They "repeatedly questioned each other's motivation, character, ability and tactics. . . ."[33]

Similar to their 1977 battle, the death penalty was a hot topic:

Koch: "The person who raises it continually happens to be Mario Cuomo. He gets in there and he says, 'I'm against the politics of electrocution,' as though, if you're for the death penalty, that somehow or other you are immoral."

Cuomo: "I resent your constant reference to morality and the death penalty. Again you're pandering. I have not only not made it a moral issue, I specifically refused to discuss it as a religious or moral issue."

Clashing over their positions on the Metropolitan Transit Authority, Cuomo charged, "You don't know what you're talking about."

Koch replied, "What he said on the MTA absolutely boggles my mind."[34]

At the August 18 debate in Buffalo, Cuomo said to Koch: "You can't be believed." Koch said of Cuomo: "I think he's squirming."[35]

And so it went in the remaining debates leading up to Primary Day.

As the campaign was heating up during the summer, questions about Koch's sexual orientation resurfaced.

"A flyer . . . in New York City in July used the old 'Vote for Cuomo Not the Homo' taunt," Koch wrote in his memoir. "And when Mario Cuomo was asked for his comment, he did not disown the piece; his only comment was 'That issue is irrelevant.'"

Koch continued:

And that was not all. At the end of July it was reported [in the *Albany Times Union*] that Bernard Ryan, Mario Cuomo's northeastern campaign coordinator, had recently appeared before a political-science class at Albany State College and during his remarks had once again repeated the false 1977 homosexual-brawl-in-Koch's-Greenwich Village-apartment slur. There were various explanations as to how the old lie had found its way into the classroom, but no one denied that he had rekindled the slander. And Mario Cuomo, true to form, did not either admonish or fire him.[36]

By late August, the race had tightened up as it came into the home stretch.

The Koch team flooded the airwaves with commercials that pounded away at Cuomo.

One displayed a ticking stopwatch with a voice saying: "You have twenty seconds to think of one major accomplishment of Mario Cuomo as Lieutenant Governor." After seconds of silence, the voice continued: "Time's up. Maybe that's the reason you should vote Ed Koch for Governor. He's got a record to run on."[37]

The Cuomo campaign adopted a slogan that struck a chord with Koch's Catholic and Jewish supporters in the city: "When you vote for Cuomo, you get Koch for Mayor."

Cuomo was stressing the "you get two for the price of one" theme in Brooklyn, Queens and Staten Island. He played on the fears of Koch's center-right supporters who dreaded the thought of the leftist president of the City Council, Carol Bellamy, succeeding to the office of mayor if Koch became governor.

As Primary Day gets closer, there is the confident Cuomo versus the self-doubting Cuomo. In his diary entry of August 20, 1982, he wrote: "The truth is, I have more knowledge of State problems: I think a better capacity to negotiate and a more consistent philosophy."[38]

Then there is the less confident Cuomo rationalizing why he could lose and second-guessing: "Dedicated liberals suspect me because I'm a Catholic; the Italians and other middle-class ethnics are put off by my position on the death penalty."[39]

Despite the millions of dollars Koch expended and the genius of Dave Garth, his campaign was failing. Traveling the state, Koch appeared to be going through the motions, sleepwalking. And many voters sensed his heart wasn't in the race.

Smelling blood, a number of unions, angry over Koch's city budget cuts and layoffs, broke for Cuomo.

At the union convention held at the Concord in late August, the State Council of Service Employees International Union (SEIU) disendorsed Koch and went for Cuomo, even though its leader, Gus Bevona, didn't think he could beat the mayor.

This was followed by the endorsement of the New York State United Teachers Union and the AFL-CIO.

One blow to Cuomo late in the campaign was Koch receiving the endorsement of Cuomo's boss, Governor Hugh Carey.

Reacting to press inquiries, Cuomo jokingly said, "I told Carey to lay off those PCBs." (Cuomo was referring to an outlandish Carey statement that "he would drink a glass of PCBs"—polychlorinated biphenyl, used in industry and a poisonous environmental pollutant—"to prove PCB wasn't as dangerous as people had been led to believe.")[40]

But that was not Cuomo's last word on the subject. A *Times* profile of Cuomo published on October 31, 1982, reported that he "poured out" his "resentment" when asked why Carey endorsed Koch:

> "He thought Koch was going to win," Mr. Cuomo replied, and then went on to talk of Mr. Carey's prospects. "What's his future? He's going to have to live here with Harry Helmsley at '21' for the rest of his life," he said, a reference to the Manhattan real-estate tycoon and the swank restaurant. "And Engie and he living in Westchester," Mr. Cuomo continued, referring to the Governor's second wife, Evangeline Gouletas Carey. "With whom? With the real estate people and the money people and the '21' people. They're all going to be with Koch. It's all one big circle."

> Then Mr. Cuomo offered his own version of what Mr. Carey was thinking: "This guy Cuomo can't win. Why should I be neutral and be left out? What do I get if I'm neutral?"[41]

The Carey endorsement was too little too late. The momentum, thanks to union and minority support, particularly African-Americans, was moving toward Cuomo and nothing could stop it. And, of course, Koch's *Playboy* comments had killed him upstate.

On September 23, 1982, Mario Cuomo beat Ed Koch 52.34% to 47.66%. His victory, the *Times* reported, was due to "an unusual coalition of liberal Democrats, labor, minorities and upstaters."[42]

Upstate, Cuomo carried 55 of the 57 counties, beating Koch 2 to 1. In New York City, Cuomo only lost to Koch 50.25% to 49.75%. The incumbent mayor carried his city by a mere 3,886 votes.

As for the ethnic vote, Frank Lynn reported in *The New York Times*, "Mr. Koch won heavily Jewish districts by up to 2-to-1 while Mr. Cuomo won black, liberal and Italian districts by up to 2-to-1. Mr. Cuomo won Staten Island and Manhattan and better than half of the city's assembly districts."[43]

There was one other surprise primary night: Westchester County Executive Alfred DelBello, Koch's lieutenant governor pick, beat Cuomo's running mate Carl McCall. Although in the fall DelBello would help Cuomo in Westchester, the marriage would turn out to be not one made in heaven.

In his victory speech, Cuomo said, "I look forward to locking arms with Mayor Koch and another great Democrat, Governor Carey." Cuomo boasted that he won because of the message his campaign promoted around the state.

However, the reality was the Cuomo-Koch primary had nothing to do with ideas or conflicting philosophies. If there was any message, it was that Koch really didn't want to be governor. He didn't know the state and seemed indifferent to learning about it.

No doubt Cuomo's slogan, "If you vote Cuomo for governor, you get to keep Koch as mayor," also had an impact.

But there was also an element of luck. For the first time since he entered politics, most of the breaks went Cuomo's way and many of those breaks were not of his making. The question now was, would his luck hold out until Election Day.

Cuomo vs. Lehrman

One primary that did not get as much attention as the Cuomo-Koch showdown was the Republican gubernatorial battle between newcomer Lewis Lehrman and the candidate of the aging and decrepit GOP establishment, Paul Curran.

Back in 1977, at a dinner at Gallagher's Steak House, N.Y. Conservative Party Chairman Dan Mahoney, Executive Director Serf Maltese, Brooklyn leader Mike Long, and several other key party leaders had met with entrepreneur Lewis L. Lehrman to hear his pitch to become a gubernatorial candidate. Lehrman was native of Pennsylvania with a B.A. from Yale and an M.A. from Harvard, and who was now living on Park Avenue. He told his dinner guests the story of how he had helped build his family company, Rite Aid, into one of the nation's top pharmaceutical retailers, and how, now that he had financial independence, he looked forward to doing something in the political arena. The idea of running for comptroller in 1978 was kicked around, but Lehrman made it clear that even though he was a political neophyte, he intended to run for governor in 1982. Mike Long recalls that he and Lehrman hit it off that night because: "I was confrontational with him . . . I looked at him and said, 'You mean you're telling us exactly what you are going to do five years from now.' And Lew replied, 'That's exactly what I'm doing.'"[44]

Over the next five years, Lehrman attended Conservative Party functions and gave speeches around the state. He was also active on the Republican side, and after he donated generously to the financially strapped GOP, he was rewarded with the chairmanship of the 1978 platform committee. Lehrman took the job seriously. He held hearings all over the state and took advantage of the opportunity to meet as many Republican leaders as possible. Upon reporting the platform to the Republican state committee, he learned an important political lesson. His report was all but ignored, and Lehrman realized, as he put it, that "ideas don't always rule."

Lew Lehrman was what Republican insiders pejoratively labeled "a true believer." The old-line establishment opposed him because he was devoted to the fundamental principles of conservatism. Although his optimistic vision was in tune with Ronald Reagan's—lower taxes and supply-side growth—New York's Republican hacks considered Lehrman an outsider, and they feared they would be left out in the cold if he were elected.

At the 1982 Republican state convention, Lehrman became the party's designee, but the old guard managed to muster 25% of the delegates for an uninspiring candidate, a former U.S. Attorney named Paul Curran. Curran's convention showing guaranteed him a spot in a Republican primary. The establishment was prepared to lose with Curran rather than lose control of the party to the likes of Lehrman.

In a series of primary debates, Lehrman and Curran went for the jugular. In the hottest of the debates, sponsored by the *Buffalo Courier Express*,

Curran attacked Lehrman's character, and Lehrman replied: "When people like Paul Curran talk about character, I think it's time to start counting the silverware." Pointing to Curran's "old boy" reputation, Lehrman "accused Curran of having 'two standards of morality' and said 'his principal backer' [Nassau County Republican Chairman Joe Margiotta] is a convicted felon."[45]

It wasn't pretty, but it was effective. On Primary Day, Lehrman flattened his opponent:

Lehrman	464,231	80.6%
Curran	111,814	19.4%

To win big, Lehrman spent big. "Mr. Lehrman's landslide victory," the *Times* reported, "capped a 13-month campaign in which he spent a record $7 million, more than half of it his own money, with much of it on television advertising that transformed a political novice into a formidable candidate."[46]

The battle lines were now drawn and the two champs, liberal Mario Cuomo and conservative Lew Lehrman, came out fighting.

Mario Cuomo's strategy in the five-week fall campaign was threefold:

1) Attack Reaganomics. Believing that Reagan's tax cut policies were "a disaster," Cuomo wanted to hang them around Lehrman's neck like an anvil.
2) Run on Governor Hugh Carey's fiscal and tax cutting record. To win, Cuomo had to put aside his pride and embrace a man he had come to despise. Throughout the campaign he boasted about the "Carey-Cuomo record."
3) Because he could not come close to raising and spending the kind of campaign money Lehrman had at his disposal, the debates mattered for Cuomo. As in the primary, he wanted plenty of debates.

However, Lehrman did not cooperate. Because his campaign had so much money, he saw no reason to accept multiple debates. He even declined the honor of participating in the quadrennial *New York Times* debate.

The first debate on October 7, 1982 was sponsored by the *New York Post* and held at the Sheraton Centre. And both Cuomo and Lehrman came out fighting. The debate became so intense that the moderator and panel had no role in asking substantive questions. The debate was basically a free-for-all.

In his opening statement, Cuomo boasted about the Carey record and blamed the state's woes on Republican Nelson Rockefeller.

> For more than seven and a half years, I have been part of the governmental effort that brought back this state from virtual bankruptcy in 1975.
>
> We had been pushed there by sixteen years of Republican administrations that made us the most heavily taxed state in the United States and that drove out of New York hundreds of thousands of jobs.
>
> Our remedy has been to reduce taxes by some $2.6 billion dollars, to slow the growth of government to under the rate of inflation. And to bring nearly a half million new job opportunities back.[47]

He went on to castigate Reaganomics alleging it cost the state $2 billion in revenue, destroyed jobs and businesses and caused crime and drug addiction to grow. And he told Lew Lehrman that "You proposed Reaganomics" to President Reagan.

Lehrman attempted to promote his plans for economic renewal and stated that he preferred to "go forward" and not dwell in the past.

But the Cuomo assault put Lehrman on the defensive. When Lehrman explained his differences with President Reagan over his tax cuts and spending, Cuomo retorted, "I don't blame you from running away from Reaganomics."

Instead of going on the defensive, Lehrman should have turned the tables on Cuomo by saying something along these lines:

> Mario, you claim you were part of the governmental effort that brought back the state from virtual bankruptcy in 1975, but

you were nowhere to be seen. You weren't part of the negotiations with the city and the federal government. You didn't take part in the creation of the Municipal Assistance Corporation or the Emergency Financial Control Board. Governor Carey, Felix Rohatyn, Dick Ravitch—they were the ones who saved the city while you were in your State Department office issuing fishing licenses.

Obviously, Governor Carey has no respect for your role in his administration because he endorsed your opponent Ed Koch to succeed him.

Such a response might have put Cuomo on the defensive and turned the course of the debate.

Throughout the debate, Cuomo was sharp-tongued, outlandish, quick on his feet, unable to avoid a wisecrack. He harped on the Republican's inexperience, saying Lehrman had no practical knowledge of government and that his campaign produced only naïve term papers written by "slick researchers." He pushed Lehrman to debate on his terms—namely to answer his specific charges and not simply promote a vague governing philosophy.

Cuomo was on such a roll, he even took shots at the panelists. When they grabbed back the job of moderating the debate for a few seconds, one discombobulated panelist blurted out, "What about jobs?" Reacting, Cuomo yelled at the panelist for not posing a "creative question."

Cuomo took plenty of credit for the accomplishments of the Carey administration, implying he had been a key figure in decisions made under Carey. He summed himself up as a "Progressive Pragmatist" who managed to balance fiscal discipline and social justice. But as we've seen, as lieutenant governor, Cuomo had next to nothing to do with achieving fiscal austerity.

Cuomo accused Lehrman of "Talk Show Conservatism"— of using lots of one-liners—even as he, himself, used plenty of liberal (and sarcastic) one-liners. Here are a few examples: "I have more experience in state government than my opponent has years in the state." Concerning his proposals, he quipped: "These are ideas I didn't purchase this year."

Although Cuomo and Lehrman both made strong closing statements, the consensus was that Cuomo had won the debate.

The question raised after that first confrontation was, had Mario gone overboard? Had he taken too many cheap shots, as when he had stared at Lehrman's wrist and said: "That's a very expensive watch, Lew"?

The liberal *Times* columnist Sydney Schanberg, put it this way: "Mario Cuomo is very good at debates. . . . [But] one question raised on Thursday in the first debate of the general election campaign for governor . . . was whether Mr. Cuomo might damage himself by overdoing it, thereby creating sympathy for his opponent."[48]

At the *Daily News* debate held on October 25 at the Plaza Hotel, there was more of the same.

Cuomo considered Lehrman a fraud. His conservative positions on the death penalty and taxes, etc., Cuomo believed, were merely driven by polls. In other words, to disagree with Mario's sacrosanct positions means one is siding with the misinformed public.

There was more of the same at the last debate sponsored by the public television show *Inside Albany*. Summarizing the confrontation, the *Times* wrote, "[The candidates] sharply disagreed on how the state should spend—and even on the very nature of the state's financial outlook for next year."[49]

Toward the end of the campaign, what really upset Cuomo operatives was Lehrman's targeted social policy mailings to Catholics and Orthodox Jews.

Throughout the campaign, Cuomo studiously avoided public discussion of his various positions: pro-abortion, pro-gay rights, and pro-state funding of abortion. That's because he flipped on these issues and because they offended practicing Catholics and social conservatives. Hence, there was a fear that Lehrman's endorsement of "traditional values" would hurt Cuomo.

In the final days of the campaign, it appeared that the Lehrman mailings had had the desired effect: the undecided vote stood at 19% by October 26. And since the rule of thumb says the undecided vote generally breaks toward the party out of power, the Cuomo camp was nervous, particularly since internal tracking polls predicted the election was too close to call.

On Election Day, Tuesday, November 2, 1982, New York voters faced the clearest philosophical choice in recent political history. In the closest election since the 1954 Harriman-Ives race, they chose Mario Cuomo as New York's fifty-second governor.

	Cuomo Dem.	Lehrman Rep.	Lehrman Cons.	Bohner R. to L.	Cuomo Lib.
Upstate New York	1,542,975	1,808,042	171,441	39,105	52,398
Bronx	168,775	51,339	7,351	2,104	7,691
Brooklyn	283,896	118,257	15,085	3,245	12,540
Manhattan	241,478	78,727	6,468	1,898	28,765
Queens	277,732	155,808	22,207	4,456	12,374
Staten Island	44,751	36,568	7,601	1,548	1,838
Total New York City	1,016,632	440,699	58,712	13,251	63,208
Total State	2,559,607	2,248,741	230,153	52,356	115,606
Percentages	49.3%	43.2%	4.4%	1.0%	2.2%

The voter breakdowns revealed some interesting trends. While Cuomo carried the traditional Democratic strongholds of Manhattan, Brooklyn, The Bronx, and Queens, he managed to get 51.1% of the vote in the Republican bastion of Staten Island, thanks mostly to the Italian vote. But overall, Lehrman's last-minute mailings appeared to pay off. Statewide he received a majority of the Catholic vote. This was most evident in traditionally Democratic, heavily Catholic blue-collar Erie County which Lehrman lost by only 1,200 votes:

Cuomo	178,337	49.8%
Lehrman	177,146	49.5%
Bohner	2,375	0.7%

By contrast, Hugh Carey had received 64% of Erie County's vote in 1974 and 52% in 1978.

The most interesting results, however, were those in the Republican-dominated counties of Nassau and Westchester. Lehrman actually lost Westchester County, with Cuomo receiving 155,593 votes to Lehrman's 148,764. Experts tend to agree that many old-line Westchester Republicans declined to support Lehrman because they actually wanted the Cuomo-DelBello ticket to win. They reasoned that if elected, DelBello would have to resign his post as Westchester's county executive. This would clear the way for Republican Andrew O'Rourke to take over. The Westchester Republicans figured they would get more patronage more easily from County Executive O'Rourke than from Governor Lehrman, so they stabbed Lehrman in the back.

Lehrman's poor showing in Nassau County was even more startling: Lehrman carried the county by a mere 19,000 votes, or 50.8%. Why? Well, in 1981, Nassau County's long-time Republican boss, Joseph Margiotta, had been convicted of fraud and extortion. During the campaign, Lehrman had publicly referred to Margiotta as a convicted felon and had refused to appear on the same stage with him at a huge Nassau Republican rally. (Margiotta's conviction was appealed and eventually reviewed by the U.S. Supreme Court, which ruled against him. He began a prison sentence in 1983.) Conservative Party Chairman Mike Long agrees with other political insiders that word went out to Nassau's Republican County Committee that Lehrman had to be punished for slighting Boss Joe. This becomes even more plausible when you consider that Republican Comptroller Ned Regan carried Nassau with 60.6% of the vote.

The race was so close that on election night Lehrman refused to concede. This did not, however, stop Cuomo from declaring victory at 12:45 a.m. in the Sheraton Centre's ballroom.

"We won," he said, "because people . . . people and the passion of belief are still more important than money. And now on to Albany."

Lehrman told reporters that he viewed the race "as a contest of ideas, strong personalities. . . . It's a test of endurance and character." As for his opponent, Lehrman noted, "I haven't made the personal comments about him that he's said about me. I think he became increasingly desperate in the last few weeks for whatever reason. I don't know. Maybe he saw it was working as a political tactic—attacks work."

Cuomo, on the other hand, revealed a trait that would resurface after future victories: He was a sore winner.

In his hotel suite at 1:30 in the morning, Cuomo told reporters, "We have been given a very solid vote of confidence. I feel very good about that. It got very close to being what they used to call a landslide."

That statement was delusional. Receiving 51.5% of the vote is not a solid victory and it is nowhere near a landslide.

Cuomo went on to add, "Besides, the plurality will be like 100% in a month. Nobody will remember it was 3%. Incidentally, that's not a small plurality."

Apparently, Cuomo could not accept that 48.5% of the votes were cast against him.

Told that the Lehrman camp procured a court order impounding election machines just in case a recount was needed, the impetuous Cuomo said: "I'm not concerned about this lawsuit. I tell you as an attorney, it's what you do when you know you're going to lose."

Cuomo capped off his victory night by announcing his 24-year-old son, Andrew, would serve as the head of his transition team. He described Andrew as "24 going on 68."[50]

PART II

GOVERNOR MARIO CUOMO

1983-1994

CHAPTER 9

1983 - YEAR ONE

Most newly elected officials go on vacation to recover from their exhausting campaigns. Not Mario Cuomo. He hit the ground running the day after the election, and for several reasons.

For one thing, it was in his nature. Cuomo did not know how to vacation. For another thing, he had only eight weeks to organize his staff, name a cabinet, and prepare to face a budget deficit that was projected to hit $1.8 billion in the fiscal year that would begin on April 1, 1983.

More immediately, there was an inaugural address to be delivered on January 1, a State of the State speech to be delivered on January 6, and a budget to be constructed and unveiled by January 31.

As for his approach to making appointments, Cuomo wrote confidently: "I can do it in a way that no one else has been able to do it in a long time, because I came singularly free of contracts. I don't owe Governor Carey anything except respect. I don't owe the politicians anything. The unions—10% of my money came from public employees. . . . I mean, if they could buy loyalty they didn't."[1]

Cuomo was moving fast; by the end of the first week of December, he had named all his cabinet members. He was boasting that he was probably ahead of any previous gubernatorial transition in New York.[2]

Cuomo was also sitting in on meetings with Governor Carey to discuss strategies to be employed with a special "lame duck" meeting of the Legislature to deal with the pending state, city, and Metropolitan Transit Authority fiscal crises. Subsequently, a deal was cut with Senate Republican Majority Leader, Warren Anderson of Binghamton, that prevented MTA fare increases for 1983, but the other issues were unresolved.

As the first of January approached, Cuomo began to underplay his own expectations. He worried that the inaugural address he had drafted "was a piece of garbage." It was, he wrote, "so familiar to me and so trite and

167

hackneyed."[3] However, his self-critical foreboding was misplaced. The speech did not "bomb," as he feared it might. In fact, it was praised by the liberal media as the beginning of a new era in Albany.

Throughout his political career, Cuomo would say that campaign speeches and inaugural and State of the State addresses were poetry whereas budgets and policies were prose.

The inaugural address was classic Cuomo political "poetry." It was beautifully delivered, contained the usual liberal nostrums, and attacked the Reagan administration.[4]

He said he had "no intention of using Washington as a scapegoat," but then went onto stress that he would "not allow the National Administration to escape responsibility for its policies," especially "what we believe is the cruelty and economic recklessness of the unemployment that these policies produce and the mistakes."

Cuomo took a shot at Reagan's defense policies that were to bring down the Soviet Union and end the Cold War: " . . . we will point out what we believe is the mistake of an excessive multiplication of nuclear weapons that denies us the resources we need."

Cuomo repeated a theme from his campaign that New York was one big family:

> Those who made our history taught us above all things the idea of family, mutuality, the sharing of benefits and burdens fairly for the good of all. There's an ideal essential to our success and no family that favored its strong children or that in the name of evenhandedness failed to help its vulnerable ones would be worthy of the name. And no state or nation that chooses to ignore its troubled regions and people, while watching others thrive, can call itself justified.

> We must be the family of New York. Feeling one another's pain, sharing one another's blessings, equitably, honestly, fairly, without respect to geography or race or political affiliation. Those who made our history taught us more. By a willingness to sweat for a lifetime just to give their children something better, they taught us the virtue of hard work. These things, then, I pledge as I begin my term.

Calling himself a "progressive pragmatist," he said, "I believe we can balance our lives and our society even as we balance our books."

In his closing paragraph, Cuomo did a twist on St. Thomas More's final words on the scaffold before his beheading: "That I might be the state's good servant and God's, too."

The next bit of political poetry came in Cuomo's State of the State address delivered to a joint session of the Legislature on January 5.

When preparing the speech, Cuomo told his staff:

> I want to put a stress on doing more with less. I want to make a point about the diversity of the state being at once its strength and its vulnerability. Now, I will come up before I'm through with thirty points, forty points, and they aren't all for the State of the State, but they're the beginning of a thought process. To say that we have fiscal problems and the most we can hope for is to balance the budget—that's not government. A budget that's balanced but doesn't do good things—that's a failed government. We have a harder obligation than that. Our obligation is to balance the budget and do good things. We have to balance the budget without raising the taxes and still do good things. And I think we can do more with less. I don't believe that's political poetry. We're going to do it![5]

In his address to the Legislature, Cuomo began by calling out the names of several key legislators on both sides of the aisle, congratulating them and appealing to them to work together in the coming months.

He painted a dire picture of the state's finances, although he did not get into specifics, avoiding any mention of tax increases and spending cuts. He merely generalized, saying the state must "draw fully on our resources without punishing private enterprise."[6]

He called for the issuance of $7 billion in bonds to rebuild New York's infrastructure.

He called for reducing bloated state bureaucracies, yet also "proposed about a dozen new councils, committees, funds, offices, commissions, authorities and boards—not to mention an expanded Urban Development Corporation, a restructured Public Service Commission and possibly a dismembered Metropolitan Transportation Authority."[7]

A generous assessment of Cuomo's first State of the State was that it was an artful balancing act. While "cash was limited," *The New York Times* observed, "his ambitions clearly weren't."[8]

Senate Majority Leader Anderson offered caution: "[Cuomo] had said that his inaugural address presented the soul of his administration. Now he has set forth its parameters—what he would like to do. Apparently, we will have to wait until February 1 to find out what he can afford to do."[9]

The time for fine poetry was over. Now Cuomo faced the arduous task of presenting a balanced budget to the Legislature in mere prose.

The Budget Battle

As Cuomo and his new finance team scrambled to put together an operating budget for the 1983–1984 fiscal year, they had to find a way to fill the projected deficit of $1.8 billion.

There were two reasons for the record-breaking deficit: In Hugh Carey's last year in office, Democratic and Republican legislators revolted against his fiscal conservatism. They overrode his vetoes of over $300 million in line-item spending without coming up with revenue to fund the restored expenditures.

The other reason was the national recession sparked by Fed Chairman Paul Volker's significant increase in interest rates intended to crush the spiraling inflation of the Carter years.

Unemployment in New York had hit 9%, and many of the state's major employers (e.g., Eastman Kodak) had recently been forced to lay off large numbers of employees. In Lackawanna, Bethlehem Steel, which was more than half the city's property tax base, had announced in January that it was going to permanently close its plant there and lay off 15,000 workers.

Economists were predicting that by mid-1983, New York would lose another 100,000 jobs.

These dreary projections seriously impacted state budgetary projections. In addition to declining revenues in hard economic times, state expenses go up. "Every 1% increase in joblessness," the *Times* pointed out, "costs the state $100 million in revenues, increases unemployment insurance by $200 million and boosts welfare spending by tens of millions more."[10]

As the February 1, deadline approached, Cuomo was leaking his plans by dribs and drabs.

As early as January 2, Cuomo hedged on his promise not to raise the personal income tax, the corporate tax, and the sales tax, which are about 85% of total revenues. He said he "never 'pledged' not to raise taxes but simply said increases would be 'counterproductive' and should be a last resort. 'I have not changed the position I took during the campaign, so far.'"[11]

On January 17, Cuomo announced he had no choice but to cut "good programs" and "raise some revenue." As for cuts, everything was on the table including layoffs.[12]

He did reject across-the-board cuts because "it treats everyone alike. It's Marie Antoinette—'Let them eat cake.' It's a kind of evenhandedness I don't approve of. You treat the cripple and the person who's gifted the same way. I don't regard that as equity. It might be evenhanded and even, but it is not fair."[13]

Cuomo also equivocated on his campaign pledge that the states assume "$360 million in local Medicaid costs from local governments."[14] He said he had not decided if the state could afford to do it.

Then on January 21, it was reported that the governor "had been advised to raise taxes, lay off workers and increase fees to close the budget gap—but added he had not made any decisions."[15]

Five days later, he announced that he would not raise the personal income tax, sales tax, or corporate income tax. However, he said his budget would include "program cuts and hinted that more than $800 million in new and increased taxes, fees and other revenue-raising measures would be required" to close the deficit gap.[16] Up to 10,000 state employees could also lose their jobs.

The fact that almost half of all state employees worked at mental-health facilities and prisons posed a problem for Cuomo because he ran on a platform to protect the neediest and to be tough on crime.

So instead of across-the-board cuts, he directed his commissioners to examine every function and target layoffs.

To set an example and to show he was "sharing the pain," Cuomo ordered that the executive budget, which had been $6.1 million in Carey's last year, be cut by 10%.

Showing disregard for the position he had previously held, Cuomo cut his lieutenant governor's staff from 38 to 17.

Cuomo proudly contrasted his bold cost-cutting with the judicial branch, whose budget was slated to rise by $5 million, and the legislative branch, which was to increase by $73 million.

Despite the boasting, the governor's "symbolic act" turned out to be a hoax. *The New York Times* revealed that he did not shrink his staff, "because Cuomo used the payrolls of various state agencies to add dozens of executive-chamber employees." [17]

On January 31, 1983, Mario Cuomo unveiled his $31.5 billion budget calling it "progressive but realistic."[18]

Although it did not raise corporate or personal income tax rates, there were tax increases on liquor, tobacco, home heating oil, real estate transfers, and retail sales.

Drivers' license fees would jump from $1.00 a year to $4.00. Chauffeur licenses would go from $2.00 to $8.00 annually. Registration fees for automobiles would go up 50%.

State University students were also affected. The governor called for tuition to go up 23.8% to $1,300 a year. City University tuition would be $1,200 a year, up $150. Dormitory fees would also go up by $150.[19]

Total state employees would decline by 14,000 out of a total of approximately 216,000; 8,500 would be laid off, and 5,600 by attrition.

To tackle the $1.8 billion deficit Cuomo "produced $530 million in savings—$219 million through work force reductions, $250 million in reductions in other programs and $61 million through a Medicaid cost-containment program."[20]

The rest came from $485 million in tax increases and $437 million "in provisions that strengthened tax laws and enforcement and speeded up the collection of taxes."[21]

Then there were the fiscal gimmicks: Cuomo proposed raiding state surplus fund balances to the tune of $139 million and putting off "until the following fiscal year $60 million in costs for the last [state] payroll of the coming year."[22]

Even though this was to be an austerity budget to handle the "direst" deficit ever, Cuomo managed to increase spending over the previous year's level. "Aid to local governments rose by $434 million, or 4.1%, while state programs went up $237 million, or 5.3%."[23]

Cuomo looked to expand the New York State Police and to create 7,000 new prison beds. To expand correctional facilities, he looked to expand the authority of the Urban Development Corporation which was originally created to build affordable housing for the poor.

The proposal that was to catch the most flak was his call for the poorer school districts to receive more of the $75 million increase in school aid than wealthier districts.

Reactions to the budget proposal were for the most part muted. Democrats did not want to dump on the freshman governor, although there were whispers that changes would be made.

Republican Warren Anderson was also cautious in his comments. "At this point in time," he said, "we do not rule anything in or anything out."

He did, however, question the governor's change in the school-aid formula. "It is one thing for all concerned to share equally in the pain—that's only fair. It is quite another thing for some to be treated as more equal than others, as in the winners-and-losers school-aid formula proposed by the governor."[24]

Later in the week, Anderson released a memo to the media stating that Cuomo's claim of "shared sacrifice" was false.

New York City, he complained, "stood to receive more than half the revenues from the billion-dollar state-wide tax increase, while paying only 35% of the new taxes; he also charged that the city would receive two-thirds of tax revenues collected outside the city and suffer fewer layoffs."[25]

Meanwhile Democrats were grumbling that Cuomo's "Republican Budget" depended too much on nuisance tax increases that would most hurt people with low incomes. They also were bellyaching that the layoffs were excessive and the revenue estimates too conservative.

As soon as the ink was dry on the governor's proposal, the battle of the budget was on. Cuomo now had to buckle down and do some serious negotiating with the Republican Senate and the Democratic Assembly if he was to have a budget passed by March 31, the end of fiscal year.

The budget process in New York is very different from the federal government's process. In Washington, the president proposes a budget plan but Congress is free to do whatever it wants with it. Hence, the president's budget is often described as "dead on arrival."

It is very different in New York, thanks to the efforts taken by Governor Alfred E. Smith in 1927. A constitutional amendment he proposed was added to the state Constitution that aimed to put an end to "extravagance, waste and irresponsibility" by giving the governor responsibility for drafting the budget.

Under this system, the governor deals from his budgetary deck of cards and the :egislature must play the hand dealt to it. The Legislature has the power to "take action," which means that it can accept the governor's budget as is, or it can reduce spending, eliminate spending, or add to a spending measure. However, the governor can exercise his veto power to reject any of these spending changes.

The Legislature's main job in the budgetary process is to appropriate money—and until it performs that function it has not "taken action." So, if the Legislature says "no" to the governor's budget and refuses to appropriate money by the April 1 deadline, it is responsible for shutting down the government.

Although the governor knew he had the upper hand in negotiations, he still wanted an on-time budget—something Carey failed to achieve in his last years in office—and that meant compromise. "That's the key to decision making," he told his staff on February 1. "When you compromise and both sides are unhappy. That's this budget."[26]

Secretary to the governor, Michael Del Giudice, speculated on how the negotiations would proceed:

> There are four main actors, and they all have to win. Each has to have something that reflects the wishes of his conference. [Republican Senate Leader] Warren Anderson will win by moving some dollars out of New York City to upstate and suburban school districts. [Speaker] Stanley [Fink] will win by getting some social programs put back and funded by responsible revenue measures. [Senate Minority Leader] Ohrenstein will win by retaining most of the money for New York City, and he'll take credit for avoiding some layoffs." And Governor Cuomo would win, Del Giudice

added, by having a balanced budget without raising any of the big-three taxes, by getting new money for the homeless, and by having the budget passed on time in a spirit of partnership—of family.[27]

And that's almost the way it worked out.

In March, there were numerous closed-door meetings and plenty of public posturing. For example, Cuomo showed his seriousness by issuing layoff notices to 2,500 state workers in March, to take effect on April 1.

He argued that it would be unfair to ask businesses to pay more taxes and for local municipalities to receive fewer state dollars if he was not willing to right-size the state government. "We cannot build a private economy," he declared, "on the public payroll."[28]

After the layoff notices went out, Cuomo sent a handwritten note to the human resources director saying, "What can we do to make the truth clear to them. I don't want them to think that they have been used cynically in this process."[29]

But the approved budget, as described below, proves they *were* used.

On Friday, March 18, it was announced that there was indeed a budget deal—but, the details still had to be worked out.

After more negotiations and outright buyoffs of individual legislators with pork-barrel projects for their districts, the Legislature passed a budget in the early morning of March 28.

A jubilant Cuomo proclaimed, "Say hallelujah, it's the miracle of New York—it really did work. It's the family of New York—it really works."[30]

But all the tough talk and the public relations campaign portraying Cuomo as the master negotiator who would put the state on the road to fiscal righteousness turned out to be a mirage. The deal maker agreed to spend $945 million more than Carey's last budget, which could hardly be called "austerity."

Here's the overview of the budget outcome:

- The authorized budget was $80 million higher than Cuomo's original proposal;
- Cuomo agreed to restore $360 million of his proposed cuts;
- Cuomo, who claimed his original revenue projections were solid, raised them by $80 million;

- The proposed nuisance taxes were dropped. Instead, Cuomo agreed to a 10% capital gains tax on real estate sales that exceeded $1 million. This tax was directed primarily at commercial real estate developers;
- The 9,400 proposed layoffs of jobs determined to be not essential by Cuomo's commissioners were reduced to 3,100 of which only 1,000 were actually terminated.
- Cuomo dropped his school-aid "fairness" redistribution formula;
- Cuomo shelved his plan to start paying down the accumulated deficit.

Despite these very significant compromises, Cuomo declared victory. He was "very grateful" that the Legislature approved a "better budget than the one I gave you."[31]

In his 1984 *New Yorker* profile of Mario Cuomo, Ken Auletta summed up the reaction to Cuomo's budgetary performance:

> Legislators emphasized their success in restoring most of Cuomo's proposed cuts. People close to Speaker Fink complained that Cuomo had caved in to Anderson and the Senate Republicans too easily, and had lost some credibility in the process. "The Governor wanted layoffs," one person said. "There won't be any. The Governor wanted the 'save harmless' removed. It's not going to be removed. The Governor wanted three hundred million dollars in program money not to be spent. All of it has been restored. So—tough he hasn't been. He hasn't been tough and he hasn't been easy. He's been agreeable. The fact is that he was willing to pay a price for an early agreement." Referring to the Governor's tendency to invest his words and actions with a moralistic tone, a Democratic Senate aide said, "Why did he call them 'principles' if they weren't principles? If Cuomo's role as governor was to be a mediator, he did an excellent job. But that's not what the prophet does."[32]

In an off moment, perhaps realizing he had negotiated away plenty to boast the first on-time budget in four years, Cuomo quipped "Can you imagine? We're all cheered for complying with the law."[33]

Cuomo's Management Approach: "Control Freak"

For most of his career, private and public, Mario Cuomo was a one-man band. He would work long hours because he needed to have total control over all decisions, even routine ones. As a rule, he would not delegate. Also, outside of his wife and son, Andrew, he trusted very few people. "Even in his present position of eminence," one associate told the *Times*, "Mario Cuomo trusts no one completely who isn't a member of his own family."[34]

This was most evident in his political campaigns: he tried to be candidate and campaign manager at one and the same time. This approach often led to chaos. Staff members feared Cuomo's wrath if they did not go to him for approval. They were afraid to speak or negotiate in his name. This approach caused the wheels of progress to come to a halt as recommendations piled up on Cuomo's desk.

During the transition in the fall of 1982, Cuomo confirmed this management approach: "I want myself in the center of the wheel and a lot of spokes out to the agencies."[35] In other words, he would not delegate authority to executive chamber subordinates; he wanted his fingers in every governmental pie. And considering the size of the state government, this approach could prove to be disastrous.

> To call Cuomo a "hands on" manager is to grossly understate his role in running state government. Cuomo is his own chief negotiator . . . and he often serves as his own press secretary (he has been known to talk on the telephone with the same reporter two or three times in one day). He calls his aides dozens of times to remind them about one thing or another and asks: "How come I'm the only one who's thinking of these things?"[36]

The distrustful Cuomo would not permit his secretary—the official title for chief of staff—to be a powerful gatekeeper, as was the case in the Carey administration.

In fact, the first appointment announced by a governor-elect is almost always chief of staff. This was not to be with Cuomo. The appointment of Michael Del Giudice as secretary was the fourth announcement.

Cuomo told Ken Auletta that Del Giudice "would not control access to the Governor; commissioners would not report to him; he would not have teams of deputies; and he would not have the freedom Morgado [Carey's chief of staff] had had to speak or act in the Governor's name."[37] In other words, Cuomo would be the center of all things in his administration. And as a result, he would bog himself down by doing too many things, including writing his speeches and answering his mail. He even insisted on shining his own shoes.

During his first year in office, Cuomo spent time every day determining his daily schedule. As for speaking engagements, he would sit with his scheduler and sift through the hundreds of requests that would arrive in his office and make instant decisions on which to accept.

The governor's speech writer said Cuomo frequently cancelled meetings to go over drafts of upcoming speeches. "I don't think Cuomo can keep this up," the writer complained. "You can't hover over each speech forever."[38]

One top Democratic Assembly aide, Ralph Laws said, "my own sense is that he may have a fatal flaw in not being able to delegate to a few strong people. I think that could do him in. . . ."[39]

Senator Warren Anderson voiced a similar concern: "[Cuomo] tries to do too much himself; he's his own bottleneck sometimes."[40]

Norman Adler of District Council 27—a key union leader who came out strongly for Cuomo in 1983—bluntly assessed Cuomo's approach to governing: "My principal worry is that Mario has almost a compulsion for detail, I just wonder whether he's learning that he can't be one of the most important figures in the national Democratic Party and chief executive of the state and spokesman for the liberal philosophy and at the same time worry about what's going on in the clearing of the Thruway north of Syracuse. Mario was elected governor. He's like a guy who owns a department store and cleans its windows himself."[41]

By March 1983, *The New York Times* was reporting that "Cuomo Holds A Tight Rein on Decisions." Defending his loose chain of command, Cuomo thundered, "No bill will go up, no appointment will be made without crossing my desk."[42]

Cuomo went on to say: "I don't like having too strong a dependence on anybody. I'm sleeping less and less. I work all the time. I'm not say[ing] that's a virtue. It's not. It really isn't. I'm always busy. I was busy when I was Lieutenant Governor, if you can believe that."[43]

On another occasion, after a question was raised about his management style, Cuomo said, "Delegate what? I was elected to govern. I wasn't elected to let other people govern. To the extent that my strength allows me to bring myself to bear, that's what I ought to do."[44]

As criticism mounted that his administration was "confused or disorganized" leading to numerous snafus, Cuomo doubled down: "My instructions to [my staff] are, 'Do not make a policy decision the Governor is supposed to make'. If there were any confusion, if there were any ball being dropped, I was the quarterback who dropped the ball."[45]

Assessing Cuomo's tight rein on his inner circle, a long-time top supporter of Cuomo, District 37 chief Victor Gotbaum said, "I'm not sure how much leeway he gives them. With other people, when I'm talking to their No. 1 person, I don't have to worry. But you don't have that feeling with Cuomo."

Annoyed by Gotbaum's comment, Cuomo replied that he did not approve of the governor's management because "[Gotbaum] doesn't know how to get what he wants."[46]

Cuomo's management style pretty much left Lieutenant Governor Alfred DelBello out in the cold. DelBello, who had previously served as the Mayor of Yonkers (and was the first Democrat to be elected Westchester County Executive in 1973 and was re-elected in 1977 and 1981) had won the 1982 Democratic primary for the number two post but had supported Ed Koch for governor. Cuomo made light of that fact and told reporters, "I have the advantage of having written out what the role of lieutenant governor should be . . . [DelBello] brings some strengths I don't have. He has run a large government. He has been in government longer than I have."[47]

But Mario Cuomo never forgot a slight, and for DelBello to have supported Koch for governor was unforgiveable.

Cuomo's first move was to slash DelBello's staff in half. DelBello was not free to wander the state to promote himself as Cuomo had when he was lieutenant governor. Cuomo would tolerate nobody else in his administration to share the limelight. As Ken Auletta reported, Cuomo "now visits many of those same indignities [he endured under Carey] on Lieutenant Governor Alfred DelBello."[48]

When DelBello publicly complained that Cuomo ignored his advice, the governor told the *Times,* "He obviously chose Koch over me. He had to adjust to his own disillusioned expectations."[49]

DelBello resigned his post out of disgust in December 1984.

The one exception to Cuomo's one-man rule was his son, Andrew.

In public life, Mario trusted only his wife and children. During his campaigns for mayor and governor, he came to depend on Andrew for advice and to carry out his orders. He might best be described as the enforcer who played an indispensable role in Cuomo's Executive Chamber.

The Rise of Andrew Cuomo

Born on December 6, 1957, Andrew Mark Cuomo, was the second-born of Mario and Matilda's five children. Growing up in Queens, he was a product of the Catholic education system graduating from St. Gerard Majella's parish grammar school, Archbishop Molloy High School in 1975 and Fordham University in 1979.

While attending Albany Law School from 1979–1982, he shared an Albany apartment with his father, who was serving as lieutenant governor.

As described in earlier chapters, as Mario plotted his political comeback after he lost the 1977 Mayor's race, Andrew worked at his side as friend, adviser and campaign manager. In the 1978 race for lieutenant governor, and in the 1982 gubernatorial battle, Andrew oversaw the daily management of the campaigns. After Cuomo beat Koch in 1984, Andrew was the nuts and bolts guy in the campaign against Lew Lehrman, and he also became the liaison with the state Democratic Party.

Andrew went on to direct the transition team during the post-election interregnum and on January 1, 1983, he became Special Assistant to the governor. *The New York Red Book* blurb on Andrew reads: "He ran Mr. Cuomo's campaign for Governor. A crucial advisor to the Governor, he is often relied on by him to oversee important matters, including appointments and political ties. Andrew Cuomo is paid $1.00 a year."

The Albany crowd quickly dubbed him "Prince of Darkness" and "Darth Vader" because he was responsible for firing holdovers from the outgoing Carey administration.

One long-time political operator told the author, "I watched grown men shake with fear when they heard Andrew was coming to see them. If Andrew showed up in your office you knew something was amiss or he would not be there. Andrew was not shy about badgering people verbally, humiliating them, demoting them or dismissing them."

Many in the Executive Branch believed Andrew enjoyed playing "thug." His role in his father's administration was similar to the role Joe Percoco would play (before he went to jail) in Andrew's gubernatorial administration.

Andrew, who claimed he was only his father's "messenger carrier," decided after serving two years in the Executive Chamber that it was time "to walk his own path" and after a one-year stint in Manhattan District Attorney Morgenthau's office, joined a law firm. As described later in this book, it was not to be always smooth sailing, as he and some of his partners became embroiled in litigation over an investment they made in a Florida savings and loan.

Cuomo and the Media

Complaints about Cuomo's style also extended to the members of the press. The governor insisted on being the principal spokesman for the administration, so he regularly spoke to the press. But he disdained them. "Reporters," he said, "are like epidemics. They follow catastrophes."[50] Another time Cuomo said that "he is adept at talking to school children . . . because he deals with them the same way he does with reporters. Only the children," he added, "get it right."[51]

Cuomo's press conferences, one reporter complained, did "more to confuse than clarify." Cuomo rarely answered a question directly. He often answered questions with questions, sometimes posing questions to himself and even debating himself. The Albany reporter for the *Watertown Times*, Paul J. Browne, described Cuomo's press conference style as answering questions "by posing others a more thoughtful press corps should have raised were it not slave to the quick fix, easy resolution eagerly awaited by editor and headline writer alike."[52]

Cuomo extended this questioning style to every aspect of his life. On one occasion, he grilled a 10-year-old boy in the halls of the State Capitol: "And how do you know you're 10 years old? Your daddy says so? How do you know your daddy's right?"[53]

Although Cuomo claimed his government was transparent, reporters had a hard time prying information out of the administration. And Cuomo, who could be verbally brutal with those who disagreed with him, was thin-skinned when *he* was criticized by the press. He was known to call reporters or editors at their homes late at night or very early in the morning to complain about their stories. He even threatened to ruin a journalist's career for what Cuomo perceived as an unfriendly article. The *Times* reported that "the Governor has also berated writers, accused them of doing the bidding of editorial boards and attacked their ethics."[54]

Cuomo's governing style and his bad relations with the press would change little during his twelve years in office. And some would later argue it prevented him from running for president and cost him in his quest for a fourth term in 1994.

Despite all the complaints, rookie mistakes, clashes with the Republican-controlled Senate over Medicaid costs and pension benefits, Cuomo would boast that his first year in office was a success. He did, after all, successfully negotiate an on-time budget.

CHAPTER 10
1984 – THE YEAR OF THE SPEECHES

Managing the state's executive branch was not the only job that kept Mario Cuomo busy during his first year in office; he also moved quickly to take control of the State's Democratic Party.

Two weeks after his election, Cuomo met with top party officials, Don Manes of Queens, Meade Esposito of Brooklyn, Stanley Friedman of The Bronx, and Manhattan's Danny Farrell. He made it clear that he wanted to replace the incumbent state chairman, Dominic Baranello, with his friend Bill Hennessy.[1]

Cuomo moved fast for several reasons. First, he wanted to get rid of Carey loyalists and to clean out holdovers who either had opposed his candidacy or might give him trouble down the road. Second, he wanted to put in a person loyal to him. Although Hennessy was Carey's transportation commissioner, he had made it clear to Cuomo as early as September 1981 that he would support him for governor. Hennessy quit his government job in January 1982 to be available to help Cuomo, particularly in upstate New York.

Third, Cuomo needed to control the party apparatus if he were to have any influence on the selection of the 1984 Democratic presidential nominee. New York was to have the second largest delegation to the national convention, and Cuomo wanted its members to follow his instructions.

And it did not take Cuomo very long to begin dabbling in national politics.

To create a positive relationship with the Democratic Party's National Chairman, Charles T. Manatt, Cuomo hosted a fundraiser in New York City for the D.N.C. shortly after his inauguration.

In May, he addressed national party leaders and major contributors at a Democratic Strategy Council meeting in Washington, D.C. According to the *Times*, Cuomo "warned the presidential candidates against appealing to special interests and impressed some listeners as a figure who could stir the Democratic ethnic working-class constituency that strayed to Mr. Reagan in 1980."[2]

Although he was leaning towards former Vice President Walter Mondale over the other top contender, Senator John Glenn of Ohio, he made an effort to appear neutral and urged New York Democrats to remain uncommitted until October 1983.

The appearance of neutrality also gave Cuomo the ability to host several Democratic presidential forums in various parts of the state in September 1983.

During the summer, Cuomo's top political adviser, Tim Russert (later host of "Meet the Press"), contacted the Mondale and Glenn campaign chiefs and told them that "Cuomo was very concerned that neither of the frontrunners was being sufficiently specific in his issue positions, and that he intended to press them in the forums to spell out where they stood."[3]

There were to be three forums: the first in Syracuse on September 26, where Glenn would be questioned; the second on September 28, where Mondale would appear; and a third in New York City that would feature both candidates.

These gatherings not only gave candidates an opportunity to shine, but gave New York and its governor plenty of attention. Cuomo, political journalists Jack Germond and Jules Witcover observed in their book, *Wake Us When It's Over: Presidential Politics of 1984*, was "officially neutral going into [the forums], but he made no secret of his view that Glenn was using his celebrity and favorable public opinion polls, rather than specific issues to advance his cause. And in this regard, Cuomo began to see similarities between Mondale's contest with Glenn and his own against Mayor Ed Koch of New York in the 1982 gubernatorial primary."[4]

Hence, when Glenn declined to answer Cuomo's question about his policy differences with Mondale at the Syracuse forum, saying he preferred to state his own views and avoid misstating Mondale's positions, Cuomo called Glenn the "celluloid" candidate—referring to the movie about Glenn based on Tom Wolfe's *The Right Stuff* that was to debut in the fall.

At the Rochester forum, two days later, Mondale happily described his many differences with Glenn and claimed he was the "real Democrat" while

Glenn was "Reagan lite" because he supported some aspects of "Reaganomics."

At the final forum held at Manhattan's Town Hall, the host was U.S. Senator Daniel Patrick Moynihan and the all-star panel included the former congresswoman from Texas, Barbara Jordan, *Making of the President* author Theodore H. White, Professor James Barber of Duke University, and Edwin Newman, formerly of NBC News. (Although Cuomo was technically co-host, he had to stay on the sidelines because of his "celluloid candidate" comment. That "acerbic phrase," journalist William Henry observed, was "a prime example of Cuomo's gift for finding the lethal 'mot juste'" to compromise himself.)[5]

While Mondale came across as an "aloof" and "condescending" frontrunner, Senator Glenn—well coached for the occasion—"presented himself as an anti-politician. Or rather more than a politician . . . He equally emphasized that he had been a military pilot, a war hero, a company president in three private businesses."[6]

Seething over Cuomo's wisecrack, Glenn struck back when answering an odd question from Professor Barber comparing Glenn's heroics to "Evel Knievel flying over the Grand Canyon on a motorcycle." Glaring directly at Cuomo, Glenn said, "As far as the 'celluloid' charge, I wasn't doing *Hellcats of the Navy* [a Reagan film] on a movie lot when I went through 149 missions. That wasn't celluloid. That was the real thing. And when I was on top of that booster down there getting ready to go, it wasn't *Star Trek* or *Star Wars*, I can guarantee you that. It was representing the future of this country, and I was very proud to take part in that."[7]

The audience applauded loudly as Cuomo sat stone-faced.

Asked later in the evening if his reply to Cuomo's attack was personal, Glenn said, "Damn right it was personal, because his comments about me were personal. I meant them to be personal."[8]

The bruised Cuomo, however, did have another opportunity to stick it to Senator Glenn. To overshadow the premiere of *The Right Stuff* in New York theaters in the second week of October, Governor Cuomo and Senator Moynihan jointly endorsed Mondale for president on October 13, 1983.

The price to be paid for Cuomo's support was high. He wanted the New York Mondale campaign to be run by Andrew Cuomo, and for Dave Garth to handle television. Cuomo also wanted to be seriously considered to give the convention keynote speech, and he wanted to be on the vice presidential short list.[9]

Mondale "grudgingly" accepted Cuomo's terms. "But Cuomo," as *Newsweek's* Peter Goldman and Tony Fuller reported, "made Mondale dance for his favor, and once bestowed, it seemed neither warm nor dependable. He said for quotation that he found Mondale as stimulating as polenta, an Italian cousin to cornmeal mush, and he threatened three times to withdraw his endorsement before a vote had been cast. Mondale's men guessed that Cuomo saw the campaign as a way to further his own higher ambitions and that he therefore would not care greatly if Mondale lost to Reagan in November, clearing the way for himself in 1988."[10]

Mondale and his people also had to endure a poorly run campaign organization in New York, including the twenty-six-year-old Andrew Cuomo's failure to return their phone calls.[11]

A week after the Town Hall debate, Cuomo was the guest of honor at a fundraiser held at the Washington D.C. home of former New York governor W. Averell Harriman.

Claiming he had no interest in seeking the presidency or being the vice presidential candidate because he made a pledge to serve out his full term as governor, Cuomo did lecture the gathering that "with the suitable approach, voters could be persuaded that 'even though Mr. Reagan has a nice face, he lies.'"[12]

Cuomo, however "made no secret of the fact that he would like to be the keynote speaker at the Democratic convention in San Francisco." He said, "I would be flattered."[13]

The Convention Speech

Despite Mondale's lukewarm relationship with the New York governor, after Cuomo made it clear he would not take the V.P. spot, Mondale did turn to him to give the keynote speech.

According to campaign chronicler Elizabeth Drew, "Mondale chose Cuomo as the keynoter because he admires his speaking ability—Cuomo's inaugural address, when he became governor of New York, in January 1983, made a big impression on Mondale—and because Cuomo's politics, an unembarrassed affirmation of the Party's liberal tradition and an ability to talk about middle-class values, fit with what Mondale wants emphasized. . . ."

Drew went on to point out that "giving a keynote address is a perilous act."[14] That's because the designated speaker is expected to give a rousing speech at the beginning of a national convention that grasps the attention of the delegates and emotionally arouses them to go forth and "fight the good fight."

And if the speaker fails to move the convention, it's curtains. A rising political star could quickly fade into oblivion.

In 1952, for instance, General Douglas MacArthur hoped that his keynote address at the Republican Convention would promote his hopes to be on the national ticket as vice president if Senator Taft were nominated for the top spot. But MacArthur's nineteenth-century, melodious speaking style didn't cut it. He quickly lost the audience, whose chatter drowned out his voice. His political ambitions also drowned that night.

The keynote speaker at the 1976 Democratic National Convention, Senator John Glenn, also fell flat on his face. The national hero came across as a dull insurance salesman and as a result, Jimmy Carter nixed him as his V.P. running mate.

When preparing a major address to the public, Mario Cuomo took nothing for granted. He would work very hard on the text and was known to drive his speechwriters crazy, sometimes spending hours practicing and polishing his delivery from a podium. He would measure every phrase, underline for emphasize, and make numerous changes to improve the flow of his words.

The drafting of his keynote address to the Democratic National Convention began in early 1984. Cuomo incorporated his "family themes" from his 1983 inaugural address with an indictment of Ronald Reagan's policies. He tried to separate the well-liked president from what he considered Reagan's disastrous policies. "He meant," wrote journalist William Henry, "to portray the president as unseeing, out of touch, not heartless or cruel."[15]

On the big night, July 16, 1984, Cuomo was in top form. The hours of practice paid off. His oratory electrified the convention. He proved to be the "ethnic Ronald Reagan."

After thanking the audience, he said that he would skip "the temptation to deal in a nice but vague rhetoric" and went immediately on the attack— with what some may argue was indeed "vague rhetoric."[16]

Cuomo attacked President Reagan's notion that America is "a shining city on a hill."

"A shining city," he continued, "is perhaps all the president sees from the portico of the White House and the veranda of his ranch, where everyone seems to be doing well."

"The hard truth," he declared, "is that not everyone is sharing in this city's splendor or glory." In this different part of the city, Cuomo said:

> . . . there are more poor than ever, more families in trouble, more and more people who need help but can't find it.

> Even worse, there are elderly people who tremble in the basements of the houses there.

> There are people who sleep in the city's streets, in the gutter, where the glitter doesn't show.

> There are ghettos where thousands of young people, without an education or a job, give their lives away to drug dealers every day.

> There is despair, Mr. President, in faces you never see, in the places you never visit in your shining city.

> In fact, Mr. President, this nation is more a "Tale of Two Cities" than it is a "shining city on a hill."

> If the President only visited other places he might begin to understand the plight of millions of Americans.

To make his point, Cuomo cited several examples of distressed areas, including Lackawanna, New York. In that western New York city, he said, "thousands of unemployed steel workers wonder why we subsidized foreign steel while we surrender their dignity to unemployment and to welfare checks. . . ."

He then went on to accuse President Reagan of subscribing "to a kind of social Darwinism. Survival of the fittest."

The Republicans believe the wagon train will not make it to the frontier unless some of our old, some of our young and some of our weak are left behind by the side of the trail. . . . We Democrats believe that we can make it all the way with the whole family intact.

To beat Reagan, the Democrats had to persuade Americans "to look past the glitter, beyond the showmanship . . . to reality, to the hard substance of things." And to achieve that end, it must be done, "[n]ot so much with speeches that bring people to their feet as with speeches that bring people to their senses."

Cuomo went on to remind his audience that Democrats pursuing "progressive principles" for fifty years prior to 1980, "created a better future for our children, using traditional Democratic principles as a fixed beacon, giving us direction and purpose, but constantly innovating, adapting to new realities: Roosevelt's Alphabet programs, Truman's NATO, the G.I. Bill of Rights, Kennedy's intelligent tax incentives and the Alliance for Progress, Johnson's civil rights, Carter's human rights, and the nearly miraculous Camp David peace accord. Democrats did it . . . and Democrats can do it again."

Nearing the end of his speech, Cuomo called "the struggle to live with dignity is the real story of the shining city." And it was a story he had lived:

I watched a small man with thick calluses on both hands work fifteen and sixteen hours a day. I saw him once literally bleed from the bottoms of his feet, a man who came here uneducated, alone, unable to speak the language, who taught me all I needed to know about faith and hard work by the simple eloquence of his example. I learned about our kind of democracy from my father. I learned about our obligation to each other from him and from my mother. They asked only for a chance to work and to make the world better for their children and to be protected in those moments when they would not be able to protect themselves. This nation and its government did that for them.

And that they were able to build a family and live in dignity and see one of their children go from behind their little grocery store on the other side of the tracks in South Jamaica where he was born, to occupy the highest seat in the greatest state of the greatest nation in the only world we know is an ineffably beautiful tribute to the democratic process.

He closed by urging Americans "For the good of all of us . . . for the love of God," to vote for Democrats. "Please make this nation how futures are built."

The rhetoric was indeed soaring; but what of the substance?

NBC's John Chancellor, the network's senior liberal political commentator, "remarked on the air that [the Cuomo speech] seemed not to be about the America he knew."[17]

The picture Cuomo painted was the Great Depression portrait, not present-day America. That may help explain why he opined on the marvels of New Deal programs, but not the Great Society programs of the 1960s.

What Cuomo failed to note was that Ronald Reagan voted for Franklin Roosevelt four times and was an enthusiastic supporter of New Deal programs.

Ronald Reagan made it clear time and again that he did not leave the Democratic Party, it left him. The takeover of the Democratic Party by extreme leftists that gave the nation the Great Society social experiments drove Reagan and millions of working-class Americans, particularly inner city and suburban ethnic Catholics, into the arms of the Republican Party.

Reagan portrayed himself as the antithesis of cultural liberalism by stressing the very themes Cuomo promoted in his speech: work, family, neighborhood, peace, and freedom.

Reagan told the millions of working-class Democrats who voted for him in 1980:

> The secret is that when the Left took over the Democratic Party, we took over the Republican Party. We made the Republican Party into the party of the working people, the family, the neighborhood, the defense of freedom, and yes, the American Flag and the Pledge of Allegiance to one Nation under God. So, you see, the party that so many of us grew up with still exists except that today it's called the Republican Party.[18]

Interestingly, Cuomo never mentioned the "Great Society." When praising President Lyndon Johnson, he only referred to "civil rights." It is fair to say that omission was by design. That's because, as described in Chapter 2 of this book, it was the hastily conceived and dubious Great Society social welfare programs that helped destroy millions of families. As Daniel Patrick Moynihan concluded as early as the mid-1960s, the U.S. welfare systems caused an "entire sub-culture of dependency, alienation and despair."

And lest we forget, it was Democratic tax-and-spend social policies on welfare and policing that turned the City of New York into the crime and welfare capital of the nation and drove the city to the edge of financial bankruptcy.

The despair Cuomo described in his address was not Ronald Reagan's fault. The erosion of traditional American values lay at the feet of the Democratic Party.

And Cuomo later admitted as much when he told *The New Republic* in April 1985, that the takeover of the Democratic Party by leftist McGovernites drove out working- and middle-class folks who "felt alienated by a new Democratic Party which he thought neither understood nor related to him."[19]

As for Cuomo's claim that the Democratic Party represented "the Family of America," columnist Richard Grenier wrote in the November 1984 issue of the *American Spectator*:

> Now it so happens that I am a very patriotic American, and I think we are one people, and have great obligations to one another, as well as obligations to our country as a whole, to defend it, for example, and keep it safe. But without pausing to compare Ronald Reagan's "safety net" with the far skimpier safety net of Franklin D. Roosevelt, not to mention that of his immediate Democratic predecessor Woodrow Wilson, I would like to point out to Mario Cuomo that no matter how many times he calls America a "family" it is still not a family. In the closing months of 1984, it is perhaps not inappropriate to point out that no matter how many times the hero of George Orwell's most famous novel calls his national leader "Big

Brother," he is still not his brother. A family is father, mother, children, grandpa, grandma, some aunts, uncles, nephews, nieces, and cousins. The "Family of America" Mario Cuomo is talking about is of necessity no family at all but a giant, impersonal state—a state which is to some degree destructive of family. When you take your child to a daycare center you are not leaving him with your sister but with a stranger, and the kind of care this stranger will provide your child is anybody's guess.

When Cuomo mentioned President John F. Kennedy, he praised his "intelligent tax incentives." But he failed to mention that JFK was "a supply sider" who believed in trickle-down economics, just like Reagan. It was Kennedy who popularized the economic phrase, "A rising tide lifts all boats."

In August 1963, in a nationally televised speech, Kennedy declared, "our tax rates are so high as to weaken the very essence of the progress of a free society, the incentive for additional return for additional effort." He called the permanent and significant tax rate cuts "to remove a serious barrier to long-term growth."

Fighting for his tax plan, Kennedy warned Congress that failure to act "increases the chance of recession." Tragically, his efforts were cut short by an assassin's bullet on November 22, 1963.[20]

Although Kennedy's successor, LBJ, was a New Deal Democrat, Johnson believed he had an obligation to advance JFK's tax plan. Hence, he engineered a deal that "took the 24 rates of the income tax down from the range between 20% and 91% to between 14% and 70%, phased in over two years." The corporate tax rate declined from 52% to 48%.[21]

The upsurge: economic growth between 1965 and 1969 averaged 5% annually; median family income grew at a "pace 50% higher than in the previous eight years"; automobile sales went up by 60%; and the flow of capital out of tax shelters fueled a boom in new business formation. Also, the federal tax cuts, contrary to Keynesian predictions, resulted in over a billion dollars in new tax receipts and "state and local revenues went up by 40% over the standard baseline, inflation plus population growth from 1963 to 1969."[22]

Sadly, Kennedy's tax reforms were undone by Johnson, Nixon, Ford, and Carter causing several recessions and stagflation in the 1970s.

Kennedy's efforts, however, were not in vain. His policy inspired the supply-side economics of the Reagan Administration that brought federal income tax rates down to two brackets, 28% and 15%, the corporate rate down to 34%, and produced 4% average annual growth, a stock market that went up 15-fold, and 44 million new jobs between 1983 and 2000.

Cuomo was right to praise "Kennedy's intelligent tax incentives," the very incentives that Ronald Reagan adopted.

While Cuomo praised the "progressive principles" from which he claimed the nation profited, he accused Reagan of believing a "kind of social Darwinism. Survival of the fittest."

Reagan and the Republicans, he said, "believe the wagon train will not make it to the frontier unless some of our old, some of our young, and some of our weak are left behind by the side of the trail. The strong will inherit the land."

This claim is absolute nonsense. Reaganomics, like Kennedynomics, proved "A rising tide lifts all boats." More importantly, those who subscribed to the notion that "the strong will inherit the land" were actually Cuomo's cherished Progressives.

Back in 1912, under the banner of a "New Nationalism," Progressives called for a centralized administrative state manned by expert managers and planners, who would use "scientific methods" to enhance human welfare.

Believing that social progress "required the individual to be controlled, liberated and expanded by collective actions," progressive intellectuals perceived human persons as "lumps of human dough" to be formed on the "social kneading board."[23]

That molding was to be done "by the best and the brightest, those who, uniquely, ignored profit and power to serve the common good—which is to say, the Progressives themselves."[24]

These Progressive experts denied inalienable rights, which their hero, Woodrow Wilson, called "nonsense." The editors of the progressive journal, *The New Republic*, spoke for the movement when it ridiculed individual liberties as "quaint and retrograde." The leading progressive legal scholar, Roscoe Pound (1879–1964), author of *Social Control Through Law*, argued the ten amendments in the Bill of Rights "were not needed in the [Founders' time] and they are not desired in our own."[25]

Believing that the state superseded even God, Progressives encouraged government officials to embrace eugenics—"the social control of human breeding" to rid the nation of perceived undesirables.

Progressive-era eugenics "required agreement upon three things only—the primacy of heredity, human hierarchy rather than human equality, and the necessary illiberal idea that human heredity must be socially controlled rather than left to individual choice."[26]

In 1911, New Jersey Democratic governor, Woodrow Wilson, signed into law forcible sterilization legislation aimed at "the hopelessly defective and criminal classes." Numerous states and municipalities followed Wilson's lead.

In America's inner cities, Anglo-Saxon Progressives took aim at Catholic and Jewish immigrants. They looked upon Eastern European immigrants as inferiors who "out-bred their biological betters" and agreed (with Wilson) that "low-standard races" were undercutting genuine American workers by accepting very low wages.

The dark side of the Progressive movement helps explain why Franklin Delano Roosevelt, a staunch Wilsonian, banned the term "progressive" and instead called himself a "liberal" when he ran for president in 1932.

FDR ran away from the Progressive movement because he knew "the intellectual champions of the regulatory welfare state proposed using it not to help those they portrayed as hereditary inferiors, but to exclude them."[27]

Reagan was no social Darwinist. In fact, throughout his first term, Reagan remained popular because millions of working-class folks, whose faith was in America's institutions in the 1970s, felt renewed confidence under Reagan. According to the Democratic pollster Stanley Greenberg, Reagan knew how to speak to the forgotten middle class, many of whom were life-long Democrats:

> Reagan reached out to ordinary people: he touched them first with his essential honesty and then with his heartfelt proposal to lift their financial burden by cutting tax rates. He sought to restore faith in the market and in entrepreneurship in order to allow people once again to believe that American business could

194

lead America to a new age of growth and prosperity. For a moment, it all seemed quite magical; it was, as the campaign ad suggested, "morning in America."[28]

Mario Cuomo's "Tale of Two Cities" address was grand oratory, but as ABC's David Brinkley pointed out, "Cuomo had preached only to the already converted."[29]

Time magazine's William Henry had this take on the speech:

It was the classic New Deal argument, movingly spoken. But Cuomo took it too far. He began to envision the unemployed, the dispossessed, the homeless sleeping on city streets. As he talked, he evoked a nation reminiscent of fifty years before, at the height of the Depression, an America remembered from his own childhood. The scenes he described were distant from the lives of ordinary suburban Americans of 1984. The deprivation he so piteously depicted seemed all but impossible in a modern, prosperous welfare state. And indeed, many of the people whose griefs he most graphically described were the victims, not of Reagan's policies, but of their own mental illness, and ironically of the liberal push in the 1970s to get such people out of institutions in favor of the purported panacea of "community-based release." They wandered unwashed in their overcoats in midsummer, stood on street corners shouting at unseen phantoms, sought winter warmth above subway grates, because they were unable to cope with life. No party, no program, no philosophy would heal their psychic wounds.[30]

In its totality, Governor Cuomo's speech to the Democratic National Convention offered the usual high-toned partisan bromides comparing the virtues of his party's social and economic policies with the vices of greedy, mean-spirited Republicans represented by Ronald Reagan. Variations on this theme had been the more or less constant mantra of Democrats ever since the New Deal, echoed endlessly by everyone from city councilmen to presidential candidates and their media epigones. Cuomo's gifted oratory gave it a certain lift—buoyed by his supporters' hopes that he would someday become president—but it offered little, if anything, that hadn't been touted by his party for half a century. It was essentially FDR on steroids. And like FDR, Cuomo's flowery rhetoric masked a wily political strategy first pithily captured by Harry Hopkins in the 1930's: "Spend, spend, tax, tax, elect, elect."

While Cuomo electrified his party's base, after the "high" wore off many Democrats had, over time, buyer's remorse—including Mario Cuomo. In later years, he confessed he regretted ever having given the speech. "Frankly," he said, "I'm sorry I went."[31]

Why regret the speech? Probably because the left wing of his party held him to the standards *he* established and found him wanting. Dr. Donna Shalala, former president of City University's Hunter College (and secretary of Human Services in the Clinton Administration), was quoted by *The New York Times* as describing Cuomo "as a powerful and articulate spokesman for social and political issues: yet when it came to implementing those views she concluded 'I'm confused by Cuomo.'"[32]

But in July 1984, Cuomo was basking in the warm glow of the many accolades he received for his soaring rhetoric.

And it was not to be his only major speech that year.

The Road to Notre Dame

On October 6, 1984, Terence Cardinal Cooke, seventh archbishop of New York, died from leukemia. Several days earlier, he signed a farewell letter that was read in all archdiocesan parishes three days after his death. In that letter, the staunchly pro-life cleric reiterated the fundamental teaching of the Church that every human person was precious from the moment of conception to the moment of natural death. The ailing cardinal declared:

> We are made in God's image and likeness, and this fact gives a unique dimension to "the gift of life." We have even more reason to be grateful. It is tragic that in our time, concepts which are disastrous to the well-being of God's human family—abortion, euthanasia and infanticide—are falsely presented as useful and even respectable solutions to human, family and social problems. Human life is sometimes narrowly viewed in terms of

being inconvenient or unwanted, unproductive or lacking arbitrarily imposed human criteria.

From the depths of my being, I urge you to reject this anti-life, anti-child, anti-human view of life and to oppose with all your strength the deadly technologies of life-destruction which daily result in the planned death of the innocent and the helpless. Together we must search for ways to demonstrate this conviction in our daily lives and in our public institutions. In doing so, we must never be discouraged or give up. Too much is at stake—"the gift of life" itself.

The "gift of life," God's special gift, is no less beautiful when it is accompanied by illness or weakness, hunger or poverty, mental or physical handicaps, loneliness or old age. Indeed, at these times, human life gains extra splendor as it requires our special care, concern and reverence. It is in and through the weakest of human vessels that the Lord continues to reveal the power of His love. . . .[32]

Cardinal Cooke's successor, the Most Reverend John J. O'Connor, installed as archbishop on March 19, 1984, was as militantly pro-life as his predecessor, but he had a different personality in public and in private. While Cooke was a low-key conciliatory person who lacked oratory skills, O'Connor was the exact opposite.

Serving twenty-seven years in the U.S. Navy, O'Connor was the first Catholic priest to be appointed senior Chaplain at the Naval Academy and the Navy's first Catholic Chief of Chaplains. Rear Admiral O'Connor had also earned advanced degrees in theology, psychology, philosophy, and a Ph.D. in political science.

The "Admiral," as many on his N.Y. staff affectionately referred to him, was a demanding taskmaster who did not fear confrontation in his chancellery or the public square.

Archbishop O'Connor threw down the gauntlet on June 24 when he said during a press conference, "I do not see how a Catholic in good conscience, can vote for an individual expressing himself or herself as favoring abortion." When asked if a pro-abortion Catholic elected official should be excommunicated, O'Connor replied, "I'd have to think about that."[34]

His comments, not out of the ordinary for a Catholic prelate, did not make any headlines. But two months later, Governor Cuomo complained to *The New York Times*, in an interview he requested, that "The Church has never been this aggressively involved [in politics]. Now you have the Archbishop of New York saying that no Catholic can vote for [Mayor] Ed Koch, no Catholic can vote for [City Comptroller] Jay Goldin, for [City Council President] Carol Bellamy, for [U.S. Senator] Pat Moynihan or Mario Cuomo—anybody who disagrees with him on abortion. . . . The Archbishop says, 'You Mario, are a Catholic who agrees with me that abortion is evil'. . . . The archbishop says, 'OK, now I want you to insist that everybody believes what we believe.'"[35]

O'Connor responded in the Brooklyn Diocese's newspaper, *The Tablet*, "I have never said, anywhere, at any time 'no Catholic can vote for Ed Koch'. . . . My sole responsibility is to present . . . the formal official teaching of the Catholic Church. I leave to those interested in such teachings [to judge how] the public statements of office-holders and candidates [match up.]"[36]

As mentioned earlier in this book, Cuomo, in his unsuccessful candidacy for lieutenant governor in 1974, said he would have voted against the 1970 pro-abortion law.

Three years later, while running for mayor, television commercials created by Cuomo's political consultant, Gerald Rafshoon, had "emphasized Mr. Cuomo's adherence to traditional values and family life."[37]

But after losing to Ed Koch in 1977, Cuomo began moving to the left on social issues. When Cuomo was gearing up to run for governor in 1982, he wrote this somewhat cryptic letter to Elaine Lytel, a public affairs specialist for the Planned Parenthood Center of Syracuse:

February 3, 1982

Dear Elaine:

It was good to see you again on Monday.

As we discussed, my position on abortion has been consistent although public opinion was varied from time to time. It was stated as part of our platform when Governor Carey and I ran in 1978, and has been the Administration's policy since then. I believe in and support choice. I believe in the use of Medicaid funds to insure that we have procedures available to women unable to pay for professional services. I believe in commitment to the major concerns of maternal and child health. I will continue to be an aggressive advocate on both state and federal levels for WIC, teenage pregnancy prevention and assistance, CHAP and family access to health care.

I'm sure questions will come up repeatedly over the next few months as we move into a campaign season. I think they should. If I am not available to answer inquiries in person, please make liberal use of this letter as a statement of my position.

Sincerely,
Mario M. Cuomo
Lieutenant Governor[38]

Despite becoming a "I'm personally opposed to abortion but who am I to impose my views" Catholic politician, Cuomo had avoided picking fights with the Church on social issues.

So why now?

Kenneth L. Woodward, *Newsweek*'s religion editor, who interviewed Cuomo for a 1986 cover story, had this take:

Why had Cuomo decided to create a public controversy where none had existed? The explanations ranged from the purely political to the patently psychological to the traditional ethnic conflict between Irish and Italian Catholics, and all of them were probably true. Tim Russert, at the time a counselor to Cuomo, thought the governor felt snubbed at O'Connor's inaugural Mass when he gave a pulpit shout out to Cuomo's party rival, Mayor Ed Koch—"How'm I doin' Mr. Mayor?"—but not to Cuomo. The major reason, I believe, was that invitation to speak at Notre Dame [on September 13, 1984]. For an Italian grocer's son from Queens, this was an opportunity as big in its own way as his invitation to keynote the Democratic Convention. And what better way to ensure the attention of the national press than to pick a fight with the archbishop (and soon to be cardinal) of New York?[39]

This perspective is very different from the one described in the Cuomo biography by Robert McElvaine:

> Christopher Cuomo [the youngest child] jumped up and started to cry, [after he heard Archbishop O'Connor's statement] his mother told me. "What are you saying—excommunicate my father?" the boy exclaimed. "And Mario got so white, so pale, and he stands up and leaves the room," Matilda Cuomo recounts. "They hit us like a hammer in the head."

> When Mario Cuomo is hit in the head, he responds. As his wife said to herself right after the O'Connor interview, "Boy, did he pick on the wrong person."[40]

Years later, Cuomo told historian Charles R. Morris, in an interview for his 1997 book *American Catholic*, that he told his son that he couldn't be excommunicated. "And even if he is the archbishop, he's wrong."

"But" Cuomo continued, "I was so upset—can you imagine someone saying you could be excommunicated—I couldn't sleep and I said to Matilda, 'I have to answer that.' And she said, 'Mario don't. Nothing's happened. Just leave it alone.'"

Here's Morris' summary of Cuomo's version of the making of the Notre Dame speech:

> As Cuomo tells it, he worked for five weeks on a response, to the exclusion of almost all his other activities, consulting with a number of theologians. At the time he had a long-standing invitation to address Richard McBrien's theology seminar at Notre Dame. "I called Father McBrien and canceled my talk," Cuomo said. "There had been a lot of publicity about my abortion position and I didn't want to embarrass them." McBrien at first agreed, but later called to say that he and Fr. Theodore Hesburgh, the university president, thought Cuomo should come anyway in the interest of the free exchange of ideas. "By then I'd finished this long and complicated paper," Cuomo said, "and

it dawned on me that Notre Dame was the only forum I had. I couldn't call a press conference to read an hour-long paper.[41]

And so, Cuomo changed his mind and decided to travel to Indiana to give what is arguably his most famous and significant speech—and the most wrongheaded.

Meanwhile, the abortion issue erupted again three days before Cuomo's Notre Dame speech.

On September 10, shortly after Geraldine Ferraro, the Democratic Party's vice-presidential candidate, a pro-choice Catholic congresswoman from Queens, New York, denied she had ever misrepresented Church teaching, Archbishop O'Connor made public a copy of a letter Ferraro had signed and sent to fifty Catholic congressmen/congresswomen in 1982. In that letter, she wrote that an organization called Catholics For a Free Choice "shows us that the Catholic position on abortion is not monolithic and that there can be a range of personal and political responses to the issue."[42]

O'Connor replied that the "only thing I know about her is that she has given the world to understand that Catholic teaching is divided on the subject of abortion. . . . As an officially approved teacher of the Catholic Church, all I can judge is that what has been said about Catholic teaching is wrong. It's wrong."[43]

The outrage on the left about O'Connor's criticism of Ferraro was summed up in a *New York Times* editorial: "It might as well be said bluntly: . . . [the] effort to impose a religious test on the performance of Catholic politicians threatens the hard-won understanding that finally brought America to elect a Catholic president a generation ago."[44]

The O'Connor-Ferraro brouhaha only increased the media-frenzy, and once again, put the national spotlight on Cuomo as he prepared to fly to the University of Notre Dame on September 13.

The Notre Dame Speech, September 13, 1984

Throughout his tenure as the state's chief executive, Governor Cuomo did not like to leave New York for extended periods of time. After his convention address in San Francisco, he jumped on a plane that night to get back home.

Likewise, his trip to South Bend, Indiana, was in and out in one day. The flight out to Notre Dame, however, was an eerie one. "A storm had rocked the plane so severely," Kenneth Woodward wrote after an interview with the governor, "that one of [Cuomo's] aides—probably [Tim] Russert—pulled out his rosary beads and the governor, himself, was moved to nervous prayer."

Mrs. Cuomo, who had advised Mario not to give the speech ("Mario," she said, "drop it. Better that you be wrong than the Church."), was also on the plane. And after one "heart-stopping plunge" during the flight, Cuomo told historian Charles Morris, "Matilda is in the back, her face is white, she's looking at me, and I know what she's thinking."[46]

Cuomo titled the speech he delivered, "Religious Belief and Public Morality: A Catholic Governor's Perspective."[47]

Cuomo began his speech by describing himself as "an old-fashioned Catholic who sins, regrets, struggles, worries, gets confused, and most of the time feels better after confession." "The Catholic Church," he added, "is my spiritual home."

"I accept the Church's teaching on abortion" he continued. But then he asked, "Must I insist you do?" Cuomo went on to argue that one cannot impose one's moral views. "Our public morality then—the moral standards we maintain for everyone, not just the ones we insist on in our private lives—depends on a consensus view of right and wrong. The values derived from religious belief will not and should not be accepted as part of the public morality unless they are shared by the pluralistic community at large by consensus."

He appealed to Cardinal Joseph Bernardin's "seamless garment" position saying, "Abortion has a unique significance but not a preemptive significance." "Abortion," he contended, "will always be a central concern of Catholics. But so will nuclear weapons. And hunger and homelessness and joblessness, all the forces diminishing human life and threatening to destroy it."

Arguing that a consensus to ban abortion did not exist, Cuomo concluded: "I believe that legal interdicting of all abortions by either the federal government or the individual states is not a plausible possibility and, even if it could be obtained, it wouldn't work. Given present attitudes, it would be Prohibition revisited, legislating what couldn't be enforced and in the process creating a disrespect for law in general."

Of Cuomo's attempt to protect his political flanks, historian Richard Brookhiser wrote: "Cuomo had found, in consensus and prudence, a way of having religion when he wanted it and not having it when he didn't."[48]

The consensus argument was even too much for the very liberal bishop of Albany, Howard Hubbard:

> While I support wholeheartedly the governor's position on capital punishment, there is no consensus in our state or nation on this matter. Quite the contrary. The polls show that 60% to 70% of the population favors the death penalty.

> Also, polls indicate that the vast majority of the citizens in New York are opposed to recent legislation about the mandatory usage of seat belts. Yet contrary to citizen consensus, the governor supports such legislation because it would save several hundred lives a year. Why not a similar concern about saving the thousands of human lives which are terminated annually through abortion on demand?[49]

The renowned theologian Monsignor William B. Smith, academic dean at St. Joseph's Seminary in Yonkers, New York, agreed:

> The governor's style was smooth and slick, but the content was specious and misleading. He is obviously a competent man, but a couple of points were horrendous, one being the complete ignoring of the human rights issue. Human rights do not rest on consensus. Respect for the human rights of blacks, Jewish people—any minority—does not rest on consensus. This is why we call them inalienable rights. He relied on the 15-year-old rhetoric of Planned Parenthood [that] we're trying to impose our morality on others. The Supreme Court didn't establish a consensus; it destroyed one. The laws in the 50 states weren't there because the Catholic Church put them there.[50]

Journalist Kenneth Woodward had this take on Cuomo's thesis:

. . . I found Cuomo's line of argument fraught with pious dissembling. First, he mischaracterized the Church's teaching on abortion as simply one "belief" among others that loyal Catholics like himself accept on faith—in other words, a plank in a sectarian belief system imposed by the bishops in their role as official Church teachers. The clear implication was that if Cuomo belonged to some other church that found no evil in aborting the life of an unborn child, his personal belief as a loyal member would be just the opposite. Nowhere did the governor argue that he, Mario Cuomo, like millions of other Americans who are not Catholic or even religious, had through any kind of moral intuition or reasoning of his own concluded that abortion was morally abhorrent in and of itself. Instead, his argument inadvertently resurrected the hoariest of anti-Catholic slurs, namely, that "loyal" Catholics do not think for themselves.[51]

Governor Cuomo was also criticized by former Minnesota Senator and liberal icon, Eugene McCarthy, who said that "abortion is a legitimate public issue and far from sectarian, since more than just Catholics oppose it."[52]

On October 18, Archbishop O'Connor, in a speech before a Catholic medical group—with Mother Teresa of Calcutta sitting on the stage—challenged the Cuomo thesis:

You have to uphold the law, the Constitution says. It does not say that you must agree with the law, or that you cannot work to change the law. . . .

There are those who argue that we cannot legislate morality. The reality is that we do legislate behavior every day. . . . It is obvious that law is not the entire answer to abortion. Nor is it the entire answer to theft, arson, child abuse, or shooting police officers. Everybody knows that. But who would suggest that we repeal the laws against such crimes because the law is so often broken?[53]

O'Connor reminded his audience, "I have the responsibility of spelling out . . . with accuracy and clarity what the Church officially teaches. . . . I have simultaneously the obligation to try to dispel confusion about such teaching wherever it exists, however it has been generated, regardless of who may have generated it. . . . I recognize the dilemma confronted by some Catholics in political life. I cannot resolve that dilemma for them. As I see it, their disagreement, if they do disagree, is not simply with me [but] with the teaching of the Catholic Church."[54]

Governor Cuomo's Notre Dame address was perhaps the high-water mark of the so-called "seamless garment" strategy articulated by Cardinal Joseph Bernadin a few years before. However, theologians might gloss over its moral logic, the appeal of the seamless garment argument lay in its cynical political consequence: it allowed politicians to say they were "personally opposed" to abortion while continuing to support it. Mario Cuomo played this theme for all it was worth, while wrapping himself in false humility: he did not wish to "impose" his morality on non-Catholics. To do so would encourage social strife among competing moralities, contrary to the civil peace sought by Catholic social teaching. The intended effect of the governor's speech was to make the world safer for pro-choice Catholic politicians like himself. The million-plus unborn children who would lose their lives in 1984 enjoyed no such protection.

November, 1984: The Democratic Debacle

The abortion controversy did not help the floundering campaign of the Democratic presidential nominee, Walter Mondale. And his hope to attract Catholics back to the party with the choice of Geraldine Ferraro appeared to be falling flat.

On the other hand, President Reagan reached out to disaffected Catholics with great effectiveness. In Waterbury, Connecticut, a Catholic town of factory workers that had hosted John F. Kennedy's last campaign appearance in 1960, Reagan said: "You know, I was a Democrat once. . . . The only abandoning I see is the Democratic leadership abandoning the good and decent Democrats of the JFK and FDR . . . and Truman tradition."

Mondale and many others in the Democratic Party failed to grasp that for most average church-going Catholics in 1984, abortion was one matter on which they could not compromise. As a result, the most visible Catholic politicians in 1984—Mario Cuomo, Edward Kennedy, and Geraldine Ferraro—were viewed more as traitors than champions.

In contrast, Ronald Reagan was pro-life. He also had an attitude and a demeanor as president that enhanced his support among Catholics. They were impressed that Reagan stood on their side of the barricades in the brewing culture wars. And they were delighted that Reagan stood up for them and fought big government and the big taxes needed to support it. A blue-collar worker in the Northeast put it best: "The Democratic Party has been good to me—Social Security, G.I. Bill, student loans. The Democratic Party made me middle-class. But Reagan will keep me middle-class."[55]

On Election Day the American people overwhelmingly re-elected President Reagan. He carried forty-nine states with 525 electoral votes, the largest total ever received.

Sixty-one percent of Catholic voters cast their ballots for Reagan. Mondale's gamble with Geraldine Ferraro failed. The fact that Reagan handily carried Ferraro's Ninth Congressional District with 57% of the vote proves the point. As for the nation's most liberal state, New York, Reagan carried the state for the second time receiving 54% of votes cast. He romped in the suburban counties—Nassau, Suffolk, Westchester, Rockland—that surround New York City, garnering 67.3% of the vote.

While Reagan did not carry the City of New York, he carried the working-class Catholic neighborhoods of Parkchester, Throgs Neck and Unionport in the Bronx; Borough Park, Dyker Heights, Bensonhurst, and Bath Beach in Brooklyn; Bayside, Bellerose, Richmond Hill, Ozone Park, Jackson Heights, Woodside, Sunnyside and Ridgewood in Queens. Reagan won one county outright, Staten Island, 61% to Mondale's 39%.

While Democrats, nationally, were shedding tears, many in New York were happily looking to 1988.

A headline in the post-election issue of the *New York Post*, read "Cuomo 'hot property' in four." The article written by *Post* Albany Bureau Chief Frederic Dicker, declared:

> Gov. Cuomo has emerged as one of the "hottest Democratic properties" in the battle for the presidency in 1988. That's the conclusion of a half-dozen key New York and national party

leaders, who say the time is right for a "fresh face" Democrat like Cuomo to pick up the pieces from yesterday's disaster.

Cuomo, who has refused to rule out a run for President, "is certainly going to have to be considered as one of only about five potential Democratic candidates for President in 1988," said media consultant David Garth.

"I hear him mentioned all the time as a potential candidate," Garth said.

"Gov. Cuomo has become overnight one of the leading contenders for the Democratic presidential nomination," observed Assembly Speaker Stanley Fink, the politically-savvy Brooklyn Democrat.

Reagan's victory has made Cuomo "a hot property," said Cuomo political adviser and Mondale campaign activist Sandy Frucher.[56]

Even the political sage of Saddle River, New Jersey, former President Richard Nixon, agreed. "Like many successful politicians, he is, at times, a demagogue," Nixon said, "but he is a very effective one, and if he can keep his nose clean in running the state of New York, I do not see anybody on the scene who would be able to stop him."[57]

The day after the election Cuomo played a cagey game with the media. He appeared to be walking away from his convention speech when he told the *Times* "that he viewed the election not as 'an ideological contest' but rather as 'President Reagan's personal landslide.'"[58]

That same day in another interview, Cuomo appeared to be moving to the right, using what was becoming his standard style, answering a question with a series of questions:

One of the Senators . . . is supposed to have said, "We have read all of Governor Cuomo's speeches and they are New Deal." I laughed. What are you when you reduce public employees by

9,000? What are you when you say [that] need should be the criterion [for welfare benefits]? What are you when you can come out for a tax cut? What are you when you refuse to raise the basic taxes? What are you when you spend more on your defense budget, which we call corrections, than any governor in history?[59]

The key question Cuomo was evading: Was he posturing himself for a presidential run in 1988?

CHAPTER 11

THE MAN WHO WOULDN'T BE PRESIDENT

In the aftermath of the 1984 presidential election, in which Ronald Reagan received nearly 98% of the electoral votes against Democratic challenger Walter Mondale, Mario Cuomo's name jumped to the top of the list of potential 1988 nominees.

Historically, being a governor of New York automatically made one a contender, but Cuomo knew that many of his predecessors—Al Smith, Tom Dewey, Averell Harriman, Nelson Rockefeller—had failed in their quest for the White House.

Therefore, Cuomo approached his new-found national prominence cautiously. He realized that even New York's voters had moved to the right, particularly in the suburbs where Reagan had won big. He admitted as much on election night when he told the *Post*, "I will have to work harder" to be reelected in 1986.[1]

So, Cuomo began moving slowly to the center of the political spectrum.

In January 1985, for instance, he "took pains to complain when his 'state of the state' message to the Legislature in Albany was described as a throwback to the New Deal."[2]

Cuomo's 1985–1986 budget was one fiscal conservatives could embrace. The final $39 billion product contained tax cuts, much larger than Cuomo requested, that would save taxpayers that year $635 million "with annual savings climbing to $1.6 billion by 1987. . . . Moreover, more than 500,000 people who are below the official poverty line [would] fall from the tax rolls."[3] The Senate's Republican Majority Leader, Warren Anderson, boasted, "It's the greatest single decrease in taxes in the history of the state."[4]

Siding with the Republican State Comptroller, Ned Regan, the governor "accepted both a budget balanced according to GAAP, or generally accepted accounting principles, and a start on debt reduction."[5]

Further shedding his liberal image, Cuomo argued that the budget was good for all New Yorkers. "The New York State politic is embodied in that budget. . . . We're not at ideological warfare the way they are in Washington. Are we conservative? Are we liberal? All of that's irrelevant. Our politics *is* this budget and it's a consensus."[6]

As Cuomo was gearing up to run for a second term, tax revenues were growing at a rapid pace (in part because of the booming national economy under President Reagan), which permitted Cuomo to cut taxes and increase spending in the 1985–86 and 1986–1987 fiscal year. (Expenditures in his 1988–1987 budget were 30% higher than in his first budget.)

In early 1986, Cuomo made the covers of *Newsweek* (March 24, 1986) and *Time* (June 2, 1986)—a big deal back then.

The *Newsweek* story, titled "Is Mario Cuomo for Real?," declared: "He is the most interesting of all the presidential hopefuls for 1988, a complex blend of toughness, intelligence, sensitivity and combativeness. But critics say Gov. Mario Cuomo's temper is too hot, his religion too sanctimonious, his ethnic pride too thin-skinned; they fault his administration of New York State as lacking both reach and grasp."

The article pointed out that both Republicans and Democrats consider Cuomo a "mediocre administrator": "he is said to have assembled a staff that is more notable for its loyalty than its brilliance, and he is routinely criticized for his excessive reliance on a tiny coterie of advisers—his son Andrew, 28, chief among them. He is also criticized for refusing to delegate even the most picayune policy decisions—a charge he says is 'kind of silly.'"

As for the charge that Cuomo doesn't delegate beyond a few people in his inner circle, his friend, the columnist Jimmy Breslin, told *Newsweek*, "What circle? There ain't enough people to form a circle."

The *Time* cover story, "What to make of Mario," observed: "The son of Italian immigrants, a man of passion and contemplation who wrestles with ambition and doubt, Cuomo may be the Democratic Party's brightest star and best hope to recapture the White House in 1988. Does he stand for the party's liberal, big-spending past, or is he the avatar of the future? He is, in any case, that rare thing in politics, a man who can inspire."

The opening of the *Time* profile may as well have been written by Cuomo's own campaign staff. Mario is described as both a "man of strenuous action and the man of otherworldly contemplation." It continued,

"Like the titans he frequently invokes—Jefferson, Lincoln, Roosevelt—he is a man who battles inwardly between passion and reason, between his ambition and his doubts. Some believe that out of this man's head and heart may come the soul of a new Democratic Party, and perhaps the strength to lead it to the White House in 1988."

But the section about "the muscular philosopher-prince" who "has modeled himself on St. Thomas More" does concede that he "can display a kind of conspicuous moral vanity."

On Cuomo as micromanager and his reputation for being thin-skinned, a former staffer told *Time* that Cuomo "has no grasp of management systems: 'He runs a high-level mom-and-pop operation.'" Another former colleague said, "Mario cannot treat honest criticism with respect. He views it as a personal attack."

Democrats complained to *Time* "that he has not translated his popularity into programs, that he has failed to get the Legislature to pass many of his initiatives." He is accused of "never tack[ling] real change."

Cuomo, who is quick to boast that he is "the founder of the Progressive Pragmatist Party . . . a kind of frugal liberalism, conservatism with a human face," appears to contradict himself by claiming he "loathes labels." He calls them "one-word summaries of an entire philosophy."

Time reported:

> He challenges anyone to define him. "How about the money we spent on prisons?" Cuomo asks. He has built more than 6,000 new cells. "Is that liberal or conservative?" He cites his $1.2 billion transportation bond issue. "What about all the work we've done on highways, roads and bridges?" His voice rises. "Is that liberal? Maybe it's conservative." He has balanced New York's budget but has appropriated more money for the homeless than any other state. "Tell me," he says, as if cross-examining a recalcitrant witness in a Queens criminal court, "is that liberal or conservative?"

And when *Time* asked the governor if he really wants to be president:

> The question troubled him. He seems unable to deal with his own ambiguous feelings. He and Matilda have never had a

211

single conversation about the presidency, Cuomo said. Slowly he rubbed his fingers over his chin. "I see that job as a burden," he answered, "not as an opportunity." He glanced over at [a sculpture of] Lincoln's bronze hands. He views the job much as Lincoln did, Cuomo said, and as Lincoln did, he muses on the biblical phrase "Let this cup pass."

That biblical phrase is the same one an earlier indecisive, self-proclaimed Democratic intellectual politician, Adlai Stevenson, pretentiously used in his 1952 presidential nomination acceptance speech: "I have asked the merciful Father—the father of us all—*to let this cup pass from me*. But from such dread responsibility one does not shrink in fear, in self-interest, or in false humility."[7]

After essays portraying Cuomo "The Italian-American," "The Catholic," "The Governor" and "The Candidate," *Time* had this to say about his presidential prospects:

At bottom, presidential elections usually hinge on character—and Cuomo has almost too much of that. The problem is defining it and sharpening the image. If he has some of Ronald Reagan's common touch and moral authority, it is offset by arrogance and a kind of reverse snobbery; if there is a trace of Jimmy Carter in his workaholism and pietism, he also has the saving grace of humor. That could take him a long way. But for now, he chooses to wait.

The Race for Governor: 1986

If he were to be taken seriously as a 1988 presidential contender, Cuomo believed he had to win big in his 1986 re-election campaign for a second term as governor.

And by early 1986, it appeared that all the political winds were blowing Cuomo's way.

Above all, he had plenty of money: about $10 million in his campaign treasury. Next, 1986 was the second mid-term election during the Reagan years. Traditionally, the incumbent party—in this case the Republicans—fares poorly in off-year elections.

Finally, the N.Y. Republican Party was a shadow of its former self. The state GOP organization, which was dependent for years on the financial largesse of Nelson Rockefeller, was broke. The party's two statewide elected officials, Senator Alfonse D'Amato and State Comptroller Ned Regan, did not look to the state party for fundraising or grassroots organization. They did it themselves, setting up their own independent operations. Also, both D'Amato and Regan had cozy relationships with Cuomo. The operating principle was, "you leave us alone and we'll leave you alone."

Looking for a sacrificial lamb, GOP leaders convinced Westchester County Executive Andrew P. O'Rourke to accept the party's nomination for governor.

O'Rourke, who grew up in Manhattan's Hell's Kitchen, graduated from Fordham University and Fordham University School of Law. To help finance his education, he became a part-time actor appearing as a bit player on Broadway and television.

After college, he enlisted in the Air Force rising to the rank of captain. He "was on a response team throughout the Cuban missile crisis and flew missions around the world during his eight years of active duty."[8]

O'Rourke went on to serve four terms on the Yonkers City Council. After Westchester County Executive Al Del Bello was elected lieutenant governor in November 1982, O'Rourke was chosen to fill the vacancy and was subsequently elected to a full term in 1985.

O'Rourke was a good speaker, was sharp on his feet, and was a competent administrator (he was to be elected four times as County Executive and served for a total of 15 years in that post before becoming a judge)— but he lacked one thing: money.

So, O'Rourke adopted the strategy Cuomo had used against Ed Koch in 1977 and 1982: he challenged him to a series of debates all around the state.

But Cuomo wouldn't bite. The great orator and debater ducked one-on-one confrontations for months.

Since he was solidly ahead in the polls, he didn't want to give his underfunded and unknown opponent free exposure. Also, by keeping the media focused on the "debate over the debates," Cuomo escaped scrutiny. O'Rourke kept the debate issue alive by campaigning around the state carrying a life-size cardboard cutout of Cuomo.

Another reason for avoiding debates and evading the press: Cuomo's first-term record was meager. The *Times* pointed out in 1985 that Cuomo had become known and admired by many more for what "he has said as for what he has done."[9]

As Professor Gerald Benjamin, a top scholar on New York government, has written, "Mario Cuomo's chief achievement has been the alteration, through his approach to communication, of the terms of political discourse in New York."[10]

But "the talk," some Cuomo admirers told the *Times*, "do[es] not always seem connected to what is happening in government."[11]

> They say that he talks of helping the homeless, but that virtually none of the money appropriated for shelters has been spent. They say that he talks of improving treatment of the mentally ill, but that the mental health system remains tangled in dispute and delay. He talks of preserving the environment, but failed to offer a proposal to clean up toxic waste last session until too late for the Legislature to act.[12]

Citizens Budget Commission Chairman Lawrence S. Huntington, also complained about the governor's record. "The Governor has achieved enormous popularity and following for his intellectual capabilities," he said, "and that has caused people not to look at the specifics of his financial administration." He added that because people are focused on Cuomo's rhetoric, they are ignoring the fact that state spending is increasing above the rate of inflation and that the state's debt burden is growing. "It's an atmosphere," Huntington concluded "in which people are not being particularly analytical."[13]

This type of criticism continued as Cuomo sought a second term.

The New York Public Interest Research Group's Walter Hang concluded, "[Cuomo] talks about programs but he doesn't fight for them. The public has the sense this guy is a fighter, that he's really out there slugging it out. But what you see at the end of the [Legislative] session is very, very little progress, very little to show for it."[14]

On the Sunday before Cuomo was to announce his decision to run again, *The New York Times* published a lengthy article, "As Cuomo Seeks

Re-Election, Popularity Outshines Record," in which the governor gave a rather tortured justification of the fact that his popularity was "to a degree . . . based on perception and image" and not the "specifics of his record":

> "To the extent that you can be constant, to the extent that you can be perceived as believing something, it doesn't make a whole lot of difference to the public, I don't think, what you believe as long as it's not outrageous," he said, "As long as you believe it, really believe it, and are pretty consistent—that's a big plus. Sincerity, hard work, a general sense that this is a person who is trying to help other people—my guess is that the things that people relate to are kind of fundamental.

> "I think in my case impressions were formed—let's face it, you had the keynote," Mr. Cuomo continued. "The truth is, people saw the darned thing. I was amazed how many people saw it. Now, they don't remember what you said. Some of them do. They get a general impression.

> "If people see you on television," he added later, "and you didn't do anything really bad, like you're not in handcuffs, they're going to assume you did something good." Nevertheless, the Governor said he was disturbed that not enough attention was paid to his record, in Albany, and he listed as accomplishments: cutting taxes, balancing the state budget, increasing education spending by 42%, pushing through a bond issue to rebuild the state's roads and bridges, raising the drinking age to 21, enacting the country's first law requiring car occupants to wear seatbelts, expanding prison capacity by 10,000 inmates, winning passage of a low- and middle-income housing program for New York City.[15]

Putting aside that Cuomo's reply was typically cryptic; he took credit for actions that were "not all passed because of his efforts."[16] The key one being the tax cut he signed into law which was actually a Republican State Senate initiative.

Republican Senate leader Warren Anderson argued that Cuomo's first-term accomplishments were meager. "I think he's distracted." Anderson said. "He's more concerned about what he's going to say in his speeches around the country than in concentrating on the problems of New York."[17]

Despite the criticism, Cuomo enjoyed a strong lead over Republican challenger Andrew O'Rourke. Most polls had him beating O'Rourke by 20 to 30 percentage points.

Yet, as he breezed toward an easy victory, Cuomo was ornery. He appeared to have reverted back to the belligerent and angry Cuomo of the early 1970s.

The Almanac of American Politics 1988 edition succinctly described the Cuomo campaign:

> In 1986 Cuomo's reelection was certain and his Republican opponent, Westchester County Executive Andrew O'Rourke, a humorous man who had just written his first mystery novel, could do little more than get in a few quips. But Cuomo's testiness and contentiousness prevented him from showcasing his record and his philosophy as much as he might have liked. Early in the year he defensively claimed there was no such thing as the Mafia and took umbrage at a remark that there were "not many Marios" in the South; he got into an imbroglio when George Bush distorted some of his remarks and attacked him for granting clemency to a prisoner. In the fall campaign he was criticized for going to court to get a rival to his choice for lieutenant governor off the primary ballot; he got into a shouting match with O'Rourke on the radio and agreed only at the last minute to debate; he criticized O'Rourke harshly for not disclosing his legal clients and responded angrily to criticism of his top aide and 28-year-old son, Andrew Cuomo.[18]

On Tuesday, November 4, 1986, Cuomo won by the largest margin in the state's electoral history, receiving 2,775,229 votes (65%) versus O'Rourke's 1,363,810 votes (32%). He topped the previous record, 58.5%, achieved by Grover Cleveland in 1882.

Cuomo carried 56 of the state's 62 counties including Westchester—

O'Rourke's home county. As for the suburban counties surrounding New York City, whose voters had been traditionally Republican and Conservative, Cuomo racked up 62.1% of the votes. He almost topped Ronald Reagan's 1984 total of 62.3%.

Cuomo's movement rightward towards the center helps explain why he carried the suburban Republican bastions, particularly Nassau County which boasted the most powerful GOP political machine in the nation.

Back in January, *New York Times* reporter Maurice Carroll had noted Cuomo's changing tone when the governor introduced a "Work Not Welfare" proposal. "It was a considerable change," Carroll wrote, "both in the Governor's tone and in the sentiment. . . . Mr. Cuomo who has hailed the birth of the New Deal here in Albany . . . was sounding a traditional conservative theme. He did not limit it to welfare . . . [Cuomo stated], 'I'm not anxious to see the state do things the private sector does better.'"[19]

But for some observers, including many state Democrats, Cuomo's victory was pyrrhic for several reasons.

First, the turnout was the lowest in the state's recent history. Only 55% of the 8 million registered voters went to the polls to cast their votes. As a result, Cuomo received only 100,000 more votes than he did in 1982; 2,775,229 versus 2,675,213.

Second, local Democrats complained that he did nothing to defeat Republican U.S. Senator Al D'Amato and Republican State Comptroller Ned Regan. Democratic Senator Daniel Patrick Moynihan, the day after the election, bluntly stated: "Of course there was a nonaggression pact between Governor Cuomo and Senator D'Amato. That's not a theory; it's a fact. And now that the election is over, we have to recognize it as such."[20]

There were also complaints that Cuomo did not lift a finger to help Democrats wrest control of the state Senate from the Republicans. On November 6, 1986, the *Times* reported that, "While Governor Cuomo made some campaign appearances and was the host of a fundraising even for State Senate Democrats, legislators say the Governor did less and did it later than he was asked to. One official said it took him five weeks to respond to a request to make radio commercials for State Senate candidates."

Third, there were plenty of complaints about Cuomo's "rough and tumble hardball political tactics." Frederic Dicker and Deborah Orin wrote in the *Post*:

Cuomo's campaign strategy—to grind his foes into the dust—backfired badly, leaving the governor hostile and angry and looking like he worked overtime to try to snatch a kind of moral defeat from the jaws of victory.

This miscalculation calls into question not only Cuomo's personal style and commitment to fair play, but his political judgment and that of his top aides.[21]

The New York Times agreed. In their endorsement of Cuomo, the editors pointed out that the governor had appeared "authoritarian" and showed "a taste for endless, intricate, contentious argument."[22]

The Village Voice endorsement also criticized Cuomo describing him as a "swaggering pol" whose "recent political behavior has been 'a disgrace.'"

Mary McGrory, the nationally syndicated liberal columnist, criticized Cuomo's ruthless tactics and warned Democrats "that charisma and eloquence aren't everything."[23]

After declaring his victory was due to his "record of accomplishment," Cuomo downplayed questions concerning a 1988 presidential run. He said that his big win in New York "doesn't say anything about Iowa and the rest of the country. . . . I'm not sure that it makes a lot of sense to extend the significance of this and to make it national."[24]

Meanwhile, Democratic political wags on the national level were already complaining because Cuomo "refused to leave the state to stump for other Democrats and did little to help them raise money—while potential 1988 rivals like Massachusetts Gov. Michael Dukakis, [Colorado Sen. Gary] Hart, Delaware Sen. Joe Biden and Missouri Rep. Richard Gebhardt, were doing all they could."

One Republican critic, the famed political consultant, Roger Ailes, pointed out that Cuomo "showed his true colors when he got testy in the final days of the race despite a grand lead that should have left him breathing easy."

"This election," Ailes said, "has shown that Mario Cuomo can't run for national office unless he gets a personality transplant. On his best days, Cuomo makes Richard Nixon look like Dale Carnegie."[25]

The Non-Candidate for President

In late December 1986, *Washington Post* journalist Paul Taylor met with Cuomo in the State Capitol Building to discuss presidential politics. Taylor quickly realized that the fast-talking governor was "filibustering." Cuomo dominated the interview talking about the writing of his second inaugural address, and the "physiology of thinking."

Taylor finally found an opening before his allotted time was up and "jumped in and asked if he had the fire in the belly for a presidential campaign."[26]

The answer was a classic Cuomo non-answer: "If you show me someone who has fire in the belly, I'll put seltzer in the mouth," Cuomo said. "I almost certainly wouldn't want to vote for that person. I would probably be very distrustful of anyone who had that feeling about the presidency. I would think of the presidency with awe, with vast trepidation. Not because I am not aware of my own capacities, as compared to other persons'. But because that position is the most important in the universe, and I have a dramatic sense of its significance. Just governing this state—which is a formidable task—I can imagine what it would mean to be President. One mistake and you could obliterate the known world. That is a literal fact. I don't have that kind of power as governor, thank God. . . ."

Cuomo continued: "Before you would consider running for it, you would have to be able to say to yourself that there is no one more capable who could achieve it with your help. And then you would have to conclude that you could will yourself, emotionally, to exhaust yourself in the process of trying to be President. If you decide that, then you could almost convert it into a responsibility. I don't want to sound unctuous about it, but that's just the way my mind works. . . . I felt that way about the governorship. I said to myself [before deciding to get into the 1982 gubernatorial race], 'I am better than those other people out there. I am better than [Ed] Koch. I am better than [Lew] Lehrman. It gave me huge reservoirs of strength. In 1977, when I was talked into running for mayor [a campaign Cuomo lost], I started the race by saying, 'I don't think they need me. I don't believe I am as good as these other people'—and I wasn't. I could never get past that truth. In a courtroom for money, I was able to win a lot of cases for clients that people thought couldn't be won. But I have great difficulty winning cases with myself that shouldn't be won."[27]

After completing this "soliloquy" of self-doubt, Cuomo went on to describe how a run would be a strain on his family.

But in January 1987, Cuomo began to explore what it would take to run for president, beginning with a meeting with top Democratic strategists, Robert Shrum and Kirk O'Donnell.

After a seven-hour meeting, Cuomo asked Shrum and O'Donnell: "Could I do my job as governor and still do the primaries?" Cuomo told Paul Taylor, after the 1988 election, that "They didn't say if I could or couldn't, but they started talking about all the time you had to spend in Iowa. After each of them finished, I said thank you very much but concluded that I couldn't possibly do it."[28]

Then on February 19, Cuomo stated during his regular weekly appearance on the "Ask the Governor" show that he would not be a candidate for president in 1988. In his statement, he pointed out that the Democratic Party "offers a number of presidential candidates who can prove themselves capable of leading the nation toward a more sane, a more progressive and a more humane future."[29]

Everyone, particularly Cuomo's family and staff, were shocked by his withdrawal. Cuomo did not talk over his announcement with anyone. "The only thing I did was to tell [Press Secretary] Marty [Steadman] a few hours in advance to call up reporters and make sure they were listening that night, so they wouldn't get hurt."[30]

Cuomo told Paul Taylor, "I wrote the statement the night before. Actually, I wrote two statements, so that the secretaries wouldn't know. I wrote the one that I read and I wrote another one saying that I was running. It drove 'em crazy."[31]

Cuomo aide Fred Martin, who earlier in the day discussed the presidential race with the governor and Democratic fundraiser Stanley Sheinbaum of California, was floored by the announcement:

"We talked," Martin said, "about a lot of things during the day and he never said, 'I'll take myself out.' But he's been enigmatic on the subject all along, even with the people closest to him. He made clear that this would be a decision he would make on his own."[32]

Andrew Cuomo put his own spin on his father's announcement the following day. "This is not the pitch to swing at. . . . This [is] not the year."[33]

State and national reporters were skeptical about Cuomo's non-candidacy, particularly when he leaked out he would accept a draft at the national convention.

Absent Cuomo, the stable of Democratic candidates was weak. As a result, Cuomo became the most "tantalizing non-candidate." *Newsweek*'s political reporters noted that Cuomo "remained a ghostly presence, the phantom of the opera of our politics, and the shadow he cast from the wings only lengthened as the real contenders began assembling onstage."[34]

Throughout 1987, the non-candidate was very visible. He started speaking out on foreign affairs and came out against President Reagan's Strategic Defense Initiative (a/k/a/ Star Wars).

In his May 1987 commencement speech at Johns Hopkins School of Advanced International Studies, Cuomo lectured the graduates on the need for "a truly democratic foreign policy, worldwide interdependence, the need for negotiation and conciliation, and the rule of law."[35]

As was his way, Cuomo tried to show that he was the middleman between the hawks and doves.

On the one hand, he opposed isolationism saying: "There is no way . . . to make ourselves secure from one another's aggressions and mistakes by building a wall around our borders—or an impenetrable shield reaching to the stars. You know that no man is an island. No woman. No village. No town. No state. No nation either."

Yet, on the other hand, Cuomo made clear he was a Cold Warrior, insisting Americans should not abandon "our wariness of the Soviet Union. Whether they are driven by historical fears or a desire for global supremacy spawned by Marxist-Leninist principles, we should not make the mistake of tempting them with weakness."[36]

Then the man who hated being away from home actually took a weeklong trip to the Soviet Union in the fall of 1987, presumably to improve his foreign policy credentials. The trip, journalist Elizabeth Drew pointed out, included a "number of blunders," particularly when the "Soviet hosts tricked him into endorsing a proposal they had made for a joint conference on human rights violations in the two countries."[37] After realizing he was duped, Cuomo quickly backtracked.

Shortly after his return, the non-candidate gave a speech in Washington before the Council on Foreign Relations. The speech, Drew reported, "was intelligent but did not, because it could not, convey deep knowledge; yet he drew a big crowd here, of the curious and the ambitious, and he had most of it in his hand."[38]

Cuomo's foreign policy activities, his frequent meetings with national political heavyweights, kept rumors alive that he would enter the race. "The governor was not above encouraging the talk with a coquettish wink now and then—a stubborn shyness about endorsing anyone else in the field, a periodic hint that he would not resist a legitimate draft by the party convention."[39]

He loved torturing and "playing mind and word games" with inquisitive reporters about his real intentions. On one occasion, he gleefully stated "It's great for non-candidates like me. We get to stand behind the batting cage and tell the players 'Do this. Do that. Slow it down.' But we never have to go in there and make a fool of ourselves."[40]

On another occasion when a reporter asked, "Why don't you want to be president?", Cuomo answered with a question, "Who says I don't want to be president?" Reporter: "Do you want to be president?" Cuomo: "No."[41]

When the former National Chairman of the Democratic Party and top Washington lawyer Robert Strauss met with Cuomo in 1987, the governor quizzed him on how an Italian-American candidate would fare in the Southern states.

Strauss replied, "They may not like Marios and they may not like Cuomos. They may not even like liberals. But they do like balls, and you've got 'em. You've got balls that clank, when you're walking down the hall."

Taken aback, Cuomo later told friends about Strauss's balls-that-clank remark, "You couldn't exactly make a bumper sticker out of that, let alone a soundbite, you couldn't do much with it at all except maybe liven up your diary on an otherwise slow day."[42]

The 1988 Democratic Route

By late spring 1988, the candidacies of most of the announced Democratic candidates had fallen by the wayside. The campaign of Delaware Senator Joe Biden—who Cuomo called a "dumb blonde"[43]—came abruptly to an end after he was accused of plagiarism and resume-inflating. Congressman Richard Gebhardt folded after he carried only his home state of Missouri on Super Tuesday. Senator Al Gore of Tennessee withdrew after his embarrassing "anti-Jackson" (Jesse Jackson, that is) campaign backfired in the April 19, 1988 New York State primary. Senator Gary Hart of Colorado couldn't withstand the Miami Herald 1987 story on his liaison with Donna Rice, and Senator Paul Simon of Illinois quit after losing the Iowa primary.

The two candidates still standing, in early 1988, were Governor Michael Dukakis of Massachusetts and the civil rights activist, Jesse Jackson.

While the Democrat contenders were slugging it out, Cuomo was kibitzing on the sidelines, condemning the process. Sydney Blumenthal, in his work on the 1988 campaign, *Pledging Allegiance: The Last Campaign of the Cold War*, reported the following Cuomo outburst:

> So far, through no fault of the candidates, we have heard phrases. We haven't even gotten to paragraphs, even sentences. . . . Interconnectedness with the Soviets? You can't discuss immense ideas in twenty-eight seconds. You wouldn't be able to do it in a debate for the presidency. You are not going to do it in the campaign. You should think of the world as a constant set of emergencies. Can we talk about them in the campaign?

And then the man who demanded scads of debates in 1977 and 1982 went on to say:

> I'm against debates. You don't govern that way. It's the last ability I want to see in a president sitting down with Gorbachev. I would call in the media, all of you, as many as I could get in the room. Today, we're going to do the media. What we'll do, you are going to ask questions on the economy. It may take five hours, six hours, twelve hours. Every question you can think of. . . . A candidate says the same one minute's worth of intelligence for six months. One hundred debates, it's the same one hundred times. You never get beyond it. I don't want that anymore. I want to get beyond that first minute. . . . Nothing

has been said that's real. A lot of it has to do with false values interpolated into the process. These are artificial values. We made celebrity important. We said there were stars that were not playing. . . .

Mario Cuomo? That's the biggest myth of all.[44]

Dukakis, the odds-on favorite to be the nominee, was a Greek-American and represented a Northeastern state. His profile was similar to Mario Cuomo except for one aspect: Dukakis, unlike Cuomo, had no personality. He was a short, boring technocrat.

And "Mario, the unready" played head games with Dukakis just as he had with Mondale four years earlier.

Newsweek journalists described the day Dukakis made a pilgrimage to Albany to kiss the ring:

> Their relationship had been a scratchy one almost from the beginning; Cuomo seemed to hold both Dukakis and his [Massachusetts's economic] Miracle in light regard, and the Dukakis team in turn was offended by Cuomo's relentless cuteness—his refusal to choose sides, his acts of aid and comfort to various enemies, his public flirtations with the possibility of a draft at the convention. It was plain, in any case, that he wasn't going to endorse anybody before the primary. Dukakis's visit was accordingly a *pro forma* one, which didn't improve his spirits; neither did the fact that Cuomo kept him and his party waiting for ten minutes past the appointed time for their audience.[45]

Cuomo's height also intimidated Dukakis who "puffed up his chest and put his hands on his hips, the banty rooster pose he struck when he felt intimidated or self-conscious about his size."[46]

After giving Dukakis a tour of the executive chamber in the state capitol, Cuomo showed him a secret button in a drawer of the governor's huge ceremonial desk. When Cuomo pushed it, a small platform popped out from the bottom of the back of the desk.

The platform had been installed for two-time presidential candidate

Governor Thomas E. Dewey. The former governor, who was very short, stood on it when he met with reporters. During Cuomo's show and tell, *Newsweek* reported, "Dukakis was silent as stone. Some of his people thought the slight was innocent, some thought it was intended, but they could feel the pain."[47]

Both Mario and Andrew Cuomo, who had meetings with the Dukakis people on his father's behalf, dangled the possibility of an endorsement, but never agreed to follow through. This led many to wonder if the governor "was still nourishing dreams of another scenario—a collapse of the frontrunning Dukakis that could be expected to set off a new round of demands for the governor of New York to rescue his party."[48]

In the end, Cuomo's endorsement didn't matter. After Dukakis won the New York Primary on April 19, 1988 with 55% of the vote, he became the presumptive nominee.

Cuomo's refusal to run in some ways enhanced his stature in the eyes of many Democrats. And this troubled the Dukakis camp as they prepared for the July 1988 Democratic convention.

Fearing some splendid Cuomo oratory might stir a delegate stampede to nominate the New York governor, the Dukakis campaign did not want Cuomo to have a significant role at the convention. They offered him the job of introducing the person who would formally nominate Dukakis, Arkansas Governor Bill Clinton. Cuomo politely declined this minor honor. He preferred no role at the convention.

Michael Dukakis left the Democratic Convention in Atlanta with a 17-point lead over the Republican nominee, Vice President George H.W. Bush. The lead, however, quickly dissipated for two reasons. Bush's campaign manager, Lee Atwater, ran a brilliant media campaign that portrayed Dukakis as a radical out of touch liberal "on issues like the Pledge of Allegiance, furloughs for first degree murder, ocean dumping and a strong national defense."[49]

Dukakis also proved to be an awful candidate. In the second debate on October 13, 1988, he blew the opening question, and for that matter the entire debate and the election, when he failed to give a passionate or emotional answer to a hypothetical question from CNN's Bernard Shaw on how he would react if his wife was raped and murdered. His answer was robotic: "I've opposed the death penalty during all my life," and then went on to cite, "how crime was reduced in his state without it and finally going into a short monologue on the need to fight drug traffic."[50]

Five days later, October 18, 1988, the NBC/Wall Street Journal poll had Bush leading Dukakis by 17 points. In other words, Dukakis went from up 17 to down 17—a 34-point swing in 90 days.

Cuomo did do a few things for Dukakis. He defended his opposition to the death penalty and hosted a rally at the Statue of Liberty.

In the end, no manner of help from Cuomo could have saved the Democratic candidate's doomed campaign. On November 8, 1988, George Bush won 54% to 46% with 426 electoral votes to Dukakis's 112.

Seconds after Michael Dukakis conceded his loss to George H.W. Bush, Mario Cuomo became a top contender for the 1992 Democratic presidential nomination.

Cuomo's media consultant, Dave Garth, began beating the drum for the governor shortly after the polls closed. "Obviously," Garth said, "the governor will be catapulted whether he likes it or not into a position of strong consideration. Mario would have taken Bush apart in the debates. . . . Mario may be a liberal, but he's macho enough to get away with it." Garth added, "[Cuomo] has some heavy thinking to do" about 1992.[51]

Lee Miringoff, pollster for the Marist College Institute for Public Opinion, agreed. "The look toward 1992 begins immediately and the story of 1988 for Mario Cuomo leaves him in a very good position." He is one of "perhaps a half dozen prominent national Democrats who will likely vie for control of the party."[52]

True to form, during a Brooklyn press conference the day after the election, Cuomo played down his prospects for 1992. "I don't say anything about 1992. . . . I'm not eager to get into another round of speculation."[53]

When asked why he thought Bush won, Cuomo replied, "How do I know why the guy won?"[54]

As for the reason Dukakis lost, he said, "He got fewer votes."[55]

After saying, "I'm tired of polls, political prognosticators, pundits, seers, analysts," the reporters pressed on. When asked about a party leadership role, Cuomo said, "I don't aspire to that."[56]

Reporter: "Why didn't he want a leadership role in the Party."

Cuomo: "I'm choosing to be Governor. Was that a sufficient explanation? If it's not, it's not."[57] Cuomo went on to show "a gesture of contempt" when asked about the 1992 race.

"Oh please," he said, "you can do better than that. Write what you want to write. If you want to write a tawdry little story that talks about '92, go ahead."[58]

"All of us," he continued, "should be thinking about coming together to solve these [national] problems."

"This man [Bush] isn't even sworn in yet. To start suggesting plans for his undoing is not the best way to govern as a nation."[59]

Later that day, Cuomo complained to *The New York Times* about the election process: "If there's anything about his election that strikes me, that I find debilitating, it's the harshness, the crassness, the negativism. . . . You do what you have to do to win. [But] on the way there, you gouge out eyes, you lie, you cheat. I find that disconcerting."[60]

Although Cuomo's national star was rising once again, before he could contemplate a run for president he had to convince the voters of New York he deserved a third term as their governor.

The 1990 Race for Governor

During most of his tenure as the state's chief executive, Cuomo had been pretty lucky. Thanks to the booming Reagan economy, state tax revenues were rising and this gave leverage to the governor when dealing with the Legislature on spending.

The governor was also lucky that control of the Legislature was divided, with Democrats controlling the Assembly and Republicans controlling the Senate.

That split permitted the governor to play the role he cherished: "honest broker."

During the annual budget negotiations, Cuomo would step in and negotiate compromises between the demands of the Senate and Assembly leaders. Just as he had done years earlier in Forest Hills, Cuomo would split the difference, giving each side a chunk of what they wanted—often more money than the state was taking in.

As a result of Cuomo's generous budget deals, total spending was increasing at double the rate of inflation. Between 1983 and 1989, per capita spending in New York increased 55.9% while the national average was 38.2%. In addition, since Cuomo became governor, the state payroll had grown by 31,000 employees by 1989. And when the budget for 1990–1991 projected a $1.8 billion deficit, the governor and the Legislature agreed to defer $400 million income tax cuts and imposed $1 billion in new taxes.[61]

As the 1990 election season began, Cynthia Green of the Citizens Budget Commission gave *Barron's* this gloomy analysis: "Throughout the eighties, the state has engaged in deficit financing—spending more than it takes in. The state's problems are structural. They're long-term. And they're not self-correcting."[62]

This did not bode well in an election year or for the four years to follow.

But Cuomo was also once again lucky that the state Republican Party remained financially and intellectually bankrupt.

The Republican bullpen was empty. And as its May 29 state convention neared, a frantic search for a gubernatorial candidate began. As a *Times* headline read: "GOP Short of Time and a Candidate."[63]

As party leaders panicked, State Senator Roy Goodman, a member of the search committee, and a colleague, investment banker Laurence Leeds, combed their address books and under "R" came across the name of economic consultant Dr. Pierre Rinfret. They telephoned him and after a brief conversation, Rinfret agreed to be the candidate, and he said he would put up $500,000 in "earnest" money.[64]

Cuomo's luck continued to hold out thanks to the Conservative Party. The day after the GOP convention adjourned, Conservative Party State chairman, Mike Long, announced that at his party's convention on Saturday, June 2, he would recommend that members of the state committee endorse Dr. Herbert London for governor.

London, a 6-foot, 5-inch, articulate scholar, who played basketball for Jamaica High School and Columbia University, was the founding director of New York University's Gallatin Division, an adult education program that emphasized a "Great Books" curriculum. A prolific author and public speaker, London served in 1984 and 1985 as a member of President Reagan's Committee for the Next Agenda.

The split between the Republicans and Conservatives boded well for Cuomo.

But there was even more good news for the Cuomo camp. Pierre Rinfret turned out to be a political nightmare for the GOP.

For one thing, *The New York Times* claimed Rinfret's use of the title "Doctor" was fraudulent. And it was discovered that Rinfret, who swore he was a Republican, was actually a registered Independent. Worst of all, Rinfret was not coming up with the money he had promised.

All in all, he was the loosest of loose cannons. To wit:

- He called incumbent Republican Comptroller Ned Regan an idiot and endorsed his opponent, Democrat-Liberal Carol Bellamy;
- He called the man who discovered him, Senator Roy Goodman, "one of the most destructive people in this state";
- He said Republican State Chairman Patrick Barrett "hasn't been a leader," and that he should resign.

Columnists Rowland Evans and Robert Novak wrote that Rinfret "has turned out to be a worse candidate than even his critics feared."[65]

By September, Republicans were jumping off the sinking Rinfret ship in droves and endorsing the Conservative candidate.

On October 6, 1990, at the *National Review* thirty-fifth anniversary dinner, the political world shook when President Bush's Housing Secretary Jack Kemp enthusiastically proclaimed: "I endorse Herb London for governor of New York State."

Several days later, another shoe dropped when former Republican gubernatorial candidate Lewis Lehrman also endorsed London.

The incumbent could hardly believe his luck. With a campaign chest of $8 million, Cuomo was able to sit back and watch the Republicans self-destruct. He spent his money to promote a very positive image of himself. He did face his opponents in two debates, although they were oddly scheduled: one during the World Series and the other the morning of the New York City Marathon.

Yet, despite all these breaks, the Election Day results were surprising. Cuomo barely mustered 53% of the vote, down 12% from four years earlier.

Cuomo received only 2,157,087 votes versus 865,948 (22%) for Rinfret and 827,614 (21%) for London, and 2% for the Right to Life Party candidate, Louis Wein.

Cuomo's coattails were also short. He failed to carry any Democrats into the state Senate and the $1.975 billion environmental bond proposal, for which he campaigned extensively, was defeated by a large margin.

The New York Times analysis, titled "Cuomo, Omnipotence Blunted," stated that, "Mr. Cuomo, who under better circumstances rarely misses an opportunity to meet the press, was uncharacteristically silent yesterday on the subject of the election. . . . In his own race, Mr. Cuomo showed unexpected weakness . . . against opponents who early on in the race had been dismissed as sure losers."[66]

As in 1986, Cuomo appeared to be a sore winner. It actually took two full days for Cuomo to come out of seclusion. On Thursday, November 8, he admitted that New Yorkers had sent him "more of a message than a mandate" and that "New Yorkers no longer trust their government." Cuomo also said, "The signals that did go out, as regrettable as they are—the defeat of the bond issue . . . the fact that we didn't get the margins we wanted, we didn't get the exultant shout that we wanted from the people—that can be instructive to us." The *Times* reported that "the Governor pledged to heed the electorate's warning to cut spending and keep a lid on taxes." He added, "We're going to do all the hard things. We're going to bite the bullet. And we're going to do the courageous thing without punishing little people or exploiting the rich people."[67]

Mario for President?

Whenever Mario Cuomo was asked by journalists if he planned or was thinking about running for president, he would generally dismiss the question and ridicule the questioner.

Speaking before the election to the editorial board of the *Utica Observer Dispatch*, when asked, "If re-elected, did the governor plan to finish his four-year term or might he make a run for president?" Cuomo replied: "I have no plans to run, and no plans to make plans."

Later in the interview, when pressed with essentially the same question ("We don't expect you'll be announcing your candidacy for president today. Are you going to pledge to finish your full four-year term, if you're re-elected in November?"), an agitated Cuomo gave this longer reply:

I'm not even going to pledge to live for four years. That is, frankly, a dumb question, to be honest with you. How would you answer that? How does anybody even answer that who had any brains?

I don't have any plans to run. I am not delighted by the prospect, and I never have been—for a lot of reasons that are difficult to explain to people. I'm not going to rule it out, nor should I rule it out. How can you, and I never did.

What I've said always was the same thing: I have no plans to run, and no plans to make plans. . . . It's very hard for me to believe that you can't find somebody better than me in the Democratic Party. Very hard for me to believe that. And I'm not eager to believe that. . . . To be the most important leader in the free world—you think that's fun? I would regard that with great awe and circumspection.[68]

Yet, a month later, the *Poughkeepsie Journal* reported that in Hyde Park, the hometown of Franklin Roosevelt, "Cuomo hints at '92."

According to the report, the governor made a slip about the White House, "and when that little slip came out the applause was wild."

Cuomo said, "I need a little more help. I've gotten to the age where I need just a little more help. For just a few more years, you need me in the White H_ _ _. Oops! I guess I kept you a sentence too late."[69]

When presidential campaign chroniclers Jack Germond and Jules Witcover spent a day on the 1990 campaign trail with Cuomo, the governor quickly concluded that they were going to write "another dumb story" about his "ambitions for the presidency" and that he would enjoy running against the Yale elitist George H.W. Bush.

Banging his fist on a table, Cuomo declared, "That would be self-aggrandizing. It would be the height of egoism and the height of selfishness." He went on to explain that he hasn't ruled out a run because "They'd say, 'He must have colon cancer, he must have a Mafia uncle.'"[70]

Was he or was he not running? That was the question on the minds of

Democratic Party officials, political pundits, and most importantly, the potential contenders for the 1992 presidential nomination.

Liberal commentator, Michael Tomasky, believing Cuomo's shillyshallying was part of a plan, wrote in *The Nation* (October 22, 1990):

> The scenario for Cuomo's putative candidacy goes something like this: He can continue to play it coy with the press well into the campaign season, not saying whether he will or won't run, even after the others have finished dusting the snows of Iowa from their boots. As the news media become more and more impatient, and unimpressed, with the likely gaggle of candidates, calls will beckon from the Op-Ed pages and the "well-placed sources in the D.N.C." for Cuomo to jump in. As the primary season heads toward full pitch, the Jackson Factor, assuming the Reverend runs, will take hold, starting a scramble for a white candidate who's good on the stump.[71]

Cuomo's third inauguration on January 1, 1991, was a very low-key event. After taking his oath of office before 80 people—as opposed to 5,000 in 1983—there was no speech and no party and no 19-gun salute afterwards. The entire event was over in six minutes.

With the state facing a budget deficit as high as $4 billion, Cuomo thought it inappropriate to spend tax dollars on inaugural hoopla.

"The months immediately ahead of us are going to be perhaps more difficult than any since the Great Depression," he told reporters. "But the state has overcome fires and floods and Depression and wars, always bringing us to a higher ground."[72]

When asked about when he would make a decision on running for president, Cuomo gave a version of his standard answer: "If I were going to make plans, or plan to make plans, I would have to start with that question."

In a follow-up question as to what the answer to "that question" might be, the governor said, "I haven't made plans to make plans." Laughing, he added that he gave that non-answer "just to show you that nothing will be different in 1991."[73]

As Cuomo continued to deny presidential ambitions and made it clear that dealing with state's fiscal and economic problems were his only concern, he would, from time to time, make news on the national level.

In May, for instance, Cuomo made disapproving statements about the Democratic Leadership Council (DLC).

Founded in 1985, the DLC was a centrist organization that held that the leftist notions of the McGovern wing of the party should be abandoned to appeal to working-class voters. Council members included Governor Bill Clinton, Senator Al Gore, and Congressman Richard Gebhardt.

Cuomo, waving the banner of liberalism, objected to the DLC because of its "implicit position that we have something we have to apologize for, and now we have to move to the middle."[74]

Two months later at a meeting of the United States Conference of Mayors, guest speaker Cuomo attacked the Bush Administration's handling of the economy. He urged Democrats to pass a recovery plan to force Bush to take a stand on it and to dare him to veto it. He pledged to the mayors, "I'll do anything you ask me to do—as governor."[75]

At an October gathering of long-time supporters at the Regency Hotel in Manhattan, and after his standard tap-dance about not being worthy to run for president, Vincent Albanese, a big-time real estate developer, asked "Well, that's very interesting and we believe that and we understand what you're saying, but what about us? What if we thought the country needed you?"[76]

Finding himself on a spot with these loyal financial contributors, Mario had replied, "I'll tell you what I'll do, I will think about it for the first time and I'll be honest about it." He went on to say that he would have his son Andrew examine what it would take to set up a campaign, to study the political process and calendar. Pointing out it could take up to six weeks to complete the task, he also reminded his audience that the state financial problems might take precedence over a presidential candidacy.

Within an hour after the meeting adjourned, it was leaked to the press that he was thinking about running.

An annoyed Cuomo complained that he gave a courteous "perfunctory" response to friends. "I said, 'sure I'll think about it. I'm always thinking about it.' I said I'd have to be mindless not to think about it. I don't talk about it, but I think about it. Of course, I do. I said absolutely nothing. You can't honestly say you have a big story. If you're asking me did you say anything new, the answer is no."[77]

Then at an October 25th event sponsored by the Radio and Television News Directors Association held in New York City, Cuomo made unprepared remarks and took questions. When the obligatory question about running for president came up, Cuomo answered with a question; "How do you run and service government?" He thought he might have to run and leave behind unsolved a bunch of New York's pending problems. "Do you do that and announce OK now that I've told you how bad things are I want you to know I'm leaving for New Hampshire. . . . I'm going to Iowa and New Hampshire to tell people how to save the country."[78]

To put people off, Cuomo said in the summer and early fall of 1991 that while he was thinking about running, he did not have to make a decision until late November, several weeks before the December filing deadline in New Hampshire.

One person pushing for a decision in November was Ron Brown, the Chairman of the National Democratic Committee. Brown, a former Cuomo law student at St. John's University, was anxious to get all wavering candidates off the dime, particularly the N.Y. governor. That's because "the threat of a Cuomo candidacy was freezing Democratic activists and contributors, who by this point might have been choosing another candidate to support."[79]

One candidate, Senator Tom Harkin, confirmed Brown's concern. "A lot of my supporters in a lot of places," he said, "were just hanging back, waiting to see what Cuomo was going to do. I heard it constantly."[80]

Brown, frustrated because Mario refused to take his calls, leaned on Cuomo aides to get the governor to make up his mind. "I felt like we had to move the thing off dead [center]," Brown told reporters Germond and Witcover. "We had to know what the field was and who the choices were. And as long as Mario and others were out there undecided, it kept people from focusing on what we had to do to get ready for a general election campaign."[81]

Cuomo continued to duck a deadline. When asked if his cutoff date would be "Thanksgiving Day or New Year's Day or Valentine's Day or St. Patrick's Day," he answered: "All of those are possibilities."[82]

Then on Sunday, November 24, in an appearance on ABC's "This Week" show with David Brinkley, George Will, and Sam Donaldson, Cuomo had this run-in with Donaldson over his possible candidacy:

Mr. DONALDSON: But you will make a decision before Election Day next year. I mean, at some point, it'll be mooted, won't it?

Gov. CUOMO: It will—I will have to make the decision on the best evidence I have at the moment at the point when I am convinced it's bad for the Democrats for me to delay them any further, even if I don't have all the facts.

Mr. DONALDSON: But is it still not bad for them? I mean, all these guys are out there in Iowa and elsewhere, frozen in amber?

Gov. CUOMO: Oh, that's silly, Sam. Even for you, that's silly. They're not frozen in amber. Why weren't they frozen so they didn't declare? They didn't wait for me. I'm not relevant to their lives. That's silly. They're not waiting for me. They're writing their speeches, they declared for President, they're running around. They don't need me. I'm not that important.

Mr. DONALDSON: But it's important that the Governor—

Gov. CUOMO: I'm not even popular.

Mr. DONALDSON: Well, I don't know where to go. There are so many things. It's gotten to be a game—"waiting for Mario," and in just saying that, of course, I've used your first name.

Gov. CUOMO: Excuse me, can I make a suggestion? Can I make—I don't like games, so don't play it.

Mr. DONALDSON: Well—sorry, if I may—with all due respect, just because you hand down an admonition—"Don't play it"—in the game of politics, that doesn't mean that everyone's going to say, "Oh well, of course."

Gov. CUOMO: What would you suggest I do, Sam?

Mr. DONALDSON: Well, a lot of people are suggesting you make up your mind and make an announcement—

Gov. CUOMO: I have made up my mind.

Mr. DONALDSON: —and either get on with it or get off.

Gov. CUOMO: Sam, I have—I'm sorry that you're perturbed by the tremendous delay in my decision-making process, which is now into its fifth week. Imagine, I'm sure all the candidates spent maybe six or seven days. I'm sure you would do it in an hour, shaving—"Oh, time for me to run for President."

I'm spending now my fifth week as Governor of the State of New York, trying to gather all the facts, trying to decide—will it help the City of New York, which has a deficit problem which is very substantial; will it help my own state; is it too complicated; if I leave to campaign four or five days a week, will that—

Mr. DONALDSON: But you know, Governor—

Gov. CUOMO: —excuse me—when the party or the candidates persuade me, "Governor, we don't have any more time, I'm Governor, I'm committed to do it, I can't run," then that's what I'll do.[83]

Pundits on both the left and the right were frustrated with Cuomo's "This Week" performance.

From the right, George Will wrote in his *Washington Post* column: "Is the Cuomo drama bound for Broadway, which in politics means Pennsylvania Avenue? Not with the current script. Cuomo continues on the losing side of a monologue with himself, which is not easy to do but is less remarkable than this. He may go from being a fad to being a bore without an interval of being as interesting as he could be."[84]

And from the left, *Times* columnist Leslie Gelb wrote:

His lofty and powerful mind often works its way deep into the black hole of immobility and indecision. Unlike leaders who concentrate on the rule and their goals, he is forever stymied by exceptions.

He transforms everything into an argument, and often seems more interested in winning arguments than governing. He turns the slightest slight into mortal combat. . . .

Mr. Cuomo, brilliant and charismatic, has yet to master his temperament and mind, and has yet to make his record in office—and cannot be a worthy presidential candidate or president until he does.[85]

On December 16, just four days before the New Hampshire primary filing deadline, Cuomo appeared to come up with a convoluted rationale for running while grappling with a budget deficit and the uncooperative

Senate Republicans in Albany: "If you made up your mind that [the Republican Senate] were doing this only to prevent you from running, then the solution would be to run. Then they would no longer have the motive to show you up. And that would save the state, by running for president."[86]

Meanwhile, Cuomo political aides were looking for office space, organizing fund raisers and handing out economic position papers.

Cuomo had no choice but to accept December 20 as his final deadline. To be prepared, two planes were hired—one for the governor and one for members of the press—and were waiting on an Albany runway to fly him to Manchester where a car would be waiting to drive him to Concord to file a statement declaring his candidacy and to pay the $1,000 entry fee. Just in case a sudden snowstorm prevented the plan from taking off, a surrogate was on the ground ready to file.

As the clock was ticking, Cuomo prepared two statements, just as he did in 1987 when he announced he would not run for president in 1988. One announced he was in the race, the other stated he was out due to the stalled budget negotiations with the Republicans.

On the afternoon of Friday, December 20, scores of reporters and hundreds of supporters were waiting at the New Hampshire statehouse for Cuomo to arrive.

But, back in Albany, the governor was getting cold feet, and at 3:37 p.m.—one hour and a half before the 5:00 p.m. deadline—Cuomo commenced a press conference and delivered a four-minute statement. After accusing Senate Republican Majority Leader Ralph Marino and his conference members of refusing to compromise on a budget solution, "for their own purposes," he went on to say, "It's my responsibility as governor to deal with this extraordinarily severe problem. Were it not, I would travel to New Hampshire today and file my name as a candidate in its presidential primary. That was my hope and I prepared for it. But it seems to me I cannot turn my attention to New Hampshire while this threat hangs over the head of the New Yorkers that I have sworn to put first."

While Cuomo confessed, "I would be less than honest if I did not admit to you my regret at not having the chance to run for president," he went on to say that even though it was possible to enter later primaries and be a contender once the budget impasse was resolved, he decided against that alternative. He accepted advice from party chairman Ron Brown. "I accept the judgment of the national chairman of our party," he said, "that it would be in the best interest of the Democratic Party that I abandon any such effort now as to avoid whatever inconvenience and disruption to the process is created by the uncertain possibility of another candidacy."[87]

As for a draft movement, he told reporters: "You don't get drafted for the Presidency. Whoever wins the primary ought to be the candidate."

Bill Powers, the chairman of the New York Republican Party said, "After months of fence-straddling, Cuomo looked in the mirror and realized that he wasn't up to the job of running the country." And state Senator Ralph Marino said:

> We had C-Span on, and we're all watching C-Span, the world was awaiting this decision. We thought he was going to run. As we're speaking, he said he wasn't going to run, and blamed me. I about dropped the phone. It was news to me. Unnecessary. I thought he could have run, and [Lieutenant Governor] Stan Lundine carried on, which is what I thought he would do. He'd be running around the country, running for president, and telling Lundine what he wanted done. I almost had a heart attack when he mentioned my name.[88]

Most commentators were stunned and not a few were angry. In a front-page commentary in the *Times* titled, "A Cage of Equivocation," Margaret Kolbert wrote: "Gov. Mario M. Cuomo brought his strangely drawn-out agony of decision to a close today, not with a bang, but with a news conference. And even as the final uncanny act was playing out, he remained firmly on character: equivocal, eloquent and ultimately trapped by his own ambivalence."[89]

Columnist Mary McGrory wrote:

> The first half of the news conference was enough to make any Democrat who had followed him down the garden path say good riddance. The feeling was compounded when, asked if his decision represented an end to presidential aspirations, he said, in his maddening, Delphic style, that "you will have to make the analysis."

Democrats will have to accept the no as final. They will have to say that the romance that began in 1984, when Cuomo swept them off their feet with his convention keynote address, is absolutely over. He may want to be president but not enough. He would not be a happy warrior. . . .[90]

In *The Washington Post* "News Analysis," journalist E.J. Dionne wrote: "When the New York governor was talking about 'the ugly contradiction' involved in seeking the presidency at a time when doing so might endanger his own state, he seems disengaged, decidedly unhappy, thoroughly unenthusiastic. . . . The notion that one of the most powerful politicians in America could somehow be the victim of forces beyond his control may seem peculiar to Washington. But it's very much in keeping with a certain fatalism that has characterized Cuomo's political career, and his powerful sense that no individual is ever fully the master of his own fate."[91]

And *The Washington Post* published a disparaging editorial the day after Cuomo withdrew:

> Gov. Cuomo has said no. He should not now be made into the Elvis of the campaign—a declared non-candidate whose candidacy is believed to live. . . .
>
> There has been a self-defeating aspect to the endless hand-wringing over the Cuomo candidacy: the more people talk as if it were or would have been or still could be the salvation of the Democrats, the more they needlessly and unfairly disparage candidates they also hardly know. They need to put an end to the fantasy of a Cuomo candidacy that would end all their troubles. Even if Gov. Cuomo had said yes, the campaign was not going to work out that way.

Months later, the Hamlet of the Hudson gave his own cryptic analysis of his presidential ambitions:

> I have difficulty with the notion of wanting it badly. I'm not sure what that means. I'm afraid some people want the office

too much and I've always tried to guard against that. If you say, 'Did you have a great hunger for it.' I was always afraid of people who had too great hunger for it. I thought they had the process backward. It shouldn't be that you desire the office and then you go out and get it. It should be that you are better than anybody else who's available. Otherwise, it's a very difficult thing to justify.[92]

The Cuomo-Clinton Shuffle

Politicians across the nation were stunned by Cuomo's announcement, but none more than the governor of Arkansas, Bill Clinton.

The Clinton campaign viewed Cuomo as the biggest roadblock in their quest for the 1992 nomination.

In his memoir, *My Life*, Clinton conceded that "for more than two months after I announced, the campaign was shadowed by the specter that there might be yet another candidate, Governor Mario Cuomo of New York."

He continued:

> Cuomo was a huge figure in Democratic politics, our finest orator and a passionate defender of Democratic values during the Reagan-Bush years. Many people thought the nomination was his for the asking, and for a good while I thought he would ask. He took some hard shots at the DLC, at me, and at my ideas on welfare reform and national service. I was magnanimous in public, but I fumed in private and said some things about Mario I regret. I think I was so stung by his criticism because I had always admired him. In mid-December he finally announced that he wouldn't run. When some of my hard comments about him became public during the New Hampshire primary, all I could do was apologize. Thank goodness, he was big enough to accept it.[94]

And the fragile relationship between the two governors was further tested in late January 1992, when the tape recording of a telephone call between Clinton and his long-time mistress, Gennifer Flowers, became public.

At one point during the taped conversation there is a discussion concerning Cuomo's huge name recognition. Flowers tells Clinton she does not like Cuomo's "demeanor." Clinton replies, "Boy, is he so aggressive," and goes on to say that the New York governor was "a mean son of a bitch."[95]

Flowers agrees and adds that she would not be shocked if Cuomo "didn't have some Mafioso major connections." To which Clinton says, "Well, he acts like one."[96]

Upon hearing of the publication of the conversations, Clinton, who was campaigning in Houston, immediately went into damage control mode.

He told reporters that even though he had not heard the tape, nevertheless he wanted Governor Cuomo "to know if anything was said I didn't mean any offense by it."

"If the remarks on the tape left anyone with the impression that I was disrespectful to either Gov. Cuomo or Italian-Americans, then I deeply regret it."

"At the time the conversation was held, there had been some political give and take between myself and the governor and I meant simply to imply that Gov. Cuomo is a tough, worthy competitor."[97]

Cuomo would have none of it. The perturbed governor said of Clinton's apology, "What do you mean 'if.'"

"If you are not capable of understanding what was said, then don't try apologizing."

"This is part of an ugly syndrome that strikes Italian-Americans, Jewish people, blacks, women, all the ethnic groups."[98] It is "an indication of snide condescension. Bigotry."[99]

While the "comeback kid" survived the early primaries, he and his staff always kept one eye on Cuomo. Their attitude was best expressed by one Clinton aide who said, "We haven't begun to think about how Mario Cuomo will f*** us."[100]

When late in the primary season, California Governor Jerry Brown appeared to threaten the inevitability of Clinton, Cuomo struck. He summoned Brown up to Albany—as he had Mondale in '84 and Dukakis in

'88—and after a tête-à-tête, Cuomo announced that the battle for the nomination remained "wide open." (It really wasn't, but Cuomo's pronouncement jarred the Clinton operation.)

To make amends, Cuomo was put on Clinton's short V.P. list. "I'd love to pick Cuomo for one reason," Clinton said, "if you let me be in the room when they tell [Vice President] Dan Quayle."[101]

Clinton's staff people were not thrilled with the prospect of having an uncontrollable candidate on the ticket, but they were pretty certain he would decline.

And they were right—Cuomo blew them off and his name was taken off the short list.

As a consolation prize, Clinton asked Cuomo to give the nominating speech at the convention that was to be held at New York City's Madison Square Garden in July.

Cuomo being Cuomo was ambivalent about accepting the task, but his former student, Chairman Brown, leaned on him to acquiesce.

Just as he had tortured Mondale in 1988, Cuomo wouldn't share an advance copy of his nominating speech with Clinton's nervous senior staff. "What would Mario say," they asked. "Would he sound enthusiastic, as if he really meant it? Would he try to undercut Clinton on some policy question on which they disagreed?"[102]

Early on the day Cuomo was to deliver the speech, he called the one Clinton aide who was not one of the Arkansas gang and was known to be Cuomo's biggest fan in the Clinton camp, George Stephanopoulos.

Cuomo began to recite a draft of the speech. Stephanopoulos wrote in his memoir, *All Too Human*, that "Cuomo was proud of his speech, and the more he recited, the more he seemed to convince himself that Clinton really was our 'new captain for a new century.'"[103]

That night Cuomo delivered another "barnburner." After officially placing Clinton's name in nomination, an exuberant Cuomo proclaimed, "I want to clap my hands and throw my fists in the air."[104]

Speaking to Cuomo later that night, an overwhelmed Clinton said, "Oh Mario, thank you."

A comical Cuomo replied: "I gave it just the way you wrote it, except I left out the part about how handsome you are."

Clinton: "God, it was wonderful. I'll never forget it."

Cuomo: "I'm a good lawyer, like you, I can make up a case when I have to. Tonight I didn't."[105]

On November 3, 1992, William Jefferson Clinton was elected with a 43% vote plurality, the 42nd president of the United States. His election effectively ended any hopes of a Cuomo presidency.

CHAPTER 12

UNDERSTANDING THE HAMLET

ON THE HUDSON

When Bill and Hillary Clinton were listening to the nominating speech, "Clinton mused that Cuomo would make a perfect chief justice, Hillary nodded."

Later in the year, Clinton specifically mentioned that Cuomo was the one person who fit his job description for the post. Cuomo had "A fine mind, good judgment, wide experience in the law and in the problems of real people, and someone with a big heart."[1]

Many people agreed with Clinton and believed Cuomo would be a great foil for another Italian-American from Queens, Supreme Court Justice Antonia Scalia. (Interestingly, Cuomo was a fan of Scalia. When Reagan nominated him in 1986, Cuomo told the *New York Post* that he is "an intelligent and hard-working judge, a terrific judge, and should be confirmed immediately. I'll take on the whole Democratic Party if they try anything on Scalia.")[2]

Little did they know that exactly two months after Clinton was sworn in as president, March 30, 1993, Supreme Court Justice Byron R. White, a Kennedy appointee, would tender his resignation.

Ten days later on March 30, Clinton aides George Stephanopoulos and Gene Sperling were on a conference call with Governor Cuomo urging him to take the seat White was vacating.

The talking points prepared for the conversation gave these reasons Cuomo should accept the appointment:

- This will be the fulfillment of your career.
- You could read and write on the big issues.
- No other job leaves a longer legacy.

- Look at history: Frankfurter, Holmes, Brandeis.
- One hundred years from now your words will still be changing people's lives and protecting their rights.
- You've been training for this all your life.[3]

Cuomo's response to the sales pitch, "I can't believe you've descended to this level of groveling exploitation."[4]

Cuomo, who had ducked two calls from the president in the previous 24 hours, was beginning to grate on Clinton and his aides. Stephanopoulos, who describes the events in his memoir, was quickly getting annoyed with Cuomo's reprisal of Hamlet. He complained that "Cuomo didn't take the call because he couldn't decide what to do—again."[5]

Clinton was also losing his patience with Cuomo. He thought the governor should be more deferential to him now that he was president.

On April 1, Clinton finally connected with Cuomo by phone while traveling to a summit in Europe. Cuomo made it clear that he was "leaning against being considered but would think about it."[6]

An annoyed Clinton went along because he was focused on the upcoming summit with the Russian president, Boris Yeltsin.

By April 7, Stephanopoulos, who was by necessity communicating with Andrew Cuomo, said the clock had run out and a decision was needed.

Andrew, after spending hours on the phone with his father, was told "If you want me to, I'll call Clinton and take it."

However, shortly thereafter, the governor sent a fax to President Clinton declining the honor, citing his duty to the New Yorkers who had elected him.

In June, when Clinton had narrowed his choices to Ruth Bader Ginsburg and Stephen Breyer, Andrew Cuomo called Stephanopoulos and told him that Mario told political columnists Roland Evans and Robert Novak, that if the president called him and asked him to join the Supreme Court, "I would not say no to the president."[7]

A skeptical Stephanopoulos asked if this was for real. Andrew, putting him on hold, called Mario, who told him he would say "yes."

A reluctant Clinton agreed to think about it and consulted with the pro-Cuomo Hillary.

Clinton came back saying "Mario will sing the song of America. It'll be like watching Pavarotti at Christmastime."

After Andrew was told the president was interested in making the offer, he said "Mario will do it because the president wants him to. . . . *BUT* the president really has to put it to him. Unless he puts it to him, he won't do it. He needs to use strong language, has to tell Mario he has to do it."

That "But" caused Stephanopoulos to think, "Here we go again."[8]

Meanwhile, Clinton told top staff members that going with Cuomo was "the right thing to do." Nominating Cuomo would make "a big, powerful statement," he said. "If he doesn't say 'yes,' we'll announce Ginsburg tomorrow."

Shortly thereafter, Stephanopoulos was told that Cuomo called asking to speak to him. The nervous press secretary heard what he called a "soliloquy":

> George, Andrew's been trying very hard to bring me to change my view, but I feel that I would be doing a disservice to the president. I feel that I would not be able to do what we all need, including supporting the president politically. I surrender so many opportunities of service if I take the Court. I feel that I would abandon what I have to do. I don't want the president to think that I might say yes.
>
> It's important to do what you believe you can do. The only two times I didn't were disasters. That's what I'm afraid of. It would be untrue to myself. It's wrong to enter a marriage that you don't feel. I don't want to be in a position to say no. The president shouldn't call me.[9]

After hearing Cuomo out, Stephanopoulos said, "Let me be clear: If he calls you, you will not accept. Will you turn the president down?

"Yes," Cuomo replied.[10]

Mario Cuomo, one of the brightest and most dynamic Democrats of his generation, turned down opportunities to run for the nation's highest office and to be appointed to the nation's highest court. Why couldn't he bring himself to accept either?

Although Cuomo gave dubious rationales and excuses, which will be quoted later in this chapter, it's unlikely that the exact reason will ever be known.

Nevertheless, after much research, this author has concluded that there are at least four possible explanations for Cuomo's decisions not to throw his hat into the presidential ring or don a black robe.

I. The Media

On April 10, 1985, a 1,700-word news story was published by *The Washington Post* titled, "Cuomo's Record at Midterm Nicks Presidential-Timber Image." In the article, national reporter Margot Hornblower raised this question, "Mario Matthew Cuomo, governor of New York, media star, orator, new hope of Democrats: Could it be that the man is a mere politician?"

Hornblower described how Cuomo's record was "increasingly under fire" and quoted complaints lodged by editorial writers, environmentalists, good government leaders, etc. One unnamed "high-level Democratic operative" summed up the growing perception of Cuomo when he told the *Post*: "He's a visionary. His weakness is governing."[11]

The article also pointed out that many who criticized the governor insisted on anonymity because they feared retribution. One suburban congressman told Hornblower, "Mario is an Old Testament Christian rather than a New Testament Christian. He's vindictive. He has an enemies list. I sort of view him as a liberal Nixon."

Mario Cuomo was livid over the reporting and "struck back fiercely."[12]

Coincidentally, Cuomo happened to be in Washington the day the piece was published, and on a CNN appearance, he was asked about Hornblower's reporting: "All of this criticism was in the form of blind quotes except for one line," Cuomo said. "We don't do a whole lot of that in my state. . . . This article in *The Washington Post* was mostly from anonymities, which means that there's no way of evaluating who was supposed to have said this."[13] In fact, Hornblower's story contained seven on-the-record critical quotes and just four off-the-record. In any case, Cuomo went on the offensive.

He ordered one of his top aides to search for the unnamed sources. The "suburban congressman" turned out to be Democratic Representative Thomas Downey of Long Island. Downey was persuaded to send a letter to *The Washington Post* recanting his earlier criticism.

The thin-skinned Cuomo's reaction to the *Post* story was not atypical. He distrusted reporters, claimed they were lazy and incompetent, and would go after them relentlessly.

Harry Rosenfeld, the long-time editor of the *Albany Times Union*, described Cuomo's reactions to the press thusly:

> He proved to be a riveting guest although not always a charming one. Mario Cuomo sometimes turned hostile when, from his perspective, he was sorely provoked. This did not necessarily take a whole lot . . . but in any hypersensitivity competition, Mario Matthew Cuomo easily won the trophy. He personalized his disagreements and whatever motivated him also may have caused him to be overly touchy about the kind of criticisms political figures routinely engender. Cuomo's counterpunches often were perceived as bullying or arrogance. His poor relations with the press were a concern when his name was in play for the 1988 Democratic presidential nomination.[14]

Reporters would be "Mario-ed," when they received very early morning calls to their home from the governor complaining about a news article.

After Jeffrey Schmalz of *The New York Times* reported that in one speech Cuomo "had spoken in general terms, avoiding the details that could prove sticky politically," an angry Cuomo attacked him demanding to know if he had "a button on your word processor that you press and that spews out: 'Cuomo was vague, Cuomo didn't give details'?"[15]

On other occasions, Mario went so far as to threaten to destroy a journalist's career for writing what he perceived as negative comments. He told Schmalz, "I could end your career. Your publisher doesn't even know who you are."[16]

On another occasion, Adam Nagourney (then the *Daily News* Albany bureau chief) had an "intense, at times unpleasant" argument with Cuomo, during which the governor said, "I could destroy you if I wanted to."[17]

As for the governor's attitude towards the *Daily News*, Cuomo told Associated Press reporter Marc Humbert, "They'll never get another phone call from me. They can call from a burning building and say 'You're the captain of the Fire Department' and they'll have to learn how to fly."[18]

When traveling with a group of reporters around the state, Cuomo made a point of telling them, "Don't flatter yourself into thinking that you're the best way to reach the public. When I go to you, I don't reach the public directly, you do. When I go electronically, I reach the public. If I want to reach the public, I shouldn't be talking to you, I should be talking to a radio microphone."[19]

On yet another occasion, when the governor threatened to forbid his staff from making "off the record" comments to the press, he backed off when reminded he had often been an anonymous source himself.

After covering Cuomo in Albany for several years, Jeffrey Schmalz concluded, "Cuomo seems to view himself as the outsider. He takes each criticism as a threat—as if each could topple him—and he responds in kind. . . . A reporter who writes a negative article can't be doing so with any honesty; it must be because the governor did not return a phone call, or leaked a story to another newspaper."[20]

After Cuomo called reporters "spoiled" and threatened to "restrict access" and to cut down "on weekend phone calls and limiting press conferences to one topic," the Albany press corps began referring to him as Captain Queeg, "the paranoid captain overthrown in *The Caine Mutiny*."[21]

Obviously, Mario Cuomo did not like the press. In fact, he hated their questioning and despised them for poking around in his life and questioning his policies and motives.

In an April 1987 essay in the *Washington Journalism Review* titled "Cuomo Leaves The Ring: Did Press Problems Play a Part?", Michael Oreskes described an incident the day Cuomo announced he would not run for president in 1988:

> Mario M. Cuomo pulled out of the 1988 race for president with a gesture to the media. The gesture was this: Cuomo placed his fingertips against his throat and then swept them upward until they flipped off the edge of his chin.
>
> Cuomo delivered this gesture, which for family newspapers loosely translates as "shove off," at a news conference where he was asked by reporters for the thousandth time if he had any message for them about his presidential ambitions. A few

hours later, he went on a radio call-in show, his very favorite media forum, and announced, "I will not be a candidate."

He then walked out of the radio station and refused to answer any questions from the assembled reporters. Mario Cuomo was not giving anyone else control of his message this night.[22]

Oreskes, who covered Cuomo for the *Times* as Albany bureau chief (1982–1985), concluded that Cuomo's decision not to run "was heavily influenced by the fact that a Cuomo presidential campaign was going to be subjected—indeed, was already being subjected—to intense scrutiny of precisely the sort that infuriates Cuomo and sometimes exposes what critics call his 'dark side'."[23]

II. Scrutiny of the Cuomo Family

On the last day of February in 1990, Mario Cuomo's 25-year-old daughter, Madeline, had been in a traffic accident in the Albany area. Her driver's license was expired at the time, and she was charged accordingly. Except the charge was not made at the scene.

The story, first reported in the March 1 edition of the *Post*, was later picked up by the Associated Press. According to the AP, Miss Cuomo had been "charged with driving without a valid license, a full day after she was in a traffic accident" but that police said "the failure to ticket her earlier was an oversight not favoritism."

According to an Albany Police Sergeant Robert Wolfgang, "In the confusion, it was an oversight that [the officer on the scene] did not note the expiration of the license. When it was brought to his attention . . . he investigated further and issued the ticket."[24]

As a father, Cuomo was livid that his daughter's lapsed driver's license, which could be easily renewed, had become headline news. As a politician, however, he had to know that even a minor indiscretion of an elected official's relative is a story. Nevertheless, Cuomo took out his anger on the entire Albany press corps, refusing to talk to them for days.

Cuomo grew even angrier when his son Andrew became the subject of news stories.

As described earlier in this book, Andrew served during Governor Cuomo's first two years in office as a dollar-a-year Special Assistant to the governor. Wanting to branch out on his own, Andrew left Albany and joined the office of the Manhattan District Attorney Robert Morgenthau.

A year later, Andrew became a partner in the firm of Blutrich, Falcone and Miller. Originally founded by Jerry Weiss, a close friend of Mario Cuomo and his special counsel when he was lieutenant governor, Weiss left the firm after Cuomo's 1982 election, and it was reorganized. The five remaining partners included Lucille Falcone, a Cuomo family friend and fundraiser for Governor Cuomo's 1986 re-election campaign. Robert Seavey, who had served as Chairman of the Urban Development Corporation, a state agency, also joined the firm in 1986 as counsel.

A *New York Times* metro section story, published on August 27, 1986 and titled "At Andrew Cuomo's Firm, Politics and Law Intersect," revealed that the firm represented "major real estate developers who have extensive dealings with the state: Donald J. Trump, William B. Zeckendorf and Jerry I. Speyer."

Andrew told the *Times* that when he became a partner in May 1985, it was agreed the firm would no longer represent any new clients that would appear before agencies whose heads were appointed by Governor Cuomo, and Andrew added: "There is no possible conflict of interest in our representing companies that have other matters before the state. Otherwise, you would have to say, 'Andrew, you shouldn't represent anyone who has any interaction with the state.' Then I couldn't represent anyone who wants a driver's license or has a tax problem."[25]

In a *Washington Post* follow-up story published on August 29, 1986, "Cuomo Son's Law Firm Scrutinized for Dealings" and written by Margot Hornblower, William Stern, Governor Cuomo's 1982 campaign finance chairman and Chairman of the Urban Development Corporation for two years during the Cuomo's first term, revealed that he told the governor that Andrew's firm "was casting a bad light on the administration" and that "it was the Cuomo family firm, so to speak."[26]

Coming to Andrew's defense, Governor Cuomo attributed the story to the Republicans, and said, "Andrew is not a public official. He is my son. . . . There are no legal inhibitions against him practicing before state agencies. But voluntarily, the firm does not represent clients before state agencies."[27]

These were not the only stories that cast a shadow over Andrew Cuomo's business dealings. On Wednesday, December 23, 1987, *The New York Times* ran an Associated Press story titled "Florida Suit Names Andrew Cuomo: A savings group seeks to avert a takeover." According to the report, a civil suit filed in the Broward County Circuit Court "contends that Andrew Cuomo . . . and a group of business associates violated Federal regulations in an attempt to take over two southern Florida savings institutions and drain their assets."

One of those named in the suit, along with Andrew, was one of his clients, Sheldon Goldstein, a big contributor to Cuomo's 1982 campaign who gave as much as $49,000. Goldstein, the Associated Press reported, was "expected to testify in a bribery and conspiracy trial that began [in November] in Manhattan involving the rental of a building to the state of New York."[28]

Allegedly, Goldstein threatened "to destroy" Harry Partridge if he did not sell him a 50% interest in his Broome Street building the state had agreed to rent.[29]

According to the Associated Press, Andrew "when he was a special counsel to the Governor, ordered the State Office of General Services in 1983 to reverse a decision to rent the partly completed eighth floor of the building at 400 Broome St., in lower Manhattan."[30]

Partridge, who was accused of attempting to defraud the state of the $20 million value of the 10-year 400 Broome Street lease, was cleared of the charges.

Sheldon Goldstein, whose real estate management company won contracts from the state "to manage two major state supervised housing projects in New York City" during Mario Cuomo's first gubernatorial term, admitted to a state commission that he had "threatened to ruin [Partridge] in the state of New York as a window contractor."[31] Shortly thereafter, Goldstein stepped down as Chairman of the State University Construction Fund.

As for Goldstein's scheme, involving Andrew, to merge two Florida Savings and Loans, the investigation into that matter, plus the ensuing suits and countersuits that Andrew's biographer, Michael Shnayerson, claims "haunted" him and infuriated his father, as well as Madeline's driver's license controversy, may have given the governor second thoughts about running for president.

III. The Mafia Rumors

Mario Cuomo was not a member of the Mafia. He was not connected to the Mafia or any other organized crime syndicate. As a practicing lawyer, he did not have any clients involved in organized crime.

Edward McDonald, the chief of the Organized Crime "Task" Force of the U.S. Attorney for the Southern District of New York in 1987, dismissed rumors that Cuomo had met with a mob capo while in government service. The story arose because Cuomo, while a guest at a large Italian wedding, may have shaken the hand of another guest, "Sonny Franzese, a capo in the Columbo crime family."[32]

"Aside from that," McDonald told *New York* magazine, "I have never heard of Cuomo connected with any wise guys in any way whatever. It shouldn't be worth denying, but still the calls keep coming in."[33]

But the rumors about "skeletons in the Cuomo closet" persisted and they understandably irked Cuomo. "I know it's all around," he said on one occasion, "but what do you do about it?"[34]

In December 1985, in a meeting with reporters in his office, Governor Cuomo objected to the media using the term "Mafia" when referring to organized crime. Reporters were taken aback when he said, "You're telling me that Mafia is an organization, and I'm telling you that's a lot of baloney. . . . It's nothing—it's a word somebody made up."[35]

Those Cuomo remarks created such a stir in the media, that Cuomo was forced to swallow his pride and walk back his words. He conceded that there was a Mafia but that "every time you use the word 'Mafia' you suggest to people that all organized crime is Italian—it's an ugly stereotype."[36]

And after years of Mafia rumors, the media and Cuomo's political opponents came up with nothing connecting Mario and the Mob. But to keep the story alive, they turned their sights to Cuomo's father-in-law, Charles Raffa. As the governor told his biographer, Robert McElvaine, in the fall of 1987, "They gave up on me personally a long time ago. They're talking about my in-laws, frankly. It's sick, terrible."[37]

What generated interest in Mr. Raffa was a tragic event that happened on May 22, 1984.

Early that morning, the seventy-nine-year-old Raffa was severely assaulted at a vacant store he owned in Brooklyn's East New York neighborhood. The

crime took place around 9:00 a.m. and was said to have involved two assailants. Raffa was hit in the head multiple times and knocked unconscious.
When he woke up around noon, his face covered with blood, he managed to
walk out to the street.

Shopkeepers across the street saw that his "head had been sliced open"
and went to his aid.[38] The somewhat incoherent Raffa asked to be taken
home, but instead he was rushed to the Baptist Medical Center, and then
transferred to N.Y.U. Medical Center.

Raffa underwent plastic surgery for facial injuries, but he never fully
recovered from his injuries, and he was confined to a wheelchair for the
four remaining years of his life.

In the aftermath of the crime, N.Y.P.D. Deputy Inspector Charles Prestia said: "Raffa was questioned by detectives on at least seven occasions, including July 11, when he returned to the crime scene with Patrol Lieutenant
Michael Murray and other officers. But his responses were confused, and
he gave contradictory statements about what happened to him." During
various interviews, Prestia explained, "Raffa described his assailants as white,
Hispanic, and black. Sometimes he said there was one man and sometimes
he said there were two. He said he was hit. Detectives did find Raffa's blood
at the top and bottom of the basement steps. But, aside from that, he was
confused about how he was beaten."

"Several suspects were brought in for questioning, but there were no
other witnesses to the beating, and Raffa's description of his attacker was
so inconsistent that the investigation eventually died."[39]

Rumors about a cover-up began to spread like wildfire. Among them,
according to *New York* magazine, were:

- That the mugging was a mob beating that grew out of a dispute over
  arson.
- That Cuomo interfered with the police investigation of the beating.
- That the record of a Raffa arrest for arson has been erased from the
  state computer.

Although none of the buzz turned out to be true, the rumor-mills
wouldn't let the story die.

And as Governor Cuomo's name remained in the mix as a potential presidential candidate in late 1987, and despite his announcement he would not run, *The New York Times* resurrected the Raffa story.

On October 28, 1987 the *Times* published a story by Selwyn Raab, titled "Unorthodox Steps in Inquiry on a Cuomo Relative: Police handing of his father-in-law assault case is at issue."

The reporter claimed that a detective "took unorthodox steps that may have hampered the search for evidence. . . ."

One of Governor Cuomo's N.Y.P.D. bodyguards, Sebastian Pipitone, said that while off duty, he took Raffa's car from the police station several hours after the assault and had it washed.

But the N.Y.P.D. said that Pipitone had the car cleaned "as a courtesy" to the Cuomo family before delivering it to the Raffa family. The wash was needed to remove powder used by forensics to recover fingerprints. However, N.Y.P.D. records contradict Pipitone's statement. " . . . [T]he car was first dusted and examined for fingerprints four days after Mr. Raffa was attacked, not on the day of the attack."[40] The exam was ordered because a witness came forward saying he saw someone sitting in the car.

Captain Michael Murphy, the officer who was in charge of the investigation, had not been aware that the car had been washed until asked by the *Times*. "It might have hurt the investigation," he said. "We still don't know if the car was important, but he would have been better off if it had been left alone."[41]

According to Deputy Police Commissioner Alice McGillion, Detective Pipitone couldn't remember who gave him the okay or the keys to take the car or where the car was washed. However, McGillion went on to say that Pipitone "had acted properly."[42]

A month later, the *Times* published a follow-up story by Raab, "Cuomo Guard Defends Actions in Assault Inquiry."

Detective Pipitone had decided to go public about his activities. He now claimed that on the day of the Raffa assault, "he was on duty but was authorized to be at home that afternoon. Five minutes before he was to go off duty, he said he was called from Albany by Maj. Martin J. Burke, commander of the State Police Department's Protective Service Unit . . . [who] told him Mr. Raffa had been assaulted. . . ." Pipitone said he was "asked" to visit the hospital and then the 75th precinct station house "to inquire about the case" to update the Governor's office.[43]

Pipitone made it clear that he "was not there as an investigator" and that he had "no input into the case."

Later, Pipitone alleged that when a police officer said, "We have [Raffa's] car here, what are we going to do with it?" Pipitone volunteered to "take it." He had no memory who approved the release of the car.

After getting the car washed, he went back to the 75th Precinct, retrieved Raffa's personal items and dropped off the car at the governor's home in Queens County.

"I had nothing to do with nothing other than I made a decision to get the car washed before I put it in front of Mrs. Cuomo's house," he told the *Times*. "How was I to know that four days later some guy would come up and say there was someone in the car."[44]

The *Times* also reported that aides to Governor Cuomo complained to the paper's editors that "his family were distressed by the [October 28] article." They said, "the Governor and his relatives believed the report contained innuendo suggesting that Mr. Pipitone . . . or other police officers had deliberately destroyed evidence that might in some way be embarrassing to Mr. Raffa."[45]

Around the time Raab's pieces were published, a number of other articles were published alleging links between the governor and some shady characters.

On October 27, 1987 the *New York Post* ran an article, "Cuomo And The Sewer Scandal: Governor was part owner of mob-linked concrete company." The story reported that "before he entered public service in 1975, Gov. Cuomo was part-owner of a concrete company that later figured in a huge construction scandal."

The *Post* said it learned that Cuomo served as a director of the Grand Pre-Stressed concrete company "along with Vincent DeLillo, who was convicted in 1979 in federal court of conspiring to supply substandard concrete pipe for Suffolk County's $920 million Southwest Sewer District project."

According to the FBI and N.Y.P.D. sources, DeLillo was said to be "an associate of the Colombo crime family."[46]

Fabiano Palomino, Cuomo's special counsel, authorized to speak to the *Post*, dismissed the reporting saying, "Mario didn't know the DeLillos from a hole in the ground."[47]

Cuomo did own 5% of the company but he resigned from the Grand Pre-Stressed board on May 1, 1972 and sold his 10 shares [of stock] a year later to Vincent DeLillo, for which he "was paid $2,900 in 1973 and $7,100 in 1974."[48]

Palomino said that Cuomo's involvement amounted to nothing. "[Founder] Moe Hornstein took a liking to Mario. They gave him [Cuomo] a couple of shares, a minor thing there."[49]

A week later, a *Post* headline read "DeLillos Deny Mob Link."

The DeLillo's family lawyer acknowledged that his clients were "public figures involved in several federal investigations during the 1970s, but claimed that at no time has anyone alleged associations with any organized crime family."

However, the *Post* refused the DeLillos' request to retract its October story.

Between the publication of the two *Post* stories, *New York* magazine featured a cover story by Nicholas Pileggi, "Cuomo And Those Rumors: Getting To The Bottom Of All The 'Mob' Talk."

Pileggi, author of the book *Wiseguy* (made into the Martin Scorsese film *Goodfellas*) did a very credible job in reviewing and dismissing all the mob rumors that swirled around Cuomo and his family.

Cuomo forcefully told Pileggi, "I never represented wise guys. I was asked thousands of times to do appeals for this guy and that guy, but I never did one. I had friends who were prosecutors, detectives, and FBI men, and if I wasn't sure, I could go to them and they'd warn me about who anyone was."[50]

Responding to a question about the *New York* cover story, Cuomo said, "If it's a price I pay for being Italian-American, then being Italian-American is well worth the price."[51]

The persistent but unfounded rumors about Mafia connections and the media poking around Cuomo's father-in-law's businesses, may be another reason Mario choose not to enter the presidential sweepstakes.

IV. Cuomo vs. His Ex-Law Firm

In August 1985, *Newsday* published a lengthy investigative report describing the events surrounding Cuomo's civil suit, filed in the New York Supreme Court in Brooklyn, against the law firm he left when he became Governor Carey's Secretary of State in 1975.

Newsday summed up the controversy: "Mario Cuomo has demanded a share of the fees his former law firm received after he left to enter public office. He's taking the action despite an agreement to accept $100,000 in exchange for his full interest in the firm and its future fees."[52]

When Mario Cuomo was a candidate for lieutenant governor in 1975, he promised he would resign from his law firm and not practice law in the private sector to supplement his income. Although he lost that race, when Governor Carey appointed him Secretary of State on January 1, 1975, he maintained his earlier pledge and severed all ties with Corner, Finn, Cuomo and Charles.

Cuomo, who had a 40% interest in the firm, told *The New York Times* on December 19, 1974, that he would terminate all relations with the firm "but would receive some future remuneration for his contribution to projects not yet finished." He added, "This will be disclosed in accord with the Carey administration's new policy."[53]

Cuomo's statement to the *Times* did not comply with the law firm's written policy—which Cuomo helped to draw up. That policy "provided that any partner leaving the firm would be paid a flat sum covering his entire interest in the firm and any future fees the firm might earn for work in progress."[54]

Shortly after Cuomo's statement to the *Times*, he changed his mind about future compensation on cases that were in progress. He wrote to a firm partner, John Finn (a former N.Y. State Supreme Court judge), that he "had agreed with another partner, Peter Dwyer, to surrender his interest in the firm's accounts receivables and work in progress for $80,000."[55] Half that amount represented billings for work completed.

A final settlement was agreed to on January 6, 1975. The payout was still $80,000 but $50,000 was for accounts receivable and $30,000 for works in progress. The money was to be paid in $20,000 installments over four years. In addition, Cuomo was also to receive a return of the firm's capital of $20,000.

In Cuomo's financial disclosure with the state on May 28, 1975, he affirmed "that he had no financial interest in matters pending against the state, firms doing business with the state or contracts with state, county or municipal bodies."[56]

As for the question concerning "all contractual arrangements producing or expected to produce income," Cuomo answered, "Contractual agreement for past services."[57]

During the next three years two of Cuomo's former partners, Finn and Charles, died. As a result of these deaths, one of Cuomo's former law school students, Michael Nicholson (also a licensed professional engineer with an M.S. in Civil Engineering from Columbia University), who had joined the firm in 1973 and had reported directly to Cuomo, was able to acquire a 45% partnership interest in the law firm.

When on December 3, 1978 Pete Dwyer was killed in a car accident, Nicholson, the only remaining partner, "inherited the law firm, its clients and its accounts," as *Newsday* reported. He also brought in his wife, Diana, as a partner.

After Dwyer's death there were court battles concerning the value of his piece of the partnership, and over the proceeds of a "Key Man" life insurance policy. (Cuomo insisted on the policy to cover unpaid installments if Dwyer should die and cause the firm to dissolve.)

Eventually, Cuomo was paid $34,722.04 from the policy and the Dwyer family received the balance, $75,000.

By 1979 and into 1980, the law firm's client suits against various federal and state agencies were being settled.

One big payoff was a settlement with Perini North River Associates, a client Cuomo had procured before he left the firm.

In 1979, Nicholson submitted a partial legal bill to Perini Corporation for $900,000.

Perini Corporation made out the check to Michael Nicholson as Attorney, not to the law firm. (Nicholson claimed he had the check made out as such "because of the dispute with the Dwyer estate which was claiming part of the fee.")[58]

Mario Cuomo learned about the settlement payout when he received a call in 1980 from the new counselor to the Perini Corporation, Charles Molineaux.

Perini Construction had received another invoice from Nicolson for $600,000 on August 18, 1980 and Molineaux was doing due diligence before approving the payout.

Molineaux was concerned about the earlier check that was made out not to a law firm but directly to Nicholson. He was also concerned that it was deposited in a fiduciary account in a Missouri bank that had been managing investments for Diana Nicholson's family.[59]

When reviewing the 1974 fee agreement, Molineaux realized this was Mario Cuomo's former firm. (Coincidently, Molineaux was a graduate of St. John's Law School's Class of 1959 and had been introduced to Cuomo at alumni lunches held at the Lawyer's Club in lower Manhattan in the early 1960s.)

In a sworn deposition conducted by Nicholson related to his suit against Perini North River Associates in the U.S. District Court, Eastern District of New York, on March 17, 1988, Molineaux said he was told by Perini officials, "that the Cuomo firm had been retained because it was considered that Mario Cuomo had some expertise in construction matters and he had political contacts in the city."[60]

Molineaux had left a phone message at Lt. Governor Cuomo's World Trade Center office on September 25, 1980. The next morning, around 11:00 a.m., Cuomo returned the call from his car radio phone after attending the funeral mass of a fellow classmate and Dean of St. John's Law, John Murphy.

Molineaux told Cuomo that "the purpose of my call was to ask whether Michael Nicholson had—was in effect the successor to all assets of Corner, Finn and Cuomo and other firm assets."

Cuomo's response, according to Molineaux, "It's complicated. . . . There is a war on with the Dwyer estate."

Molineaux went on to say in his deposition:

I told Mr. Cuomo—I asked him if he recalled the Perini North River claim.

He seemed to recall it, although somewhat vaguely.

I told him that there had been a settlement. I told him that there had been a partial payment of a settlement and a partial payment of the fee.

He indicated that he knew nothing about that. I told him that we were about to make a further payment of the fee and I said we were talking about a fee of over a million dollars. I did not tell him the amount.

He said, "I will call you back."

Concerning the "call back" that took place later that day, about 4:00 p.m., Molineaux was asked:

Q. What did you discuss with Mr. Cuomo at that time?

A. I didn't discuss very much because he did most of the talking. Mr. Cuomo—

Q. Did he call you or did you call him?

A. No, he called me back.

Q. What did he say?

A. He started out by saying, "I am furious." He went into a tirade about you [Michael Nicholson] and Mrs. Nicholson to the effect that things had been concealed from him, that—I think he used the word "incredibly."

He had been asked to furnish a statement allegedly for tax purposes to the effect that he had no claim on the assets of the firm, that this was not true, that he was going to write me a letter and the letter would request that we make no further payment on the Perini fee matter.

I was concerned at that point that Perini might face a claim from Mr. Cuomo and from the estate of Dwyer with respect to the payment that had already been paid.

I asked Mr. Cuomo to put in the letter, that he said that he was going to write, a statement to the effect that prior payments paid by Perini were paid out in good faith.

He also told me rather pompously that he was retaining an attorney. . . .

My response was to request that he state in such a letter that the prior payment had been made in good faith and he agreed to do that.

He said that his attorney would call me, which he then did.

The attorney who called Molineaux was Fabian Palomino—the lieutenant governor's law school chum and special counsel.

Palomino read a draft of a letter dated September 26, 1980. Molineaux pointed out that it did not contain the language he requested. He then told Palomino, "in my prior conversation with Mr. Cuomo, Mr. Cuomo had agreed to state in the letter that prior payments made by Perini Corporation to Mr. Nicholson had been made in good faith."

Palomino then agreed to include such language.

Based on Molineaux's advice, Perini Corporation held back the $600,000 payment.

Cuomo's version is different from Molineaux's deposition. Here's what he said to *Newsday* in July 1985, during a five-hour tape-recorded interview, "flanked by two lawyers," concerning this matter:

As Cuomo recalls it, Molineaux said he had heard that Cuomo might be leaving state office and asked why, Cuomo replied that he couldn't afford to stay in public service: " . . . I've got the kids and it's tough . . . I'm not making any money." According to Cuomo, Molineaux expressed surprise saying that he thought Cuomo had shared in the initial $900,000 paid to Nicholson on the Perini claim. Cuomo added: " . . . I was paralyzed, you know. You're talking to me about a million-dollar fee. . . ."

Cuomo said Molineaux told him that Nicholson had just

submitted a second bill for an additional $600,000 and—in response to Molineaux's questions—had stated that Cuomo had no share in the fees because he had surrendered his entire interest in the fees when he took office in 1975. This, said Cuomo, is what had prompted Molineaux's friendly call. Cuomo said that he told Molineaux that he was entitled to a share of the fees.

Said Cuomo: "He [Molineaux] says: 'You know what you've got to do... You better send me a note, a letter, that says "Hold everything."' And I said, I'm going to do that right away. . . . "

The next day, on Sept. 26, 1980, Cuomo wrote Molineaux: . . . "This is to make clear that whatever writings have been entered into and whatever transactions between me and the firm [Cuomo's former law firm], none of them properly foreclosed my right to participate in the Perini fee and, indeed, any compensation for construction claims that were outstanding."

Cuomo asked Molineaux to make "no further payments until the various claimants are able to resolve this disagreement." Since Cuomo's letter, Perini has made no further payments and has gone to federal court in a dispute over the amount of the legal fee.[61]

Cuomo also admitted to *Newsday*, "There's no question that I made an agreement and signed it. That's absolutely clear. But I certainly didn't make a deal for $80,000 to give up millions of dollars in fees. That's dumb. I'm not."

In the affidavit Cuomo had filed in the State Supreme Court in Brooklyn, he asked the court to void his 1975 agreement with the firm because much to his "dismay and disappointment," he "realized that the representations made to me by Peter Dwyer as to the value of my partnership share for work in progress, which representations I relied upon to enter into the liquidation agreement, were the result of either mutual mistake or fraud."[62]

Cuomo also alleged that "Nicholson, then a salaried employee of the firm, fraudulently led him to believe that the claims being worked on by the office were 'without value.'"[63]

During the *Newsday* interview, Cuomo referred to Nicholson several times as a "liar" and a "cheat."

In his affidavit, he alleged:

> The Nicholsons' attempts at subterfuge, first in hiding the Perini fee, and then by trying to trick me into relinquishing my claim and believing that I had relinquished my claim to that fee are clear evidence that the Nicholsons knew that I was entitled to share in that fee. Otherwise, why did they go to such great lengths to weave a web of lies and deceit concerning the fee and my right to share in it. . . .[64]

When *Newsday* asked his reaction to Nicholson's complaint that Cuomo might use his office to "further his court case," the governor said "All of this is being done in the open where everyone can see it. . . . I could have gone to the bar association. I would have had this kid [Nicholson] disbarred. . . . You know what I could have done as governor?.... This man [Nicholson] is desperate to stay away from the witness chair. You know why? He will perjure himself to the end, and I'm going to get him. If he gets in that chair and lies, then the law has to be served. . . ."

As for Cuomo's claims that he cheated and lied to him, Nicholson said "that Cuomo supervised all of those accounts while he was with the firm and that Cuomo was the only partner who had the knowledge and experience to estimate the potential value of each case."[65]

Nicholson claimed he had nothing to gain by lying. At the time he was only an employee for a year. "Only partners share in fees. I had no idea that I would ever become partner, much less take over the firm. Who could know then that the three remaining partners would all be dead in four years? Not me. Not Cuomo. Besides, we all expected he'd come back to the firm within two years."[66]

Cuomo made the claim against Nicholson, despite law firm files that reflect "Cuomo kept in touch with the status of potential claims until he left the firm."

As the senior partner at the firm, Cuomo also received "formal status reports on all cases being handled by the office."[67] A March 1, 1974 report in the M.M. Cuomo files, noted "the impending Perini claim shows Nicholson as the associate assigned to the case and reads '20% of recovery substantial.'"[68]

The Cuomo-Nicholson suits dragged out for years. In fact, when it finally got to trial in 1989, it was the oldest case in the State Supreme Court in Brooklyn.

The case, "a thicket of suits and countersuits," the *Times* reported, had been "so bitter that at one point a judicial referee felt compelled to warn the lawyers that the first one to throw a punch would be fined $250."[69]

Then, a few days before Governor Cuomo was scheduled to take the stand in April 1989 and testify in the trial, a settlement was announced, but monetary figures were not disclosed.

Both sides claimed victory. Nicholson's lawyer said, "I would say this is a total victory for the Nicholsons vis-a-vis the Governor. The Governor has given up any right he has or ever may have had to the fees earned by the Nicholsons since Cuomo left the practice."[70]

Cuomo's lawyer said, "The Governor is delighted and pleased by this arrangement and is satisfied he will receive his due. The truth happens to be that this is an unconditional victory for the Governor." He added that Cuomo "had been waiting to testify for nine years and had been stymied by the long delays in the trial."[71]

Was this long drawn-out lawsuit, with all the charges and counter-charges, a factor in Cuomo's decision not to run for president?

Possibly.

In an April 29, 1997 letter Charles Molineaux sent to Robert Greene, the *Newsday* assistant managing editor who headed the team that reported on Cuomo's lawsuit in August 1985, he wrote: "I enjoyed visiting with you Saturday night at the reunion. It was a surprise to learn that the Nicholson-Cuomo litigation had gone on for so long. If, as you indicated, your taped interview of Cuomo was ultimately a significant reason for his not running in 1992, you have the ingredients for a great article (or even a book): Why 'Cuomo Didn't Run.'"[72]

It is in the realm of probability that Cuomo's distrust of the media, his fear of investigative reporting into the lives of family members, the Mafia whispers, and the lawsuit against his firm were factors in his decision not to seek federal office.

Cuomo, of course, had a different take on not running for president:

If I made a mistake in terms of running for president, the mistake was not in refusing to run in '91. It was in running for governor in '90, a decision I made because the state was in trouble. So do I have any regret? No. Look, I am the luckiest person I know. I have been given much, much more than I ever deserved. Life, you discover after you've lived it for a while, is largely a matter of circumstance and good luck. Yes, it helps to work hard; it helps to try to stay as honest as you can. But your health is not something that you can control. Having a Matilda is not something that everybody gets. Having five fantastic kids is not something you can earn for yourself. Being in the right place at the right time in 1982, when everybody else dropped out of the race because Koch came in—that you couldn't have arranged except through prayer. So I've been so lucky. The people of this state were so good to me. Letting me serve for three terms! My God. And I had no money, I had no friends. I had no reputation to begin with. How could I ever admit to regretting anything? I made a lot of mistakes, and they let me stay anyway for three terms.[73]

As for the Supreme Court:

I had a chance to go on the Supreme Court of the United States, and my whole family was more disappointed in my deciding not to do that than in my deciding not to run for president—much more. Because most of my family thought, *Gee, this is natural for Pop, and this is his thing, it's what he likes—he doesn't like the cocktail parties; he doesn't like asking people for money and all this other garbage of politics.* But I said no because we learned so much in twenty years of politics and twelve years of the governorship and eight other years serving. . . . I learned so much that I thought it would be a waste to just bury that under a black robe and limit myself to the very important work of a justice of the Supreme Court. I mean, what I am saying now about America's condition—if I were a judge, that would be still one more voice quieted on this subject.[74]

CHAPTER 13
MARIO CUOMO: PUBLIC INTELLECTUAL

When Mario Cuomo was elected New York's lieutenant governor in November 1978, the post-election edition of *The New York Times* had a photograph of Cuomo with his wife at a polling place in Queens with the caption "A Practical Intellectual."

To distinguish himself from the hacks who dominated New York's political scene, Cuomo portrayed himself as a public intellectual who reluctantly entered the electoral arena because he had a moral obligation to teach his values to the public. "Sometimes," *Time* observed, "Cuomo sounds self-serving as though he is the only man in politics for the right reason."[1]

Cuomo succeeded as an intellectual in the public square, because he was brighter, better read and more articulate than most New York pols and reporters.

There was also another intellectual side of Cuomo: commentator on Catholic teaching. *Time* described him as "the cerebral Roman Catholic who has modeled himself on St. Thomas More but can display a kind of conspicuous moral vanity."[2]

In a similar vein, *Newsweek's* Kenneth Woodward wrote, "Not since Eugene McCarthy's moral crusade for the presidency in 1968 has a political leader been so intellectually, self-consciously, even aggressively Roman Catholic. . . ."[3]

During his years in public office, Cuomo wrote a number of articles for religious periodicals. These articles included, "Who Is God?" for the Jesuit magazine *America* (November 16, 1991), and for the *Catholic Lawyer*, "The Realization of Ideals In Law" (Spring 1975). And in April 1985, he gave an interview to the liberal Catholic magazine *Commonweal* defending his views as a Catholic in the political arena.

The remainder of this chapter describes and assesses Mario Cuomo's positions on abortion, the death penalty, conscience and consensus from a

Roman Catholic perspective. It also examines his religious heroes St. Thomas More and Pierre Teilhard de Chardin, S.J. and their relevance to the issues discussed.

St. Thomas More

"I believe, when statesmen forsake their own private conscience for the sake of their public duties . . . they lead their country by a short route to chaos."

St. Thomas More

A copy of the Holbein portrait of St. Thomas More hung in Mario Cuomo's office throughout his tenure as governor.

More, the patron saint of lawyers, statesmen, and politicians, was Cuomo's model because he was, in the governor's judgment, a combination of "noble hopes and goals and personal weakness."[4]

Cuomo, who won the St. John's School of Law Thomas More Scholarship, said he admired the saint's "dedication and steadfastness, his refusal to deviate, even for the king, or to keep his own head."[5] But he also told his biographer, Robert McElvaine, that he was impressed by More's "humanity, not his saintliness."[6]

"We have plenty of saints—so many that we can afford to drop a few, like St. Christopher. But More was human . . . a man of great principle, and yet he didn't go rushing to meet death. He tried to keep his life and his principles. And that is evidence of humanity. He got caught up in the ways of the world; sometimes he got compromised by it. In the end, he did the right thing, most of the time, in most people's estimate."[7]

The saint, McElvaine concludes, was "an appropriate symbol" for the governor "whose goal is also to 'do the right thing, most of the time' which he knows is the best an imperfect human can hope for."[8]

The question is, was Cuomo's take on More accurate? Did he follow the example set by More, particularly when it came to political consensus and following one's informed conscience in public life?

Thomas More was born in the City of London in 1478. The son of a lawyer, More declined to study for the priesthood and turned to the law, and in 1501, he was called to the bar at Lincoln's Inn.

A Latin and Greek scholar, he gave lectures on the Church's early Fathers. Described as a man "born for friendship," he enjoyed the company of Catholic scholars, particularly Desiderius Erasmus of Rotterdam, with whom he was very close during his adult life. Throughout Europe, More and Erasmus were considered the leading humanists of their age and were beloved for their keen intelligence and quick wit.

More was elected to Parliament in 1504 and was appointed Under-Sheriff of London in 1510. A brilliant legal negotiator, he had considerable success representing his country on commercial matters in Flanders and Calais. Those successes caught the eye of King Henry VIII who insisted More join the King's Council in 1517.

In 1521, More was named Under-Treasurer and was knighted. Two years later, he was elected Speaker of the House of Commons. He received other honors from the King including appointment as Chancellor of the Duchy of Lancaster.

When the King turned to More to support his efforts to secure a divorce from the pope in order to marry another woman, More declined stating he could not agree with the King's opinion on the matter.

Yet, despite this rebuff, the King's affection for More was so great, he named him Lord Chancellor of England in 1529.

At More's installation, the Duke of Norfolk, before giving him his chain of office, made the following remarks on the King's behalf:

> The King's Majesty has raised to the supreme dignity of Chancellor . . . Thomas More. . . . His only motive in so doing was because he saw in More all those highest gifts of nature and grace which either he or his people could desire in the Chancellor. The King, therefore . . . because of his ardent desire that his kingdom and his subjects should be governed with equity, justice, uprightness and wisdom, has made him Chancellor of the realm. . . .

St. Thomas More on Conscience

Shortly after taking office, More was ordered by the King to make another study of the divorce issue. In reviewing the matter, the King told More, "to say nothing and do nothing but what his conscience dictated, and place before his eyes God in the first place, and only in the second place the King."[10]

After an exhausting review, More, who made his judgments "grounded upon the lawe of reason and the lawe of God," reaffirmed his previous opinion. His informed conscience could not permit approval.

A displeased Henry dismissed More's findings and proceeded to successfully pressure the English clergy to accept the King as the Supreme Head of the Church in England on May 15, 1532.

The next day, More resigned his office citing he was "not being equal to the work."

Writing to his friend and fellow dissenter, Bishop John Fisher, he declared that "the fort had been betrayed even by them that should have defended it." He later complained that the "King had been allowed to get his own way because of a 'flexible Council . . . and a weak clergy,' who had failed in their duty to give him the advice he had not wanted to hear."[11]

When More refused to take the oath of the Act of Succession because it repudiated papal authority, he was imprisoned in the Tower of London on April 17, 1534. The following year, More was indicted under a revised Act of Succession for refusing to accept the King's title as Supreme Head of the Church of England.

At his trial on July 1, 1535, More was found guilty of treason based on the perjury of Sir Richard Rich. Five days later, at his place of execution, More reminded those present, "I die His Majesty's good servant but God's first."

Four hundred years later, July 1935, the Roman Catholic Church canonized Thomas More.

Mario Cuomo's hero, while serving in government, refused to abandon his informed conscience to defend an evil act and, unlike Cuomo, rejected "consensus" arguments.

For More a right conscience is judgment of the mind, the intellect. "As such," More scholar Gerard Wegemer has written, "the role of conscience is to make practical judgments in light of principles and laws recognized as true and just. Conscience does not make those principles or laws, it only applies them in particular cases."[12]

The Catechism of the Catholic Church confirms this view, "Man has the right to act in conscience and in freedom so as personally to make moral decisions. 'He must not be forced to act contrary to his conscience. Nor must he be prevented from acting according to his conscience, especially in religious matters.'"[13]

More anticipated the Catechism when he wrote: "Any man is bounden if he see peril to examine his conscience surely by learning and good counsel and be sure that his conscience be such as it may stand with his salvation."[14]

For More, the sine qua non for every citizen in the state was conscience. "Every true and good subject," More declared, "is more bound to have respect to his said conscience and to his soul than to any other thing in all the world. . . ."[15]

With no little irony, More pointed out that his belief that conscience is "the metaphysical foundation for law and justice," was affirmed by King Henry himself. "That I should perceive mine own conscience should serve me and, that I should first look unto God and after God unto [King Henry]" was the "first lesson . . . that ever his Grace gave me at my first coming into his service."[16]

During More's imprisonment, when asked if he was ready to swear to the Act of Succession, he declined, appealing to conscience:

> My purpose is not to put any fault either in the Act or any man that made it, or in the oath or any man that swears it, nor to condemn the conscience of any other man. But as for myself in good faith my conscience so moves me in the matter, that though I will not deny to swear to the succession, yet unto the oath that here is offered to me I cannot swear, without the jeopardizing of my soul to perpetual damnation.[17]

More did not swear the oath "as presented to him," biographer Peter Ackroyd observed, because "he would have concurred in the forcible removal of the pope's jurisdiction and the effective schism of the Church in England. This he could not do, even at the cost of his life."[18]

At his trial, More once again appealed to the right of conscience:

> Ye must understand that, in things touching conscience, every true and good subject is more bound to have respect to his said conscience and to his soul than to any other thing in all the world

beside; namely when his conscience is in such sort as mine is, that is to say, where the person giveth no occasion of slander, of tumult and sedition against his prince, as it is with me; for I assure you that I have not hitherto to this hour disclosed and opened my conscience and mind to any person living in all the world.[19]

When he realized he would be found guilty, due to the perjury of Sir Richard Rich, More revealed his conscience to the court:

Forasmuch as, my Lord, this indictment is grounded upon an act of Parliament directly repugnant to the laws of God and His Holy Church, the supreme government of which, or of any part whereof, may no temporal prince presume by any law to take upon him, as rightfully belonging to the See of Rome—a spiritual pre-eminence by the mouth of Our Saviour himself personally present upon the earth, only to St. Peter and his successors, Bishops of the same See by special prerogative granted; it is therefore in law amongst Christian men, insufficient to charge any Christian man.[20]

He went on to point out that the Act was a violation of Magna Carta and the King's coronation oath.

Thomas More lost his head, not an election, because he refused to forsake his private conscience for the sake of his public duties.

St. John Paul II, when declaring Thomas More Patron Saint of Statesmen on October 31, 2000 said, the saint "lived his intense public life with a simple humility marked by good humor, even at the moment of his execution. This was the height to which he was led by his passion for the truth. What enlightened his conscience was the sense that man cannot be sundered from God, nor politics from morality. . . . And it was precisely in defense of the rights of conscience that the example of Thomas More shone brightly."[21]

St. Thomas More and Consensus

"Our public morality, depends on a consensus view of right and wrong. The values derived from religious belief will not—and

272

should not—be accepted as part of the public morality unless they are shared by the pluralistic community at large, by consensus."

Mario Cuomo

To avoid a tyranny of the majority when making laws, the Founding Fathers created checks and balances that would encourage "consensus." But, as Archbishop Charles Chaput has pointed out, "consensus—which simply means the 'agreement of the people'—is never a source of truth. It says nothing at all about whether a policy is a good or a law is evil. In fact, a consensus is often wrong. A great many unjust wars and bad leaders have been very popular."[22]

During a prison interrogation, Master Thomas Cromwell told More "there is no honor which the King would be likely to deny you" if More could bring himself to "agree with the Universities, the Bishop and the Parliament of this realm," in other words, the consensus. More declined.

In another interrogation, the Duke of Norfolk appealed to consensus after he showed More the signatures on the oath saying " . . . frankly I don't know whether the marriage was lawful or not. But damn it, Thomas, look at those names. . . . You know those men! Can't you do what I did, and come with us, for fellowship?"[23]

To this consensus argument, More replied: "And when we stand before God, and you are sent to Paradise for doing according to your conscience, and I am damned for not doing according to mine, will you come with me for fellowship?"[24]

After More's favorite daughter, Margaret, took the oath, she urged her father to conform his conscience to the Act because it was "widely debated and agreed upon." Replying to her plea, More, once again, rejected consensus stating "yet is there no man bound to swear that every law is well made, nor bound upon the pain of God's displeasure, to perform any such point of law, as were indeed lawful."

More goes on to explain that man-made law must be judged by a well-formed conscience, not group consensus. "I never intend (God being my good Lord) to pin my soul at another man's back, not even the best man that I know this day living; for I know not whither he may hap to carry it."[25]

For Mario Cuomo's hero, public morality did not depend on consensus, it depended on truth.

Cuomo, the Church and Abortion

"My position on abortion is absolutely theologically sound."
—Mario Cuomo, ABC's The Week, November 24, 1991

Mario Cuomo's issue with the Roman Catholic Church's hierarchy on abortion did not begin when John O'Connor became archbishop of New York in March 1984. It actually began several weeks before Cuomo won the gubernatorial election in November 1982.

The Most Rev. Patrick V. Ahern, an auxiliary bishop of the Archdiocese of New York, first broached the subject with Lt. Governor Cuomo in a letter dated October 26, 1982.

The bishop began by stressing "how much I admire" and "how grateful I shall always be" for Cuomo's help in the West Bronx Community clergy coalition "in its attempt to save neighborhoods."

Ahern then went on to write:

> But I am absolutely stunned by your position on abortion. I have before me your letter to Elaine Lytel of Planned Parenthood and I can hardly believe it is your signature at the bottom of that letter.

> You are opposed to abortion personally. Presumably that is because you believe it takes a human life. How then can you "believe in and support choice?" How can anyone have the right to *choose* to take the life of another human being? It is like saying: "I am personally opposed to slavery, but I respect your choice to own slaves if *you* think it is alright."

> What especially distresses me is the rhetoric you have been using in discussing the issue, saying that your personal morality rejects abortion but you will not impose your personal morality on others. That formulation leaves out the essential element in the

274

problem: the poor little child whom an abortion kills. One just doesn't elude the issue that easily. . . .

It grieves me to find a man I once admired saying such indefensible things. Surely it is laudable to seek public office, but is it laudable to pay such a price?

The most serious consequence I see in your rhetoric is that it confuses and misleads people who might otherwise think straight on this issue of such enormous consequence to humanity.

I don't enjoy writing this letter, but if I leave it unwritten I shall do a disservice to two persons. You are one and I am the other.

Governor-Elect Cuomo replied to Bishop Ahern in a letter dated November 23, 1982:

As you might imagine, I did not enjoy reading your letter of October 26, any more than you did writing it.

It is painful to have lost your respect. . . .

I believe abortion is wrong. I have said so over and again, in front of both Catholic and non-Catholic audiences. With all respect to you, but contrary to the judgment you expressed in your letter, this is not "rhetoric." The five children my wife and I have brought into the world are not rhetoric either. They are, I would hope, the most basic affirmation people can make about the value of human life. . . .

In this country, thank God, we have not been totally denied the right to make our own choices as dictated by our own consciences. We have the right not to abort. But respect for the choices allowed to others by the law is at the foundation of our system. Our rules are made through the process and we live by the law—"Caesar's" law—until we change "Caesar's" mind.

As you know, these are not easy matters to articulate. Sometimes the articulation clouds basic issues. The tone of your letter would make it appear that we have adopted laws that require abortions. Of course, we have done no such thing. If abortions are requested and performed—even by many Catholics—it is, as you know, bishop, not because the State requires it, but because we have failed to convince people, even some of our own people, that it is wrong. I have tried to articulate this point, perhaps clumsily. I have tried to say that too many of us too often depend upon the law to enforce a moral standard that we have ourselves not been able to teach through our families and our churches.

Painful as your letter is, I am grateful at least that you thought enough of me to write it. I hope you will continue to share your views with me and to support me with your prayers, if not your vote, as I undertake the awesome responsibility of governing New York.

Interestingly, Cuomo sent a second letter to Ahern the next day, November 24, 1982 quoting St. Thomas More's Utopia. It read:

Consistent with my letter to you of November 23, please note the following from St. Thomas More:

"If you can't completely eradicate wrong ideas, or deal with inveterate vices as effectively as you could wish, that's no reason for turning your back on public life altogether. You wouldn't abandon ship in a storm just because you couldn't control the winds. . . . You must go to work indirectly. You must handle everything as tactfully as you can, and what you can't put right you must try to make as little wrong as possible. For things will never be perfect, until human beings are perfect—which I don't expect for quite a number of years!"

This second letter, however, was postmarked December 3, 1982 and was not received by Ahern until December 7, 1982. Hence, Ahern's reply

to Cuomo dated December 6, 1982 does not refer to the More citation.
Here are excerpts of Ahern's December 6, 1982 reply:

> I appreciate your letter of November 23rd and hasten to tell you
> that you have lost neither my respect nor my friendship. If I
> may presume to use the latter word. The last thing I meant to
> do was to offend you personally and since apparently I did, I
> apologize. Who am I to stand in judgment of another man?
> When it comes to not practicing virtue, especially courage, I
> can afford to throw stones at no one.
>
> It was not a person I wished to attack in my letter but an issue,
> one of supreme importance because it is an issue of life and
> death. Every time an abortion is done a human being is killed,
> and that is happening a million and a half times a year in the
> United States, which is a tragedy. . . .
>
> What I ask you to do is to oppose this killing. I ask you to state
> publicly that not only your own five wonderful children could
> not be killed as they made their nine-month journey to birth,
> but that no child on that journey may be killed. I ask you to
> come out publicly and denounce abortion, publicly reverse the
> position you have taken, say that, in the words of our wonderful
> Pope at the Washington Monument, you too will "stand up"
> for unborn human beings.
>
> I realize this is asking a lot of you, and I dare to ask it because I
> believe in you. You have made a mistake, and a grave one, in
> supporting "freedom of choice." It is hard to change what you
> have said. It may even be humiliating. But your friend Thomas
> More will put his hand on your head and bless you if you do it.
> God will bless you, and He will bless your Governorship.
>
> You say that "our rules are made through the process and we
> live by the law—'Caesar's Law'—or until we change 'Caesar's
> mind'." You are now Caesar. You are the Governor of New York

State. I am trying to change your mind through the only process available to me, which is to ask you to change it. And I ask you to put your shoulder behind the effort to change the minds of the other Caesars of our country. . . .

You point out that the Church has failed to convince many Catholic women not to abort. Of course it has. It has also failed to prevent a lot of husbands from killing their wives but the law still forbids them to do it. Law helps to prevent, and Mario as a lawyer you know that law also teaches. If the Supreme Court struck down the laws against homicide tomorrow, I think we would soon have a lot more homicides.

I know you have more to do just now than read letters from me and I apologize for the length of this one. But I must write it because your letter to me did not face the issue. You never once mentioned the unborn child. The issue Mario is killing human beings and it can't be set aside. I'm sorry if I bother your conscience—but that's what I'm trying to do.

On December 8, 1982, Bishop Ahern sent another letter to Cuomo addressing the Thomas More quote:

You and I are friends, I hope, and I can speak plainly to you. The quotation from St. Thomas More could hardly be more inappropriate. I am not talking about "eradicating wrong ideas or dealing as effectively as we could wish." I am not talking about legislating morality. I am talking about the government's obligation to try to protect innocent human lives instead of condoning their killing. I am not talking about "turning your back on public life." I am suggesting that you use your considerable influence in it to try to stop, or at least to minimize, this killing. I am talking about the very point in the quotation from *Utopia*: "making as little wrong as possible what you can't put right." Supporting "reproductive freedom," *after* the reproduction has taken place, is hardly doing that.

Of all the men to quote, St. Thomas More, who went to his death with gallant good humour rather than do something his government demanded of him which he knew to be wrong— over a matter less grave, I'm afraid, than the killing of millions of babies *with the government's blessing*. Can you possibly believe that St. Thomas More would not use all his brilliant talents to try to change the Supreme Court Decision of 1973, and follow through on all matters relating to it, such as government funding for abortions, to the limit of his ability and influence? Let's not involve our Saints in this bloody business. . . .

This exchange of letters began the protracted conflict between Cuomo and his Church on abortion that would go on for the rest of his life.

While Cuomo's famed Notre Dame speech on abortion and the immediate reaction to it is described in Chapter 10, what follows is an analysis of Cuomo's approach to the issue and whether or not it was "absolutely theologically sound."

The most important sentence in Mario Cuomo's Notre Dame speech is: "I accepted the Church's teaching on abortion."

What is that teaching?

Here is an excerpt from the Catechism of the Catholic Church:

The inalienable right to life of every innocent human individual is a constitutive element of a civil society and its legislation: "The inalienable rights of the person must be recognized and respected by civil society and the political authority. . . . Among such fundamental rights one should mention in this regard every human being's right to life and physical integrity from the moment of conception until death." . . . As a consequence of the respect and protection which must be ensured for the unborn child from the moment of conception, the law must provide appropriate penal sanctions for every deliberate violation of the child's rights.[26]

But instead of taking the Church's position at face value, namely that the right to life of the unborn child was a universal human right, Cuomo sidestepped the issue, defining his opposition to abortion as "our Catholic morality..." or "certain articles of our belief."

However, as Garry Wills, a noted left-wing historian pointed out, the Catholic bishops do not view their position on abortion as dogma; "it is not a religious issue when addressing the public at large. In that forum they rely on natural law, common sense and probabilistic arguments. . . ."[27]

The very liberal bishop of Albany, Howard Hubbard, agreed with Wills' observations and rejected Cuomo's distortion of the Church's position:

The abortion question is not purely an issue of Catholic doctrine. It is a basic issue of human rights, the right of the unborn child to exist. This is a burning concern shared by many Protestants and Jewish people and by people who hold no formal religious belief. In this regard, then, the issue cannot be presented simply as one religious community seeking to impose its doctrinal beliefs on the body politic.

Consequently, I would suggest that we move away from such expressions as "forcing our beliefs on others," "religious values in public affairs" or behavior that is "sinful"—expressions that punctuated the governor's talk.

Such phrases muddy the waters, because in discussing abortion the Catholic Church and other citizens do so not only under the heading of religious belief but of human rights.[28]

As for the "consensus" argument, as the theologian Msgr. William Smith pointed out, "Human Rights do not rest on consensus, that is why they are called inalienable rights." Or as Cardinal Ratzinger (the future Pope Benedict) declared in 1999, "Truth does not create consensus, and consensus does not create truth as much as it does a common ordering."[29]

Roe v. Wade, in 1973, was not a consensus decision, it was judicial fiat. The court imposed a constitutional right on states that, by way of consensus, had laws prohibiting abortion. "The court tried to short-circuit a recently begun and developing controversy over the abortion laws by taking the abortion issue out of politics. The court, thereby, prevented the

American people from arriving at such resolution of their differences as they could have achieved through the democratic process."[30]

Throughout the 1980s, public opinion polls indicated that a majority of the nation's people "supported limiting rights to the 'hard' cases—rape, incest, and immediate physical harm to the mother—and rejected the right to abortion upon demand as enshrined in *Roe v. Wade.*"[31] In other words, there was "consensus" on significantly limiting the so-called right to abortion.

But Mario Cuomo chose not to go into the public arena and lobby to implement that consensus. He was silent even when Pennsylvania Governor Robert Casey of Pennsylvania, a pro-life Democrat, was denied a speaking role at the National Convention that nominated Bill Clinton.

Note, as Garry Wills pointed out, that while Cuomo "accepts without question" the "doctrine of the Church on abortion [h]e does not advance arguments of his own to repeat, enforce, or explain that doctrine. He simply deposits it in his own little thesaurus of faith, not to be expended outside his home."[32]

In a similar vein, *Village Voice* journalist Nat Hentoff pointed out that Mario Cuomo "has referred to his 'personal' conviction about abortion in only a perfunctory manner. Nor has he urged the reversal of *Roe v. Wade,* the Supreme Court decision declaring a constitutional right to an abortion. It is as if Cuomo had been governor of New York in the 1850s and dutifully upheld the Fugitive Slave Act while merely whispering his opposition to slavery. It is one thing for a public official to uphold the law as, of course, he must. But this need not prevent him—if he is convinced the law is wrong—from forcefully and often saying so in an effort to persuade the citizenry to help change it. This Cuomo has not done with regard to abortion."[33]

In his Notre Dame speech, Cuomo also came out against a constitutional amendment against abortion and the Hatch Amendment that would have permitted the states to decide whether or not to permit abortion—the way it was for most of the nation's history.

And he opposed "denial" of Medicaid funding for abortion. Conceding that the federal government—via the Hyde Amendment—prohibits federal funding of abortion, he said, "I believe we cannot follow that lead." The New York State Constitution's equal protection clause, he argued, "would preclude us from denying the poor—indirectly, by cutoff of funds—the practical use of the constitutional right given by *Roe v. Wade.*"

What Cuomo failed to mention was that the same court that handed down *Roe v. Wade* would, seven years later in *Harris v. McRae*, rule that "government is not obliged to subsidize abortions, and this gives the office holder some constitutional scope for exercising his moral judgment."[34]

Cuomo ignored the fact that by 1984, two-thirds of the states passed legislation prohibiting state funding of most abortions.

And he did not tell his audience in South Bend that the New York State Assembly came within two votes of stopping funding (at the cost to taxpayers of about $13.4 million) for approximately 43,000 abortions annually.

Contrary to his claim, Cuomo did have a choice in the funding matter and could have used his power to eliminate it from the state budget.

Despite his rhetoric about not imposing his personal beliefs on citizens, the governor had no problem imposing his mistaken view on New York taxpayers—particularly those who, in good conscience, do not want the taxes they pay to finance the killing of innocents.

Cuomo's Notre Dame speech was the most famous but hardly the only public statement he made about abortion—some of them quite ridiculous.

For instance, he told *The New York Times*: "Christ sums it all up for Christians. He gave a doctrine that never mentioned abortion. He wasn't terribly strong on negatives. He prescinded from politics—he refused to register in the zealot party."[35]

Was he suggesting that because Christ did not use the word "abortion," or for that matter "the death penalty," the Church's teachings are false?

Cuomo was grasping at straws. Christ reminded his followers during his Sermon on the Mount that "you shall not kill" and "adds to it the proscription of anger, hatred, and vengeance."[36]

As for his opposition to the constitutional amendment forbidding abortion, Cuomo argued in his Notre Dame speech that "it wouldn't work" . . . "it would be Prohibition revisited, legislating what couldn't be enforced and in the process, creating a disrespect for law in general."

Once again, Cuomo contradicted his assertion that laws should not be on the books that are, for the most part, unenforceable when he pushed for a law requiring people to wear car seatbelts. When asked why he supports the legislation that would be "unworkable and unenforceable," Cuomo replied. "To suggest that maybe it can't be enforced perfectly, we don't do perfect enforcement of our cocaine laws do we, and our heroin laws? You wouldn't suggest repealing those, so I think what you do is you adopt an intelligent law, and then you do everything you can to enforce it. It's wrong to say that this is unenforceable. It's not."[37]

Cuomo found himself on intellectually thin ice when pushed to give his thoughts on when life begins.

In an interview with *Newsweek*'s Ken Woodward, the governor opined on personal liberty. He quoted from one of his speeches that "only when liberty intrudes on another's right, only when it does damage to another human being, only when it takes or hurts or deprives or invades may it be limited."[38]

"But surely," Woodward injected, "abortion damages another human being."

"Not everyone agrees on when human life begins," Cuomo said. "Even theologians can't say when the soul enters the body."

"Come on Mario," Woodward replied. "All you have to do is wait 266 days and see what you get. A human embryo does not turn out to be a cat or a dog."[39]

That was not the only time Cuomo had to confront that question.

Ken Auletta, writing in the New York *Daily News* in October 1984, realized that Cuomo was dancing around the question of an unborn baby's humanity. "He did not enjoy it when a reporter asked him yes or no: Do you believe a fetus is a human life? Cuomo launched a mini-filibuster. His initial response was 'I don't know what you mean by 'a human life.'" Then he went on to incorrectly state that the Supreme Court said that a fetus is not human (actually the Court declined to comment on the humanity of the fetus.)

The reporter, refusing to give up, eventually pushed Cuomo to give an answer. He said "I have to conclude that the fetus is life or so close to life that it ought not to be disposed of casually."

Cutting through all of Cuomo's blather, Auletta summarized the governor's position thusly, "Yes, it was human. But maybe, if people did not do it 'casually' an abortion is permissible. Yes, but."[40]

What exactly does that mean? It appears Cuomo is saying as long as the decision to take a human life is a serious one and not a whim, abortion is okay.

Another peculiar argument Cuomo articulated at a press conference on August 9, 1984, was reported by Nat Hentoff in the *Village Voice*: "Is abortion murder?," Cuomo asked. "Somebody who thought it was murder, and did it, that's a murderer. But someone who didn't think it was murder, and did it, that's not a murderer."[41]

In other words, killing someone is okay as long as one doesn't believe it's murder.

To further obfuscate the issue of when life begins, Cuomo told the *Times* in August 1984: "If you want to understand the position on abortion you have to understand Aquinas and Augustine. Aquinas says it takes six weeks from conception for the soul to make it into a male body and three months into a female body."[42] (Cuomo would repeat this argument for the remainder of his life. He used it on the author several years before he died.)

The "position" of St. Augustine and St. Thomas Aquinas was not theirs. It was not a Catholic theological position or a doctrinal one. It was, as the renowned philosopher Mortimer Adler pointed out, "a biological theory that was advocated by non-Catholic Greek scientists who lived hundreds of years before Christ."[43]

Aquinas and Augustine accepted the prevailing scientific opinions just as churchmen accepted that the world was flat until proven otherwise.

As for the findings of modern science, Adler made this observation:

> So far as the abortion controversy in its classical form is concerned, the advances in medical knowledge seem to have had only one relevant effect: everything we now know about the chemical structure of the genes and their relation to life seems to indicate that the embryo is a fully potential human being from the moment of conception. It is not surprising, therefore, that the proponents of abortion in the contemporary controversy tend to disregard the question of the human status of the embryo.[44]

It should also be noted that as a theological matter, St. Thomas Aquinas "taught that all abortions are a 'grave sin' (*peccatum grave*), 'among evil deeds' (*inter malefica*), and 'against nature' (*contra naturam*).'"[45]

The clashes between Cuomo and Church leaders over abortion flared up once again, after the U.S. Supreme Court handed down the *Webster v. Reproductive Health Services* decision on July 3, 1989.

In the *Webster* case, the court upheld provisions of a 1986 Missouri law that:

1) Prohibit public facilities and employees from being involved in the performance of abortions, and prohibits public assistance for abortions when the life of the mother is not at risk;
2) Require physicians to conduct viability tests prior to performing an abortion on a fetus believed to be at least 20 weeks old.

Because pro-lifers planned to lobby other state legislatures to enact similar laws to permit the restrictions, pro-abortion groups were urging elected officials to resist such legislation.

Then on September 11, 1989, a *Times* headline read: "Cuomo Takes Abortion Stance Favoring Women's Right to Choose."

Due to the *Webster* decision that ruled "states could limit women's access to abortion," the news story reported "Mr. Cuomo came under increasing pressure to clarify his position."

In remarks to a women's group in Arizona, the governor pledged that he would not pursue state legislation to codify the Supreme Court's limitations on abortion; he also declared that abortion "must be a matter of the woman's conscience."

"I feel absurd," Cuomo said. "Like I don't know why the judgment is mine. Or an all-male court, except for one woman, or a mostly male Congress." He went on to say that it was "presumptuous for a man to make judgments about abortion."[46]

New York abortion groups were ecstatic. One spokesman said Cuomo's remarks "were the strongest he has made in favor of a woman's right to have an abortion since he took office."[47]

The president of New York's National Organization for Women said she was "very happy to see the Governor taking a leadership position." Previously "many people in the pro-choice community weren't really satisfied with the Governor's position."[48]

The man who said that he accepted the Church's position on abortion not only refused to implement constitutionally-approved restrictions, but took the radical position that a woman has the unfettered right to an abortion.

In November 1989, Cuomo picked another fight with his Church. He criticized the decision of Bishop Leo Maher of the Diocese of San Diego for denying communion to pro-abortion California Assemblywoman Lucy Killea.

Cuomo questioned how far Bishop Maher "would go in denying the Sacrament to those who don't share his views."[49]

"The issues of contraception and the death penalty raise the most obvious examples," he said.

"Would the bishop's position require that a Catholic governor be denied communion if she voted in favor of the death penalty?"

Once again, Cuomo was misrepresenting Church teachings by comparing apples to oranges.

Concerning the worthiness to receive Holy Communion, Cardinal Joseph Ratzinger laid out these principles:

> The Church teaches that abortion or euthanasia is a grave sin. The Encyclical Letter *Evangelium vitae*, with reference to judicial decisions or civil laws that authorize or promote abortion or euthanasia, states that there is a "grave and clear obligation to oppose them by conscientious objection. [. . .] In the case of an intrinsically unjust law, such as a law permitting abortion or euthanasia, it is therefore never licit to obey it, or to 'take part in a propaganda campaign in favour of such a law or vote for it. . . .'"

> Not all moral issues have the same moral weight as abortion and euthanasia. For example, if a Catholic were to be at odds with the Holy Father on the application of capital punishment or on the decision to wage war, he would not for that reason be considered unworthy to present himself to receive Holy Communion. While the Church exhorts civil authorities to seek peace, not war, and to exercise discretion and mercy in imposing punishment on criminals, it may still be permissible to take up arms

to repel an aggressor or to have recourse to capital punishment. There may be a legitimate diversity of opinion even among Catholics about waging war and applying the death penalty, but not however with regard to abortion and euthanasia.

Apart from an individual's judgment about his worthiness to present himself to receive the Holy Eucharist, the minister of Holy Communion may find himself in the situation where he must refuse to distribute Holy Communion to someone, such as in cases of a declared excommunication, a declared interdict, or an obstinate persistence in manifest grave sin (cf. can. 915).

It is obvious that equating support for abortion with support for the death penalty is ridiculous. Under Church law, abortion is inherently evil while prudential support or opposition to the death penalty are not.

Six weeks after his remarks in Arizona, on January 3, 1990, Cuomo appeared to be backtracking a bit on abortion as he was gearing up to run for a fourth term. For the first time, he mentioned abortion in his annual State of the State address before the Legislature. "I think we ought to begin a broader discussion on the subject of abortion," he said. Calling the statistics on the number of abortions performed yearly "sobering," he pledged to include in his budget funds "specifically allocated for promoting the value of abstinence for young people."[50]

Both pro-abortion and pro-life advocates were perplexed by the intent of the governor's comments:

Abortion-rights advocates said they hoped Mr. Cuomo merely proposed continued funds for sex-education programs that, while counseling abstinence, also describe the alternatives of birth control and abortion. Abortion opponents interpreted the pledge as an endorsement of "pro-chastity" programs that avoid any mention of contraception or abortion. Both sides admitted that they did not know precisely what the governor meant.[51]

The governor's spokesman quickly made it clear that, "we're not talking about funding abstinence-only programs." Any money appropriated would be used "to enhance the use of abstinence component" at existing family planning clinics that have abortion counseling.

The spokesman went on to explain that the governor was interested in bringing both sides of the issue together. "What he is saying is 'Hey folks, let's get above the disagreement. There's so much else that we can all agree on.'"[52]

On the day of the annual March for Life in Washington, January 22, 1990, Cuomo spoke before the state's pro-abortion coalition conference in Albany. He asked the members of the Family Planning Advocates conference, "Why don't we try to think of ways to encourage people in this state and in this country to think a little harder about finding ways to reduce the number of unintended pregnancies?"[53]

Calling for greater educational efforts to encourage abstinence, he said, "I think, frankly, it is a mistake to believe that history has left the alternative of restraint behind as a sociological anachronism. And all of us, I think, must do more to promote the value of abstinence, and I will do so."[54]

Meanwhile, that same day, the Most Reverend Austin Vaughan, a New York Archdiocese auxiliary bishop, serving a 15-day jail sentence for blocking access to an abortion clinic, told the *New York Post* in a phone interview that Cuomo is a "Sunday Catholic" who "is in danger of going to hell if he dies tonight."

"Abortion is an unspeakable crime," said Bishop Vaughn. "This is an unchanged and unchangeable teaching of the Church. And Gov. Cuomo has fought harder for abortion than anybody in New York State." He continued, "I find it horrendous, absolutely contradictory for someone to say they are personally opposed to abortion, then to say nobody has fought harder for abortions for poor women."

"I think," Vaughan added, "for a believing educated Catholic to take the position he's taken, he takes a very serious risk of going straight to hell."[55]

Cuomo said in a press conference the next day, "I think my soul will be judged like yours and like the bishop's by a higher and wiser power than the bishop."

But he defended the bishop's right to make his comments. "He has a perfect right to curse you to hell, ugly as it is. You [the *Post*] have a perfect right to print it. . . . Women have a right to an abortion. I will protect that right as well as I will protect his right to curse me."[56]

The governor's portrayal of the incident, however, was wrong. Bishop Vaughan did not "curse him to hell," he said Cuomo *could* go to hell.

In that same press conference, Cuomo took umbrage to Vaughan's hope Cardinal O'Connor would ban him from receiving communion.

"I certainly would not want that to happen," he said. "I'm a Catholic. If a Jew were told you cannot come to temple to have your child bar mitzvahed, or you can't come to temple, how would it make you feel?"[57]

Cuomo went on to reject the bishop's statement that his stand on abortion violates Church teaching. "I can believe abortion is wrong without saying you must believe it," he said.[58]

"The Church," he added, "is not the Pope and the College of Cardinals and all the ecclesiastics. The Church is the body of people who choose to believe. . . . The Church is all of us."[59]

Of course, when it comes to Church teaching, the sole responsibility of presenting the formal official teaching of the Catholic Church rests entirely with the pope and his bishops. Cardinal O'Connor once asked (echoing St. Thomas More), "Are we to have a Church in which everyone's judgment is equal to everyone else's? That's not a Church, it's chaos."[60]

As for the Vaughan-Cuomo clash, on January 31, 1990, Cardinal O'Connor came to the defense of his auxiliary bishop. In his *Catholic New York* column, later quoted in *The New York Times*, the cardinal described Vaughan as "one of the finest theologians I know," continued:

> I read in the newspapers that His Excellency, the Auxiliary Bishop of New York, had "cursed" His Excellency, the Governor of New York, "to hell." Indeed, the Governor is quoted as saying: "I get condemned to hell for not agreeing [on abortion]."
>
> "Not so," Bishop Vaughan told me, "very much not so," when I spoke with him after his release from prison. He went on to say that he is well aware that he has no power whatsoever to condemn anyone to hell. He would agree with the Governor completely that such an unpleasant task in exclusively the prerogative of a much higher and wiser power.
>
> He told me, too, that despite the newspaper reports, he had never suggested for a moment that he would be happy to see me refuse the Governor Holy Communion. In fact, he says he

was asked by the press whether he, Bishop Vaughan, would ex-communicate the Governor, and replied that he had no authority to do so and would not think it a good idea anyway.

That out of way, would anyone deny that the bishop has the right and even the obligation to warn any Catholic that his soul is at risk if he should die while deliberately pursuing any gravely evil course of action, and that such would certainly include advocating publicly, as the bishop puts it, "the right of a woman to kill a child." What the bishop told me he actually said was that the Governor is "quite possibly contributing to the loss of his soul." To me that sounds significantly different from "cursing" or "condemning" the Governor to hell. . . .

I do have one major concern, however, and it's not the highly confused report on who said what in the newspaper stories. It's that such stories tend to distract from the real issue, that abortion, as the Second Vatican Council puts it, in an "abominable crime." That, neither political fortunes nor ecclesiastical sanctions, is the bottom line.

Cuomo had a terse reply: "The cardinal says the bishop was misquoted, I'm glad."[61]

"A defiant Cuomo," the *Post* reported on February 2, also insisted that "his conscience—not cardinals and bishops—be his guide on whether he's risking his soul by continuing to support a women's right to abortion."

"I think the person [who] knows best what's going to happen to your soul is you. If you do something that violates your own conscience, then probably your soul is in peril. If you do something that is in accord with a well-formed conscience, sincerely formed . . . it seems to me any God of good judgment would understand that."[62]

But was Cuomo's conscience "informed"?

The *Encyclopedia of Catholic Social Thought* entry on "conscience" states that "our conscience gives us responsibility for our actions. We have the right to act in accord with our conscience that must be respected. Although we have a duty to follow our conscience, our conscience is not always in-fallible. Our conscience must be formed in the light of the word of God and the authoritative teaching of the Church."[63]

John Paul II's 1995 encyclical *Evangelium vitae* confirms the authentic teaching of the Church:

> Faced with the progressive weakening in individual consciences and in society of the sense of the absolute and grave moral illic-itness of the direct taking of all innocent human life, especially at its beginning and at its end, the Church's Magisterium has spoken out with increasing frequency in defense of the sacred-ness and inviolability of human life. . . .

> Therefore, by the authority which Christ conferred upon Peter and his Successors, and in communion with the Bishops of the Catholic Church, I confirm that the direct and voluntary killing of an innocent human being is always gravely immoral. This doctrine, based upon that unwritten law which man, in the light of reason, finds in his own heart (cf. Rom 2:14-15), is reaf-firmed by Sacred Scripture, transmitted by the Tradition of the Church and taught by the ordinary and universal Magisterium.

> The deliberate decision to deprive an innocent human being of his life is always morally evil and can never be licit either as an end in itself or as a means to a good end. It is in fact a grave act of disobedience to the moral law, and indeed to God himself, the author and guarantor of that law; it contradicts the fundamental virtues of justice and charity. Nothing and no one can in any way permit the killing of an innocent human being, whether a fetus or an embryo, an infant or an adult, an old person, or one suffer-ing from an incurable disease, or a person who is dying. . . .

Clear enough?

As for the issue of conception, the pope's words explicitly reject Cuomo's position:

Some people try to justify abortion by claiming that the result of conception, at least up to a certain number of days, cannot yet be considered a personal human life. But in fact, "from the time that the ovum is fertilized, a life is begun which is neither that of the father nor the mother; it is rather the life off a new human being with his own growth. It would never be made human if it were not human already. This has always been clear, and . . . modern genetic science offers clear confirmation. It has demonstrated that from the first instant there is established the programme of what this living being will be: a person, this individual person with his characteristic aspects already well determined. . . .

And on "conscience" he also differs with Cuomo:

In order to shed light on this difficult question, it is necessary to recall the general principles concerning cooperation in evil actions. Christians, like all people of good will, are called upon under grave obligation of conscience not to cooperate formally in practices which, even if permitted by civil legislation, are contrary to God's law. Indeed, from the moral standpoint, it is never licit to cooperate formally in evil. . . . This cooperation can never be justified either by invoking respect for the freedom of others or by appealing to the fact that civil law permits it or requires it. Each individual in fact has moral responsibility for the acts which he personally performs; no one can be exempted from this responsibility, and on the basis of it everyone will be judged by God himself (cf. Rom 2:6; 14:12).[64]

In a further attempt to defend his Arizona statement, Cuomo accepted an invitation from *Commonweal* magazine "to join in a reasoned debate on abortion, particularly in the post-*Webster* environment."

In a 3,000-word letter, printed on his gubernatorial stationery, dated March 5, 1990, Cuomo reflected on some of the magazine's "commentary of the past six or seven months."[65]

His comments were classic Cuomo—defensive, "splitting the difference," and obfuscating.

Cuomo defended his Arizona speech insisting what he said was "perfectly consistent with his position stated at Notre Dame."

He repeated the position he made before the *Webster* decision: "Here in America where the law permits women to have abortions and preserves their right not to have abortions, the terrible, hard judgment which that freedom permits must be a matter of the women's conscience."

He declined to address the issue of viability of the fetus. He conceded that the ethical and legal implications of the medical data should be explored, but added, "we should proceed with the caution the facts dictate and without raising expectations that any law dealing with viability—even if enforced and obeyed—would lower the abortion rate more than minimally."

On the question of counseling, he argued that family planning centers "either through counseling or referral" must give "information about the full range of options available, including birth control and abortion."

Cuomo was very defensive about *Commonweal's* criticism that he signed with eight other governors an amicus brief to the Supreme Court on the case *Turnock v. Ragsdale* which concerned abortion clinic standards in Illinois that the signers considered unreasonable.

"The *Ragsdale* amicus brief that I joined," he wrote, "was in no way an argument for expanding abortion rights. I do not regret nor apologize for being party to it."

However, the fact is the amicus brief "explicitly (and unnecessarily) asked the court not to overturn *Roe v. Wade*." The *Commonweal* editors pointed out this key sentence in the amicus brief: "It would be unprecedented for this Court, having recognized a fundamental constitutional right to withdraw that right and throw the abortion issue back into the political arena."

If Cuomo believed that abortion was wrong as the Church teaches, why would he object to overturning *Roe v. Wade* and putting the issue where it belonged, with the fifty states?

In his letter to *Commonweal*, Cuomo also criticized pro-life appeals to the natural law. "The reality or concept of the natural law is not one congenial to our society," he declared.

But this nation was founded by appealing to the natural law as stated in the second paragraph of the Declaration of Independence: "We hold these truths to be self-evident, that all men are created equal, that they are endowed by their Creator with certain inalienable Rights, that among these are Life, Liberty and the pursuit of Happiness." And because these rights come from God, governments are created "to secure these rights" not to grant them. Hence, the Catholic argument that the Court in *Roe v. Wade* failed to "secure" the rights of the innocent unborn.

As for a law requiring parental notification, Cuomo conceded that it could be beneficial in some cases but "not necessarily as a way of preventing abortions but of helping to provide a minor the support she needs at such a time." Cuomo went on to say it would be a complex law to write but he would give "most careful attention" to any notification bill the Legislature would send him. However, he did not promise to have his office draft a bill that he would introduce to the Legislature and lobby for.

On restricting abortions, Cuomo wrote, "If it were my judgment that theoretically doable legal restrictions on abortion (e.g., limitations of medical funding) were fair and would engender a greater respect for life in our state, then I would have to be disposed to advocate for such change."

However, he suggested restrictions were not possible and hid behind the equal protection clause in New York's Constitution, ignoring, once again, the restrictions handed down in the *Webster* case by the Supreme Court.

The editors of *Commonweal* did not buy into most of Cuomo's explanations and focused their major disappointments in this opening sentence, "We begin this promised reply to Governor Mario Cuomo's letter by announcing he is right. We do not agree with everything his letter said, and the letter does not contain everything we wished it would have." The editor's continued:

> we reserve our greatest emphasis for what we've described as our chief disappointment with his response. Casting about for an entry point, we turned to another great national debate and read these words:
>
> 'He who molds public sentiment, goes deeper than he who enacts statutes or pronounces decisions. He makes statutes and decisions possible or impossible to be executed.'

Thus Abraham Lincoln, joining Judge Stephen Douglas in debate over the 1857 Dred Scott decision, which permitted the extension of slavery to the territories of the United States and determined that slaves had no constitutional protections. Was Judge Douglas personally opposed? "He does not give any opinion on that—but, because it has been decided by the Court . . . he is, and you are, bound to take it in your political action as law." Lincoln bore in on Douglas's silence about the content of Dred Scott because Lincoln not only opposed the decision but feared it would lead to a second one extending slavery to the states that prohibited it.

There are no perfect historical analogies, but this one is close. Douglas treated *Scott v. Sandford* as sacrosanct, the law of the land. *Roe* supporters pay *Roe* similar reverence. . . . But, with the *Webster* decision of last July, a question that had seemed closed now appears to be open; the states are in a position to test how far the Supreme Court will reshape its 1973 ruling. . . .

Shaping new state laws and regulations is a long, arduous, and conflict-filled process. Out of the ambivalence shared by a majority of Americans, some consensus needs to be formed—a consensus that will be shaped in part by the intelligence and persuasive skills that political leaders bring to the public debate. And now our question, our principal question: Why hasn't Governor Mario Cuomo stepped forth as a molder of consensus?

To ask the question is emphatically not to suggest that he has done nothing; on the contrary, he has done more than some of his critics to keep abortion from being treated as a settled question. . . .

And yet, and yet. Those of us who believe abortion is wrong—and we accept that Governor Cuomo so believes—need to do many things. Although, in the face of social and cultural pressures favoring abortion, legislation cannot prohibit it, other legislative measures can help reduce the number of abortions. . . .

But public officials do not affect public policy only through legislation and regulation; they also effect change through their powers of persuasion and their use of the public platform they are accorded for purposes of political leadership. Like Mr. Lincoln, Mario Cuomo has the oratorical skills to enlighten and persuade the public. Note his words on child care in the State of the State message: "No infant should come into a world that does not care if it is fed properly, housed decently, educated adequately; where the blind or retarded child is condemned to exist rather than empowered to live."

Here is moral wisdom married to rhetorical power. On abortion itself, Mr. Cuomo offers less of both. If indeed he takes abortion seriously as a direct assault on life, the tenor of his finely calibrated comments do not finally seem to connect with that reality.

The editors of *Commonweal* were justified in not letting Cuomo off the hook. During his 12 years as New York's governor, Cuomo did nothing to limit abortions. Until the end of his life, he argued that abortion was merely a religious matter, and, therefore, the Church's position on abortion could not be imposed on others.

Cuomo, the Church, and the Death Penalty

Throughout his political career, Mario Cuomo had been an outspoken opponent of the death penalty. His position was consistent and honorable and he paid a price for it in the political arena.

Political analysts agree that his anti-death penalty stance was a significant contributing factor to his defeat in the 1977 mayor's race and in his bid for a fourth gubernatorial term in 1994.

As governor, Cuomo vetoed death penalty legislation all eleven times that it came to his desk. Despite overwhelming state-wide consensus in favor of the death penalty, Cuomo imposed his will on the electorate. Cuomo explained his position thusly: "I have studied the death penalty for more than half my lifetime. I have debated it hundreds of times. I have heard all the arguments, analyzed all the evidence I could find, measured public opinion when it was opposed to the practice, when it was indifferent, and when it was passionately in favor. Always I have concluded the death penalty is wrong because it lowers us all; it is a surrender to the worst that is in us; it uses a power—the official power to kill by execution—that has never elevated a society, never brought back a life, never inspired anything but hate."[66]

However, his characterization during his years in elective office of the Roman Catholic Church's position on the death penalty was misguided.

To adequately explain the matter, it requires the author to describe his clash with Cuomo over the death penalty.

In early August 1994, while waiting to appear on a Syracuse radio talk show, the writer heard Cuomo say to the host, "My Church teaching I accept and I don't impose on you or anyone else. Incidentally, I feel that way about the death penalty as apparently do most Catholics. Because as you know the Catholic Church teaches [that] the death penalty is wrong, but that does not stop Catholic legislators from your area or elsewhere from voting for it."

The Catholic legislator Cuomo was referring to was his Republican-Conservative opponent in the 1994 governor's race, State Senator George Pataki of Peekskill.

Knowing that Cuomo misrepresented Catholic teaching on capital punishment, the author wrote an op-ed for *Newsday* (August 23, 1994) titled "The Governor's Dead Wrong to Cite Church."

Here are pertinent excerpts:

> The Roman Catholic Church has always acknowledged the state's power to impose the death penalty. . . . According to the Church, punishment exercised by a duly recognized government has three functions:
>
> • Retributive, which forces the criminal to pay for his crime and vindicates the rights of the offended;

- Corrective, which rehabilitates the offender;
- Deterrent, which forestalls similar crimes by warning the entire community.

The death penalty is viewed as retribution insofar as it attempts to adequately punish the most serious criminals—murderers and traitors. St. Thomas Aquinas wrote that in order to promote the common good "the state executes pestiferous men justly and sinlessly in order that the peace of the state may not be disrupted. . . ."

Pope John Paul II has often appealed for compassion and clemency for condemned murderers and the U.S. Catholic bishops stated that the death penalty should not be imposed in the United States. Yet they have never decried the Church's stand on capital punishment. As a matter of fact, the American bishops also insisted that "the state has the right to take the life of a person guilty of a serious crime. . . ."

I would recommend that Governor Cuomo refer to the newly issued Catechism of the Catholic Church that states:

"Preserving the common good of society requires rendering the aggressor unable to inflict harm. For this reason, the traditional teaching of the Church has acknowledged as well-founded the right and duty of legitimate public authority to punish malefactors by means of penalties commensurate with the gravity of the crime, not excluding, in cases of extreme gravity, the death penalty."

The closing paragraph most likely annoyed Cuomo:

Frankly, I'm disappointed with the Governor—he knows better. Mario Cuomo was well trained in Catholic philosophy and ethics at St. John's University. But sadly, in his desperation to retain his power and perks at the executive mansion he'll resort to any tactic—even misrepresenting the teachings of his Church.

Three days later, August 26, 1994, a *Newsday* op-ed piece appeared titled, "The Church Says It's Wrong" authored by Mario Cuomo:

> A recent piece by George J. Marlin, who is supporting another candidate in the governor's race, argued in favor of capital punishment. That is not unusual. But in his piece, he wrote that the official teaching of today's Catholic Church supports death as a punishment. That is unusual, inappropriate and misleading.
>
> In citing the new Catholic Catechism (Section 2266) as a justification for the death penalty, he omitted the following language: "If bloodless means are sufficient to defend human lives against an aggressor and to protect public order and the safety of persons, public authority should limit itself to such means, because they better correspond to the concrete conditions of the common good and are more in conformity to the dignity of the human person."
>
> On December 6, 1983, Cardinal Joseph Bernardin, in a much-reported lecture, spoke about a consistent ethic of life in our culture—a "seamless garment." He said it is important to note that in the case of capital punishment "there has been a shift at the level of pastoral practice." The cardinal explained that in today's Catholic Church the action of the bishops, and Popes Paul IV and John Paul II has been directed against the exercise by the state of capital punishment. "The argument has been that more humane methods of defining the society exist and should be used. . . ."
>
> One of the last letters issued by the saintly Bishop Francis Mugavero of the Brooklyn Diocese was headlined "Capital Punishment a Barbaric Response to Crime." He called it a "savage act" that "often is an act of revenge that appeals to our baser instincts." And, in a full-page commentary in 1989, His Eminence John Cardinal O'Connor concluded: "It is a sad

commentary that the death penalty is once again proposed as the cure for the ills of our times. What a tragedy, that civilization has brought us no further than this, that we cannot teach moral values in our public schools, but we can execute those who have rejected the very public values we cannot teach."

Frankly, I have not argued my position against the death penalty as a religious issue, but it would be wrong to allow the supporters of death to fool anyone into believing that their position is favored by the Catholic Church, when the truth is just the opposite.

While it is true that Cuomo did not argue against the death penalty based on Church teaching, nevertheless, his take on the Church's stance was seriously flawed as the author explained in a response titled "Stating the Church's Position" published in *Newsday* on August 31, 1994:

The issue in dispute between Gov. Cuomo and myself, as reflected in our opposing New York Forums, is, "What is the authentic teaching of the Catholic Church on capital punishment in contemporary society?" First, let's check the latest authoritative statement of the supreme authority in the Church, which one finds in the recently issued Catechism of the Catholic Church.

As the governor knows, the Catechism affirms the Church's traditional teaching on capital punishment and thus recognizes the right of the state to take the life of those guilty of grievous crimes. It does not require the state to exercise that right which is a prudential option, but it does admit that the state and only the state possesses that right. The Catechism also urges mercy, but recognizes that the choice is up to the state.

The great value of the Catechism is that it is promulgated by supreme authority to be used throughout the whole Church. . . . The Catechism, therefore, supersedes any other Catholic voice, however esteemed.

Cardinal Bernardin's thesis of the seamless garment, cited by the governor, has been used widely by those who wish to blur the obvious distinction between abortion and capital punishment in order to strengthen opposition to the latter. Anyone who cannot see the obvious distinction between taking the life of an innocent child and the life of a serial murderer cannot be taken seriously as a teacher of morals or as a political leader.

Cardinal John O'Connor told the author that he had followed the Marlin-Cuomo exchange and said that Cuomo's view of Catholic teaching was misinformed. Later O'Connor waded into the death penalty debate and had the last word on the subject. He told the N.Y.C. Police Department's Holy Name Society members in a homily at St. Patrick's Cathedral that while he was personally opposed to capital punishment:

> True formal official Church teaching does not deny the right of the state to exercise the death penalty under narrowly defined conditions. . . . The traditional teaching of the Church has acknowledged as well-founded the right and duty of legitimate police authority to punish malefactors by means of penalties that are commensurate with the gravity of the crime—not excluding, in cases of extreme gravity, the death penalty. . . .

> Perhaps I will, therefore, shock everyone if I say that in accordance with Catholic teaching, a good Catholic can responsibly be for or against the death penalty under certain restricted conditions.[67]

Cuomo and Pierre Teilhard de Chardin, S.J.

In his memoir, *Getting Religion: Faith, Culture and Politics from the Age of Eisenhower to the Era of Obama*, journalist Kenneth Woodward writes of his first encounter with Mario Cuomo:

> It was early September 1984 and *Newsweek*'s editors had invited the governor of New York over for an off-the-record lunch. . . . We were

waiting at the elevator on the fortieth floor for Cuomo, and when the doors opened the name of his favorite Catholic theologian [Teilhard de Chardin] were the first words we heard from his lips.

It appeared as though the governor had been having a deep discussion with his two aides on the ride up from the lobby. But my own surmise was that Cuomo had timed his opening words to impress his *Newsweek* hosts. Teilhard's daring theological interpretation of evolution had been the rage when Cuomo and I were both undergraduates, and the governor had every reason to believe that *Newsweek*'s editors knew nothing of the long-deceased Jesuit's work. Quite likely the governor, who relished his reputation as an intellectual Catholic, wanted to throw the editors off their game and begin our noontime conversation with the ball firmly in his own court.

Sure enough, the lunch began with Cuomo going on about Teilhard for five minutes before editor-in-chief Rick Smith could turn the discussion towards politics. I waited until the main course was served before telling Cuomo, as politely as I could, "Governor, I think you've got Teilhard's theory wrong." Cuomo shot me a quick glower, the kind reporters in Albany who criticized him often saw, and the conversation moved on.[68]

When Teilhard's most famous work, *The Divine Milieu*, became available in print in the late 1950s (it was actually written in 1927) it became "must" reading for progressive-minded Catholics who fancied themselves erudite intellectuals. And for one of his readers, Mario Cuomo, Teilhard helped rationalize his developing world view.

However, while Teilhard's avant-garde writings may have been considered chic by Cuomo and like-minded Catholic progressives in the early sixties, there was a dark side to his thought, both theologically and sociologically.

Pierre Teilhard de Chardin (1881–1955) joined the Society of Jesus in 1899. After completing his studies in philosophy and theology, he was ordained a priest in 1911. Afterwards he took up the study of paleontology.

After receiving his doctorate in 1922, he taught geology for a short time at the Catholic Institute in Paris. He was let go due to his unorthodox views on original sin and exiled himself to China.

Teilhard worked on excavations which discovered the so-called "Peking Man." He remained in China doing research until the end of the Japanese occupation in 1945.

Back in France in 1946, despite his reputation as a renowned paleontologist, he was denied a teaching post at the College of France, and the Vatican refused permission to publish his manuscripts due to his unorthodox opinions.

Teilhard moved to the United States in 1952 and settled in New York City to work for the Wenner-Gren Foundation for Anthropological Research.

On Easter Sunday, April 10, 1955, Teilhard died of a heart attack. He is buried in the Hyde Park, New York cemetery of what was then the St. Andrew-on-Hudson Jesuit novitiate and is today the property of the Culinary Institute of America.

While there was an underground industry that circulated his manuscripts in the 1940s and early 1950s, Teilhard's works began to be formally published only after his death.

"The fascination which Teilhard de Chardin exercised for an entire generation," Christoph Cardinal Schönborn has written, "stemmed from his radical manner of looking at science and Christian faith together. This unity of vision, in which he intended to unite natural science and Christian faith, was of course also problematical. Critics have shown that he could not do complete justice to both sides. His vision of evolution as an upward movement that ceaselessly produces higher and ever higher forms is more of a philosophical speculation than a scientific theory. On the other hand, his naturalization of Christ as the driving force of evolution inevitably ran up against contradiction in theological terms."[69]

Teilhard's belief that our word is evolving meant that "the static concepts of the spiritual life must be rethought and the classical teachings of Christ must be reinterpreted."[70]

Teilhard's theories, which make Christ "dependent on the cosmogenic process" leaves no room for Christ's incarnation and overthrows, "the traditional conception of an eternal transcendent God."[71]

Teilhard's evolutionary views also led him to reject "the doctrine of the creation and fall of Adam and Eve and more pointedly . . . the doctrine of original sin, which he called 'an absurdity.'"[72]

When the Catholic theologian and philosopher Dietrich von Hildebrand met Teilhard at a dinner held at Fordham University in 1949, after questioning his ideas by referring to St. Augustine, Teilhard "exclaimed violently: 'Don't mention that unfortunate man; he spoiled everything by introducing the supernatural.'"[73]

That remark, von Hildebrand wrote, not only confirmed his impression of Teilhard's crass naturalism, but by criticizing St. Augustine, "the greatest of the Fathers of the Church, betrayed Teilhard's lack of a genuine sense of intellectual and spiritual grandeur."[74]

Von Hildebrand was not the only leading Catholic philosopher to reject Teilhard's views.

The great Thomistic philosopher Etienne Gilson concluded that Teilhardian theology "is one more Christian gnosis, and like gnosis from Marcion to the present, it is theology-fiction."[75]

Another renown Catholic philosopher, Jacques Maritain, agreed. He called "Teilhardian gnosis" an "ideology fabricated by the initiates and given circulation by the popular press—presents itself as a doctrine." Maritain concluded, "In the matter of doctrine, we are here in the regime . . . of the Great Fable."[76]

Then there is the critique of Teilhard's concept of evil by the dogmatic theologian Charles Cardinal Journet.

In Teilhard's judgment, the cardinal observed, "Evil in our modern perspective of a Universe in a process of cosmogenesis, *no longer exists*, because the Multiple, since it is multiple, that is to say essentially subject to the play of probabilities of change in its arrangements, is absolutely unable to progress toward unity without engendering Evil here or there—by statistical necessity."[77]

By rejecting Teilhard's position, Journet concludes: "we are being faithful to all traditional Christianity, we are accepting Christian revelation as it has been preserved and developed in the course of centuries by the divinely assisted magisterium. . . . If, on the contrary, we accept Teilhard's vision of the world, we know from the start—we have been duly warned—which notions of traditional Christianity will have to be transposed, and which we must bid farewell: Creation, Spirit, Evil, God, and, more particularly, original Sin, Cross, Resurrection, Parousia, Charity."[78]

While these learned philosophers and theologians pinpointed the flaws in Teilhard's ideology, many merely abstracted simple ideas he advanced and hung their hats on them, particularly the following:

> The active way of life is not inferior to the contemplative life; activity can be adoration, not simply by intention but by the fact that it is essential in the uniting of the whole universe in the Mystical Body of Christ.

> The man who dedicates his life to research or worldly activity renounces the shelter of the cloister, accepts the vicissitudes of the unpredictable world of business, and becomes, when animated by the proper spirit, the Grand Detaché to an even greater extent than does the contemplative.[79]

And so it was with Mario Cuomo who proudly called himself a "Teilhardian."

Throughout his adult life, he referred to Teilhard in numerous speeches and reflected on him in his diaries.

In 1982, for instance he told *The New York Times* he was a devotee of Teilhard because the French Jesuit wrote a book that opens up with these words: "To those who love the world." According to Cuomo, Teilhard "never talks about heaven and hell. He never talks about sin, except as an experience all of us go through. All life is good, all living is good. God intended you to make the most of it in human terms, by following the instincts that you have as a human being."[80]

In a sermon Cuomo delivered on November 27, 1983, at St. John the Divine, the seat of New York's Episcopal Church, he lectured that the "great Jesuit scientist and theologian Teilhard de Chardin . . . reoriented our theology and rewrote its language. His wonderful book *The Divine Milieu*, dedicated to 'those who love this world,' made negativism a sin."[81]

He continued: "Teilhard de Chardin glorified the world and everything in it. He said the whole universe—even the pain and imperfection we see—

is sacred, every part of it touched and transformed by the Incarnation. Faith, he said, is not a call to escape the world but to embrace it. Creation isn't an elaborate testing ground but an invitation to join in the work of restoration and completion."

For Cuomo, Teilhard's writing helped him and many in his generation "to realize that salvation consisted of something more than simply escaping the pains of hell." Teilhard's views encouraged him "to be involved in government because it is very much a part of the world God loves."

Many people, particularly members of the press, accepted Cuomo's view of Teilhard because his cosmology is obscure. But as the theologian Rev. George Rutler pointed out, Teilhard's "sociology is not obscure enough; indeed, it is not easy to conceal, except possibly from those munificent and kind politicians who take only the best from their theologians, Teilhard's benign regard for the early stages of the Fascist experience, his verbal assaults on the racial worth of the Chinese and his campaigns against black African membership in the fledgling United Nations."[82]

Yes, it appears that Cuomo overlooked or ignored Teilhard's "disregard for the weakest and poorest among humanity."

Here are excerpts from Teilhard's writings that spell out his pseudo-scientific views on his fellow man:[83]

On the Chinese:

Do the yellows—[the Chinese]—have the same human value as the whites? [Fr.] Licent and many missionaries say that their present inferiority is due to their long history of Paganism. I'm afraid that this in only a 'declaration of pastors.' Instead, the cause seems to be the natural racial foundation . . . Christian love overcomes all inequalities, but it does not deny them.

On Equity of Races

The philosophical or 'supernatural' unity of human nature has *nothing* to do with the equality of races in what concerns their physical capacities to contribute to the building of the world. . . . As not all ethnic groups have the same value, they must be dominated, which does not mean they must be despised—quite the reverse. . . . In other words, *at one and the same time* there should be official recognition of: (1) the primacy/priority of the earth over nations; (2) the inequality of peoples and races. Now the *second* point is currently reviled by Communism . . . and the Church, and the *first* point is similarly reviled by the Fascist systems (and, of course, by less gifted peoples!).

On Controlling Births:

For a complex of obscure reasons, our generation still regards with distrust all efforts proposed by science for controlling the machinery of heredity, of sex-determination and the development of the nervous systems. It is as if man had the right and power to interfere with all the channels in the world except those which make him himself. And yet, it is eminently on this ground that we must try *everything*, to its conclusion.

On Eugenics:

We must recognize . . . the vital importance of a collective quest of discovery and invention no longer inspired solely by a vague delight in knowledge and power, but by the duty and the clearly-defined hope of gaining control (and so making use) of the fundamental driving forces of evolution. And with this, the urgent need for a generalized eugenics (racial no less than individual) directed, beyond all concern with economic and nutritional problems, towards a biological maturing of the human type and of the biosphere.

And then there was this genocidal reflection:

What fundamental attitude . . . should the advancing wing of humanity take to fixed or definitely unprogressive ethnical groups? The earth is a closed and limited surface. To what extent should it tolerate, racially or nationally, areas of lesser activity?

More generally still, how should we judge the efforts we lavish in all kinds of hospitals on saving what is so often no more than one of life's rejects?... To what extent should not the development of the strong . . . take precedence over the preservation of the weak?

Not a pretty picture of the man whose writings convinced Cuomo "that God really wanted people to work to improve life on earth."

What Cuomo and fellow Teilhardians may have been most impressed by was the connection between the Frenchmen's evolutionary theory and the false assertion that objective truth is malleable. In other words, Teilhard may have provided Progressives with a justification for moral relativism.

CHAPTER 14

THE LAST TERM - 1991-1994

In early 1990, Andrew Cuomo told his father, "Don't run for a third term. You've had eight great years. There's a recession hitting us. . . . The next four years are going to be terrible and [if] you're around here that will be the end of you because people will forget the first eight years and remember the next three. . . . So, let's run for president."[1]

Governor Cuomo ignored his son's advice, but he quickly learned that Andrew's predictions about troubled financial waters ahead would come to pass.

New York's Fiscal and Economic Crisis

Governor Cuomo was fortunate that the State of New York participated in the 92-month "Reagan Economic Boom" that began in July 1981 and continued through November 1992.

During the nation's second longest peacetime economic expansion, the U.S. economy expanded by one-third with the growth rate averaging 3.5% per year. The nation's GDP increased by $2 trillion for an annual growth rate of 3.6%. Non-farm employment increased by 116.1 million.

New York gained 1 million jobs in the 1980s versus 50,000 in the 1970s.

Jobs in the construction industry between 1982 and 1989 increased by 25%. Customer service jobs grew by 50%. And the finance, insurance and real estate expanded 64%—for a total of 100 thousand jobs.

The only job sector that experienced decline was manufacturing. In 1980, manufacturing represented 20% of New York jobs. By 1989, it had dropped to 14%.

This economic boom generated plenty of tax revenues. The largest portion of state revenues, the Personal Income Tax (PIT), grew from $8.2 billion in 1982 to $15.3 billion in 1990; an 87% increase.

With all this money flowing into the state coffers, Governor Cuomo was able to "split the difference" with demanding legislators. Over time, the Republican-controlled Senate got the tax cuts they wanted and the Democratic-controlled Assembly got increased spending.

The tax cuts in the state's 1985 Tax Act (which were greater than Cuomo wanted), dropped the top rate on earned income from 10% to 9%. Unearned income (i.e., dividends, interest) declined to 13%, down 1 percentage point.

Reacting to the Reagan Tax Reform Act of 1986, which ended many tax loopholes and expanded income subject to being taxed, New York passed the Tax Reform and Deduction Act of 1987 (TRDA).

Albany had to act because "if state tax rates had remained unchanged from the levels adopted in 1985, the broadening of the federal definition of gross income alone would have brought about a significant 'windfall' state tax increase estimated at $1.7 billion to $2.3 billion."[2]

Unhappy with the governor's plan that would have kept the maximum PIT at 9%, and widened tax brackets and increased tax credits, legislators decided to ignore his proposal. The resulting Act, the *Times* reported, "is very much a legislative one—drafted by the leaders of the Legislature without the Governor as part of a concerted effort by lawmakers this year to assert their independence from him. It is a blend of two early plans, one by the Democratic-controlled Assembly and the other by the Senate."[3]

TRDA returned the tax "windfall" and then some to taxpayers. It was estimated that an average person's taxes would decline 20%.

The plan that would be phased in over four years would have only two tax brackets, down from 12 brackets, and instead of tax rates that went from 2% up to 9%, it would now have only two rates, 5.5% and 7%. The marriage penalty was to be eliminated and the standard deduction "would increase to $13,000 from $3,800 for married couples to $10,500 from $3,800 for heads of households, and to $7,500 from $2,800 for single payers."[4]

The 13% tax on unearned income was to be eliminated. All income would be taxed equally.

Also, taxes for the state's 800,000 lowest earners would be zero.

Tax expert Michael J. McIntyre, writing in the *Albany Law Review*, described the historic tax law thusly:

Prior to the reform acts, the New York personal income tax employed a quixotic mixture of separate and joint filing provisions to adjust tax burdens imposed on individuals. Its relief mechanisms for low-income families were complex and inadequate. Its separate filing rule was impossible to administer fairly and imposed unjustifiable penalties on marital partners who earned substantially unequal incomes. Single parents with dependent children were taxed far more heavily than their economic condition warranted.

The reformed system, when fully effective . . . will provide simple and fair tax relief to the poor and will impose substantially equal tax burdens on family members enjoying comparable standards of living. By any reasonable standard, the reform should be judged a success.[5]

While Cuomo and the members of the state Legislature took a deep bow over the tax cuts, they also wanted their cake and to eat it. Spending continued to grow at twice the inflation rate:

The Cuomo Years State Funds Spending[6]
(dollars in millions)

Fiscal Year	State Funds Spending
1983-84	$20,994
1984-85	$23,585
1985-86	$25,855
1986-87	$28,094
1987-88	$30,442
1988-89	$33,300
1989-90	$35,358
1990-91	$36,242
1991-92	$37,078
1992-93	$38,131
1993-94	$39,430
1994-95	$43,311

Cuomo's budgets during his tenure grew by 123%, while the compounded inflation rate was 65%.

Spending on public education grew from $10.8 billion in 1982 to $22.7 billion by the time Cuomo left office—an increase of 109%.

Welfare expenditures increased from $13.2 billion in 1983 to $30.4 billion in 1992. New York was the #1 state in welfare spending—$1,017 per capita versus the national average of $517.

All the "Reagan Boom" tax revenue that was flowing into the state was not enough to pay all the bills. Hence, to "balance" his budgets, Cuomo resorted to employing a variety of fiscal gimmicks.

He raided revenues from various dedicated funds to finance his operating budget. From the Dedicated Highway and Bridge Trust Fund and the Dedicated Mass Transportation Trust, he grabbed $516 million. From the Court Facilities Fund surplus—$33 million.

In addition, over $4 billion was bilked from the treasuries of the Common Retirement Fund for State Employees, the State Insurance Worker's Compensation Fund, the Mass Transportation and Highway Funds, and the Medical Malpractice Insurance Association Fund.

Cuomo's "one-shot" revenues used to plug his operating deficits totaled more than $8 billion.

Cuomo's most notorious "one-shot" revenue scheme to balance his budget was the selling of Attica Prison to the Urban Development Corporation for $200 million dollars, raised via bonded debt.

To allow the UDC to meet the principal and interest payments on this debt, the state leased the facility and paid rent to the UDC. In effect, Cuomo saddled taxpayers with more than $560 million in principal and interest payments on bonded debt over thirty years to get $200 million in one-shot revenues.

The state was not the only government facing a fiscal squeeze. New York's municipalities were charging the highest property taxes in the nation to balance budgets thanks to more than 2,000 unfunded mandates—costly regulations and programs—imposed on them by Albany.

By the early 1990s, state-mandated programs accounted for over 60% of most county governments' spending.[7]

For example, Suffolk County was forced to cut its discretionary spending by $45 million in 1992. However, these savings did not help balance the operating budget because state-mandated spending increased by $70 million. "The county spent 53% of its General Fund on mandated programs in 1991, compared to 44% in 1988."[8]

The biggest burden was local Medicaid contributions. Throughout the Cuomo years, Medicaid costs soared due to the ever-expanding covered medical services.

Medicaid costs skyrocketed 150% between 1982 and 1990. In Cuomo's last term, it was expected to increase at least another 28%.

But unlike other states, New York mandates county government and New York City to pick up a piece of the Medicaid tab. In 1991, for instance, when total Medicaid costs were $11.9 billion, localities had to put up $2.3 billion, 21% of the total.

For most counties, Medicaid contributions were the single largest budget item—often more than 35%.

Testifying at a 1993 hearing on Medicaid before the New York Senate's Social Services Committee, Oneida County Executive Raymond Meier stated:

> When I started putting my testimony together for today, I thought about something I used to do when I was a little kid back in the 60s. We used to watch these pretty awful horror movies that usually started with some unspeakable monster coming in with an insatiable appetite and crushing and eating everything in sight, and that reminds me a lot of Medicaid. And it's not entirely fair to say that this is the monster that ate Oneida County, but it is accurate to say that this is the monster that's eating things like all the aid to libraries and cultural organizations and public works projects, for programs for kids and seniors, and literally eating our taxpayer's money alive.[9]

During the Cuomo years, Medicaid was New York's fastest growing budget item. The state spent more per capita than the combined expenditures of America's two largest states, California and Texas.

Medicaid Per-Capita Spending 1993
Ten Largest States

New York	$965	Michigan	$329
New Jersey	442	Pennsylvania	322
Ohio	421	California	309
Illinois	395	Texas	309
North Carolina	353	Florida	302
		U.S. Average	$394

Per-Recipient Spending – 1993
10 Largest States

New York.	$6,402	North Carolina	$2,729
New Jersey	4,391	Michigan	2,627
Illinois	3,314	Texas	2,415
Pennsylvania	3,177	Florida	2,368
Ohio	3,130	California	1,996
		U.S. Average	$3,042

Total Medicaid Spending – 1993

New York	$17.6 billion	18.2 million population
California	$9.6 billion	31.2 million population
Texas	$5.6 billion	18.0 million population

Source for Charts: U.S. Dept. of Health and Human Services, Health Care Financing Administration; U.S. Bureau of the Census.

An additional gimmick that was used to give the appearance of a balanced budget was financing the deficits with short-term debt that became known as "spring borrowing." These Tax Revenue Anticipation Notes (TRANS), which were issued annually, permitted the state to cover up its accumulated deficit which grew from $2.9 billion to $6.2 billion between fiscal years 1982 and 1991.

STATE OF NEW YORK GENERAL FUND OPERATING RESULTS
AND ACCUMULATED DEFICITS UNDER
GENERALLY ACCEPTED ACCOUNTING PRINCIPLES,
FISCAL YEARS 1982–1991 (dollars in millions)

Fiscal Year	Annual Surplus/ (Deficit)	Year-end Accumulated Deficit
1982	($552)	$2,901
1983	(1,076)	3,986
1984	(345)	4,331
1985	(106)	4,437
1986	156	4,281
1987	1,001	3,279
1988	(141)	3,420
1989	(1,136)	4,557
1990	(673)	5,230
1991	(1,035)	6,266

Source: Citizens Budget Commission Report, March 1992

To further cover up their fiscal excesses, in June 1990 the Legislature passed, and Governor Cuomo signed into law a bill creating the Local Government Assistance Corporation (LGAC). Although hailed by Cuomo as "the most sweeping fiscal reform in a generation," LGAC was just another fiscal gimmick.

LGAC is a non-self-supporting corporate governmental agency dependent on annual appropriations of state sales tax revenue. It was authorized to bond out $4.7 billion of New York State's accumulated deficit.

After years of reckless spending, Cuomo and his Albany cohorts were once again sticking it to the taxpayers—this time with billions of dollars in interest to be paid out over the 30-year life of the bonds.

Furthermore, this "reform" legislation did not eliminate Albany's budgetary abuses. The governor and the Legislature could pile up new deficits, since the budget doesn't have to be balanced according to generally accepted accounting principles.

Throughout the Cuomo years, bonded debt incurred by the state was also growing by huge leaps and bounds. In 1990, New York's bonded debt surpassed that of California by $17.7 billion, despite the fact that the Golden State's population was 12 million greater than the Empire State's.

New York's tax-supported debt in Cuomo's third term stood at $1,320 per capita. The figure for the median U.S. state was $391.

The Cuomo Years[10]
Total Outstanding State and Authority Debt in NYS
(in millions)

	1982	1992	Change	Percent Change
General Obligation	$3,734.1	$5,081.3	$1,347.2	36.1%
Lease-Purchase/ Contractual Obligation	4,062.0	16,745.0	12,683.0	312.2%
State-Guaranteed Authority	501.0	498.0	(3.0)	-0.6%
Authority Debt with Moral Obligation	12,541.0	8,460.0	(4,081.0)	-32.5%
Total State Debt	20,838.1	30,784.3	9,946.2	47.7%
Other Authority Debt	9,397.1	31,361.2	21,964.1	233.7%
Total State and Authority Debt	$30,235.2	$62,145.5	$31,910.3	105.5%

Cuomo's spending spree and his role as a so-called honest broker who split the difference on spending with the Legislature came to a halt when the recession hit the nation in July 1990.

That recession, which ended in March 1991, was one of the shortest and mildest of the post-World War II era. The U.S.'s Gross Domestic Product (GDP) declined only 1.4% compared to a 2.7% decline in the recession of 1981-1982.

However, the State of New York, unlike the nation as a whole, took a major economic hit.

The Empire State's job loss was three times that of the rest of the nation. Over 20% of the jobs lost in the United States were lost in New York.

Effects of 1990–1991 Recession

Jobs lost July 1990-March 1991 nationally	1,337,000
Jobs lost July 1990-March 1991 in New York	272,000
Percentage of nation's job loss in New York	20.4%
Percentage of nation's job base in New York	7.3%

Even after the recession was declared over, New York continued to lag the nation in job creation. By early 1993, while the nation's work force had grown by 2.1%, New York's had declined another 3.2%:

Total Payroll Jobs
(in millions)

	NYS	Rest of Nation
May 1990	8.264	101.519
July 1990	8.225	101.476
March 1991	7.953	100.411
February 1994	7.766	103.366

Source: New York State Dept. of Labor

Total manufacturing jobs in the state took a major hit. For the first time in the twentieth century, people employed in that sector dropped below 1 million. Hardest hit were the upstate regions, as the following chart reveals:

Percent of Manufacturing Jobs Lost, By Upstate Regions
New York State, 1980–1992

Region	Percent Decline
Albany-Schenectady-Troy	-26.0%
Binghamton area	-24.2%
Buffalo area	-30.0%
Cattaraugus County	-27.0%
Chautauqua County	-20.3%
Cortland County	-11.5%
Delaware County	-34.4%
Elmira area	-25.7%
Fulton County	-30.6%

Genesee County	-28.1%
Jefferson-Lewis	-23.5%
Niagara Falls area	-36.6%
Orange County	-21.7%
Poughkeepsie area	-25.6%
Rochester area	-18.0%
Steuben County	-12.2%
Syracuse area	-19.1%
Ulster County	-16.0%
Utica-Rome area	-31.4%
NYS Total	-26.7%

Source: New York State Department of Labor

As expected, this economic downturn severely impacted the state's fiscal condition.

To close a budget deficit for the fiscal year 1989–1990, the governor approved $1 billion in tax and fee hikes. In addition, the state deferred the last two phases of the tax cut approved in 1987.

Despite these measures, the state's Budget Division announced in November 1989 that anticipated revenues were $254 million below estimates. In January 1990, total revenues were projected to be off by $983 million. When the state closed the books for the fiscal year on March 31, 1990, revenues were $1.8 billion lower than estimated the previous July.

In fiscal year 1990–1991, there was more of the same. The personal income tax cuts were deferred once again and taxes and fees were hiked another $1.7 billion.

Interestingly, probably because it was a gubernatorial election year, Cuomo was very low-key during the budget negotiations. As a result, in many political and media circles, the question asked was, "Where's Mario?"

A *Daily News* column by Ken Auletta ("Gov's 'quiet' leadership has been nearly inaudible on the budget") concluded that "Cuomo failed to exert the kind of leadership of which he is capable. He has been cute rather than courageous, timid when he should have been bold."

One frustrated adviser to the governor told Auletta that Cuomo had been almost a "bystander watching the deficit grow, hatching plots to stick Republicans with blame, denying the obvious." He went on to complain that Cuomo "missed an opportunity. There's no one running against him.

The issue in the country and the Democratic Party is 'leadership.' Why didn't he step up with a plan to close the gap?"[11]

Nevertheless, the result was similar to the previous fiscal year: revenues continued to drop. By the end of the 1990–1991 fiscal year, tax revenues were $2.0 billion below estimates made public in July 1990.

The fiscal meltdown continued during fiscal year 1991–1992. Taxes were raised to the tune of $1.4 billion, the 1987 approved income tax cut was deferred again, and yet spending increased.

Once again, the tax increases did not produce the revenue to fill the fiscal hole.

With a pending deficit of $875 million and a projected deficit for the next fiscal year of $3.6 billion, Cuomo, in late November 1991, unveiled a trial balloon financial plan for 1992–1993 that would "raise no taxes and includes significant reductions in virtually every area of state spending."[12]

After analyzing the proposal, Change-NY, an Albany fiscal think tank, concluded it was merely "smoke and mirrors."

Here is a summary of its findings:

- Taxes would rise by $359.8 million over two years under the governor's plan, contrary to the governor's claim that his proposal "raises no taxes";
- The governor's plan includes $165.8 million in one-shot fiscal measures, adding to the $7.3 billion in one-shot measures approved since 1985, and the plan also proposes the issuance of deficit notes ($95 million) for the fourth year in a row;
- The proposed Medicaid "cuts" focus primarily on shortchanging providers of Medicaid services, rather than reforming Medicaid service delivery or scaling back Medicaid services;
- New York's Cadillac-style welfare system is totally exempted from any cuts or significant reforms;
- The 1,500 in proposed staff reductions for FY 1991–1992 are noticeably modest considering that the state workforce increased by 18,193 between 1983 and 1991;
- No significant restructuring of state government is proposed. Instead, the governor's plan only cuts a number of minor agencies, boards, and

commissions to save $125,000 this year, which amounts to .0009% of the state's $13.9 billion state-operations budget.[13]

It turned out that Cuomo's actual budget proposal, released in January 1992, called for spending to increase by $3.2 billion over the previous year's expenditures. Taxes and fees were slated to increase by $1.9 billion. And the final phases of the 1987 tax cuts were to be deferred for the third time.

After the usual squabbling with the Legislature, Governor Cuomo signed off on a $37 billion budget approved by the Legislature in the first week of April.

Spending was to be increased 3% and most of which would cover the ever-increasing welfare and Medicaid costs.

The budget called for tuition at state colleges to go up by $500. (Between 1990–1992, tuition had jumped more than 95%.) In addition:

- Hospitals and nursing homes would have to pay new state charges totaling $250 million;
- Commercial health insurance companies would have to pony up an additional $135 million in levies;
- Owners' paging services would be charged a monthly state fee— "beeper tax"—of $1;
- A four-year driver's license fee would go from $16 to $20;
- Corporations would be required to register annually with the state and pay a $50 fee;
- The state would take a 20% cut of any court-awarded punitive damages.

State Comptroller Edward Regan had this to say about the budget: "We expected this year to be a very good year in terms of restructuring. It hasn't worked out that way."[14]

Tom Carroll, the president of Change-NY, had a similar reaction. "This was supposed to be the year of historic reform. Instead, we got more of the same; more taxes, more runaway spending, more one-shot fiscal gimmicks, more pork-barrel projects and more legislative perks and privileges."[15]

As Cuomo contemplated seeking a fourth term, a January 1994 article about his State of the State address in the *Times* was headlined "Echoes G.O.P. Ideas."

The *Times* noted that the Address included "three long-standing Republican themes—improving the State's business climate, fighting crime and reforming welfare."[16]

Because the state's economy was improving, Cuomo was considering "phasing out or reducing several taxes, many of which had been established over the past four years to plug budget gaps."

The tax cuts he hoped to propose would total about $500 million. The key cut would be the one placed on corporations. Cuomo was considering dropping it from 15% to 12.8%.

"Here's the message," Cuomo bellowed. "New York State believes in business; we want the jobs you produce; we want you to do well. And if you're prepared to create jobs for our people, we'll do everything we can do to make it worth your while. We need you. We want you."[17]

A surprised Ralph Marino, Senate Republican Majority Leader, told the *Times*, "After 11 years, the Governor has finally embraced much of the Senate Republican agenda to combat crime, revitalize our economy and re-store the pride and productiveness that earned New York its reputation as the Empire State. The failed policies of the past are now clear to everyone."[18]

On January 19, 1994, Governor Cuomo released an election year budget that he described as "pro-business."

The budget would increase spending over the inflation rate and called for cutting only 160 state jobs out of a total of 151,000. It included $210 million in business tax cuts and created an income tax credit for families earning under $25,000 a year.

To manage the $3 billion projected deficit, Cuomo called for another de-ferral of the 1987 personal income tax and the extension of the hospital tax.

To generate additional income, he proposed a new lottery game, and fees for pistol permits and gun-license renewals. One-shot revenues were pegged at $78 million.

The budget also called for "curbing Medicaid costs by $185 million to keep growth of Medicaid spending to 8%. It would do that by reducing payments to hospitals by about $45 million and cutting payments to nurs-ing homes by $50 million, primarily by allowing them to keep only 75% of their profits. It would also cut $54 million in client services by eliminat-ing coverage for non-emergency transportation costs and restricting inpa-tient psychiatric services."[19]

On the expense side, Cuomo wanted to increase school aid by $198 million, with 44% of it, $88 million, going to New York City's Department of Education. The State University system would receive $77 million and City University, $37 million.

It was Cuomo's hope that his "prudent" budget "would help improve the state's bond rating, which is the second lowest among the 50 states, after Louisiana."[20]

The battle of the "three men in a room" (a phrase created in the Cuomo years), that included Cuomo, GOP Senate Majority leader Ralph Marino and Speaker Sheldon Silver, began in earnest in March. Both legislative leaders disputed Cuomo's revenue figures claiming there would be an additional $450 to $488 million by the end of the 1994–1995 fiscal year.

With this additional money, Republicans wanted to increase tax cuts and Democrats wanted to restore proposed Medicaid cuts.

Cuomo, the newly minted "fiscal conservative," unhappy with legislative counter-proposals, attacked the Republicans. "I've tried to get them to spend less, but they are going to say, let's spend, spend, spend. That's what they've been doing for the last years."[21]

On April 1, 1994, for the tenth consecutive time, the state's fiscal year began without an approved budget.

While the power brokers were still far apart on spending and tax-cut plans, legislative leaders made it clear that Cuomo's Keno lottery proposal and his plan for the state to grab $70 million in unclaimed bottle deposits were dead.

In late April, Cuomo unveiled a "split the difference" compromise plan. The *Times* reported that the plan "seeks to steer a middle course between competing Senate and Assembly tax reduction plans, incorporating aspects of both while proposing to phase in many of the cuts to reduce the impact on future budgets. The plan includes several tax cuts sought by the Senate Republicans, including eliminating by September the state's 5% tax on hotel rooms costing more than $100 a night and phasing out a 15% surcharge on corporate taxes. But while the Senate proposed eliminating the surcharge by 1996, Mr. Cuomo calls for gradually reducing it to zero by 1999."[22]

Rejecting Cuomo's claim that the GOP's "phase-in would leave a large hole in the budget," Senator Marino called Cuomo's compromise a "token" cut and said, "The Governor is sending the wrong message to struggling businesses."[23]

Two weeks later, the governor rejected a legislative budget plan that he claimed would spend $150 million more than the state could handle and would create a $500 million hole in the next year's budget.

Attempting to make the legislators look like the bad guys, Cuomo declared, "All I know is that with a billion dollars more, they couldn't satisfy themselves in an election year. I am not going to, in what may be the final stage of my career, be selling out for votes. You can't do it. You have to pay for tax cuts."[24]

One Democrat Assembly aide described Cuomo's public behavior this way. "I think he's looking to make himself a political victor in the context of a late budget. I think this is Mario Cuomo the candidate and not Mario Cuomo the Governor speaking."[25]

As the state entered the seventh week without a budget, Cuomo displayed his darker side. Blaming legislators for the delay, he called legislators "dummies," "greedy," and accused them of engaging in "politically brutal conduct." He even compared them to pigs "working with two hands to feed themselves from the trough."[26]

The governor admonished legislators for packing the budget with $100 million in "members' items"—money to finance favored projects in their districts—better known as "pork."[27] Cuomo justly condemned a proposed $25 million "members' item" for a swimming pool in Nassau County, which he called a "Taj Mahal."

An aide to Cuomo, asked about the governor's tough guy strategy, told the *Times,* "Some people say, what do we have to lose? If the governor vetoes [budget] bills, he can go to the public and say: Here, we had almost a billion-dollar surplus and they still want to spend more."[28]

As the budget impasse dragged on, both the governor and the Legislature were beginning to feel the heat from municipalities and school districts. New York City leaders were claiming they needed the $750 million in delayed state aid to balance the city's budget for the fiscal year that was to end on June 30, 1994.

School district superintendents and the powerful teachers' unions were complaining that money would have to be borrowed to fill a fiscal hole if $1.3 billion in state aid did not arrive by June 1.[29]

Finally, after 68 days without a budget, Cuomo and legislative leaders announced on June 7, 1994 "that they had finally cobbled together the last details of the $34 billion state budget . . ."[30]

The Republicans claimed victory because they worked into the budget business tax cuts twice the size Cuomo presented in his January proposal. The cuts would be approximately $450 million in 1994–1995 and when completely implemented in future years would total $1.7 billion.

Democrats were taking credit for expanding a "health insurance program to an additional 24,000 children of low-income parents not eligible for Medicaid."[31]

And they all claimed credit for providing more aid to school districts and the City of New York.

As for the "pork" members' items the governor ridiculed, the budget contained almost all of them, including the "Taj Mahal" swimming pool.

Despite the fact that the governor had been forced to abandon most of his objections, he still claimed victory: "This need not have been late, but it is arriving brimming with good news and evidence of our strong recovery."[32] His office also issued a 23-page document boasting how $9.6 billion in tax dollars would be spent across the state "from a new science library in New York City to landfill improvements in Clinton County, to repairs to Buffalo's downtown music hall."[33]

As usual, public interest groups were not satisfied. "Advocates for the poor," the *Times* reported, "said the budget did not restore money for social service programs that underwent deep cuts during the recession. Anti-tax groups said the tax cuts did not go far enough, while labor groups said they went too far. And environmentalists said the budget provided the bare minimum to protect open spaces and to clear up landfills."[34]

The budget also had fiscal critics. Mitchell Moss, director of New York University's Urban Research Center said, "The budget process was hijacked by the politics of spring, meaning positioning for the November election."[35]

John Zagame, executive director of the Association of Counties, concluded that the budget merely rearranged "the deck chairs on the Titanic." He added "Never has so much time been wasted by so many on so little without addressing the most pressing, critical, underlying problem the state faces—which is how to address out-of-control Medicaid costs."[36]

Despite Cuomo's boasting about projects, and his rosy fiscal projections that he would tout throughout the 1994 election cycle, the budget was built on a foundation of sand.

The multi-year financial projection, offered by the governor's Division of the Budget shortly after the release of Cuomo's budget proposal for fiscal year 1994–1995, predicted a $1.4 billion budget gap for fiscal year 1995–1996.

However, in the aftermath of the November election, the budget director revealed that the revised structural deficit projection for 1995–1996 was no longer $1.4 billion, but $4.8 billion.

Mario Cuomo and his budget office were remarkably silent on this development, and the state's fiscal watchdog, Democratic State Comptroller Carl McCall, if he really didn't have a clue, was asleep at the state's ledger.

The Revival of the Republican and Conservative Parties

After the 1990 Pierre Rinfret debacle, Republican U.S. Senator Alfonse D'Amato, concerned about his own re-election bid in 1992, decided it was time to begin rebuilding the defunct state GOP organization—and to make peace with the Conservative Party.

Over dinner, the Conservative Party Chairman, Mike Long, and D'Amato agreed that Cuomo was vulnerable if he decided to seek a fourth term and that it was essential for the Republicans and Conservatives to work together to achieve a gubernatorial victory.

D'Amato convinced a former aide, William Powers, to become state GOP chairman. Powers' mandate was to rebuild the feeble party from the bottom up.

Powers went on to become the most successful party chairman in decades, helping the party win back ten county executive seats and mayoral offices in Yonkers and Syracuse.

At the same time, non-partisan conservative groups, determined to save the state from the excesses of liberalism, began to sprout up. Members of New York City's Club for Growth—including New York Republicans Dusty Rhodes, Bruce Bent, Richard and Virginia Gilder, former Ambassador Alfred Klingon, and economist Larry Kudlow—were taking active roles in the plan to win back the statehouse.

D'Amato also broke his non-aggression pact with Cuomo and began to attack him publicly.

At the opening session of the Association of Towns of the State of New York convention at Manhattan's Hilton Hotel in February 1992, the two keynote speakers, Cuomo and D'Amato, publicly clashed.

In his remarks, D'Amato criticized the state welfare spending and the state budget. Cuomo, who was the next speaker, failed at least three times to grab the microphone from D'Amato. Finally, he got hold of the mic, and believing D'Amato had left the ballroom, defended welfare expenditures and made a wisecrack at the senator's expense.

As it turned out, D'Amato remained in the back of the room "making faces, rolling his eyes, crossing his arms and shaking his head."[37] And after Cuomo's reference to D'Amato, he yelled at him and walked up to the podium. D'Amato said he wanted to discuss their differences when the governor was done.

"I am finished," Cuomo said, but he held onto the mic and remained at the podium.

"Mario, I thought you were done," D'Amato said.

Cuomo then put his arm around D'Amato and said: "Lemme ask you a question, Al. . . . What percent of the federal budget is welfare?"

D'Amato responded by complaining about federal mandates on state government, and state mandates on local government.

After Cuomo rebutted with an impassioned defense of welfare, he said, "See ya 'round, Al," and walked away.[38]

In 1992, thanks to a weak opponent, State Attorney General Robert Abrams, D'Amato confounded all the pundits and pollsters by winning a third term with a 49% plurality. The 289,000 Conservative Party votes and the 224,000 Right to Life Party votes gave D'Amato the margin of victory.

One year later, the Republican and Liberal parties got behind Rudy Giuliani in his second face-off with Mayor David Dinkins.

Four years earlier, Dinkins, the Manhattan borough president, knocked off Mayor Ed Koch, who was seeking a fourth term, in the Democratic primary. In the November battle, Dinkins beat Giuliani by a razor-thin margin of 47,000 votes out of 1.787 million votes cast.

Dinkins, a lackluster chief magistrate at best, was very vulnerable when he sought a second term in 1993. The city finances were a mess and with crime rampant, the declining quality of life in the city became a major issue in 1993.

Giuliani, a former prosecutor who led the U.S. Attorney's office for New York's Southern District, ran to the right on crime but was a man of the left on cultural issues. He supported abortion, government funding of abortions, distribution of condoms in schools, and so-called gay rights. He did not rule out raising taxes and opposed tuition tax credits and vouchers for school choice.

For Mike Long, Giuliani's fusion Republican-Liberal ticket smacked of the days of John Lindsay. So, to send a message to the GOP that Conservatives would not buy a Democratic-lite candidate, this author became the Party's standard bearer in the 1993 race for mayor.

While the author's candidacy received the endorsement of nationally prominent Republicans including William F. Buckley Jr., William Bennett, Edward Meese, George Will, and Pete du Pont, it wasn't enough to stop Giuliani, who beat Dinkins by a margin of 71,598 votes.

Looking at the big picture, Mike Long concluded it had been worth the effort. He said: "By standing up for our principles, by being the moral compass and by rejecting the mounting pressure to join a Conservative-Liberal fusion to save the city, we proved to the Republicans running to unseat Cuomo that they just can't assume we'll go along for the ride. They know they will have to earn our support by promoting ideas based on the principles of conservatism."[39]

By mid-1993, D'Amato's search for a viable gubernatorial candidate began in earnest. His first instinct was to approach millionaires—men who could fund their own campaign. These included Donald Trump, First Boston CEO John Hennessy, former Smith Barney Chief Frank Zarb, and Oppenheimer mutual fund boss Jon Fossel. To keep control of the selection process, D'Amato even circulated his own name.

Since none of the millionaires had taken D'Amato's bait, he began looking at the half-dozen men who had declared an interest in running.

Two of them were unacceptable to the Conservative Party: Richard Rosenbaum, Rockefeller's former state chairman, and the former congressman from Manhattan's very liberal East Side, Bill Green.

Then there was Evan Galbraith, a long-time friend of *National Review* editor William F. Buckley Jr. He lacked the common touch and was not taken seriously by party leaders.

Next was J. Patrick Barrett, a former state GOP chairman and former CEO of Avis. He had plenty of money but wanted to be crowned. Since that was not going to happen, Barrett never got around to throwing his hat in the ring. That left Herbert I. London and George E. Pataki.

London was the favorite son of the Conservative Party but he was viewed by D'Amato and many Republican leaders as a zealot, albeit an eloquent one, who couldn't raise money.

As for Pataki, he was an obscure freshman state senator who had previously served four uninspiring terms in the state Assembly.

With the 1994 election season rapidly approaching, D'Amato decided to throw in his lot with Senator Pataki.

Born in 1943, George Elmer Pataki grew up on a 15-acre apple farm in Peekskill, New York. After graduating from high school, Pataki received an academic scholarship from Yale University, from which he graduated in three years, and then went on to receive a law degree from Columbia University in 1970.

He joined the white-shoe firm of Dewey Ballantine but lasted only four years, claiming "the pot of gold at the end of the rainbow wasn't an attraction for me."[40] Others suggested he didn't have the drive for working the long hours to achieve partner.

After joining the White Plains law firm, Plunkett and Jaffe, Pataki became involved in local politics. He worked as a part-time aide to Republican-Conservative State Senator Bernard Gordon; became Chairman of the Peekskill Republican Committee; and in 1981, was elected mayor of Peekskill with 69% of the vote.

In 1984, he beat the incumbent Democratic Assemblyman William J. Ryan in his first Assembly race. He would serve four terms in all as an assemblyman.

But as a minority member of the Assembly, Pataki and his GOP confreres had little to do. Most of their time was spent playing basketball in the legislator's gym, hanging out at local bars, and grinding out press releases criticizing Governor Cuomo.

Bored in the Assembly, Pataki took on State Senator Mary Goodhue in the 1992 Republican primary. Goodhue, 71, was a relic of the Rockefeller era, and Pataki, 47, ran with the backing of the Conservative

Party and with financial support from the money men behind Change-NY. Pataki beat Goodhue by 58 votes. In November, he easily won election to the State Senate in a four-way race, receiving 54.5% of the votes cast.

Because he had taken down a Republican incumbent, Pataki was shunned by many of his new colleagues, particularly the Senate majority leader Ralph Marino. But Pataki didn't care; he preferred to promote a maverick image that could jump-start a 1994 run for governor.

As a freshman senator, Pataki made his mark by voting against the budget deal Marino forged with Cuomo and Assembly Democrats. He also boasted he declined any member-item goodies.

As the May 25, 1994 GOP convention neared, Pataki held a delegate lead, but Herb London's support was nearing the 25% level which, if achieved, would give him an automatic ballot spot in the primary and would guarantee him the Conservative nomination.

Working behind the scenes to secure London's 25% were Senator Marino and Mayor Giuliani—neither of whom wanted a Republic governor who would overshadow them.

Journalist Wayne Barrett, in his biography of Giuliani, described the GOP convention maneuverings this way:

> Giuliani was Cuomo's covert ally at the convention, quietly working to get 25% of the delegates to vote for Herb London, the 1990 Conservative Party candidate for governor, who was positioning himself to challenge George Pataki in an upcoming Republican primary. Pataki, then a little-known state senator handpicked by Al D'Amato to run against Cuomo, was engaged in an all-out war to block the 25% and avoid a primary with London. Yet the officially neutral Giuliani got much of the Queens delegation to vote for London during the nail-biting three-hour roll-call vote.

> Peter Powers [a Giuliani aide] called delegates the weekend before the convention, looking for London votes. . . . London had little chance of defeating Cuomo, who'd routed him in 1990,

and the attempts to get him on the ballot by Giuliani and Senate Republican leader Ralph Marino were widely seen as indirectly benefiting Cuomo.[41]

On May 23, 1994, after three hours of balloting, Pataki received 72.4% of the delegates' vote to London's 22.1%.

London, realizing he didn't have the financial resources to go the petition route to challenge Pataki in the gubernatorial primary, and after hours of negotiations, agreed the following day to be the Republican-Conservative candidate for State Comptroller.

Not everyone was happy with the outcome. On the Republican side, Richard Rosenbaum declared he would challenge Pataki in the primary and went on to file the required petitions.

At the Conservative Party Convention, die-hard London supporters switched their allegiance to Robert Relph, the Jefferson County Chairman, and with their backing he received 28% of the delegate vote and pledged to enter the primary.

On Primary Day, September 13, Pataki defeated Rosenbaum 73% to 27% in the Republican Primary, and he beat Relph with 78% of the vote in the Conservative Primary.

Cuomo's Last Hurrah

As the fall campaign began, Democratic political insiders detected Mario fatigue among New York's voters.

Many liberals were tired of the Cuomo tap dance. They accused him of pandering to the right by spending over $600 million to build prisons while underspending on the homeless and poor. Welfare grants, they grumbled, as a percentage of the poverty level, declined from 108% to 67% during the Cuomo years.[42] Gays were disenchanted. Homosexual activist Gabriel Rotello, writing in *Newsday*, described the governor this way:

> [Cuomo's] hot air has long obscured the fact that not-with-standing his ineffectual support of gay-rights and hate-crimes bills in Albany, the governor's record on matters gay is mediocre at best. No leadership on issues like multicultural education.

Never in 11 years has he appointed a single openly gay judge or state commissioner. Begrudging on AIDS. No state domestic partnership registry.[43]

Feminists were also unhappy. Irene Natividad, chairperson of the National Women's Political Caucus, complained: "There's no getting around the fact that he could do more [for women] . . . and we're looking to see him do more."[44]

The Black and Puerto Rican Legislative Caucus groused about Cuomo's "lack of urgency" when it came to minority and poverty issues.[45]

Then there was the Mario fatigue—Democrats who were angry that Cuomo did nothing to build their party. They were tired of being bullied and ordered around by the governor and his minions. And they were tired of the Cuomo grudges that went back to the 1982 primary battle with Ed Koch.

The Cuomo grudge was most evident in Nassau County Democratic circles.

In 1974, when running in the Democratic Primary for lieutenant governor, he lost the county badly, receiving only 26% of the vote.

In 1982, most of Nassau Democratic Party leaders endorsed Ed Koch, who easily carried the county with 62% of the vote.

Neither Mario nor Andrew forgot the drubbing they took in that primary. They believed the county organization had pushed the electorate to come out for Koch—an argument most Nassau pols reject. (Back in those days, the Democrat organization was feeble due to the dominance of the GOP machine.)

As a result, Cuomo did not lift a finger for Nassau Democrats. He never campaigned for them in general elections and never dispensed any political goodies to them.

The exceptions were the four Nassau Democrats who endorsed him in the gubernatorial primary: Harold Berger, Arnold Brown, Thelma Sardone, and Mary Dwyer.

At Nassau County Democratic dinners, Cuomo would typically thank those early supporters publicly from the podium and then, privately, stop only at their tables.

Cuomo's disinterest in building the Nassau Democratic Party, which in the 1990s was turning politically purple; i.e., moving from GOP red to Dem blue, would come back to haunt him in his bid for a fourth term.

In September 1994, Cuomo's standing with liberals, feminists, minorities, and the Democratic establishment was best described by Jacob Weisberg in a *New York* magazine August 1994 cover story titled "Is it Time for Him to Go? Mario Cuomo just might lose this election and that might not be bad." He wrote, "The current anti-Cuomo mood is not just routine dissatisfaction. There is a deep sense of weariness with Cuomo, a feeling of anger, even betrayal."

After twelve years in office, with what most pols considered meagre accomplishments, Cuomo had a hard time articulating a rationale for seeking a fourth term. He told the *Times* that he was "running again because I don't think I've gotten enough good things done."[46]

Cuomo's political guru, Dave Garth, did not help Cuomo's cause when he was asked to name some of the governor's accomplishments and responded: "Haven't you seen the new rest stops on the Thruway? They're really something."

Hoping to energize his faltering campaign, Cuomo made a number of "Hail Mary" passes that, for the most part fell short.

First, he tried to portray himself as a fiscally conservative "supply-sider."

On September 28, 1994, the *Times* reported that "Mr. Cuomo said he had not lost confidence in the liberal vision of government as a force for good. But he also paid homage to a father of supply-side conservatism, Arthur B. Laffer, whose philosophy Mr. Cuomo ridiculed during the Reagan and Bush administrations. 'To some extent it works,' said Mr. Cuomo, who signed tax cuts in 1987 and 1994 and has said he will propose more tax cuts next year if he is re-elected."

Cuomo went on to pledge to commence the next installment of the personal income tax approved in 1987. And he also promised to trim business taxes and utility taxes.

Next, the man who vetoed death penalty legislation every year in office based on his deep-seated belief that capital punishment was corrosive to society, called for a voter referendum to decide the fate of the death penalty. This crass political move angered some voters who admired his career-long adherence to opposing the death penalty regardless of the political consequences.

Then, to shore up lagging support in Long Island, Cuomo proposed a

$9 billion government takeover of the ailing Long Island Lighting Company, that was forced by Cuomo to close down its Shoreham nuclear plant before it opened, and to stick the cost to ratepayers with ever-increasing electrical rates.

The proposal was panned as an election year sop by most Long Island pols and utility analysts.

The most dramatic "Hail Mary" pass was the announcement by Mayor Rudy Giuliani on October 24, 1994 that he was crossing party lines to endorse Mario Cuomo. Giuliani said:

> From my point of view as the mayor of New York City, the question that I have to ask is, "Who has the best chance in the next four years of successfully fighting for our interests? Who understands them, and who will make the best case for it?" Our future, our destiny is not a matter of chance. It's a matter of choice.
>
> My choice is Mario Cuomo.
>
> I've come to the conclusion that it is George Pataki who best personifies the status quo of New York politics—a candidate taking as few positions as possible, all of them as general as possible, taking no risk and being guided, scripted, and directed by others.
>
> Senator Pataki has almost uniformly voted against the interests of the city and often the metropolitan region. . . . Mario Cuomo is his own man. I prefer dealing with someone who is his own man.[47]

While outraged Republicans were calling the mayor "Judas" Giuliani, the initial reactions of the public boded well for Cuomo as Pataki's poll numbers plummeted: in just four days, Pataki's numbers dropped from a 7-point lead to a 13-point deficit.

However, shortly after the endorsement, Giuliani overplayed his hand. Instead of campaigning for Cuomo in New York City and the surrounding suburban counties, where he was popular, he decided to do an upstate tour. Hitting all the major upstate cities (where New York City mayors have never been popular), he was a complete flop. He was greeted at every stop with boos and signs saying, "Traitor" and "Let's Make a Deal," referring to accusations that, to get the mayor's endorsement, Cuomo had agreed to take away aid from upstate cities and give it to Giuliani. Even Cuomo realized the trip was a mistake: "I spoke to [political consultant David] Garth on the phone. I said this is not a good thing for him to do. I said Rudy would be seen as the Mayor of New York. They would think I was going to give all the money to him."[48]

The backlash had an impact on the polls, and Pataki's numbers began to improve. Because the Giuliani endorsement was announced fifteen days before Election Day, the Pataki campaign had enough time to recover. If Giuliani had waited another week, the chances for a Pataki comeback may have been next to impossible. (The word after the election was that Rudy's early endorsement was also designed to help the financially broke Cuomo campaign raise money.)

In the final days, the Cuomo campaign attempted to push center-right voters toward the Independent Party candidate, multimillionaire founder of Paychex, Tom Golisano, who described himself as a fiscal conservative and social liberal.

This was a sound strategy because the Pataki campaign's ABC approach— "Anybody But Cuomo"—said very little of substance about issues and repeated one message, "Mario Cuomo has been too liberal for too long." While Pataki consultants were running a shallow campaign to avoid making waves, they failed to offer a credible alternative to Cuomo.

This approach was risky in 1994 because of Golisano's insurgent candidacy.

With Golisano hitting 8% statewide in public opinion polls, with higher numbers upstate, Cuomo was hoping Golisano might siphon off enough votes to cost Pataki the election.

Cuomo's handlers pointed out that Pataki, a self-proclaimed reformer, had accepted legislative perks including payments made to legislators "in lieu of expenses" and "member's items," goodies totaling several millions of dollars.

This revelation annoyed conservatives who had been told otherwise, and the *Times* asked in an editorial whether "Pataki's rejection of the budget but acceptance of its pork raises a central question about him: Was he trying to have it both ways, or merely looking out for his district before taking a risky but principled stand against his own party?"[49]

The Cuomo campaign also called out Pataki on abortion. A commercial was aired that painted Pataki as a flip-flopper on the issue. In the ad, a woman asked: "How can you possibly trust a man like that?"[50]

There was truth to the charge. Pataki did play both sides of the abortion issue. To conservatives he boasted that he never cast a pro-abortion vote in the state Legislature. This was true because he voted annually against the state budget which contained money to fund abortions for the poor.

But Pataki upset many conservatives when he reacted to the Cuomo attack by declaring he was pro-choice. He told the *Times* in October, "I am pro-choice. Regardless of what happens with *Roe v. Wade*, I don't think politicians in Washington or Albany should tell my wife what she can or cannot do. Period."[51]

Pataki pushed the envelope even further when he said, "We are not going to deny Medicaid funding and we are not going to put any legal impediments to abortion in this state. . . . Ultimately, I believe the most important right here involved is the right of the woman to control her body and to control her decision."[52]

While the barrage of Cuomo attacks put Pataki on the defensive, what was unknown, as voters prepared to go to the polls, was if it was enough to turn the tide in the governor's favor.

On Election Day, Cuomo voted early in the morning with his wife Matilda at P.S. 178 in Queens County. He told the media gathered at the polling station, "Election days are like waiting . . . for the jury to come back. You try the case, you work[ed] for years, you put the proof in, it takes months and months, but then the jury goes out, you don't know what they're going to conclude."

"You don't sleep," Cuomo added. "You don't sleep because you know you have to think about what happens if you win, what happens if you lose. If you win, there's a tremendous amount of work to do. If you lose, you have to find work, you have to find a place to live."[53]

When a reporter asked if he was confident about winning, he replied: "I don't live that way. You know, we worked very, very hard. And then the prayer we say is not 'Lord, let me win.' The prayer we say is 'Lord, let me understand the outcome and deal with it.'"[54]

Later that day, Cuomo did what he had been doing every Election Day, he went to a mid-day Mass at St. Francis of Assisi Church on West 31st Street in Manhattan.

That evening, as votes were being tabulated, Cuomo was watching the Knicks game in a suite at Manhattan's Sheraton Hotel.

As the result began to dribble in, the race appeared too close to call. But as the evening wore on, the tide turned in Pataki's favor.

At 10:51 p.m., ABC News declared that State Senator George Pataki had beaten Governor Mario Cuomo by a plurality: 49% versus 45% for Cuomo, 4% for Golisano, and 1% for the Right to Life candidate Robert Walsh.

	Cuomo Dem.	Pataki Rep.	Pataki Cons.	Walsh R. to L.	Cuomo Lib.	Pataki TCN	Golisano Ind.
Total Upstate	1,265,156	1,787,269	285,624	57,807	39,685	42,802	200,974
Bronx	153,477	40,401	4,757	1,499	6,323	1,656	1,937
Brooklyn	285,625	100,703	10,945	2,433	13,510	3,248	3,976
Manhattan	282,299	58,775	4,354	1,492	17,611	1,906	3,742
Queens	237,732	123,496	15,060	3,239	12,564	3,474	5,314
Staten Island	48,614	45,413	7,865	1,280	2,308	954	1,547
Total NYC	1,007,747	368,788	42,981	9,943	52,316	11,238	16,516
Total State	2,272,903	2,156,057	328,605	67,750	92,001	54,040	217,490

To the crowd gathered in the Hilton's ballroom, Cuomo said:

> I'm sorry we kept you so long but it was a close race and a com-plicated one, and we had to make sure you got your money's worth. . . . George Pataki is the next governor of the State of New York. We will all respect him, we will work with him, we congrat-ulate him and his wife Libby . . . [booing] . . . Don't spoil it, you are the classiest group in America, and don't you ever spoil it. . . .
>
> Long ago, long before our first victory in 1982, this state had al-ready given me and my family more opportunity and reward than we had any right to expect. Then it added three terms as governor of the greatest state in the nation. I don't have the words to describe

the deep sense of gratitude and debt that I feel for that immense opportunity. I had great plans for this state in the coming years and I have great hopes for us still. For the strength of our people, the scope of the great gifts that nature has given us and all the good that we inherited from those who came before us. . . .

I'm sure we made mistakes as governor but I'm as proud as I can be of what we've accomplished together. And I'm just absolutely convinced that there's an enormous amount more we can do. . . .

I have one main regret this year that I was not able to make the case clearly enough to gain for you, all of you, the victory that your good work deserves. I'm sorry to have let you down, because you deserved another four years.[55]

As Pataki and his supporters were basking in the victory, Cuomo left the Sheraton and traveled up to Albany arriving at about 1:00 in the morning. Even in defeat, Cuomo could not shed his workaholic practices. He spent the remainder of the night preparing to leave office and to begin a new life. "There's too much to do," he said. "We never made plans for losing."[56]

After talking on Wednesday to Governor-elect Pataki on the phone, Cuomo worked on a to-do list to prepare the transition and to put together the framework for the next budget.

Musing that "life goes on," Cuomo went on to say, "I don't have regrets. I do have concerns about the future."[57]

Cuomo friend and long-time adviser, Sandy Frucher, after speaking to the governor, told *Newsday*, "He's certainly not dwelling on the past or wallowing in what could have been or should have been or what we did wrong or could have done better."

What Happened?

Mario Cuomo lost to George Pataki for a number of reasons. Here are ten:

1) Upstate and suburban voters turned against him; and they came out in droves to vote. In many counties, voter turnout exceeded 70% of registered voters.

For example, Erie County, which encompasses the very Democratic city of Buffalo, went Republican for the first time in 36 years.

In the upstate counties overall, Cuomo received only 32% of votes cast, versus 46% in 1990; 62% in 1986; and 42% in 1982.

As for the suburbs of NYC voters, only 43% supported Cuomo, versus 50% in 1990, 59% in 1986; and 47% in 1982.

Pataki outpolled Cuomo upstate and in suburbia by approximately 800,000 votes, a comfortable margin necessary to overcome Cuomo's New York City totals.

2) While Cuomo easily carried New York City with 70% of the vote—down slightly from 72% in 1990—voter turnout was down. Only 44.8% turned out to vote.

3) While a key constituency, African-Americans, cast 86% of their votes for Cuomo, their turnout was also down. In 1990, African-Americans were 10% of the statewide votes cast; in 1994 that number dropped to 8%.

4) Cuomo's support among women dropped from 57% in 1990 to 50% in 1994.

5) A significant number of white voters deserted Cuomo. He was supported by only 39%, down from 48% in 1990.

6) Catholics also had had it with Cuomo. His support among these mostly working-class folks went from 54% in 1990 to 37% in 1994. That result helps explain why Cuomo and Pataki split the Union vote, 48% to 48%.

7) As for key issues, Cuomo took a drubbing from voters who considered the death penalty, rising crime, and high taxes the most important issues.

Cuomo did extremely well in one area, character. For those voters for whom the issue matters, 82% supported Cuomo versus 16% for Pataki.

Vote Share	Issue	Cuomo	Pataki
16%	Death Penalty	21%	75%
13%	Crime	39%	57%
24%	Taxes	23%	72%

8) The Giuliani endorsement did not have the appeal the Cuomo camp had hoped for. Giuliani failed to attract enough suburban voters and failed to curtail Pataki's upstate advantage. In fact, Giuliani's hapless campaigning

might very well have increased the anti-Cuomo turnout in upstate counties.

9) He simply stayed on too long. Marist College public opinion pollster, Lee Miringoff, concluded, "Cuomo was not immune from the anti-incumbent buzz that's been laid at the doorsteps of elected officials across the nation."[58]

10) Finally, the hope that the Independent candidate, Tom Golisano, would be a spoiler and deny Pataki a victory, failed to materialize.

Golisano, who spent millions of his money on TV ads and mailings, had reached a high of 8% in the polls, but on Election Day his vote dissipated to 4%. Voters who changed their minds about Golisano went to Pataki helping to cement his slim victory of 174,000 votes over Cuomo.

The outcome of the 1994 gubernatorial election was best described by political analyst, Michael Barone. "Pataki's victory," he wrote, "can be summed up as a near unanimous decision by upstaters and farther-out suburbanites that the huge state and city governments were destroying jobs and communities. The New York version of the welfare state, for all the attractiveness of its champions, was repudiated."[59]

The Legacy

Several days after the election, Cuomo sat down with Kevin Sack of the *Times* for an hour and a half. Cuomo, known for his gallows humor, mentioned a call he received from a friend who was a rabbi. After telling Cuomo his defeat would be "liberating," the governor replied, "Rabbi, thank you very much, but who wanted to be liberated?"

Cuomo went on to say that he was entertaining several job offers and hoped to move to Douglas Manor, a very private and expensive enclave on the eastern end of Queens County. As for his job search, Cuomo said, "The objective is to find things that allow me to make a living but still allow me to be free to share what it is that I've learned over all these years."

As for being rejected at the polls on November 8, at first he made light of it saying, "Maybe the people just didn't like Mario Cuomo."

He added: "It is difficult to know exactly what the negative votes are saying because they're probably saying more than one thing. It is clear that they're saying that much of America is unhappy. This is not a joyous vote.

This is condemnatory, frightened, angry. Now the question is why. I think a lot of people are saying government doesn't appear to be using my money well, therefore I resent their taking it."[60]

As a guest on PBS's "The Open Mind" on December 8, 1994, Cuomo conceded to host Richard Heffner that many Americans' unhappiness helps explain why they "threw out a lot of incumbents, especially a mega-incumbent like Mario Cuomo. . . . So, I obviously lost, too. And that was clear that they wanted something else. It was generally clear that most people—not everyone—but most people felt that we lacked the efficacy in government that government should be capable of."

As for mistakes, Cuomo, like many who lose elections, blamed not his message, but the delivery of the message: "I failed to communicate with my people the way I should have. And I made some other mistakes, as well. I didn't travel enough. I should have traveled a lot more than I did. That was another mistake. I insisted on staying close to home and staying at my desk and working hands-on, and taking the red-eye back from California if I happened to be there. . . . So, I made mistakes, but I did not make a mistake in what I perceived the American people to be. We are everything I thought we were, still growing, and with biceps larger than our age ought to justify. We're stronger than we're smart, but that's because we're young."[61]

On December 16, 1994, Cuomo made his first post-election appearance before the National Press Club in Washington, D.C.

He began his remarks by joking, "You know by now that I was elected a private citizen—effective January 1. It wasn't my first choice."[62]

Discussing problems that disturbed voters, Cuomo stated that "Government did not create all these problems, but government didn't solve them either. And the people know that. Many of them are frightened, resentful, even angry."

He then went on to say, "The Conservative-Republicans measured that seething unhappiness with polls, then designed some painless home remedies which they strung together into a new political agenda that they call now the 'Contract with America.' And they tell us it will solve our problems. I don't think so. . . . But the truth is the contract fails to deal substantially with the fundamental problems we face. It's not a plan—it's an echo of selected polls."

Political proposals based on polls—that's the same criticism Cuomo lobbed at Lew Lehrman back in 1982. It appears that those who disagree with Cuomo's worldview are always driven by political expediency, never by political principles.

In December, Cuomo devoted his time to winding down his administration and preparing to vacate the Executive Mansion that had been his home for 12 years.

His last day in office was spent at his daughter Maria's home in Westchester County. He joked that he did not own a car and asked "If anybody can find a '56 Bel Air Chevy in reasonably good shape. . . ."

While talking to a reporter about his future and the nation's infrastructure, " . . . when he met the gaze of his youngest granddaughter, 9-month-old Catherine, [h]e imagined they were in one of those movies in which a baby's thoughts can be heard."

"She's saying, 'This bum will never learn. He lost and here he is talking.'" Catherine's next look, Cuomo said, "sounded like 'Go and get yourself a job.'"[63]

Hitching a ride to Albany from a family member on January 1, 1995, Cuomo sat in the front row on the stage where George Pataki was sworn in as the state's 53rd governor.

As he rose to give his inaugural address, Pataki walked over to the Cuomo's and shook Mario's hand and kissed Matilda on the cheek.

During his speech, he turned toward Cuomo and said, "I want to gratefully acknowledge the assistance of Governor Cuomo in preparing for this change in administration. The governor's three terms in office have earned him a rightful place in the history of our state. And Governor, now after 12 years, I hope you will permit me—on behalf of all the people of New York—to thank you and Matilda for your devoted service."[64]

With those kind remarks, New York's Cuomo Era came to a close.

As for the Cuomo legacy, Professor Mitchell Moss, Director of New York University's Urban Research Center, said: "Mario Cuomo's legacy will be that he kept liberalism alive during the Reagan and Bush administrations, that he was the Democratic Party's leading rhetorician."[65] Norman Adler, a former Cuomo political consultant, concluded: "He will be remembered more for himself than what he left behind. Really fine public rhetoric done of aspiration not achievement. Mario Cuomo could never match his words. It wasn't possible."[66]

And there were these sentiments from Cuomo's friend, the noted journalist Pete Hamill: "In his more than two decades in public life, including 12 as governor, Mario Cuomo didn't end crime, cure AIDS or eradicate poverty. But he didn't add to the general stupidity either. A citizen could disagree with him, and many did; but the disagreement was always on a reasonably high level. He did not reduce civic discourse to an argument in a saloon."[67]

But perhaps, Mario Cuomo's legacy was best described by his son, Andrew Cuomo, New York's 56th governor. He told the *New Yorker* that he regarded his father as "more accomplished as a speech-giver than as a governor."[68]

PART III

THE LIBERAL LION IN WINTER

CHAPTER 15

MARIO CUOMO: CORPORATE LAWYER

Shortly after leaving office, Mario Cuomo joined the "White Shoe" law firm, Willkie, Farr and Gallagher. Founded in the late nineteenth century, it was the kind of corporate law firm that had refused to give Mario Cuomo the courtesy of an interview after he graduated number one in his St. John's law school class.

The only other ex-politician the firm had accepted as a partner in its hundred year-plus history was Wendell Willkie, the 1940 Republican nominee for president who lost to Franklin Roosevelt. Cuomo would tell friends that the partners told him that he was qualified to join the firm because, "You lost the election."

Cuomo decided to join the legal big leagues for several reasons; first and foremost—he needed to make some money.

After twenty years as a public servant, he had next to nothing in savings. Shortly after leaving office, he told the author over breakfast at the Waldorf Astoria that he accepted speaking fees as governor—a practice that George Pataki publicly criticized but then practiced himself—to help finance the education tuitions of his five children.

Cuomo told the *Times* that after conceding to Pataki on election night, it hit him while flying in the state helicopter to Albany, that "I have no home, I have no job, I have no money," and he had only $200,000 in life insurance.

"I got to thinking," he said, "that if the plane [sic] had gone [down], Matilda would have to live with one of the kids because I didn't have any money. How could I get myself into this predicament?"[1]

Although he told the author that he would have preferred to move back to Queens County, preferably the Douglas Manor neighborhood in the Northeastern part of the county, Matilda wanted an apartment in Manhattan.

The down payment for the seven-room Sutton Place apartment the Cuomos bought came from the fee he received for appearing in a Doritos commercial with former Texas governor Ann Richards, that played during the 1995 Super Bowl.

Cuomo did not portray himself at Willkie, Farr and Gallagher as a celebrity "rainmaker." In fact, he took on corporate legal matters, performed his own research, and wrote his own briefs.

One key Cuomo client was the Philadelphia Stock Exchange whose C.E.O. was Meyer "Sandy" Frucher, a longtime Cuomo political crony.

Cuomo would joke that his job was now to help people get rich. He told one audience, "If you have a merger or a big company you want to sell, I'm the guy you see."[2]

Another reason Cuomo preferred being at a law firm is that it permitted him to stay active in the public arena. He planned "in whatever small way I can to participate in the dialogue."[3]

His old nemesis, Ed Koch, called him shortly after the election and told him: "Mario, do not be depressed. There is a life after death. Look at me and you will do everything I'm doing and more."[4]

And Koch was right.

Cuomo went on to give a couple of dozen speeches annually to various groups, hosted a talk radio show that played in 35 cities, and later co-hosted with Alan S. Chartock a show called "Me and Mario." And he turned his attention to writing books.

During his public life, Cuomo had already published two volumes of his diaries, a collection of his speeches, *More than Words* (1993); edited *The New York Idea: An Experiment in Democracy* (1994); and edited and wrote an introduction with Harold Holzer to *Lincoln On Democracy: His own words, with Essays by America's Foremost Civil War Historians* (1990).

In the fall of 1995, *Reason to Believe* was published by Simon and Schuster. The work was a critique of Newt Gingrich's "Contract with America." Cuomo argued that the Republicans, who took control of Congress after the 1994 election, introduced a "new harshness" and were walking "out on sixty years of the most humane and intelligent progress any government has ever achieved . . . seduced by a new mythology that insists the strongest among us are sufficient unto themselves and the rest are not worth the bother."[5]

The book was classic Mario, the moralizing "New Dealer." Discussing *Reason to Believe* in an interview on Richard Heffner's show, "The Open Mind," Cuomo said:

> . . . I have always believed that there is a moral obligation to live this way, that I am my brother's keeper. A moral obligation. In every family, in every society, you have a moral obligation. Just on the basis of what is right and wrong, whether it's good for you or not good for you. Put that aside. You have a moral obligation to take care of people. Every religion understands that. . . . It is not going to hurt you to strengthen your family. Eventually, as a family grows strong, everybody grows strong.[6]

As ever, Mario Cuomo was a walking contradiction.

On the one hand, there was the man who grew up in a Queens neighborhood and understood the importance of the family, the parish, and the neighborhood.

He knew that immigrants, like his parents, depended on their families for support. The family was the basis of his religious tradition and offered stability against the established social orders of hatred toward immigrants. Marriage and family instilled in immigrant families the character to achieve moral excellence in their daily activities.

Cuomo grasped when he entered politics in the 1970s that the reform movement in the Democratic Party was controlled by elitists who despised the values of the working-class Democrats who had overwhelmingly supported FDR, Truman, and JFK.

On "The Open Mind," Cuomo boasted: "No, I haven't changed at all. The emphasis was on the language of compassion. If you look in the book, for example, you'll see, in 1974, my first political speech to the New Democratic Coalition in this city, the City of New York, I said, in my first political speech ever, that one of the things that the liberals are doing wrong is you are pushing the middle class out of the Democratic Party and to the right."[7]

About that he was right. Millions of inner-city ethnic Democrats did indeed go on to become Nixon and Reagan Democrats.

On the other hand (and here is the contradiction), Cuomo went on to say, "and with a heavy hammer forged by the coalition of wealth and power on the extreme right, with the middle class, [the Republicans are] going to forge a hammer that beats the poor into oppression. That began with Reagan just a few years after that, when the old Democrats, the blue-collar Democrats got pushed out."[8]

What Cuomo appeared not to accept is that working-class folks left the Democratic Party because the Liberal Experiment—the Great Society's welfare programs—destroyed New York City not only financially, but culturally. The very group that Cuomo wanted to "strengthen"—poor families—were the ones hurt the most by the social policy ideology embraced by the Democratic Party.

And on the eve of the publication of *Reason to Believe*, hoping, perhaps, for more media attention, the former governor "lashed out for the first time since last year's bitter campaign, at the man who unseated him: Gov. George Pataki."[9]

On WCBS's "Morning Edition," Cuomo pointed out that Pataki had carried out most of his agenda including cuts in aid to New York City. He was particularly livid that Pataki was increasing the city's mass transportation fares. New York City, he said, "has a lot of people who are not yet making it" and he accused Pataki of not caring about them.[10]

The November 19, 1995 edition of the Sunday *Times Book Review* published a shockingly brutal review of *Reasons to Believe* by editorial writer Brent Staples.

Staples points to Cuomo as a "signal figure" responsible for the decline of the pre-Clinton "Republican Lite" Democratic Party "both as the former Governor of New York, one of those big tax-and-spend machines that helped to earn government its current disdain, and as one of the big-gun Democrats who failed to step forward in 1992 to challenge that mighty team of Bush and Quayle."[11]

Reason to Believe, Staples wrote, "traffics heavily in folksy liberal axioms and visits every station of the old Democratic cross." Cuomo's "castigations" of Republicans "seem stale and almost beside the point. These are shouts after a train has long since left the station."

Cuomo is accused of a tone that "is often patronizing and avuncular." As New York's chief executive, Staples charged Cuomo of governing "with a kingly hand, remaining aloof from the legislators, except perhaps to chide them like unruly children. No surprise, then, that the stirring rhetoric never found its way into policy. Mr. Cuomo talked the talk but he could not walk the walk."

"*Reason to Believe*," the reviewer concluded, "is a vexing book from an enigmatic politician who had access to central arenas of debate but rejected it. This book is a stump speech by a candidate who lost his nerve but wants his say anyway."

Despite this brutal drubbing from the *Times* review, Cuomo was loath to say that the voters rejected "his vision of an expansive government."[12]

In a *Times* article, "Out of Office with Mario M. Cuomo, Keeping the Faith," published three days after the review was run, Cuomo said, "I will not accept the thesis that this is a rejected philosophy at all. I don't think there's anything in my book that's been rejected."[13]

However, Cuomo implicitly implied what he explicitly denied when he described the fight he had with his publisher over the book's title. Cuomo wanted to name the book "One Nation." Simon and Schuster wanted "Common Sense." Reacting to that suggestion, Cuomo said, "If it was common sense, I'd still be Governor."[14]

Cuomo's next literary project was a book on Abraham Lincoln.

Cuomo took a serious interest in Lincoln decades earlier after he received as a gift the 9-volume *Collected Works of Abraham Lincoln*.

As mentioned above, he had collaborated with a former campaign aide, Harold Holzer (who subsequently distinguished himself as a Lincoln and Civil War scholar) to edit *Lincoln on Democracy*, and after completing that work, Cuomo had "hoped to find an opportunity to look again into the Lincoln theme and find a way to not only advance and reconsider his rich and beautiful prose, but also to interpret and apply his wisdom for the modern world."[15]

Hearing Lincoln quoted by President George W. Bush and other political leaders in the aftermath of the terrorist attack on the World Trade Center and the Pentagon, gave him his opening. "If Lincoln," Cuomo asked, "can be helpful in providing insight and comfort concerning one of the most significant events in our nation's history that occurred 136 years after his death, why not consult him concerning other serious challenges we face?"[16] *Why Lincoln Matters Today More Than Ever* (2004) was Cuomo's attempt "to do just that."[17]

While Cuomo cautions readers that "Conservatives and liberals alike should always resist the impulse to make Lincoln over in their own image,"[18] he proceeds to throw that caution to the wind.

After spinning his views and prescriptions concerning the state of America, its unfinished work, and "America's Global Role," Cuomo devotes the remainder of his book to his crystal ball reading of "What would Lincoln say?" on a number of issues that Lincoln probably never thought about including identity politics, environmental laws, the minimum wage, and government support of stem-cell research.

Cuomo not only dismissed President George W. Bush's post-9/11 actions and his views on various social issues, but when discussing his book in an interview, he questioned Bush's intelligence.

On a segment of "The Open Mind" devoted to *Why Lincoln Matters*, Cuomo said Lincoln "was such a magnificently intelligent and cogent person . . . something we miss today . . . not just with President Bush . . . there's never been, never been a president more intelligent and perhaps not as intelligent as Lincoln."

Later in the interview, after concluding that Lincoln had "intellectual command" and "understanding" of the constitutional issues concerning war, he said "this president [Bush] had nothing like it . . . [H]e didn't appear to be a man of great curiosity . . . he's still not a man of great curiosity."[19]

While Cuomo made it clear he frowns upon Lincoln's suspensions and violations of numerous civil rights, he made this questionable claim: "President Bush's excesses are worse than even the serious misappropriations of power by Lincoln."[20]

In his review of Cuomo's book, journalist Andrew Ferguson, author of *Land of Lincoln*, made this trenchant observation:

Cuomo may be blasting Bush, but he is patronizing Lincoln. How do you condescend to such a personage? It could be possible for Cuomo only if Lincoln isn't real to him, except as a rhetorical cudgel. Lost in the solipsism of the modern polemicist—you can easily imagine the book serving as the basis for a special episode of the *O'Reilly Factor*—Cuomo can't come to terms with either the figure of history or the man of myth. When Lincoln seems to agree with him, Cuomo lapses into sentimentality, misty-eyed at the thought that a man so like himself could have once been president; when Lincoln's record is deficient, Cuomo turns into a scold, snarling at his own political opponents. Whichever way the analysis swings, it's all about Mario. Lincoln himself remains untouched.[21]

And Alan Wolfe, writing in the left-wing Catholic magazine *Commonweal*, observed that Cuomo's work ventured too far into "counterfactual history":

Do we really need to know what position Lincoln would have taken on stem-cell research or whether he would support the interstate highway and space programs? Cuomo ventures too often, at least for my taste, into the realm of the imagination, even offering a speech that Lincoln would have given as an address to Congress in 2004. Although relying on Lincoln's own words and applying them to our own situation, the speech sounds Cuomoesque-a compliment, I hasten to add. Still, it raises the question why Cuomo does not simply address the current situation in his own words, for surely we need them.[22]

Throughout the remainder of the twentieth century, and in the early twenty-first century, Cuomo defended, at various forums, his "New Deal" outlook and his views on social issues, particularly abortion.

He continued to argue that opposition to abortion was based on religious beliefs, not human rights or the "inalienable rights" his hero Abraham Lincoln defended.

For example, Cuomo wrote that: "President Bush's policies on abortion and stem-cell use are specifically predicated on his belief that human life begins with the fertilization of the egg. Nothing in the Declaration of Independence, the Constitution of the United States, our federal statutes, or our high-court rulings declares that to be the law; it is a purely religious tenet held by the president and millions of other Americans."[23]

As for when life begins, he continued to insist the Church's position was nothing more than based on blind faith, and on a January 12, 2009 appearance on "The Open Mind," he went on a tirade about it:

CUOMO: A principle of abortion is life begins at conception. Great. What's conception? Well, you know . . . with the egg and the thing, they come together . . . bing. Oh, and that's human life right away? Yeah. That . . . who says so?

HEFFNER: Your co-religionists say so.

CUOMO: Oh really?

HEFFNER: Don't they?

CUOMO: Well, the Catholic Church says so. Absolutely.

HEFFNER: Okay.

CUOMO: But the Catholic Church says a lot of things. They say there's a heaven, they say there's a hell. There's a lot of things I believe because I choose to be a Roman Catholic and I accept it on faith. What is faith? Faith implies the lack of knowledge. If you could do it intellectually, on knowledge, you wouldn't need faith. Faith is the willing suspension of your insistence on an intellectual proof. . . .

I'm a Roman Catholic. And they give me rules and I have to live by them to stay in the club. But that's different than saying to people who don't have a religion . . . you should believe it because the priest told me to believe it and I chose to believe it. What they have a right to is proof. Give me a biologist. Give me a scientist who tells me human life is there in conception. As distinguished from life. Because there's life in every cell.

Give me some evidence, Mr. President. You say life begins at conception. That means no woman could ever have an abortion under any circumstances; under any circumstances, because that's a human life . . . under any circumstances . . . she was raped, it was incest. Her life is at stake. There would be no rationale for her to kill a separate human being.[24]

In October 2002, Cuomo participated in The Pew Forum Dialogues on Religion and Public Life, co-chaired by E. J. Dionne, Jr., Senior Fellow at the Bookings Institution, and Laura Spelman of the University of Chicago. The topic was "One Electorate Under God? A Dialogue on Religion and American Politics."

In his presentation titled, "In the American Catholic Tradition of Realism," Cuomo revisited his Notre Dame personally-opposed-but thesis, insisting "Catholics who also hold public office have an additional responsibility. They have to create conditions under which all citizens are reasonably free to act according to their own religious beliefs, even when those acts conflict with Roman Catholic dogma regarding divorce, birth control, abortion, stem-cell research, and even the existence of God."[25]

Cuomo also added that a public official may argue against abortion not just because my bishop says it is wrong, but also "because I think that the whole community, regardless of its religious beliefs, should agree on the importance of protecting life, including life in the womb, which is, at the very least, potentially human and should not be extinguished casually. I even, as a public official, have the right to do all of that."[26]

And then Cuomo falls back on his long-time "consensus argument."

While possessing the right "to make public law match my religious belief," he asks "Should I try?"

His answer is, once again, no. That's because, he explains, "*As I understood my own religion* (emphasis added), it required me to accept the restraints it imposed in my own life, but it did not require that I seek to impose all of them on all New Yorkers."[27] To do so would, in Cuomo's judgment, not "produce harmony and understanding" and it might "be divisive, weakening our ability to function as a pluralist community."

Religious values, he concludes, "will not be accepted as part of the public morality unless they are shared by the community at large."[28] In other words, consensus.

One of the responders to Cuomo's presentation was Professor Robert P. George, Professor of Jurisprudence and Director of the James Madison Program in American Ideals and Institutions at Princeton University. Dr. George soundly critiqued Cuomo's arguments, and rejected how Cuomo "understood my own religion."

> The trouble for Cuomo is that prolife principles are not mere matters of dogma nor are they understood as such by the Catholic Church, whose beliefs Cuomo claims to affirm, or by prolife citizens, whether they happen to be Catholics, Protestants, Jews, Muslims, Hindus, Buddhists, agnostics, or atheists. Rather, prolife citizens understand these principles and propose them to their fellow citizens as fundamental norms of justice and human rights that can be understood and affirmed even apart from claims of revelation and religious authority. . . .

It will not do to suggest, as Cuomo seems to suggest, that the sheer fact that the Catholic Church (or some other religious body) has a teaching against these practices, and that some or even many people reject this teaching, means that laws prohibiting the killing of human beings in the embryonic and fetal stages violate the right to freedom of religion of those who do not accept the teaching. If that were anything other than a fallacy, then laws against killing infants, owning slaves, exploiting workers, and many other grave forms of injustice really would be violations of religious freedom. Surely Cuomo would not wish to endorse that conclusion. . . .

After more than two decades of bobbing and weaving on the subject of prenatal homicide, it is time for Mario Cuomo to face up to the fact that people who oppose abortion and embryo-destructive research oppose these practices for the same reason they oppose postnatal homicide. Catholics and other prolife citizens oppose these practices because they involve the deliberate killing of innocent human beings. Their ground for supporting the legal prohibition of abortion and embryo-destructive research is the same ground on which they support the legal prohibition of infanticide, for example, or the principle of noncombatant immunity even in justified wars. They subscribe to the proposition that all human beings are equal in worth and dignity and cannot be denied the right to protection against killing on the basis of age, size, stage of development, or condition of dependency. . . .

Of course, it is possible for a person wielding public power to use that power to establish or preserve a legal right to abortion and even to provide public money for it while at the same time not wanting or willing anyone to exercise the right. But this does not get Cuomo off the hook. For someone who acts to protect legal abortion necessarily wills that abortion's unborn victims be denied the elementary legal protections against deliberate homicide that one favors for oneself and those whom one considers to be worthy of the law's protection. Thus one violates the most basic precept of normative social and political theory, the Golden Rule. One divides humanity into two classes: those whom one is willing to admit to the community of the commonly protected and those whom one wills to be excluded from it. By exposing members of the disfavored class to lethal violence, one deeply implicates one-self in the injustice of killing them—even if one sincerely hopes that no woman will act on her right to choose abortion. The goodness of what one *hopes* for does not redeem the evil of what one *wills*. To suppose otherwise is to commit yet another fallacy.[29]

As his years out of office went by, several of Cuomo's opponents in the public square went on to their heavenly reward. In September 1999, John Cardinal O'Connor, the eighth archbishop of New York, had a cancerous tumor removed from his brain. Additional tests revealed that the cancer had spread to other areas of his body.

One of O'Connor's last public appearances was at an eightieth-birthday fundraising party for him held at the Waldorf-Astoria on January 15, 2000. Five million dollars was raised for Catholic Charities. At the event, the ailing cardinal told his flock that while he would now "fade into the woodwork," and conceding "I will go one day. Some wonder how soon."[30]

In a gracious *New York Times* op-ed piece, Cuomo said this of his longtime adversary:

> I have felt the force of the cardinal's strong advocacy on the subject of abortion, but I also know about his equally vigorous efforts on behalf of the rest of the Catholic agenda. Over the last decade and a half, his New York Archdiocese has educated, housed, cared for, comforted and counseled hundreds of thousands of Catholics and non-Catholics. None of the great American philanthropies have done more for the most vulnerable among us. And in some cases the archdiocese has led the way for the rest of the private charities. . . .

> And, of course, there are personal deeds that tell us even more about the cardinal: unpublicized visits to AIDS patients to comfort

them in their last hours; long, personal letters to Catholic leaders, filled with humble admissions of his own imperfection and gentle attempts to save them from committing what he thought were grave and dangerous errors of judgment; scores of homilies to small groups of communicants at daily Mass.

All of these were private acts of conscience and compassion by an extraordinary prince of the Church who has always been a priest first.[31]

On Wednesday, May 3, 2000, Cardinal John O'Connor died at 8:05 p.m. of cardiopulmonary arrest.

Cuomo's other political nemesis, Edward I. Koch, died on February 1, 2013. Cuomo had this to say about his former opponent on William O'Shaughnessy's radio show:

I knew Ed Koch for most of the quarter of a century that we both became involved in politics. During those years we had our ups and downs, but no politician I know ever equaled Koch's mastery of the media. All of it—television, radio, newspapers, public appearances. It made him, perhaps, the best-known political leader in New York City's history. That was made clearer by the unprecedented media coverage his passing received. He deserved to be well known. Ed devoted his life to two great loves: the world of politics and his family. He spent his entire adult life in public service as a soldier, mayor, congressman, writer of books and columns. In the end he was more than a uniquely honored mayor. He was an institution that became an ineradicable part of our city's history, like the Statue of Liberty and the great bridges. New Yorkers will never stop answering his question, which was 'How Am I Doing?' And they'll answer it with their reply. 'You did good, Ed. You did good!'"[32]

Sadly, Koch held grudges to the very end. In an interview taped with the proviso it could not run until after he was dead, Koch called Cuomo a "prick."

When his 1986 opponent, Andrew O'Rourke, died in January 2013, Cuomo made these comments on WVOX radio:

> It's very difficult to talk about Andy without sounding like you've made an effort to cover him as some kind of heroic figure. I really do think he is—was, and always will be, in my memory—a heroic figure, because he was such a powerful coming together of good things. His intelligence, his vision, his sense of humor, his sense of fairness made all the political labels meaningless. Liberals are supposed to be Democrats, and businesspeople are supposed to be Republicans . . . all of that. Once you meet and see what he is and see his goodness and his charm and see his intelligence, you say, who needs categories, political categories? Just get the best human beings you can to serve you as public servants. He was a wonderful public servant because he was a wonderful human being. He's a great loss to Flora, his wife, and to his children.[33]

While Cuomo continued to practice law and to be relevant in the public arena, when he turned seventy in 2002 his political focus was no longer on himself, but on his oldest son Andrew, who had his eye on restoring the Cuomo name by recapturing New York's executive mansion.

CHAPTER 16
THE RESTORATION

Andrew Cuomo blamed himself for his father's loss to George Pataki in 1994.

When the governor announced his quest for a fourth term, he turned to his son to manage his campaign. "He knew he was in trouble," Andrew wrote in his memoir. "He knew he was in trouble and he had no one around him who could run it effectively. My father enjoyed the intellectual and had little time for the operational."[1]

Andrew declined the job because he enjoyed serving as President Clinton's assistant secretary at the Department of Housing and Urban Development (HUD), and had bought a house for his growing family in the Washington, D.C. area.

Observing the campaign from a distance, however, Andrew realized it "was like watching a slow-motion automobile crash."[2]

A couple of weeks before Election Day, Andrew took a vacation and traveled up to New York to pitch in. But it was too little, too late.

Andrew continued to work in the Clinton Administration and was named Secretary of HUD in January 1997. And after completing his term of office on January 20, 2001, Andrew returned to New York and "unofficially" announced his intentions to run for governor in 2002.

After George Pataki took office on January 1, 1994, he got off to a good start. Thanks to the skills and efforts of its brilliant budget director, Patricia Woodworth, the fledging administration struck a tax-cutting deal with Speaker Shelly Silver.

Pataki also ordered a hiring freeze, ordered a moratorium on new state regulations, and signed the death penalty into law.

But before long, there was a change in attitude, particularly among the governor's gatekeepers. Pataki's original financial backers, conservatives motivated by principle, were unceremoniously cut out of the loop. Political apparatchiks concluded that it would be easier for Pataki to win re-election if he traded contracts and access for campaign support than if he cast his lot with "true believers" demanding fiscal restraint.

Pataki moved to the left, and began a spending spree that paved the way for him to be re-elected in 1998. He beat his underfunded opponent, Peter Vallone, the speaker of the New York City Council, 54% to 33%.

Watching Pataki's behavior as governor, some political observers began to sense that he was a slacker—a part-time governor who preferred to spend his time dining, fundraising, socializing on the Upper East Side, and hitting the summer cocktail circuit in the Hamptons.

These perceptions led many Democrats to believe that Pataki could be vulnerable if he sought a third term in 2002. And one of those believers was Andrew Cuomo.

However, Andrew's campaign to obtain the Democratic nomination was a disaster. He was oblivious to the facts that his time in Washington had alienated him from the party faithful, that the establishment was comfortable with the other announced candidate, State Comptroller Carl McCall, and that a large number of Democrats were not eager to have the "Prince of Darkness" become the "King of Darkness."

Then speaking at a Democratic Party dinner after Carl McCall, he responded to McCall's claim that Gov. George Pataki didn't do anything on 9/11 by saying "That's not fair, Carl. He did do something. He was there to hold Giuliani's coat."[3]

Though Pataki's inept management of the rebuilding of Ground Zero would cause people to call it "Pataki's Pit," the critical reaction to Cuomo's remark was so severe that Pataki was turned into a victim.

While Mario Cuomo stayed in the background throughout the campaign, he did make phone calls on his son's behalf, and he and Matilda donated $200,000 to the campaign.

And when he sensed the campaign was adrift, Mario drafted "a forty-page manifesto for how to right the ship."

In his biography of Andrew Cuomo, *The Contender*, Michael Shnayerson reported that, "Andrew was hardly about to read the manifesto, let alone change his whole campaign to comply with it, so the tensions grew."[4]

One reporter recalled, "There were some very intense conference calls. His father was screaming 'You have to drop out now.'"[5]

Andrew's campaign went from bad to worse and he finally realized that his quest was hopeless.

On September 3, 2002, with his parents, wife, three daughters, and former President Bill Clinton at his side, Andrew withdrew from the race. "While it's harder for me to step back than step forward," he said, "today I step back. We need healing now, maybe more than ever before. I'm not going to start dividing now."

After a *New York Times* reporter asked Andrew if his poor showing in the polls was due to his personality, he insisted, "He wasn't a negative. The negative here is that I was running against the first African-American. It was his turn."[6]

In November, George Pataki was elected to a third term by a plurality. He received 49% of the vote to Democrat McCall's 34% and 14% for the Independent Party candidate, Tom Golisano.

That humiliating defeat and the subsequent collapse of his marriage to Kerry Kennedy forced Cuomo to re-evaluate his life and to begin the process of reinventing himself and plotting his comeback.

During the next four years, Cuomo worked for real estate developer Andrew Farkas, where he earned several million dollars and, according to journalist Wayne Barrett, received over "$800,000 in identifiable campaign contributions from varied Farkas company, family members, and business associates."[7]

That cash, plus an energetic bout of retail politicking throughout the state, enabled Cuomo to secure the 2006 Democratic nomination for state attorney general and easily prevail in the general election, as did Eliot Spitzer who was elected New York's 54th governor. Governor Eliot Spitzer's call girl scandal that led to his resignation on March 17, 2008, and the ascendency of his hapless lieutenant governor, David Paterson, to the governor's chair, permitted Cuomo to set his sights on the executive chamber.

As Andrew prepared to run for governor in 2010, this author met with him several times to discuss public policy issues. Impressed, I dropped a note to his father that said they were the most satisfying discussions I've had with an elected official in years. I also wrote several op-ed pieces expressing support of legislation he proposed that would permit local communities to be given referendum power to reform, consolidate, or to eliminate municipal subdivisions.

When Andrew announced he would seek the office of governor in May 2010, he declared that New York "had slipped from being a 'national model' under his father to a 'national disgrace.'"[8]

In September 2010, Cuomo received unexpected help when Republican primary voters chose Tea Party hero, Carl Paladino, as their gubernatorial candidate over the GOP establishment's choice, former Congressman Rick Lazio.

Paladino, a businessman from Buffalo, revealed in television and print interviews that he knew little about the workings of state government or its fiscal problems. Moreover, he was gaffe-prone.

For instance, Paladino said in March 2010 that the new federal health care law would kill more Americans that the 9/11 terrorist attacks. It was also revealed that he had forwarded to friends and admirers insensitive, racist, pornographic, and stupid emails.

While Mario Cuomo played no public role during the fall campaign, he worked in the background for his son.

After the *New York Post* published an October 3, 2010 op-ed by this author, "Tale of Two Cities: What went wrong with Buffalo and the South Bronx—two of the nation's poorest areas," the former governor called me the next day.

We discussed the piece, and he described what he had done during his time in office for these cities, how technology should be the new economic engine for the state, and what he expected his son to do if he became the state's chief executive.

Several days later, I received a letter from Mario Cuomo along with a copy of the book he had edited in 1994.

The letter read, "George - Regarding Centers for Advanced Technology, see pages 65 to 67, 70, 234, 246, 259, of my 'The New York Idea: An Experiment in Democracy' ... and anything else you might be interested in. Sincerely, Mario."

On Tuesday, November 3, 2010, Andrew Cuomo easily beat Carl Paladino, 63% to 33%, becoming the first son of a New York governor to be elected to the same post.

On election night, Andrew brought his father to the stage and they joined arms in a victory salute to the cheers of the assembled crowd.

The next day, Mario appeared on Westchester County's WVOX radio boasting that he would not be shocked if Andrew's name was mentioned as a presidential contender. He told host William O'Shaughnessy, "If Andrew, with his bright mind, comes up with good ideas and is able to implement them, then of course he ought to be considered for a higher place ... it should depend upon what he produces."

Saying Andrew was "smarter than his old man," he added, "He'll learn from what I did that didn't work well and he will also learn from what I did that did work well."[9] And he recommended his son pick up on the technology programs he described in his book, *The New York Idea*.[10]

Despite Mario's joy that Andrew was elected, the relationship of the 52nd governor with the 56th one was not always amicable. "Theirs was a fraught relationship," the *Times* reported. "Andrew Cuomo called his father 'Mario, not Dad.' The two were as likely to communicate through the public forum of a newspaper, interview—or through aides drafted into reluctant service—as, say, over the table at a family dinner."[11]

Mario would get upset when he would hear Andrew making "unkind comparisons between their records."[12] And Andrew would get angry when he heard of "even the most oblique criticism of what he was doing from his father."[13]

No doubt #52, who built more prison cells than any other governor, got perturbed when #56 boasted, "I am proud that I'm going to go down in the history books as the governor who closed more prisons than any other governor in the history of the state of New York."[14]

Although this author and Andrew Cuomo were philosophically on the opposite sides of the political divide, I was appointed to his transition team and later to his fiscal and economic advisory board.

Because of the state's fiscal and economic woes, Andrew Cuomo's inaugural at the state capital on January 1, 2011, was a small event. Only 200 were invited versus many thousands at George Pataki's first inaugural.

At a reception after the swearing-in, the author and Mario Cuomo chatted about our October conversation and the tough budget issues the new governor faced.

Officially, Andrew Cuomo's first-term agenda as governor was one of center-right fiscal policy and social liberalism.

His first mission was to tackle a projected deficit of $10 billion for the fiscal year beginning April 1, 2011.

To eliminate the structural deficit, Cuomo spared no facet of state spending. He used effectively the powers of his office to negotiate a budget that was passed on time and included real spending cuts of about 2%; caps on Medicaid and education spending; and no fee or tax increases.

To placate leftists unhappy over the budget cuts, the governor's next move was to push for passage of a same-sex marriage law. To secure passage, Cuomo convinced Republican Senate leader Dean Skelos to break his promise to New York's archbishop, Timothy Cardinal Dolan, that he would not permit a roll call on this issue.

Even though Cuomo was on a roll and very popular by the end of his first year in office, there were rumblings that the old Andrew had returned. There were stories that he was back to micromanaging, brow-beating his staff, bulling anyone who got in his way, and serving as his own enforcer.

Unlike his father who twisted Church teaching to rationalize his "who am I to impose my religious views" on the subject of abortion, Andrew could care less what the Church taught on any issue.

While his father looked to St. Thomas More as a model in public life, Andrew looked to Niccolò Machiavelli.

In an essay titled "How a leader's philosophy directly affects an organization culture," Peter deMarco described a 2007 meeting he attended at the office of the Secretary of Housing and Urban Development: "One of Cuomo's first acts after taking over as Secretary of HUD in 1997 was to distribute the book by Niccolò Machiavelli, *The Prince*, to his key aides ... telling them: 'This is my leadership philosophy.'"[15]

By the time Andrew's re-election campaign began in 2014, he managed to upset voters on both the left and right side of the political spectrum.

Upstate voters angry over the governor's extreme views on abortion, same-sex marriage, and gun control came out in droves to vote for the Republican-Conservative candidate Rob Astorino, Westchester's County Executive.

From the left, Cuomo was challenged in a Democratic primary by a radical left-wing law professor, Zephyr Teachout. While he won the primary, Teachout's 33% showing was impressive.

On Election Day, Tuesday November 4, 2014, Andrew Cuomo was re-elected to a second term with only 54% of the vote versus 63% four years earlier. Rob Astorino received 40% and the Green Party candidate received 5%.

The number of popular votes Cuomo received had significantly declined. In 2010, he garnered 2,911,721 votes. His vote count in 2014 was 2,069,460, a drop of 28%

During the 2014 campaign, Mario Cuomo played no discernable role. On election night, he did make an appearance with his victorious son and gave him a fist bump. It was Mario Cuomo's last public appearance. The 82-year-old former governor was ailing from a heart condition.

Inaugurals are generally happy events. There are New Year's Eve bashes in Albany for supporters, a private swearing-in at midnight with friends and family; and a public swearing-in at the Capitol building on January 1.

There was to be no such hoopla for Andrew Cuomo's second inaugural.

He preferred to be in New York City so he could be close to his father who was receiving hospice care at his Manhattan apartment.

Andrew read his second inaugural address to Mario. "He said it was good—especially for a second termer! See? My father's a third-termer."[16]

After being sworn in at the new World Trade Center, Andrew rushed up to Buffalo for another inaugural event at 4 p.m.

In his address, Andrew referred to Mario several times. "We, as my father said so well, we are 'the family of New York' ... a collection of the most daring, bold, accepting people from every country on the globe," Cuomo said.[17]

As Andrew was completing his Buffalo inaugural event, Mario Matthew Cuomo died at 5:15 p.m.

The family statement read in part, "the Governor passed away from natural causes due to heart failure this evening at home with his loving family at his side."[18]

The passing of Mario Cuomo made the front page of every newspaper in America. And the tributes poured in.

The *Times* headline read, "Governor, Governor's Father and an Eloquent Liberal Beacon." The article described him "as a tenacious debater and spellbinding speaker at a time when political oratory seemed to be shrinking to the size of the television set.... In an era when liberal thought was increasingly discredited, Mr. Cuomo, a man of large intellect and often unrestrained personality, celebrated it...."

The *Times* added: "A man of contradictions who enjoyed Socratic arguments with himself, Mr. Cuomo seemed to disdain politics even as he embraced it. 'What an ugly business this is,' he liked to say. Yet, he reveled in it, proving himself an uncommonly skilled politician and sometimes a ruthless one."[19]

Over at the *New York Post*, the editors wrote:

> Few figures in American political life were as stirring as Mario Cuomo, the three-term governor of New York and father of its current executive, who died Thursday at 82. That we seldom agreed with him does not detract from this record....
>
> In his politics, Cuomo was a passionate and forceful proponent of the classic Democratic liberalism championed by two of his heroes, Franklin Roosevelt and Adlai Stevenson. Unlike many of today's politicians, he never shied away from robust debates with his foes. And his oratorical gifts never failed to elevate both the content and the tone of public discourse.
>
> In the end, though, his advocacy served a political and governing philosophy whose most notable successes, in our view, were strictly rhetorical....
>
> Still, he was a giant of the political scene who loved his family, loved his state and loved the cut-and-thrust of old-fashioned politics. Mario Cuomo, RIP.[20]

At the *Daily News*, columnist Mike Lupica declared that Cuomo's death "was, and is, the country's loss.... Everyone who ever knew Mario Cuomo ... knew about the beauty in the man's soul, all the good in him.... This was a great man, as great as this city ever produced."[21]

And *Post* Albany editor, Fredric U. Dicker, who covered Cuomo for 20 years, wrote:

> Mario Cuomo was one of the nation's greatest orators, but his sometimes-dazzling speeches—like his keynote to the Democratic National Convention in San Francisco in 1984—almost always lacked answers to the problems they addressed. . . .

He was someone who claimed to have foresworn political labels but was actually a quintessential political liberal and, usually, proud of it. People who knew him well often joked that Mario Cuomo was someone who was ready with a question for every answer.[22]

Unlike the funeral masses of governors Alfred E. Smith and Hugh Carey, Cuomo's was not held at St. Patrick's Cathedral. Instead, the service was at the Jesuit Church of St. Ignatius Loyola on Park Avenue at 84th Street on Tuesday, January 6, 2015.

In Governor Andrew Cuomo's eulogy, he said the essence of his father was that "He was not interested in pleasing the audience—not in a speech, not in life. He believed what he believed, and the reaction of the audience on the powers that be or the popularity of his belief was irrelevant to him."

Andrew described his father, not as a politician but as a public intellectual, a humanist who "had strong feelings of right and wrong based on his religion, philosophy, and life experiences."

Mario was at his core "a philosopher and he was a poet, an advocate, and a crusader. Mario Cuomo was the keynote speaker for our better angels. He was there to make the case, to argue and convince, and in that purist mindset he could be a ferocious opponent and powerful ally."

But most "central to understanding Mario Cuomo," Andrew believed, is that he was from Queens. "Mario Cuomo's birthmark from the outer borough was deep, and he wore it with pride. He had a natural connection with the outsider looking in, the person fighting for inclusion, the underdog, the minority, the disenfranchised, the poor. He was always the son of an immigrant. He was always an outsider, and that was his edge."[23] And as one who grew up in the outer boroughs of Brooklyn and Queens, the author believes this best explains Mario Cuomo, the man: The street-smart guy who defended the little guys and loved to verbally torture the Manhattan elites he despised.

Mario Cuomo was buried not far from the neighborhoods he lived in throughout his life, St. John's Cemetery in Middle Village, Queens.

As for his tombstone, when asked what he would like it to say, he said: "Mario Cuomo, 1932-" and, "He tried."[24]

From George Clinton in 1777, New York's first chief executive, to

Andrew Cuomo, the current incumbent, the Empire State has had some remarkable governors, including Martin Van Buren, William Seward, Grover Cleveland, Theodore Roosevelt, Charles Evans Hughes, Al Smith, Franklin D. Roosevelt, Thomas E. Dewey, Nelson Rockefeller, and the father of the current incumbent, Mario M. Cuomo. These and some others not mentioned have much in common, not least that each aspired to be president of the United States—and four were elected to the highest office in the land. And among all the fifty-six men who have served as New York's governor, none was more complicated, endearing, brilliant, pugilistic, and exasperating than Mario Cuomo.

NOTES

Chapter 1

1. Warren Moscow, *The Empire State* (1948), p. 32.
2. Richard Norton Smith, *Thomas E. Dewey and His Times* (1982), p. 547.
3. Rudy Abramson, *Spanning the Century: The Life of W. Averell Harriman, 1891–1986*, p. 520.
4. Ibid.
5. Michael Kramer and Sam Roberts, *I Never Wanted to be Vice-President of Anything!: An Investigative Biography of Nelson Rockefeller* (1976), p. 198.
6. Cary Reich, *The Life of Nelson A. Rockefeller: Worlds to Conquer, 1908–1958* (1996), p. 731.
7. Garry Wills, *Nixon Agonistes: The Crisis of the Self-Made Man* (1970), p. 32.
8. Robert H. Connery and Gerald Benjamin, *Rockefeller of New York: Executive Power in the Statehouse* (1979), p. 418.
9. William Rodgers, *Rockefeller's Follies: An Unauthorized View of Nelson A. Rockefeller* (1966), p. 39.
10. Kramer and Roberts, p. 215.
11. Ibid., pp. 216–17.
12. Frank Gervasi, *The Real Rockefeller* (1964), p. 229.
13. Kramer and Roberts, p. 216.
14. Gervasi, p. 229.
15. Connery and Benjamin, p. 434.
16. Ibid., p. 58.
17. Ibid., p. 59.
18. Ibid., p. 113.
19. Ibid., p. 63.
20. Peter D. McClelland and Alan L. Magdovitz, *Crisis in the Making: The Political Economy of New York State since 1945* (1981), p. 144.
21. Kramer and Roberts, p. 146.
22. McClelland and Magdovitz, p. 292.
23. Kramer and Roberts, p. 142.
24. Connery and Benjamin, p. 190.
25. Ibid.
26. McClelland and Magdovitz, p. 374.

27. Connery and Benjamin, p. 220.
28. McClelland and Magdovitz, p. 417.
29. Ibid., p. 258.
30. Kramer and Roberts, p. 145.
31. George J. Marlin and Joe Mysak, *The Guide Book to Municipal Bonds* (1991), pp. 22–23.
32. Richard Norton Smith, *On His Own Terms: A Life of Nelson Rockefeller* (2014), p. 637.
33. McClelland and Magdovitz, p. 7.
34. Ibid., p. 29.
35. Ibid., p. 54.
36. Ibid., p. 93.
37. Ibid., pp. 97–98.
38. Ibid., p. 211.

Chapter 2

1. Marlin and Mysak, pp. 4–6.
2. Ibid.
3. Ibid.
4. George J. Marlin, *The American Catholic Voter: Two Hundred Years of Political Impact* (2004), pp. 173–74.
5. Ibid., p. 174.
6. Chris McNickle, *To be Mayor of New York: Ethnic Politics in the City* (1993), p. 93.
7. Ibid., p. 104.
8. George J. Marlin, *Fighting the Good Fight: A History of the New York Conservative Party* (2002), p. 94.
9. Ibid., p. 95.
10. Ibid.
11. William F. Buckley Jr., *The Unmaking of a Mayor* (1966), p. 141.
12. Marlin, *Fighting the Good Fight*, p. 102.
13. Vincent J. Cannato, *The Ungovernable City: John Lindsay on His Struggle to Save New York* (2001), p. 391.
14. Marlin, *Fighting the Good Fight*, p. 93.
15. Joshua B. Freeman, *Working-Class New York: Life and Labor Since World War II* (2000), p. 25.
16. Ibid., p. 172.
17. E. Michael Jones, *The Slaughter of Cities* (2004), p. 200.
18. Kenneth T. Jackson, *Crabgrass Frontier: The Suburbanization of the United States* (1985), p. 206.

19. Edward C. Banfield, *The Unheavenly City Revisited* (1974), p. 36.
20. Ibid.
21. Ibid., p. 16.
22. Jones, p. 200.
23. Ibid., p. 359.
24. Freeman, p. 170.
25. Banfield, p. 16.
26. Kenneth T. Jackson, *The Encyclopedia of New York City* (1995), p. 362.
27. Ibid.
28. Ibid.
29. Robert Fitch, *The Assassination of New York* (1993), p. 279.
30. Freeman, p. 165.
31. Ibid., p. 147.
32. McClelland and Magdovitz, p. 113.
33. Ibid., p. 128.
34. Freeman, p. 143.
35. Ibid., pp. 144–45.
36. Ibid., p. 168.
37. Source: New York City Council on Economic Education.
38. McClelland and Magdovitz, p. 71.
39. Ibid.
40. Fred Siegel, *The Future Once Happened Here: New York, D.C., L.A., and The Fate of America's Big Cities* (1997), pp. 47–48.
41. John F. Cogan, *The High Cost of Good Intentions: A History of U.S. Federal Entitlement Programs* (2017), p. 83.
42. Ibid., p. 45.
43. Ibid., p. 87.
44. Ibid., p. 80.
45. Ibid., p. 347.
46. Ibid., p. 91.
47. Ibid., p. 94.
48. Ibid., p. 180.
49. Ibid., p. 223.
50. Ibid., p. 228.
51. George J. Marlin, *Narcissist Nation* (2011), excerpted from pp. 160–63.
52. Ibid.
53. Ibid.
54. Ibid.
55. Charles R. Morris, *The Cost of Good Intentions: New York City and the Liberal Experiment, 1960–1975* (1980), p. 69.
56. Ibid., p. 71.

57. Richard Norton Smith, *On His Own Terms*, p. 483.
58. Siegel, p. 61.
59. Steven Weisman, Editor, *Daniel Patrick Moynihan: A Portrait in Letters of an American Visionary* (2010), p. 552.
60. Buckley, pp. 265–66.
61. Weisman, pp. 94–95.
62. Jackson, *The Encyclopedia of New York City*, p. 298.
63. Cannato, p. 526.
64. Ibid., p. 532.
65. Ibid., p. 528.
66. Ibid., p. 531.

Chapter 3

1. Robert S. McElvaine, *Mario Cuomo: A Biography* (1988), p. 72.
2. Ken Auletta, "Governor I," *The New Yorker*, April 9, 1984.
3. Ibid.
4. Ibid.
5. McElvaine, p. 170.
6. Cannato, p. 505.
7. Mario Cuomo, *Forest Hills Diary: The Crisis of Low-Income Housing* (1974), p. 20.
8. Marlin, *The American Catholic Voter*, p. 137.
9. Andrew Greeley, *Neighborhood* (1977), p. 119.
10. Cuomo, *Forest Hills Diary*, p. 8.
11. McElvaine, p. 172.
12. Cannato, p. 509.
13. Cuomo, *Forest Hills Diary*, p. 177.
14. Ibid., p. 185.
15. Ibid., p. 116.
16. Ibid., p. 200.
17. McElvaine, p. 194.
18. Cuomo, *Forest Hills Diary*, p. 138.
19. McElvaine, p. 194.
20. Ibid., p. 196.
21. Ibid., p. 199.
22. Auletta, "Governor I."
23. Nat Hentoff, *The Village Voice*, "Cuomo Rising: Will New York's Great Smart Hope Run for Mayor?", April 18, 1977.
24. Marlin, *Fighting the Good Fight*, p. 155.

25. Cannato, p. xx.
26. Jack Newfield and Paul Du Brul, *The Abuse of Power: The Permanent Government and the Fall of New York* (1977), pp. 150–51.
27. Cannato, p. xi.
28. Marlin, *Fighting the Good Fight*, p. 155.
29. Auletta, "Governor I."
30. McElvaine, pp. 202–03.
31. *New York Times*, September 23, 1971.
32. McElvaine, p. 204.
33. Ibid., p. 205.
34. Ibid., p. 204.
35. *New York Times*, August 13, 1974.
36. Hentoff, *The Village Voice*.
37. McElvaine, p. 209.
38. *New York Times*, August 24, 1974.
39. Ibid.
40. Seymour P. Lachman and Robert Polner, *The Man Who Saved New York: Hugh Carey and the Great Fiscal Crisis of 1975* (2010), pp. 58–59.

Chapter 4

1. Marlin, *Fighting the Good Fight*, p. 221.
2. Lynne A. Weikart, *Follow the Money: Who Controls New York City Mayors?* (2009), p. 34.
3. *Long Island Business News*, September 24, 2010.
4. Newfield and Du Brul, p. 28.
5. Charles Brecher and Raymond D. Horton, *Power Failure: New York City Politics & Policy Since 1960* (1993), p. 20.
6. McClelland and Magdovitz, p. 310.
7. Mallory Factor, *Shadowbosses* (2012), p. 241.
8. Raymond D. Horton, *Municipal Labor Relations in New York City: Lessons of the Lindsay-Wagner Years* (1972), p. 73.
9. Ibid., p. 75.
10. Ken Auletta, *The Streets Were Paved with Gold* (1979), p. 47.
11. *New York Times*, February 12, 1969.
12. Auletta, p. 48.
13. Ibid., p. 32.
14. Ibid., p. 97.
15. Kim Phillips-Fein, *Fear City: New York's Fiscal Crisis and the Rise of Austerity Politics* (2017), p. 199.
16. Ibid., p. 200.

Chapter 5

1. McElvaine, p. 212.
2. Ibid., p. 217.
3. Newfield and Du Brul, p. 310.
4. Lachman and Palmer, pp. 182–83.
5. McElvaine, p. 234.
6. *New York* magazine, October 3, 1977.
7. *New York Times Magazine*, October 30, 1977.

Chapter 6

1. Kim Phillips-Fein, p. 270.
2. *New York Times*, July 15, 1977.
3. Ibid., August 4, 1977.
4. Kim Phillips-Fein, p. 285.
5. Ibid.
6. Jonathan Mahler, *Ladies and Gentlemen, The Bronx is Burning* (2005), p. 282.
7. Ibid., p. 283.
8. McNickel, p. 263.
9. *New York Times Magazine*, July 21, 1977.
10. Ibid.
11. Mahler, p. 231.
12. Ibid., p. 232.
13. *New York Times Magazine*, September 5, 1977.
14. Curtis Stephen, "New York 1977: The Night The Lights Went Out," July 12, 2017, curtisstephen.com.
15. Arthur Browne, Dan Collins and Michael Goodwin, *I, Koch: A Decidedly Unauthorized Biography of the Mayor of New York City, Edward I. Koch* (1985), p. 140.
16. Jonathan Soffer, *Ed Koch and the Rebuilding of New York City* (2010) pp. 128–29.
17. Mahler, p. 109.
18. Mahler, pp. 109–10.
19. Hentoff, *The Village Voice*, April 18, 1977.
20. Ibid.
21. Mahler, p. 294.
22. Ibid., p. 295.
23. McElvaine, p. 243.
24. *New York* magazine, October 3, 1977.
25. Ibid.

26. Mahler, p. 292.
27. Edward I. Koch, *Mayor: An Autobiography* (1984), p. 37.
28. Mahler, p. 304.
29. Koch, p. 40.
30. Soffer, p. 137.
31. Ibid.
32. *New York* magazine, October 3, 1977.
33. Soffer, p. 136.
34. Ibid., p. 135.
35. *New York* magazine, October 3, 1977.
36. Soffer, p. 138.
37. George J. Marlin and Brad Miner, *Sons of Saint Patrick: A History of the Archbishops of New York from Dagger John to Timmytown* (2017), pp. 268–69.
38. Jack Newfield and Wayne Barrett, *City for Sale: Ed Koch and the Betrayal of New York* (1988), p. 125.
39. Soffer, p. 139.
40. Koch, p. 34.
41. Ibid.
42. Soffer, p. 139.
43. Ibid., pp. 139–40.
44. Michael Shnayerson, *The Contender: Andrew Cuomo, a Biography* (2015), p. 38.
45. McElvaine, p. 254.
46. *New York Post*, November 9, 1977.
47. Koch, p. 33.
48. McElvaine, p. 253.
49. Ibid., pp. 253–55.
50. Ibid., p. 254.
51. *Daily News*, September 20, 1977.
52. Ibid.
53. *New York Times*, September 21, 1977.
54. Ibid.
55. *Time*, June 2, 1986.
56. Soffer, p. 141.
57. Cuomo post-election comments from *New York Times*, *Daily News*, *New York Post* editions of November 9, 1977.
58. McElvaine, p. 250.
59. Mahler, pp. 306–07.
60. Ibid., p. 313.
61. Ken Auletta, *Hard Feelings* (1980), p. 277.
62. *New York* magazine, September 5, 1977.
63. Mahler, p. 294.
64. Marlin, *Fighting the Good Fight*, p. 277.

Chapter 7

1. E. J. McMahon, "The Tax Reform That Wasn't," *Albany Government Law Review*, May 2012.
2. Ibid.
3. Auletta, *Hard Feelings*, p. 162.
4. Ibid., p. 165.
5. Ibid., p. 169.
6. Daniel C. Kramer, *The Days of Wine and Roses are Over* (1997), p. 161.
7. Ibid.
8. McElvaine, p. 264.
9. Ibid., p. 265.
10. Aulella, *Hard Feelings*, p. 166.
11. McElvaine, p. 267.
12. Ibid.
13. Marlin, *Fighting the Good Fight*, p. 247.
14. McElvaine, p. 267.
15. *New York Post*, November 8, 1978.
16. Ibid.
17. McElvaine, p. 270.
18. Ibid., pp. 270–71.
19. Ibid., p. 271.
20. Aulella, *Hard Feelings*, pp. 173–74.
21. Kramer, p. 276.
22. The Empire Center for Public Policy, "Deja Vu All Over Again: The Right Way to Cure New York's Looming Budget Gap," October 1, 2002.
23. Ibid.
24. Kramer, p. 283.
25. Ibid., p. 282.

Chapter 8

1. McElvaine, p. 278.
2. Ibid.
3. Mario Cuomo, *Diaries of Mario M. Cuomo: The Campaign For Governor* (1984), p. 71.
4. Ibid., p. 78.
5. *New York Times*, June 13, 1981.
6. Ibid.
7. Cuomo, *Diaries*, p. 102.
8. Ibid., p. 103.

9. Ibid., p. 104.
10. *New York Times Magazine*, October 31, 1982.
11. Cuomo, *Diaries*, p. 105.
12. Ibid., pp. 113–14.
13. Ibid., p. 119.
14. Soffer, p. 225.
15. Ibid.
16. *How'm I Doing?: The Wit & Wisdom of Ed Koch* (1981), p. 56.
17. Ibid., p. 35.
18. Ibid., p. 36.
19. Browne et al., p. 241.
20. Koch, *Mayor*, p. 30.
21. Ibid., pp. 330–31.
22. Cuomo, *Diaries*, p. 112.
23. Browne, et al., p. 247.
24. Cuomo, *Diaries*, p. 121.
25. Ibid., pp. 119 and 254.
26. Ibid., p. 133.
27. Koch, *Mayor*, pp. 333–34.
28. Soffer, p. 230.
29. Cuomo, *Diaries*, p. 153.
30. Soffer, p. 232.
31. *New York Times*, July 8, 1982.
32. Ibid., July 13, 1982.
33. Ibid., July 29, 1982.
34. Ibid.
35. Ibid., August 19, 1982.
36. Koch, *Mayor*, pp. 335–36.
37. Browne, et al., p. 260.
38. Cuomo, *Diaries*, p. 264.
39. Ibid., p. 255.
40. Ibid., p. 296.
41. *New York Times Magazine*, October 31, 1982.
42. *New York Times*, September 24, 1982.
43. Ibid.
44. Marlin, *Fighting the Good Fight*, pp. 260–61.
45. Ibid., p. 262.
46. *New York Times*, September 24, 1982.
47. Quotes from the first debate were transcribed from the taping that was posted by the Empire Center for Public Policy on its web site.
48. *New York Times*, October 9, 1982.
49. Ibid., October 30, 1982.

50. Post-election comments compiled from the November 3, 1982 editions of the *New York Post, Daily News* and *New York Times.*

Chapter 9

1. Auletta, "Governor I."
2. Cuomo, *Diaries*, p. 366.
3. McElvaine, p. 304.
4. Excerpts of Cuomo's Inaugural Address from transcript published in *The New York Times*, January 2, 1983.
5. Auletta, "Governor I."
6. *New York Times*, January 6, 1983.
7. Ibid., January 9, 1983.
8. Ibid.
9. Ibid., January 6, 1983.
10. Ibid., January 9, 1983.
11. Ibid., January 2, 1983.
12. Ibid., January 18, 1983.
13. Ibid.
14. Ibid.
15. Ibid., January 21, 1983.
16. Ibid, January 28, 1983.
17. Auletta, "Governor I."
18. *New York Times*, February 1, 1983.
19. Ibid.
20. Ibid.
21. Ibid.
22. Ibid.
23. Ibid.
24. Ibid.
25. Ken Auletta, "Governor II," *The New Yorker*, April 16, 1984.
26. Ibid.
27. Ibid.
28. *New York Times*, March 28, 1983.
29. Ibid.
30. Ibid., March 29, 1983.
31. Ibid.
32. Auletta, "Governor II."
33. Ibid.
34. *New York Times Magazine*, September 14, 1986.
35. Auletta, "Governor I."

36. *New York Times Magazine*, February 10, 1991.
37. Auletta, "Governor I."
38. Auletta, "Governor II."
39. Ibid.
40. Ibid.
41. Ibid.
42. *New York Times*, March 14, 1983.
43. Ibid.
44. Auletta, "Governor II."
45. *New York Times*, August 23, 1983.
46. Ibid.
47. Auletta, "Governor I."
48. Auletta, "Governor II."
49. Ibid.
50. *New York Times*, May 29, 1983.
51. Ibid.
52. Ibid.
53. *New York Times Magazine*, May 15, 1988.
54. *New York Times*, May 29, 1983.

Chapter 10

1. Cuomo, *Diaries,* pp. 363–64.
2. *New York Times*, September 29, 1983.
3. Jack W. Germond and Jules Witcover, *Wake Us When It's Over: Presidential Politics of 1984* (1985), p. 102.
4. Ibid., p. 103.
5. William A. Henry, *Visions of America: How We Saw the 1984 Election* (1985), p. 84.
6. Ibid., p. 83.
7. Germond and Witcover, p. 106.
8. Ibid.
9. Peter Goldman and Tony Fuller, *The Quest for the Presidency 1984 Election* (1985), p. 173.
10. Ibid.
11. Ibid.
12. *New York Times*, September 29, 1983.
13. Ibid.
14. Elizabeth Drew, *Campaign Journal: The Political Events of 1983–1984* (1985), pp. 522–23.
15. Henry, p. 185.

16. Excerpts of the 1984 Cuomo Convention speech from *More Than Just Words: The Speeches of Mario Cuomo*, pp. 21–31.
17. Henry, p. 186.
18. John Kenneth White, *The New Politics of Old Values* (Second Edition, 1988), p. 147.
19. Ibid., p. 83.
20. George J. Marlin, "Return of Kennedy, Reagan Policies Would Grow Economy," *Newsmax*, September 30, 2016.
21. Ibid.
22. Ibid.
23. George J. Marlin, "Progressivism's Dark Side," *The Catholic Thing*, April 2, 2016.
24. Ibid.
25. Ibid.
26. Ibid.
27. Ibid.
28. George J. Marlin, *The American Catholic Voter: Two Hundred Years of Political Impact* (2004), pp. 298–99.
29. Henry, p. 186.
30. Ibid., p. 185.
31. *New York Times Magazine*, February 10, 1991.
32. George J. Marlin, *Squandered Opportunities: New York's Pataki Years*, pp. 1–2.
33. George J. Marlin and Brad Miner, *Sons of Saint Patrick: A History of the Archbishops of New York from Dagger John to Timmytown* (2017), p. 283.
34. Ibid., p. 297.
35. Ibid., pp. 297–98.
36. Ibid., p. 298.
37. *New York Times*, October 31, 1982.
38. Marlin, *Squandered Opportunities*, pp. 5–6.
39. *First Things*, March 2015.
40. McElvaine, pp. 92–93.
41. Charles R. Morris, *American Catholic* (1997), pp. 425–26.
42. Arthur M. Schlesinger, Jr., Editor, *History of American Presidential Elections Supplemental Volume 1972–1984* (1986), p. 302.
43. Marlin and Miner, p. 298.
44. *New York Times*, September 15, 1984.
45. *First Things*, March 2015.
46. Morris, p. 426.
47. Excerpts of the Cuomo speech, "Religious Belief and Public Morality" from *More Than Just Words: The Speeches of Mario Cuomo*, pp. 32–35.
48. Marlin and Miner, p. 299.

49. Ibid., pp. 299–300.
50. Ibid., p. 300.
51. *First Things*, March 2015.
52. Kenneth J. Heineman, *God Is A Conservative: Religion, Politics and Morality in Contemporary America* (1998), p. 142.
53. Marlin and Miner, p. 300.
54. Ibid.
55. Marlin, *The American Catholic Voter*, p. 302.
56. *New York Post*, November 7, 1984.
57. Goldman and Fuller, p. 368.
58. *New York Times*, November 8, 1984.
59. John Kenneth White, p. 134.

Chapter 11

1. *New York Post*, November 7, 1984.
2. Jack W. Germond and Jules Witcover, *Whose Broad Stripes and Bright Stars? The Trivial Pursuit of the Presidency 1988* (1989), p. 38.
3. *New York Times*, April 4, 1985.
4. Ibid., April 6, 1985.
5. Ibid.
6. Ibid.
7. Arthur M. Schlesinger, Jr., *History of American Presidential Elections Volume VIII* (1985), p. 3293.
8. *The Journal News*, Westchester, January 4, 2013.
9. *New York Times*, January 7, 1985.
10. Ibid.
11. Ibid.
12. Ibid.
13. Ibid.
14. *New York Times*, May 18, 1986.
15. Ibid.
16. Ibid.
17. Ibid., March 15, 1986.
18. Michael Barone and Grant Ujifusa, *The Almanac of American Politics 1988* (1987), p. 789.
19. Lee M. Miringoff and Barbara L. Carvalno, *The Cuomo Factor* (1986), p. 115.
20. *New York Times*, November 6, 1986.
21. *New York Post*, November 5, 1986.
22. Ibid.
23. Ibid.

24. Ibid.
25. Ibid.
26. Paul Taylor, *See How They Run: Electing the President In An Age of Mediaocracy* (1990), p. 123.
27. Ibid., pp. 123–24.
28. Ibid., p. 125.
29. McElvaine, p. 413.
30. *New York Times*, February 20, 1987.
31. Taylor, p. 126.
32. *New York Times*, February 20, 1987.
33. *New York Times Magazine*, May 15, 1988.
34. Peter Goldman and Tom Mathews, *The Quest for the Presidency: The 1988 Campaign* (1989), p. 52.
35. McElvaine, p. 382.
36. Ibid., pp. 382–83.
37. Elizabeth Drew, *Election Journal: Political Events of 1987–1988* (1989), p. 38.
38. Ibid.
39. Goldman and Mathews, p. 53.
40. Taylor, p. 127.
41. Ibid.
42. Goldman and Mathews, p. 53.
43. Sidney Blumenthal, *Pledging Allegiance: The Last Campaign of the Cold War* (1990), p. 152.
44. Ibid., pp. 207–08.
45. Goldman and Mathews, p. 161.
46. Ibid.
47. Ibid., p. 162.
48. Germond and Witcover, p. 317.
49. Gary Maloney, Editor, *The Almanac of 1988 Presidential Politics* (1989), p. 6.
50. Germond and Witcover, p. 446.
51. *New York City Tribune*, November 10, 1988.
52. Ibid.
53. *New York Post*, November 10, 1988.
54. *New York Times*, November 10, 1988.
55. Ibid.
56. *New York Post*, November 10, 1988.
57. *New York Times*, November 10, 1988.
58. Ibid.
59. *New York Post*, November 10, 1988.
60. *New York Times*, November 10, 1988.
61. Ibid., September 13, 1990.
62. Marlin, *Squandered Opportunities*, p. 12.

63. Marlin, *Fighting the Good Fight*, p. 284.
64. Ibid.
65. Ibid., p. 286.
66. Ibid., p. 290.
67. *New York Times*, November 9, 1990.
68. *Utica Observer Dispatch*, September 23, 1990.
69. *Poughkeepsie Journal*, October 18, 1990.
70. Jack W. Germond and Jules Witcover, *Mad As Hell: Revolt At The Ballot Box 1992* (1993), p. 115.
71. *The Nation*, October 22, 1990.
72. *New York Times*, January 1, 1991.
73. Ibid.
74. Germond and Witcover, *Mad As Hell*, pp. 115–16.
75. Ibid.
76. Ibid., p. 117.
77. Ibid, p. 118.
78. C-Span Transcript of Radio and Television News Directors Association Event.
79. Germond and Witcover, *Mad As Hell*, p. 119.
80. Ibid.
81. Ibid., p. 122.
82. Ibid.
83. ABC News This Week with David Brinkley, Show #526, November 24, 1991 Transcript.
84. *Washington Post*, November 26, 1991.
85. *New York Times*, November 26, 1991.
86. Germond and Witcover, *Mad As Hell*, p. 123.
87. Cuomo quotes from C-Span taping and *New York Times*, December 21, 1991.
88. Hy Rosen and Peter Slocum, *From Rocky to Pataki* (1998), p. 122.
89. *New York Times*, December 21, 1991.
90. *Washington Post*, December 26, 1991.
91. *Washington Post*, December 21, 1991.
92. Ibid.
93. Germond and Witcover, *Mad As Hell*, p. 129.
94. Bill Clinton, *My Life* (2004), p. 380.
95. Steve Kornacki, *The Red and the Blue: The 1990s and the Birth of Political Tribalism* (2018), p. 122.
96. *Los Angeles Times*, January 29, 1992.
97. Ibid.
98. Ibid.
99. Kornacki, p. 123.
100. Peter Goldman et al., *Quest for the Presidency 1992* (1994), p. 232.
101. Ibid., p. 280.

102. Ibid, p. 288.
103. George Stephanopoulos, *All Too Human* (1999), p. 84.
104. Peter Goldmark et al., p. 288.
105. Ibid., p. 289.

Chapter 12

1. Stephanopoulos, p. 167.
2. *The Nation*, October 22, 1990.
3. Stephanopoulos, p. 166.
4. Ibid.
5. Ibid.
6. Ibid., p. 167.
7. Ibid., p. 170.
8. Ibid., pp. 171–72.
9. Ibid., pp. 173–74.
10. Ibid., p. 174.
11. *Washington Post*, April 10, 1985.
12. *Washington Journalism Review*, April 1987.
13. Ibid.
14. Harry Rosenfeld, *Battling Editor: The Albany Years* (2019), pp. 48 and 51.
15. *New York Times Magazine*, May 15, 1988.
16. Ibid.
17. *Washington Journalism Review*, April 1987.
18. Ibid.
19. *New York Times Magazine*, May 15, 1988.
20. Ibid.
21. *Washington Journalism Review*, April 1987.
22. Ibid.
23. Ibid.
24. Associated Press, March 1, 1990.
25. *New York Times*, August 27, 1986.
26. *Washington Post*, August 29, 1986.
27. Ibid.
28. *New York Times*, December 23, 1987.
29. Ibid.
30. Ibid.
31. Michael Shnayerson, *The Contender: Andrew Cuomo* (2015), p. 70.
32. *New York* magazine, November 2, 1987.
33. Ibid.
34. *New York Times*, January 19, 1986.

35. Ibid.
36. Ibid.
37. McElvaine, p. 410.
38. *New York* magazine, November 2, 1987.
39. Ibid.
40. *New York Times*, October 10, 1987.
41. Ibid.
42. Ibid.
43. *New York Times*, November 30, 1987.
44. Ibid.
45. Ibid.
46. Ibid.
47. Ibid.
48. Ibid.
49. Ibid.
50. *New York* magazine, November 2, 1987.
51. Saladin Ambar, *American Cicero: Mario Cuomo and the Defense of American Liberalism* (2018), p. 107.
52. *Newsday*, August 25, 1985.
53. Ibid.
54. Ibid.
55. Ibid.
56. Ibid.
57. Ibid.
58. Ibid.
59. Ibid.
60. Deposition of Charles B. Molineaux, taken by Defendants, pursuant to subpoena, at the offices of Buckley, Treacy, Schaffel, Mackey & Abbate, Esq., 115 Broadway, New York, New York 10006, before Susan B. Ratner, a Shorthand Reporter and Notary Public of the State of New York, on March 27, 1988, commencing 9:10 a.m.
61. *Newsday*, April 25, 1985.
62. Excerpt from Cuomo's affidavit published in *Manhattan Lawyer*, May 24–June 3, 1988.
63. *Newsday*, April 25, 1985.
64. *Manhattan Lawyer*.
65. *Newsday*, April 25, 1985.
66. Ibid.
67. Ibid.
68. Ibid.
69. *New York Times*, April 14, 1989.
70. Ibid.

71. Ibid.
72. Excerpt of letter Molineaux sent to Greene dated April 29, 1997.
73. *New York* magazine, 30ᵗʰ Anniversary Issue, *Mario Cuomo: Keeping the Faith*
74. Ibid.

Chapter 13

1. *Time*, June 2, 1986.
2. Ibid.
3. *Newsweek*, March 24, 1986.
4. *New York Times Magazine*, September 14, 1986.
5. McElvaine, p. 80.
6. Ibid., p. 82.
7. Ibid.
8. Ibid.
9. Thomas Stapleton, *The Life and Illustrious Martyrdom of Sir Thomas More* (1966), p. 19.
10. Ibid., p. 136.
11. Anne Murphy, *Thomas More* (1966), p. 54.
12. Gerard B. Wegemer and Stephen W. Smith, *A Thomas More Source Book* (2004), p. XXIII.
13. *Catechism of the Catholic Church*, Libreria Editrice Vaticana (1994), p. 439.
14. Richard S. Sylvester, *St. Thomas More: Action and Contemplation* (1972), p. 9.
15. Gerard B. Wegemer, *Thomas More on Statesmanship* (1996), p. 183.
16. Ibid., p. 184.
17. Peter Ackroyd, *The Life of Thomas More* (1998), pp. 360–61.
18. Ibid., p. 364.
19. R. W. Chambers, *Thomas More* (1965), pp. 336–37.
20. James Mason Cline, Editor, *Roper's Life Of More* (1950), p. 77.
21. *Columbia*, November 2002.
22. Charles Chaput, *Render Unto Caesar* (2008), p. 146.
23. Robert Bolt, *A Man for All Seasons* (1962), p. 132.
24. Ibid.
25. Wegemer, *Thomas More on Statesmanship*, pp. 210–11.
26. *Cathechism*, p. 548.
27. Garry Wills, *The New York Review of Books*, June 28, 1990.
28. Ellen McCormick, *Cuomo vs. O'Connor* (1985), p. 73.
29. Charles E. Rice, *What Happened to Notre Dame?* (2009), p. 81.
30. Frances Canavan, *The Human Life Review*, Winter 2009.
31. Kenneth L. Woodward, *Getting Religion* (2016), p. 386.
32. Garry Wills, *The New York Review of Books*.

33. Nat Hentoff, *John Cardinal O'Connor* (1988), p. 149.
34. Canavan.
35. *New York Times*, August 3, 1984.
36. *Catechism*, p. 545.
37. McCormick, p. 80.
38. Woodward, p. 38.
39. Ibid.
40. McCormick, p. 66.
41. *Village Voice*, September 4, 1984.
42. *New York Times*, August 14, 1984.
43. McCormick, p. 57.
44. Ibid., p. 58.
45. Msgr. William B. Smith, *Modern Moral Problems* (2012), p. 19.
46. *New York Times*, September 11, 1989.
47. Ibid.
48. Ibid.
49. *New York Post*, November 8, 1989.
50. *New York Times*, January 7, 1990.
51. Ibid.
52. Ibid.
53. *New York Post*, January 23, 1990.
54. Ibid.
55. Ibid.
56. *New York Post*, January 24, 1990.
57. Ibid.
58. Ibid.
59. Ibid.
60. Marlin and Miner, p. 306.
61. Ibid., pp. 307–08.
62. *New York Post*, February 2, 1990.
63. Michael L. Coulter et al., *The Encyclopedia of Catholic Social Thought, Social Science and Social Policies*, Volume I (2007), p. 231.
64. Quotes from John Paul II's *Evangelium Vitae*, March 25, 1995, Libreria Editrice Vaticana.
65. Quotes are from a copy of the March 5, 1990 Cuomo letter on the governor's stationery, and from *Commonweal* Editor's March 23, 1990 response to the Cuomo letter.
66. *Daily News*, October 2, 2011.
67. Marlin, *Squandered Opportunities*, p. 123.
68. Woodward, p. 382.
69. Christoph Cardinal Schönborn, *Chance or Purpose: Creation, Evolution and a Rational Faith* (2007), p. 142.

70. Frank N. Magill, *Masterpieces of Catholic Literature* (1965), p. 1054.
71. Scott Ventureyra, *Crisis*, January 20, 2015.
72. Peter A. Kwasniewski, *Latin Mass* Winter/Spring 2019.
73. From an excerpt of Dietrich von Hildebrand's *Trojan Horse in the City of God* (1967), posted on Absolute Primacy of Christ web site.
74. Ibid.
75. Jacques Maritain, *The Peasant of The Garonne* (1968), p. 119.
76. Ibid., p. 120.
77. Kwasniewski.
78. Ibid.
79. McGill, p. 1054.
80. *New York Times*, October 31, 1982.
81. From the texts of the "Sunday Service, St. John the Divine, New York City, November 27, 1983" found in *Diaries of Mario M. Cuomo*, pp. 462–68.
82. George William Rutler, *Beyond Modernity: Reflections of a Post-Modern Catholic* (1987), p. 92.
83. The excerpts are from John P. Slattery's *Pierre Teilhard de Chardin's Legacy of Eugenics and Racism Can't Be Ignored*, published in Religion Dispatches-Rewire News, May 21, 2018.

Chapter 14

1. From the transcript of The Open Mind (PBS) interview of Mario Cuomo, March 12, 2003.
2. E. J. McMahon, "The Tax Reform That Wasn't," *Albany Government Law Review*, May 2012.
3. *New York Times*, April 4, 1987.
4. Ibid.
5. Michael J. McIntyre, 51 *Albany Law Review* (1987).
6. Executive Budget, U.S. Department of Commerce.
7. The Empire Foundation for Policy Research Report, "Taking Credit and Shifting The Blame: New York's Mandate Game," December 1991.
8. Ibid.
9. Marlin, *Squandered Opportunities*, p. 19.
10. Ibid., p. 17.
11. *Daily News*, April 1, 1990.
12. Cuomo statement released November 25, 1991.
13. Change-N.Y. Report, "The Governor's Deficit-Reduction Plan: A Short-Sighted Response to A Long-Term Problem," November 1991.
14. *The Daily Gazette* (Schenectady), April 11, 1992.

15. *Ithaca Journal*, April 11, 1991.
16. *New York Times*, January 6, 1994.
17. Ibid.
18. Ibid.
19. *New York Times*, January 19, 1994.
20. Ibid.
21. *New York Times*, March 3, 1994.
22. Ibid., April 27, 1994.
23. Ibid.
24. Ibid., May 8, 1994.
25. Ibid.
26. Ibid., May 20, 1994.
27. Ibid.
28. Ibid.
29. Ibid.
30. Ibid., June 8, 1994.
31. Ibid.
32. Ibid.
33. Ibid.
34. Ibid.
35. Ibid.
36. Ibid.
37. *Post Star*, Glen Falls, February 18, 1992.
38. *Associated Press*, February 18, 1992.
39. Marlin, *Fighting the Good Fight*, p. 315.
40. *New York Times*, October 21, 1994.
41. Wayne Barrett, *Rudy Giuliani* (1992), pp. 229–30.
42. *Mother Jones*, February–March 1987.
43. *Newsday*, November 24, 1993.
44. *Mother Jones*.
45. Ibid.
46. *New York Times*, September 28, 1994.
47. Ibid., October 25, 1994.
48. Barrett, p. 302.
49. *New York Times*, October 24, 1994.
50. Ibid., September 30, 1994.
51. Ibid., October 10, 1994.
52. Ibid.
53. *Newsday*, November 9, 1994.
54. Ibid.
55. Ibid.
56. *Daily News*, November 10, 1994.

57. *Newsday*, November 10, 1994.
58. *Daily News*, November 9, 1994.
59. Michael Barone, *Almanac of American Politics*, 1996, p. 898.
60. *New York Times*, November 13, 1994.
61. From the transcript of The Open Mind, December 8, 1994.
62. From the C-Span transcript.
63. *Daily News*, January 2, 1995.
64. New York State Red Book 1995, p. 23.
65. *Daily News*, November 9, 1994.
66. Ibid.
67. *Newsday*, November 10, 1994.
68. *The New Yorker*, January 5, 2015.

Chapter 15

1. *New York Times*, December 17, 2000.
2. Ibid., November 22, 1995.
3. Ibid., November 20, 1995.
4. Ibid., December 17, 2000.
5. Mario Cuomo, *Reason to Believe* (1995). Quote is from the jacket cover.
6. The Open Mind transcript, November 14, 1995.
7. Ibid.
8. Ibid.
9. *New York Times*, November 13, 1995.
10. Ibid.
11. *New York Times*, November 19, 1995.
12. Ibid., November 22, 1995.
13. Ibid.
14. Ibid.
15. Mario M. Cuomo, *Why Lincoln Matters* (2004), p. 180.
16. Ibid., p. 181.
17. Ibid.
18. Andrew Ferguson, "Cuomo's Lincoln," *The Weekly Standard*, July 5, 2004.
19. The Open Mind transcript, May 26, 2004.
20. Ibid.
21. Andrew Ferguson.
22. Alan Wolfe, *Commonweal*, September 10, 2004.
23. Cuomo, *Why Lincoln Matters*, p. 43.
24. The Open Mind transcript, January 12, 2005
25. E. J. Dionne, Jr., Jean Bethke Elshtain, and Kayla M. Drogosz, Editors, *One Electorate Under God?* (2004), p. 13.

26. Ibid., p. 14.
27. Ibid.
28. Ibid., p. 15.
29. Ibid., pp. 101–05.
30. Marlin and Miner, p. 329.
31. *New York Times*, January 17, 2000.
32. William O'Shaughnessy, *Mario Cuomo: Remembrances of a Remarkable Man* (2017), pp. 220–21.
33. Ibid., p. 209.

Chapter 16

1. Andrew M. Cuomo, *All Things Possible* (2014), p. 196.
2. Ibid.
3. Ibid., p. 214.
4. Michael Shnayerson, *The Contender* (2015), p. 216.
5. Ibid.
6. Ibid., p. 219.
7. Wayne Barrett, "Andrew Cuomo's $2 Million Man," *The Village Voice*, September 5, 2006.
8. Michael Barone, *The American Political Almanac 2012* (2011), p. 1107.
9. *New York Post*, November 4, 2010.
10. William O'Shaughnessy, *Mario Cuomo: Remembrances of a Remarkable Man* (2017), p. 196.
11. *New York Times*, January 2, 2015.
12. Ibid.
13. Ibid.
14. Ibid.
15. George J. Marlin, "Andrew Cuomo: N.Y.'s Machiavellian Governor," *The Catholic Thing*, January 11, 2017.
16. *Newsday*, January 2, 2015.
17. *Daily News*, January 2, 2015.
18. *Newsday*, January 2, 2015.
19. *New York Times*, January 2, 2015.
20. *New York Post*, January 2, 2015.
21. *Daily News*, January 2, 2015.
22. *New York Post*, January 2, 2015.
23. William O'Shaughnessy, pp. 255–70.
24. Ibid., p. 125.

INDEX

Tables are indicated by a "t" after the page number. "MC" refers to Mario Cuomo.

Raffa, Charles (MC's father-in-law), 253–56
Rafshoon, Gerald, 104, 107, 134, 198
Rangel, Charles, 92, 109, 148
RANS (Revenue Anticipation Notes), 81
Ratzinger, Joseph (Pope Benedict XVI), 280, 286
Ravitch, Richard, 86
Reagan, Ronald
abortion controversy and, 205–6; MC's critiques of, 168; MC's Democratic National Convention speech on, 187–90, 193; New York State, election results in, 120, 135; popularity of, 194–95 Reagan Economic Boom, 309; Reaganomics, 158, 159, 193; Tax Reform Act (1986), 310
Reason to Believe (Cuomo), 346–49
recessions, 170, 316–18, 317–18*t*
Regan, Edward (Ned)
MC and, 209, 217; on MC's 1991–1992 budget, 320; MC's gubernatorial campaign, 147; Nassau County, election results in, 163; Rinfret and, 229; state Republican Party and, 213
Relph, Robert, 330
Republican Party (New York State), 213, 228, 325–30
Republican Party (U.S.), 5, 26, 27, 28, 213
Revenue Anticipation Notes (RANS), 81
Rhodes, Dusty, 325
Rice, Donna, 223
Rich, Richard, 270, 272
Right to Life Party, 326
Rinfret, Pierre, 228–29
Robert McElvaine, 106
Rockefeller, Nelson ("Rocky")

agencies created by, 15, 16*t*; on Carey as governor, 74; Carey on financial management by, 76; fiscal policies of, 4; as governor, 4–12; gubernatorial campaigns, 8–9, 11, 27; Levitt and, 14; Medicaid and, 45; mentioned, 367; NYC financing under, 81; as presidential candidate, 209; Republican Party, control of, 12; resignation as governor, 19; scatter-site housing projects and, 57; shadow government under, 10–11, 17; spending spree (1959–1973), 11–21, 13*t*
Rockland County, growth in, 3
Rodgers, William, 9
Roe v. Wade, 280–81, 282, 294
Rohan, Patrick, 53
Rohatyn, Felix, 148
Roman Catholic Church
on conscience, 270–71; MC and death penalty and, 296–301; teachings of, MC as commentator on, 267; *See also* abortion
Ronan, William J., 9, 12
Roosevelt, Eleanor, 8
Roosevelt, Franklin Delano, 24, 31, 38–39, 78, 194, 367
Roosevelt, Theodore, 38, 367
Rosenbaum, Richard, 327, 330
Rosenfeld, Harry, 248
Rotello, Gabriel, 330–31
Rubin, Marilyn, 144
Russert, Tim, 184, 199
Rutler, George, 306
Ryan, Bernard, 153
Ryan, William J., 28, 328

Sack, Kevin, 339
same-sex marriage law, 363
Samuels, Howard, 68, 69–70
Sardone, Thelma, 331